THE SPANISH INQUISITION

Henry Kamen

THE SPANISH
INQUISITION

WEIDENFELD AND NICOLSON
20 NEW BOND STREET LONDON WI

272-246
18 128

160560

Printed in Great Britain by C. Tinling & Co. Ltd.,
Liverpool, London and Prescot

For
Karen

CONTENTS

ILLUSTRATIONS

PREFACE

T HIS is a small book on a big subject, but the need for a new study of the Spanish Inquisition has long been felt and this is the excuse for the present volume. My aim has been to create a synthesis of what has been written on the subject of the Inquisition since the appearance in 1906 of the great work of Henry Charles Lea, whose unsuperseded researches are still the basis for all serious students. Since Lea's work there have appeared in English only two or three brief general histories, notably that by Cecil Roth which came out in 1937. Meanwhile many historians, French, Spanish, and American, have by their labours thrown greater light on individual aspects of the Inquisition. Lea's work itself has long been out of print, while its sheer bulk and its minute attention to juridical and administrative matters have made it unsuited to the general reader.

Essentially this is not an account of the Inquisition so much as a tentative interpretation of its place in Spanish history. The dead bones of institutional history can only be given life in the context of the human beings who make up society, and it is with this in mind that I have tried to trace the career of the Holy Office. If I have sinned in adopting a particular thesis or opinion to the exclusion of others, I hope the evidence is on my side. In two respects the scope of this book has been restricted. The Spanish Inquisition existed uniformly throughout the Spanish empire from Manila and Lima to Sicily, but I have dealt only with the tribunal as it existed within peninsular Spain, including the Canaries and the Balearic Islands but excluding Portugal. I have in addition found it impossible, in a subject which covers three hundred years of Spanish history, to give adequate space to the discussion of events and themes not directly central to the narrative. For further information the reader is referred to the bibliographical notes, which are necessarily brief and not meant to be an exhaustive *apparatus criticus*.

Some technicalities should be excused. In the use of proper names I have usually kept to the Spanish spelling, with some exceptions when a regular English equivalent exists, such as 'Catalonia' instead of 'Cataluña'. For several reasons it has been impossible to reduce the various monetary units to a single denomination or even to convert them into modern equivalents. The original denominations may be of interest to historians, and for this reason I have preferred to retain them.

The complex structure of the Spanish kingdoms has created problems of terminology. For convenience I refer generally to the individual realms of Aragon, Valencia, and Catalonia as 'provinces', and use the term 'kingdom' to refer to the larger entity, Aragon, of which they formed a part. 'Castile' is used for all the peninsular realms subject to the crown of Castile. I use the word 'feudal' to refer to a pre-capitalist economic order: a social system based on the fief is termed 'institutional feudalism'.

My particular thanks go to Professor A. A. Parker and Mr V. G. Kiernan, of Edinburgh University, who have given some of my chapters the benefit of their comments and criticisms. Needless to say, the opinions and errors that remain in the book are my own. Dr S. P. Oakley very kindly helped to read the proofs. My greatest debt is of course to my wife, from whose helpful criticisms I have very much profited, and who sacrificed her leisure hours to type the entire manuscript and to help draw up the index.

H.K.

CHAPTER ONE

INTRODUCTORY

Sancho Panza: I am an Old Christian, and to become an earl
that is sufficient.
Don Quixote: And more than sufficient.

Cervantes, DON QUIXOTE, book I chap. 21

ON 19 October 1469 the princess Isabella of Castile was solemnly
married to prince Ferdinand of Aragon, so uniting the dynasties
of the two principal kingdoms in the Iberian peninsula. It was
not until 1474, however, that Isabella succeeded to the throne of
Castile, and five years after this that her husband succeeded to
that of Aragon. From this date the two kingdoms, linked by the
personal union of their rulers but otherwise independent in
government and institutions, began to pursue a policy of recupera-
tion and consolidation which has led the era of Ferdinand and
Isabella – the *Catholic monarchs*, as they were called – to be considered one of the most glorious in Spanish history. Spain and
Europe were on the threshold of a great period of creation and
expansion, a period which saw the emergence of new economic,
political and cultural forces out of the restraints imposed by the
feudal order and mediaeval ways of thought. In the events of the
next generation, Spain was to participate fully as a political
power which soon became one of the strongest in Europe.

The Iberian peninsula at the end of the fifteenth century was
divided among the three monarchies of Portugal, Castile and
Aragon. Portugal dominated the Atlantic coastline of the peninsula, and it was from here that the Portuguese, under the
influence of Prince Henry the Navigator, had begun the pioneer-
ing voyages which were to earn the first-fruits of trade and
colonization in Asia and America. The kingdom of Aragon
(comprising the three provinces of Valencia, Aragon and

Catalonia) looked out from the eastern coastline of the peninsula to an empire that had once stretched across the Mediterranean as far as Greece. Between these two dynamic powers lay Castile, hemmed in between its neighbours but in population and wealth far exceeding both of them. The crown of Castile contained within itself two thirds of the territory of the peninsula and three quarters of the population, at a time when the total land mass covered 225,000 square miles and the total population included about 11,350,000 people. With a population density greater than that of its neighbours, Castile created more room for living by pressing southwards against the last remnants of the Moors who had once occupied the greater part of the peninsula and who now retained their only foothold in the Moorish kingdom of Granada. The persistence of what appeared to be a foreign enclave on Castilian soil meant that of all the realms of the peninsula it alone continued to be fired by the spirit of the reconquest of Spanish territory which had inspired Christian Spaniards for the last four centuries; consequently, Castile alone had adapted its forms of society to the needs of this lengthy crusade against the Muslim invaders.

The Reconquest meant the slow and systematic extension of Christian power over all those lands that had been Muslim since the eighth century, and so involved the clash of Christian and Muslim armies and societies. What the Reconquest destroyed, however, was the racial and religious coexistence, which despite incessant armed conflict had distinguished the society of mediaeval Spain. It was claimed by a contemporary that when the Christians went to war against the Moors, it was 'neither because of the law (of Mahommed) nor because of the sect that they hold to',[1] but because of the lands they occupied, and for this reason alone. For long periods in mediaeval Spain, close contact between the peoples of the peninsula had led to a mutual tolerance among the three main communities of Christians, Jews and Moors. Within the territories of each community, dissident minorities were tolerated to a degree that makes it sometimes possible to consider racial or religious divisions as irrelevant: Christians (*mozárabes*) existed under Moorish rule and Muslims (*mudéjares*) under Christian rule. Political considerations were obviously uppermost in such a policy. The different communities shared, moreover, in a common culture which blurred any racial prejudices, and military alliances were often made irrespective of religion. Saint Ferdinand, king of Castile from 1230 to 1252, called himself 'king of the three religions', a singular claim in an increasingly intolerant age in Europe. These observations show us that the notion of a 'crusade' was largely absent from the earlier periods of the Reconquest, and that the communities of Spain had come to coexist in a relatively 'open' or free society which reflects immense credit on the ideals of the time. Obviously, however, this coexistence depended on the political and military balance maintained between the three communities. When this balance was upset by the outstanding Christian advances that followed the defeat of the Moors at Las Navas de Tolosa in 1212, the fabric began to fall apart. Bit by bit the law of the conqueror established itself. By the end of the thirteenth century the Moors retained little more than Granada. In the fourteenth century the pogroms commenced.

It was, of course, nothing new for minorities to suffer persecution, and massacres, particularly of Jews, had occurred repeatedly before this time. On 30 December 1066, five days after William the Conqueror was crowned king of England in Westminster Abbey, about four thousand Jews were massacred by the Moors in Granada. About the middle of the twelfth century the arrival from Africa of the intolerant Almorávide Moors led to widespread killing, destruction and forced conversion of the Jews and Christians. These outbreaks, however, were exceptional. What made the situation in the fourteenth century different was that 'it was no longer possible for Christians, Moors, and Jews to live under the same roof, because the Christian now felt himself strong enough to break down the traditional custom of Spain whereby the Christian population made war and tilled the soil, the Moor built the houses, and the Jew presided over the enterprise as a fiscal agent and a skilful technician'.[2] In this way the possibility that Spain might see the evolution of a multi-racial society based on mutual tolerance was explicitly rejected by the men who now came to rule the peninsula.

Ferdinand and Isabella inherited a realm that had been reduced to political and financial chaos by dynastic and personal quarrels among the nobility. The primary task therefore was pacification. The development under the Catholic monarchs of peace-keeping brotherhoods or *hermandades* to pacify the country-side and to act against recalcitrant nobles, was one of the many important reforms of the period. But pacification was only part of the solution. The crown also had to come to terms with the ruling circles of the nobility. The policy adopted by Ferdinand and Isabella was to be of consummate importance in the history of Castile.

To understand this policy let us look at the position of the nobility. Out of a population of about nine million people in Castile and Aragon in 1482, it has been calculated that about 0.8 per cent consisted of the higher nobility and about 0.85 per cent of the town aristocracy, giving a rough total of 1.65 per cent as the ratio of nobles to the rest of the population.[3] This tiny proportion of individuals, however, exercised ownership directly or indirectly over 97 per cent of the soil of the peninsula. To demonstrate this we have only to note that virtually the whole of the great province of Andalucia was owned by noble houses and the archbishop of Toledo; this picture could be repeated for most other regions of Spain. Besides this landed predominance in an age where land was the principal means of production and subsistence, the noble houses could claim incomes of fantastic proportions. The Marquis of Villena at the beginning of the reign boasted an income of 100,000 ducats a year, where one ducat was equivalent to eight days wages of a skilled worker. In modern terms this would mean an annual income of over £1,000,000, fantastic by any standards but shocking for the level of life in fourteenth century Spain. The higher clergy were very much in the same category. The Spanish church had an annual income of over 6,000,000 ducats, and the archbishop of Toledo alone received an annual income of some 80,000 ducats. Since most of this income came from land, and Spain like other countries remained overwhelmingly agricultural, it is clear that the aristocratic classes controlled the economic development of the country.

The Catholic monarchs have usually been credited with reducing the power and influence of these classes.[4] This belief rests on the fact that at the Cortes or parliament of the realm held at Toledo in 1480, grants made to nobles without sufficient cause were revoked, so that an annual sum of 80,000 ducats was reclaimed for the royal treasury. This and other measures, such as the razing of castles and the development of the *hermandades*, certainly hit at the pockets of some nobles and trimmed the nails of political disaffection. What was not achieved, however, was any diminution of the social and economic power of the nobility. The Cortes of Toledo certainly ordered the return of grants made since 1464, but all grants made before the accession of Henry IV of Castile in 1454 were explicitly confirmed; this meant that all the most important profits made by the Castilian nobility were left untouched. The Catholic monarchs seem in fact to have been more concerned with pacification than with reformation, and this attempt at a compromise led inevitably to an implicit alliance between the crown and the ruling classes. This followed the general trend in western Europe, where the rise of the new monarchies was based on alliances with the feudal nobility against the urban middle classes. The results of this policy in Castile are what directly concern us, for it was events in Castile that led to the rise of the modern Spanish Inquisition.

The understanding reached between the Castilian nobility and the crown was to be of paramount economic and social importance. The compromise of 1480 became the basis of the supremacy of the landed aristocracy. The consequences of this were soon to be seen in the agrarian crisis of 1504, when the big landowners were able to extend their power by buying out independent cultivators.[5] The higher nobility, however, were not conscientious cultivators: like the crown, they were interested in immediate financial returns. This tendency explains the support given by the crown and aristocracy to the guild of sheepowners, the Mesta, whose rights to pasturage were favoured by the government at the expense of agriculture, so that productive lands were ordered to be left uncultivated to feed the flocks of sheep wandering over the plains of Castile: the results on the primarily agricultural economy of Castile need not be discussed.[6] Of the three million sheep in the flocks of the Mesta at the beginning of the sixteenth century, the greater part was owned by small-property men; but wealthy nobles like the Dukes of Béjar and Infantazgo, and great monasteries like those of the Escorial and Guadalupe, came to own the biggest flocks. Royal support eventually turned the Mesta into a cornerstone of crown finance. In one other important respect the legislation of the Catholic monarchs surrendered the economy of Castile into noble hands. By the Laws drawn up at Toro in 1505, the nobles were allowed to found *mayorazgos* or entailed estates, with the result that as the years went on the hereditary possessions of the great noble houses grew through purchase, marriage and inheritance. As elsewhere in Europe, these great estates proved to be anything but beneficial to the national economy.

In a state where the government was aristocratic in spirit as well as in personnel, the values of the old nobility were bound to take precedence over the needs of the economy. The prevalence of these values can be illustrated by the last stages of the Reconquest, initiated in February 1482 by the capture of Alhama, a small town on the confines of the kingdom of Granada. The war of Granada ended finally in January 1492 with the surrender of the great city of that name. Glorious as the campaigns were to the martial spirit of the nobility of Castile, even more glorious were the profits registered: with the exception of the regions in eastern Granada, which were apportioned among cultivators of lower Andalucia, the whole of the newly conquered kingdom was granted to the aristocracy as compensation for what they had lost in 1480.[7] This was merely a continuation of the old pattern of the Reconquest, whereby the nobility, and above all the military orders of Santiago and Calatrava, were given the task of resettling conquered lands with Christian men. Invariably the only territory retained by the crown was in the big urban centres; for the rest, the nobles, the military orders, and the Church, came into full possession.[8] The fortunes made at Granada were in line with this pattern. The secretary of the Catholic monarchs, Hernando del Pulgar, was one of those who received a grant of six hundred acres of land in the kingdom. But it was the great ones who made the most: the Marquis of Moya, the Duke of Medina Sidonia, the Duke of Alba (who received the city of Huéscar), the Marquis of Zeñete, and scores of others.[9]

With the nobility in control of important sections of central and local administration, with their power over the economic direction of the country confirmed, and with their military and social ideals justified by the completion of the Reconquest, we come to the critical question in the evolution of the modern Spanish state. Was Castile to develop as an 'open', free and complex community, with differing ideals contributing to a common way of life, or was it to adopt a single ideal to the exclusion of all others? This question was decided in the course of the late fifteenth century, and the decision was confirmed by the success of the Castilian aristocracy at the siege of Granada. From that time the train of events was plain and inexorable. On 2 January 1492 the Catholic monarchs entered in state into the city of Granada. Just under three months later, on 31 March 1492, they decreed the expulsion of all Jews from Spain.

The motives and circumstances leading up to this step we shall discuss later. What must be stressed is that there was nothing surprising or extraordinary about the fact of expulsion. The Jews had in the course of their history been expelled from most of the countries of Europe, for reasons which usually varied between fanaticism and greed. Spain, or mediaeval Spanish society, must take the credit for having tolerated this minority longer than most nations: the expulsion of 1492, for instance, occurred more than two centuries after the expulsion of the Jews from England, decreed on 18 July 1290 by Edward I. The importance of 1492, then, consists not in the expulsion itself but in its historical context. The expulsion was, in its widest interpretation, an attempt by the feudalistic nobility to eliminate that section of the middle classes – the Jews – which was threatening its predominance in the state. It was a refusal of the old order to accept the new importance of those sections of the community that controlled the capital and commerce of the towns. This reaction was not a new one nor was it sudden; it developed during the fourteenth century, at the very time that the Christian reconquests of the thirteenth century had destroyed racial coexistence in the peninsula. Thus the consciousness of conflicting interests came to the fore at the same time as a sharpened awareness of the potential religious and racial danger presented by the two great Jewish and Moorish minorities in Spain.

The edict of 1492 did not, as we know, solve the problem. The thousands of Jews who preferred to remain in Spain and be 'voluntarily' baptized, continued the old conflict under new forms. Old and new converts – *conversos*, or New Christians (to distinguish them from Old or non-Jewish Christians) – continued to maintain the hold of their class and race on trading and capital. It was to examine the genuineness of their conversions that the Inquisition had been established by papal decree in November 1478. Since the expulsion had not, however, eliminated these classes, the Inquisition continued to function with renewed vigour. What emerges from this situation is that the Inquisition was neither more nor less than a class weapon, used to impose on all communities of the peninsula the ideology of one class – the lay and ecclesiastical aristocracy. Their beliefs and ideals were henceforth to be the norm of Castilian life: at its best this attitude flowered out into heroic spirituality, at its worst it degenerated into the worst of all racialisms – the racialism of a single class.

In this way, by consolidating their economic supremacy through the land, and by eliminating dissident minorities from the peninsula, the nobles took upon themselves the direction of the fortunes of Spain. We shall have occasion to examine the material consequences of this situation in the course of our story. It is worth noting, meanwhile, that the crown had now abandoned its traditional role of arbiter over the different communities of the nation and had chosen to identify itself with the one class it considered essential to its own existence.[10] This view is confirmed by the refusal of Ferdinand to listen to the representations made by the municipalities of the chief cities of Spain against the economic results likely to follow the introduction of the Inquisition and the consequent flight of conversos.[11] The king maintained that spiritual reasons were more important than mere material considerations of the national economy, and so helped to put into practice the 'crusading' ideals of the Castilian nobility.

What was startling about this new situation was that the ideals of the nobility were not confined to them as a class, but permeated the whole of Spanish society. The peculiar structure of Castile, in which institutional feudalism had never taken root, partly because of the demands made on society by the constant struggle against the Moors, resulted in the complete absence of a servile peasant class; so that even though noble and peasant were at opposite ends of the social ladder, each was as free from feudal obligations as the other. In this free society, therefore, it was possible to move up and down the ladder without any stigma being attached to oneself. Particularly after the elimination of the more dynamic section of the urban middle class –

8

the Jews – there remained little to separate a lord from his peasant. By the time of Cervantes it was possible to observe with Don Quixote that 'there are two kinds of classes in the world: those who draw and derive their descent from princes and monarchs, and whom time undoes bit by bit until they are totally ruined; and others who take their beginnings from the common people and rise from rank to rank until they become great lords; the difference being that some were what they are no longer, and others are what they once were not'.[12] With such great social mobility between these two classes, it is not surprising that the lower classes should have considered themselves as good as their betters. As the maiden Dorotea says to her noble lover Fernando in *Don Quixote*, 'Although a peasant and labouring girl, I consider myself the equal of you who are a lord and knight.'[13] When Francesco Guicciardini went on an embassy to Spain in 1512, he was quick to note that the pride in nobility played a big part in the character of the ordinary Spaniard.[14] In succeeding centuries the situation remained unchanged. In the time of Philip IV, the writer Saavedra Fajardo observed that the distinction between nobility and common people was less marked in Spain than in Germany. As late as the nineteenth century, in the time of Isabella II, Balmes claimed that there was no country in the world where there was more levelling of classes than Spain, and that in Spain a man of the humblest class of society would stop in the road the highest magnate in the land.[15] This familiarity between the classes meant that the lower orders came to accept the ideals of their betters, the nobility; the practice of chivalry, and the concept of 'honour' which sprang from this,[16] found a ready home in the imagination of peasant and labouring communities. Commentators from the sixteenth century onwards were virtually unanimous in considering the growing disdain for manual labour in Spain to be a result of the unfortunate yearning for nobility among wide sections of the population. The concept of 'honour' bred a reactionary anti-capitalist and anti-labouring outlook which was certainly not peculiar to Spain alone; but which in Spain attained an influence equalled nowhere else. Over and above this was the fact that the lower classes identified themselves with the 'crusading' spirit of the nobility: they too were heirs of the Reconquest, they too had been Christians before the entry of the new Jewish and Moorish converts into the faith. Unmistakeably, therefore, we now see the rise of the distinction between Old Christians and New Christians. It was nothing extraordinary for Sancho Panza, a simple man of the people, to consider being an Old Christian equivalent to, and adequate for, nobility.

The success of the Castilian nobility was to have pernicious effects of deeper importance and of greater duration than it could ever have realized. For us the problem is to consider how a nation can be constricted and hedged about by the narrow vision of its own ruling classes, so that an 'open' community having creative links with the world outside is forced to recoil upon itself and live off itself, closing off all external communication and so becoming a 'closed' society. At the heart of this development lies the Spanish Inquisition. It was the Inquisition that protected the faith and morals of the peninsula so that native and foreign heresies, and above all the Protestant Reformation, never took root in Spain. At the same time Spain withdrew from active participation in the intellectual life of Europe, and devoted itself to the ideals of a resurgent Church and military aristocracy: the sixteenth century, when a dynamic Spain established its hegemony over Europe, America, and the Atlantic and Pacific oceans, was the era of its greatest triumph. This was followed by a no less remarkable period of cultural activity in Spain. Thereafter the closed society found that it had exhausted its own resources: the tumult and the shouting died, and it became painfully clear that a common speech with the external world must be sought if Spain was not to decline into a stagnant backwater.

This evolution, or decline, cannot be laid entirely at the door of the Inquisition. The kind of explanation that was once fashionable among liberal and Protestant historians was not only wrong: it was superficial. The superficiality lay in leaving out of the picture all the most important social factors, and attempting to give a convincing account in terms of religious factors alone. Yet behind the religious façade, behind the question of intolerance, lie other questions which hinge on the role of the nobility. In this respect 1492 is probably the most important year in Spanish history. The fall of Granada represented the victory of Reconquest ideals. The expulsion of the Jews represented the victory of the feudalistic nobility over the class most identified with commercial capitalism. And the discovery of America meant the opening of new frontiers to the ruling classes of Castile.

These three things taken together are fundamental. The Jews, as we shall see, played some part in the discovery of America. Their expulsion meant that the aristocracy, having eliminated its richest competitors, was now free to extend its regime to the New World. And this is in fact what happened. The discovery of America led to a strengthening of the hold exercised by the dominant class.[17] It is true that the nobles played virtually no part in the conquest and opening-up of America,[18] but a century later all the best noble houses of Castile were represented in the Indies,[19] and the landed regime of America confirmed once again the dominance of the lay and ecclesiastical aristocracy. Since the state monopolized trade to the Indies, and the nobles controlled the councils of state, it was the Castilian nobility that most exploited the opportunities across the Atlantic. Above all, the military caste assumed a new and singular importance with the great expansion of trade, discovery and empire. The private and public economy of Castile became geared to a new industry – that of war – which was to multiply in victories over the next century.

Only one thing spoilt this picture. The disappearance of the Jews and the persecution of conversos created a void in the world of capital which was never satisfactorily filled by Spaniards. The merchants of the Mesta took over for a time the handling of foreign exchange on behalf of the crown, and it was in this period that the great trade fair at Medina del Campo came into its own. But business soon slipped into the hands of foreign traders and capitalists, despite an order in 1499 that foreigners were not to have public banking houses. The Genoese, who had had a foothold in Seville as early as the fourteenth century, led the way, to be followed by other Italians and then by Germans. Isabella herself relied on a Genoese banker, Agostino Italiano, to pay the dowry of her daughter Catherine of Aragon when she went to London to marry the Prince of Wales. Soon the prominent names in Spanish finance, and particularly in the trade to America, were Italian ones – Grimaldi, Centurioni, Spinola, Calvi, Cattaneo, Doria, Pallavicini. From

Philip II to Philip IV and Charles II similar names predominated – Paravicino, Guistiniani, Piquenotti, Strati, Imbrea. In addition to these were the famous names, notably the Fuggers, and several Portuguese.[20] In such company the distinguished Castilian financiers such as Simon Ruiz were decidedly in a minority. In practice, as one historian observes, 'foreigners monopolised the trade of the capital cities';[21] and how much the crown itself relied on loans from foreign capitalists is a tragic chapter in Spanish financial history. In this way, the internal management of the country fell under the control of foreign money because the ethic and ideals of Reconquest Spain refused to compromise with the new age. Spain took one step backwards, away from the new developments in Western Europe. Even in culture conservatism triumphed, according to Menéndez Pidal, who points to 'the Renaissance, the period which was in other countries radically modernist, but in Spain made a truce with traditionalism',[22] the traditionalism of scholastic Catholicism, the *romanceros*, and books of chivalry.

It is only against this background that the Inquisition can begin to be understood. Its introduction was intimately connected with the regime, ideals and society prevalent in Spain at the end of the fifteenth century, and only in this context can it be studied. As we shall see, the Inquisition began to collapse only when the regime which created it began to wither, and when the personnel of that regime, the administrative sections of the ruling class, began to question the framework of the nation's political and economic life. This brings us to the beginning of our story.

CHAPTER TWO

THE GREAT DISPERSION

> You only need to ask:
> Is this or that man a threat to us? Then
> Is he a Jew.
>
> *Bertolt Brecht,* DER JUDE, EIN UNGLÜCK FÜR DAS VOLK

'THE kings and lords of Castile have had this advantage, that their Jewish subjects, reflecting the magnificence of their lords, have been the most learned, the most distinguished Jews that there have been in all the realms of the dispersion; they are distinguished in four ways: in lineage, in wealth, in virtues, in science.'[1] Such was the fully justified boast of a fifteenth-century Castilian rabbi. Where all other countries in Europe could consider the Jews as a troublesome minority alien to their history, in the Iberian peninsula alone were they intimately and anciently connected with the mainstream of the country's history. The Jewish problem is our direct concern for without it there would have been no Spanish Inquisition.

At the heart of racial and religious persecution in mediaeval Spain lay the problem of coexistence between the three great faiths of the peninsula: Muslim, Christian and Jewish. The first great persecution of the Jews occurred in the seventh century, and made them look with relief to the Moorish invasions and the establishment of the Muslim Caliphate at Córdoba. Under the liberal Caliphate the Jews prospered socially and economically. This came to an end in the twelfth century with the overthrow of the Caliphate by a new wave of Moorish invaders, the Almorávides, who persecuted Christians and Jews alike and destroyed their places of worship. The Jews fled to Christian territory and, under the tolerant eye of Christian rulers, continued to prosper in their new surroundings. Thus although intermittent persecution did occur, some degree of tolerance was the general rule. 'In the commercial sphere, no visible barriers separated Jewish, Christian and Saracen merchants during the major period of Jewish life in Spain. Christian contractors built Jewish houses and Jewish craftsmen worked for Christian employers. Jewish advocates represented gentile clients in the secular courts. Jewish brokers acted as intermediaries between Christian and Moorish principals. As a by-product, such continuous daily contacts inevitably fostered tolerance and friendly relationships, despite the irritations kept alive in the name of religion.'[2]

Political factiousness and economic jealousy soon helped to break down the security of this prosperous minority. From the thirteenth century onwards anti-Jewish legislation, first called for in the Fourth Lateran Council at Rome in 1215, became commonplace. It was the Council of Arles which first in 1235 ordered all Jews to wear a round yellow patch, four fingers in circumference, over their hearts as a mark of identification. Such legislation was never properly enforced in Spain because of powerful Jewish opposition, but the Cortes of Castile did approve of it in 1371 at the Cortes of Toro and again in 1405 at the Cortes of Madrid, with little success. This new anti-Jewish trend was accompanied by popular riots and occasional slaughter. Finally the whole question erupted in 1391 into the worst series of massacres ever suffered by the Jews in the peninsula. Religious fanaticism was clearly the driving force but, as a contemporary chronicler observed, 'all this was more out of a thirst for robbery than out of devotion.'[3] In June 1391 over four thousand Jews were murdered in Seville alone. The pogroms of this year occurred in all the largest cities of Spain, and the ghettos or *aljamas* of Seville, Barcelona, Valencia, Toledo and other cities were totally wiped out. Those who were not murdered were compelled to accept baptism. It is from this time, the age of forcible mass conversions after pogroms, that the conversos came into existence on a grand scale.

The converso was not simply a convert. Christian society was all too conscious that converted Jews had in reality been forced unwillingly into their new faith: the converso was from the first, therefore, regarded with suspicion as a false Christian and a secret judaizer or practiser of Jewish rites. The conversos or New

Christians soon came to be distrusted even more than the Jews, for they were considered to be a fifth column within the body of the Church. New words were coined to describe them, the most common being *marranos*, a word which probably derived either from the Hebrew *maranatha* (the Lord comes) or from a description of the Jews as those who 'marran', or mar, the true faith. The conversos were thus resented by the body of Old Christians, who distrusted the sincerity of their faith and objected to the prominent part they played in Christian society. Although no longer Jews in religion, they now began to be subjected to all the rigours of antisemitism.

The roots of antisemitism are universal in character and as incomprehensible as they are deeply ingrained. The nature of the problem in Spain did not perhaps differ fundamentally from its nature in any other place or time.[4] But we can begin to understand some of the reasons for antisemitism in Spain, and for the foundation of the Inquisition, by outlining the important role played by the Jews in Spanish society. In Christian Spain the first great era of the Jews was the thirteenth century, when their science and influence reached heights great enough to justify the claim of Mosé Arragel with which this chapter opens. Jewish scientists and writers distinguished themselves at the Court of Alfonso X of Castile.[5] The medical profession was virtually monopolised by Jews, and royal and aristocratic circles relied heavily on this race for physicians: as one historian observes of the kingdom of Aragon, 'there was not a noble or prelate in the land who did not keep a Jewish physician',[6] and a similar situation also existed in Castile. The unfortunate sequel in any critical period was that Jewish doctors were accused of poisoning their patients. This was given as a contemporary reason for the expulsion of the Jews in 1492, the royal physician, a Jew, being accused of having poisoned the Infante Don Juan, son of Ferdinand and Isabella. For the next two centuries converso doctors carried on the work of their Jewish forbears, many of them suffering at the hands of the Inquisition because of prejudice or ignorance.

The most important cause of hostility to Jews, however, lay in their financial activities. In the first place they acted as taxgatherers and fiscal officials to the crown and aristocracy. In answer to a protest of the Cortes of Burgos against this practice in 1367, Henry II claimed that 'we farmed out the collection of the revenue to Jews because we found no others to bid for it';[7] and in 1469 the Cortes of Ocaña complained to Henry IV that 'many prelates and other ecclesiastics farm to Jews and Moors the revenue and tithes that belong to them; and they enter churches to apportion the tithe among the contributors, to the great offence and injury of the Church.'[8] A direct result of hostility to this situation may be seen in the serious rioting at Toledo in 1449, when murders and sackings marked the resentment of the population against converso tax-gatherers employed by the royal minister Alvaro de Luna. Right up to the time of the expulsion, moreover, Jews held prominent official positions in the financial service of the crown. 'From the beginning of the Reconquest till the capitulation of the last Moorish fortress on the peninsula in 1492, Jews were to be found in the Spanish states, especially in Castile, in key positions as ministers, royal counsellors, farmers of state revenue, financiers of military enterprises and as majordomos of the estates of the crown and of the higher nobility.'[9] Thus in the thirteenth century, under Jaime I of Aragon, the bailiffs or controllers of royal revenue in Barcelona, Gerona, Saragossa, Tarazona, Tortosa, Lérida, Valencia and other cities, were all Jews. In 1369 a Jew, Joseph Pichon, was 'chief treasurer and manager of the revenues of the realm' under Henry II, just as over a century later a Jew, Gerónimo Pérez, was one of the principal treasurers of the Catholic monarchs.[10] Needless to say, the Catholic monarchs could hardly have financed their campaign against Granada without the help of the two great Jewish financiers Abraham Senior and Isaac Abarbanel.

The chronicler of the Catholic monarchs, Andrés Bernáldez, summed up the hold of Jewish finance on the nation in this way; the Jewish exiles, he said, had been:

merchants, salesmen, tax-gatherers, retailers, stewards of the nobility, officials, tailors, shoemakers, tanners, weavers, grocers, pedlars, silk-mercers, smiths, jewellers, and other like trades; none broke the earth, or became a farmer, carpenter or builder, but all sought after comfortable posts and ways of making profits without much labour.[11]

One particular example is illuminating. In Saragossa, the capital of Aragon, the *aljama* had become by the fifteenth century a virtual bank, controlling the greater part of the capital of the Christian population. Municipalities in Aragon used to resort to the *aljama* for loans and credit, and so great was the dependence of all social classes in Saragossa on it that when it was open for business 'there appeared . . . nobles, gentry, clergy, friars from all the religious orders, representatives of nunneries, and parish officials.'[12] In fact, so identified were the Jews with fiscal administration that at the end of the seventeenth century a writer complained:

Formerly all who applied themselves to the gathering of taxes were Jews and people of low origin; yet now, when they are not so, people look on them as Hebrews, even though they be Old Christians and of noble descent.[13]

Besides their financial role in the state, however, the Jews offended the Christians by their social position. They were not only a powerful middle class: they also had dangerously close links with the aristocracy, into which several conversos had married; both these factors constituted a threat to the predominance of the nobility. It is not at first obvious why this threat should be considered a serious one. If, for instance, we adopt the very general figure of a population of nine millions for Castile and Aragon in about 1482, within this figure we can identify a middle class of over half a million persons.[14] Of this latter figure, by far the greater part represents the Jewish population of Spain. This limitation of the Jews to one social class alone is a recognizable feature of the community. It is also a probable indication of the basic weakness of the community, in not having any roots among the mass of the population. Jews were also despised for their unwillingness to take part in manual labour. As Andrés Bernáldez put it:

They never wanted to take jobs in ploughing or digging, nor would they go through the fields tending cattle, nor would they teach their children to do so; all their wish was a job in the town, and earning their living without much labour while sitting on their bottoms.[15]

This belief that the Jew refused to put his hand to hard manual work and preferred to make easy profits while others sweated, was to become a basic factor in popular antisemitism. The popular belief did, however, have some basis in reality. Jewish farmers and peasants are all but unknown in available documentation.[16] Even in the lists of *autos de fe* of the Inquisition, the farmer is virtually non-existent and the financier continuously present. This shows that the Jews were essentially an urban population, with the *aljamas* as their focus and the towns as their field of activity. The example of Badajoz, in agricultural Extremadura, shows that all the 231 conversos punished by the Inquisition between 1493 and 1599 came from the professional and commercial classes. They held posts ranging from that of mayor and municipal official to the lesser occupations of physicians, lawyers, traders, shopkeepers and manufacturers.[17] The same is true for Saragossa and other principal cities of which we have details. The fact that these examples come from cities need not be misleading, for the inquisitorial tribunal sitting in the city also took cognisance of the rural areas. Against this evidence we can cite the case of Aguilar de la Frontera, near Córdoba. Of the sixty *sanbenitos* or penitential garments hung up in churches in this region in the late sixteenth century, about nineteen belonged to *labradores*, that is, to peasant farmers.[18] This proportion is perhaps unrepresentative, but should be kept in mind as a modification to the general picture. If Jews were largely cut off from the land, however, they were not cut off from the aristocracy. Despised for their religion, they could still become converts to Christianity and, as conversos, penetrate into the upper reaches of the nobility of the realm. In this lay the threat to the noble caste and to true religion, a threat which several modern writers have categorised as 'the converso danger'. Because of this danger, they argue, it became necessary to bring the Inquisition into existence. What is not clear, however, is whether the danger is represented as one to the purity of religion or to the purity of the nobility. For the latter alternative, at least, a great deal of evidence is available.

The class of conversos had grown enormously in the course of the fifteenth century, and the number of Jews had correspondingly diminished through conversion and emigration. The massacres of 1391 were followed throughout the next century by sporadic pogroms and the inevitable conversions. But the height of antisemitic legislation was reached in 1412 when, on the advice of the zealous Valencian saint, Vincent Ferrer (who shares some responsibility for the events of 1391), and the converso Chancellor of Castile, bishop Pablo de Santa María, it was decreed that Jews and Moors should wear distinguishing badges, be deprived of the right to hold office or possess titles, and should not change their domicile. In addition they were excluded from various trades such as those of grocers, carpenters, tailors and butchers; could not bear arms or hire Christians to work for them; were not allowed to eat, drink, bathe or even talk with Christians; and were forbidden to wear any but coarse clothes. This savage legislation, which was meant to speed up the rate of conversions, forced the minority races into misery and mourning. One of the victims lamented:

> They forced strange clothing upon us. They kept us from trade, farming and the crafts. They compelled us to grow our beards and our hair long. Instead of silken apparel, we were obliged to wear wretched clothes which drew contempt upon us. Unshaved, we appeared like mourners. Starvation stared everyone in the face.[19]

Yet of course this proved to be an effective way of converting the Jews. By the mid-fifteenth century the growing numbers of conversos represented an open challenge to the old aristocracy. Marriage alliances had carried many formerly Jewish families into the heart of the Castilian and Aragonese nobility. In 1449 a petition to the bishop of Cuenca stated that all the noblest families of Spain were now of Jewish blood, and among them the Henríquez, from whom Ferdinand the Catholic descended through his mother.[20] In Aragon nearly every noble house had Jewish blood in it, and half the important offices at the Aragonese court were held by conversos. In Castile the highest ranks of the clergy were contaminated. Under Isabella the Catholic at least four prominent bishops were conversos; as well as Cardinal Juan de Torquemada, uncle of the first Inquisitor General (himself, of course, of Jewish descent); Diego Deza the second Inquisitor General; and the pious archbishop of Granada Hernando de Talavera. Three secretaries of the crown, Fernando Alvárez, Alfonso de Avila, and Hernando del Pulgar, were all New Christians.[21] Individual conversos founded powerful families of their own which contributed not only to the unease of the aristocracy but also to the dismay of the Jews. In Aragon the powerful converso family of De la Caballería 'contributed, besides a few prominent clerics, the Vice-Chancellor of the kingdom of Aragon, the Comptroller General of the royal household, a Treasurer of the kingdom of Navarre, an Admiral, a Vice-Principal of the University of Saragossa, and a prominent antisemitic writer.[22] Don Juan Pacheco, Marquis of Villena and Grand Master of the Order of Santiago, was a descendant on both sides of the former Jew, Ruy Capon. His brother, Don Pedro Giron, was Grand Master of the Order of Calatrava, while the archbishop of Toledo was his uncle. Seven at least of the principal prelates of the kingdom were of Jewish extraction, as well as the Treasurer'.[23] Among the most distinguished of Castilian converts was Salomón Ha Levi, chief rabbi of Burgos, who was opportunely converted along with his brothers in 1390, adopted the name Pablo de Santa María, entered the Church, and eventually became in turn bishop of Cartagena, bishop of Burgos, tutor to the son of Henry III of Castile, and papal legate. His eldest son Gonzalo became Spanish delegate to the Council of Constance, bishop successively of Astorga, Plasencia, and Sigüenza, and also attended the Council of Basel. His second son, Alonso de Cartagena, succeeded his father in the see of Burgos.[24]

Further citation of individual cases would be superfluous. It was accepted by all contemporaries that the blood of the aristocracy had been gravely compromised by the Jewish converts. In Aragon an assessor of the Inquisition of Saragossa drew up what became known as the *Libro verde de Aragón*,[25] a genealogical table tracing the origins of the nobility, from which it became clear that the most prominent families in the kingdom had not escaped converso infiltration. This document, which was set down in manuscript in the first decade of the sixteenth century, was soon to become a source of major scandal, for copies were passed from hand to hand, added to and distorted, until the government could no longer tolerate so vicious a slander against the leading nobles of the realm. In 1623, therefore, the extreme measure was taken of ordering all available copies of these *libros verdes* to be burnt. But already a far more powerful libel had been circulating in secret. In 1560 the Cardinal Francisco Mendoza y Bobadilla, angered by a refusal to admit two members of his family into a military order, presented to Philip II a memorandum, later to be known as the *Tizón de la Nobleza de España*, or *Blot on the Nobility of Spain*, in which he claimed to prove that virtually the whole of the nobility was of Jewish descent.[26] The proofs he offered were so incontrovertible that the *Tizón* was reprinted many times down to the nineteenth century, almost always as a tract against the power and influence of the nobility. At no time was even the slightest attempt at a rejoinder to these two publications made. The implications for a social class that affected to despise the Jews and conversos could not fail to be serious. On the one hand the nobility was claiming for itself a privileged position in return for its long services to the crown, and on the other it was being morally undermined by a racial dilution which tended to bring it into contempt. If the nobles were no longer truly Old Christians, they then had no right to true nobility. The dangerous point was obviously approaching at which membership of the nobility was in itself suspicion of debased blood, and only membership of the non-noble classes provided any guarantee against Jewish descent. In an important memoir upon the royal council presented by the historian Lorenzo Galíndez de Carvajal to the emperor Charles V, it was significantly reported that several of the most important members were of converso origin; among the exceptions, however, was doctor Palacios Rubios, 'a man of pure blood because he is of labouring descent'.[27] In that 'because' lay the ultimate threat to the interests and ideals of Reconquest Spain, and to the position of the aristocratic classes. The struggle against the minorities of the realm now became a struggle for their own existence, and for the maintenance of their name as Old Christians. The apparently negligible 'converso danger' had ultimately developed into a threat to the whole social order.

Over and above this was the religious problem. Of the thousands of Jews who in the course of the preceding century had been forced by persecution and massacre to accept baptism, very few embraced Catholicism sincerely. Many, if not most, of them continued to practise the Jewish rites in secret as well as openly, so that the authorities were faced with a large minority of pseudo-Christians who had neither respect nor love for their new faith. Throughout the provinces of Toledo, Extremadura, Andalucia and Murcia, according to a polemic written in 1488, of all the conversos 'hardly any are true Christians, as is well known in all Spain'.[28] The chronicler and royal secretary Hernando del Pulgar, himself a prominent converso, vouched for the existence of numerous secret judaizers among the New Christians of Toledo. The phenomenon was widespread enough to be commonplace. Understandably then, the ecclesiastical authorities took alarm at the large numbers of false Christians who were mocking God and the true religion. What is surprising is that the bishops of Spain seem never to have realized that the blame for this sad situation rested immediately on the shoulders of those who had provoked the forcible conversion of Jews, and that the false Christians should be made the object of missionary preaching rather than persecution.

Within Spanish Catholicism there thus existed a vast secret core of those who had never reconciled themselves to baptism. The life they led, which was to be substantially the same during all the centuries of their stay in Spain, was a furtive underground one, liable to sudden discovery or betrayal, and cut off from the religious practices of the Jewish community as a whole. Despised by the Old Christians for their race, and scorned by the Jews for their apostasy, the conversos lived for the most part in a social atmosphere they had never willingly chosen. After the foundation of the Inquisition their lot became even more difficult, for the tribunal regularly published instructions showing how judaizers could be detected. Distinctive food and clothes were therefore increasingly done without, in an attempt to throw off suspicion, and few judaizing households even dared to keep books of prayer in Hebrew or any other language, lest a servant should by chance come upon them. The result of these attempts to do without any of the outward detectable signs of Judaism, and to exist only on the internal inspiration of faith, led inevitably to a gradual decay in the Jewish forms of converso religion. Consequently, as we shall see, the later conversos possessed little or no religion, and they became a nameless community, replenished only now and then by immigrant Portuguese judaizers, but otherwise sorry remnants of a great and martyred race.

In the earlier period, however, their questionable Catholicism made them an obvious target for popular resentment; to this were often added political and other reasons. The disturbances in Toledo in 1449, to which we have already referred, aroused different political factions in the city and led to an alignment of Old Christians against New Christians. The same division of parties arose in the city in 1467, and led to the final confirmation of a notorious statute excluding conversos from any public office in Toledo. There were racial riots in 1470 in Valladolid, and three years later in 1473 the conversos were expelled from Córdoba after a murderous struggle which opened the way for further killings throughout Andalucia, one of the victims being the converso Constable of Castile, who was killed before the altar of a church at Jaén. Though the direct instrument of persecution and massacre in all these cases was the populace in town and countryside we must go beyond the populace to get at the real culprits – the Old Christians with a prominent part in both municipal and ecclesiastical administration, who resented sharing power with men of mixed race and doubtful orthodoxy. Because of them, racial antagonism and antisemitism had come to stay.

Worse, antisemitism was made official. The legislation of 1412, which had stipulated among other things that Jews were to wear distinctive badges, was reaffirmed by the Castilian Cortes at Toledo in 1480. Ferdinand enforced this and other measures with due strictness in his realm of Aragon. The Catholic monarchs now began a policy of systematic expulsion. In April 1481 Jews throughout the monarchy were ordered to be confined to their ghettos and not to live outside them. At the end of 1482 a partial expulsion of the Jewish population from Andalucia was ordered.[29] The following year Jews were expelled from the bishoprics of Seville and Córdoba. In 1486 all Jews were expelled from the dioceses of Saragossa, Albarracin and Teruel. The process was piecemeal but efficient. After the fall of Granada, to which Jewish gold (supplied principally by Isaac Abarbanel and Abraham Senior) had contributed, the Catholic monarchs decided to complete their work by ridding Spain of the Jews. On 31 March 1492 an edict of expulsion was issued, giving the Jews of Spain until 31 July to accept baptism or leave the country.

Among those faced with this choice was the great financier Abraham Senior. His services to his queen had been so great that as late as March 1492, when the government ordered its debts to him to be paid, the sum in question came to 1,500,000 *maravedis*.[30] In addition he was one of the few to receive official permission to take with him out of the country personal possessions in the form of gold and silver, should he wish to accompany his brethren into exile. But, for reasons that we can neither question nor condemn, Senior preferred to stay and accept baptism, adopting for himself and his family the new surname of Coronel. His friend and colleague Isaac Abarbanel went with his people out of the country.

The general problems raised by the expulsion of the Jews have never been adequately resolved. There is no agreement on how many people left the country, nor is there any hope of measuring the effects of the expulsion on Spain as a whole. Available estimates give a figure somewhere between 165,000[31] and 400,000 as the number of actual émigrés. The figure given for those who stayed and accepted baptism is even less certain, and has been put at about 50,000. The effects of the expulsion can only be guessed at. The sultan of Turkey is reported to have said at a later date that he 'marvelled greatly at expelling the Jews from Spain, since this was to expel its wealth'.[32] This was true to a great extent. The expulsion depleted the ranks of the urban middle classes and the commercial sectors of the population, with the result that foreigners stepped in to occupy places left vacant by the Jews. Many people benefited from seizures of Jewish property, but this was completely outweighed by what we can only presume to have been an enormous loss in trading and capital. The decree of 1492 certainly solved the Jewish problem, but it created a converso problem of dimensions comparable only to the great persecution of 1391. Thousands of Jews were forced into the external observance of a religion they hated, and waited only for better days, hoping that this trial would pass as previous ones had done. As for the sufferings of those who undertook to go into exile for the sake of their religion, the details given by Andrés Bernáldez, chronicler and curate of Los Palacios in Andalucia, go to make up a picture unfortunately all too familiar since the fifteenth century.[33] The richer Jews out of charity helped to pay the costs of the poorer exiles, while the very poor managed to help themselves in no other way but by accepting baptism. They were unable to sell their possessions for gold or silver, for the export of these metals was forbidden; so they sold houses, property and everything for the most desperate substitutes. 'They went round asking for buyers and found none to buy; some sold a house for an ass, and a vineyard for a little cloth or linen, since they could not take away gold or silver.' The ships which met them at the ports were overcrowded and ill-managed. Once they had put out to sea, storms drove them back, forcing hundreds to reconcile themselves to Spain and baptism. Others, not more fortunate, reached their desired haven in north Africa, only to be pillaged and murdered. Hundreds of others staggered back to Spain by every available route, preferring familiar sufferings to those of the open sea and road. A rabbi whose father was one of the exiles, wrote:

> Some of them the Turks killed to take out the gold which they had swallowed to hide it; some of them hunger and the plague consumed and some of them were cast naked by the captains on the isles of the sea; and some of them were sold for men-servants and maid-servants in Genoa and its villages and some of them were cast into the sea.[34]

In this way the greatest scattering of Jews until modern times was carried out by the Catholic monarchs in the name of religion. Whether religious unity was the principal motive may be judged by the fact that they still continued to tolerate within their realms a large minority of practising Muslims. The exiles, or *sephardim* as they came to be called, augmented the Jewish populations of Portugal, Africa, Turkey, Italy and western Europe.[35] They contributed with their abilities and learning to the promotion of commerce and culture in nearly all the new lands of their exile. This does not mean that Spain was entirely robbed of the services of its Jews, for between one third and one half of the community remained in the realms of Castile and Aragon, accepted baptism, and prepared to live the kind of underground life the conversos had been living for the past century or more. This number was supplemented by the many who returned from abroad, convinced that baptism was better than death in a strange land. Thus finally the Jews were forced into the Christian community. 'In this way', says the curate of Los Palacios, 'was fulfilled the prophecy of David in the psalm *Eripe me*, which says: *Convertentur ad vesperam, et famen patientur, ut canes; et circuibunt civitatem.* Which is to say: "They shall return at evening, and shall suffer hunger like dogs, and shall prowl round the city". Thus these were converted at a late hour and by force and after great suffering'.[36]

CHAPTER THREE

THE COMING OF THE INQUISITION

Sancho Panza: Since I believe firmly and truly in God and in all that the Holy Catholic and Roman Church holds and believes, and am a mortal enemy of the Jews, historians should have mercy on me and treat me well in their writings.

Cervantes, DON QUIXOTE, book II chap. 8.

THE expulsion of the Jews opened a new and bitter chapter in Spanish history. To a few wealthy men, such as Abraham Senior who immediately accepted baptism, 1492 made little or no difference. To thousands of other lesser Jews forced into choosing a new religion, the result was a bitter hatred for the Spanish Church. At one stroke the Catholic monarchs had doubled the number of false converts in the realm. Now more than ever before there came into existence a 'converso danger' on a scale to terrify the ecclesiastical authorities. It is one of the ironies of history that this was the logical result of the policy of Ferdinand and Isabella, whose declared aim in expelling the Jews was purification of the country and unity in faith. So long as the Jews remained in Spain, the well-springs of heresy among false conversos could be tapped; with their expulsion, the proportion of judaizers multiplied and Jewish practices flourished virtually unseen in a vast and ever-growing underground complex of heresy. There was thus no 'final solution'; the elimination of one problem led to the growth of an even more insidious one.

Essentially, 1492 did not alter the social life of the Jews. In the new post-1492 Christian society, the conversos occupied exactly the same social position as the Jews. As before the expulsion, they continued to be an urban population occupied in the same activities as the Jews, whether as merchants or as tax-gatherers, moneylenders, doctors, tailors and cobblers. Like the Jews, they tended to keep a communal existence very similar to the life of the ghettos. The populace found it easy enough to identify the New Christians with the old Jews, and this social identification led inevitably to religious identification. Such a process was helped not only by the conservative habits of the conversos and by the survival of Jewish practices and religious observance, but also by the impossibility many genuine converts found in adapting themselves to Christian usages such as the eating of pork.

Though the general social level of the conversos remained unchanged, many of them, as we have already seen, climbed upwards into the higher ranks of the ruling classes. Whatever their position, they were an integral part of Spanish society and contributed magnificently to it from generation to generation. It is even possible that the ghetto mentality which has always been part of the character of a persecuted minority would have disappeared entirely from the make-up of the conversos, but for two important factors—the continued existence of secret Jewish practices, and the prevalence of antisemitism. Because of these two factors the conversos were obliged to maintain almost a separate existence, on the edge of Spanish society, and in this way the ghetto mentality perpetuated itself. Such a development was all too unfortunate, in view of the important role that conversos did, and could, play if properly assimilated into the Christian body. A brief glance at a few prominent conversos will underline this. At the end of the fifteenth century the entire administration of Aragon was in converso hands; at the very moment the Inquisition began to function, five conversos – Luis de Santangel, Gabriel Sánchez, Sancho de Paternoy, Felipe Climent, and Alfonso de la Caballería – held the five most important posts in the kingdom. Sons and grandsons of conversos continued this predominance. One of them was the notorious secretary of Philip II, Antonio Pérez. The persistence of conversos in Spanish life, despite all the hostility of society, has been explained by the tendency of the Habsburgs to choose as their closest advisers men who were not from the old aristocracy. It may, however, be just as simply explained by the fact that so many of the leading families of the realm contained converso blood that it would have been impossible to ignore talented members from them. What nobody can doubt is that the converso contribution was out of all proportion to their numbers. The names of Fernando de Rojas, author of the drama *Celestina*; the great humanist Luis Vives; the Blessed Juan de Avila; Luis de León; and Saint Teresa of Avila; and of Diego Laínez, second General of the Jesuit Order; are only a beginning to the list of hundreds of likely and unlikely conversos whose names have illuminated not simply Spanish but the whole of western European history.

Since these pages do not attempt to give more than a sketch of converso history, we should direct our attention to the kind of role played by the conversos in Spanish society. As always, the most obvious sphere in which they excelled was that of finance. It is memorable that but for converso finance Columbus' first voyage in 1492 would not have been carried out: it was the Aragonese conversos Luis de Santangel and Gabriel Sánchez who protected and financed the expedition; Jews and conversos, including a Jewish interpreter, formed part of the crew; and there is the possibility that Columbus himself was descended from a family of Catalan conversos.[1] A high proportion of the great financiers of the seventeenth century were conversos, mainly of Portuguese origin thanks to the flight of conversos from the persecution in Portugal; the more distinguished of these we shall encounter later. Several Spaniards were later to regret the expulsion of Jewish financiers in 1492, and in the seventeenth century we first meet suggestions by native writers that the growing wealth of countries like Holland was due in great measure to the help of Jewish capital flowing into Amsterdam. At a later date the decline of Spain and the triumph of its enemies was blamed on the international Jewish conspiracy. Among the first writers to take this line was the otherwise distinguished novelist and poet Francisco de Quevedo, who took to imagining a typical meeting of Jewish elders from all over Europe in Salonika, where they drew up their secret plans against Christendom.[2] The Count Duke of Olivares was similarly obsessed with the power of Jewish finance, and entertained serious plans to invite the Jews back into Spain and so undo all the harm of 1492.

The other principal occupation of the converso was medicine.[3] How far they perpetuated Jewish predominance in this field is shown by a famous case. The Inquisition in Logroño (Navarre) at the end of the sixteenth century found itself in need of a doctor, but could find no Old Christian with the necessary qualifications: finally it had to have recourse to a converso, one Doctor Bélez. The Inquisition in Madrid, on being consulted about this, decreed that the tribunal should keep the converso doctor but give him no official status, in the hope that an Old Christian might some day be found. Even the crown had conversos in attendance: doctor Francisco Villalobos was court physician to both Ferdinand the Catholic and Charles V. Among other famous conversos should be mentioned doctor Andrés Laguna (1499-1560), naturalist, botanist and physician, a native of Segovia and one of the great luminaries of Spanish science. The outstanding services of conversos to medicine are amply illustrated by the number of doctors who appear in the records of the Inquisition during the sixteenth and seventeenth centuries. Why they should have played so great a part in the liberal professions it is difficult to say, but there was no difficulty in spreading the rumour that Jews became physicians because this gave them a greater opportunity to carry on their nefarious deeds.

Following a long tradition, converso families gave many sons and daughters into the hands of the Church, to be brought up in the religious orders. While this policy would have been followed only by sincere converts, no doubt many other young conversos chose the clerical life because it gave them the easiest chance of advancement. Converso students were consequently to be seen in ever growing numbers in the universities of Spain, and choice benefices and even episcopal sees went to them in preference to Old Christians. By the mid-sixteenth century it was reliably reported that a majority, if not all, of the Spanish clergy resident in Rome and seeking ecclesiastical preferment, were of Jewish origin. Once again, therefore, we have a 'converso danger' which consisted in the struggle between Old and New Christians for influential positions in the Church. From the Old Christian point of view, the danger was very real, for the Church then as always, kept its ranks open to entrants from every race and social class, and unless some method of exclusion were adopted there existed a real possibility that the gifted conversos would seize control of the Spanish Church. Those who consider such fears exaggerated and incredible need only read the polemics that grew up around the question of exclusion: the issue is important enough to warrant discussion in the course of our narrative.

With so much hostility prevalent in Spain against false converts who were secretly Jews, it is not surprising if the genuine converts took alarm and attempted to justify themselves against their judaizing brethren and against the Jewish religion in general. In so doing they contributed powerfully to the arsenal of antisemitism. Many may have been motivated by pure zeal for their new faith, but others did not stop at fomenting racial hatred. There was a long ancestry for this. From earliest times Christian writers had laid against the Jews the guilt of having crucified Christ, and there was no limit to the crimes that could be blamed on them. Consequently the same old stories appeared in every antisemitic tract ever issued. Our concern here is with converso writers who took part in these attacks on members of their own race. Among the more moderate writers was the famous convert Pablo de Santa María, with his *Scrutinium scripturarum, sive dialogus Sauli et Pauli contra Judaeos*, written in 1432 but published posthumously in 1591 at Burgos. Another distinguished author was the former rabbi Jehoshua Ha-Lorqui, who adopted the name Jerónimo de Santa Fe, founded a powerful converso family, and produced his anti-Jewish polemics in the form of a work called *Hebraeomastix*. A member of a third great converso family, Pedro de la Caballería, wrote in 1450 a treatise known in Latin as *Zelus Christi contra Judaeos*. These three converso productions were distinguished by learned theological arguments and a profound factual knowledge of Jewish rites, so that although they were full of hostility they did not contain falsifications and slanders. The same cannot be said for the work of a friar named Alonso de Espina, whose *Fortalitium fidei contra Judeos* was written in 1458 and published in 1487.

Espina is described by all Spanish historians as a converso. While he may have been of converso descent, it seems unlikely that he himself was a convert, particularly since his writings are based on deliberate distortions and fabrications of a kind difficult to expect even from an apostate. To him, says Lea, 'may be ascribed a large share in hastening the development of organized persecution in Spain, by inflaming the race hatred of recent origin which already needed no stimulation.'[4] In the 1450s he was exceptionally busy in a campaign to bring about the forced conversion of the Jews, and his tract helped by its themes and language to contribute to the general detestation of the race. For Espina the crimes of Jews against Christians were all too well known: they were traitors, homosexuals, blasphemers, child-murderers, assassins (in the guise of doctors), poisoners, usurers, and so on. Such accusations clearly sprang from fanaticism rather than knowledge, and it is little wonder if they served to stir up similar fanaticism in Spanish audiences. What differentiates Espina from the other converso apologists, however, is the fact that his accusations were clearly racialist in character and purpose, whereas the anger of Santa María and the others was more explicitly directed against the stubborn unbelief of their unconverted brethren. Espina's tract was little more than Jew-baiting, while the others were concerned about the cause of religion. For all this, it is perhaps possible to admit the existence of a specifically semitic form of antisemitism. The fact is not only that the chief anti-Jewish polemicists were former Jews, but also that the first two Inquisitors General, Tomás de Torquemada, and Diego de Deza, were both of converso origin. A later Inquisitor General, Alonso Manrique, Cardinal archbishop of Seville and Inquisitor from 1523 to 1538, was also reputed to be a *marrano*.[5] This phenomenon of men with Jewish blood leading the hunt against members of their own race has since become such a commonplace that the historian has no need to comment on its significance. In sixteenth century Spain, however, converso blood was, as we have seen, so widely dispersed that there is no reason for supposing that everyone of remote Jewish origin was conscious of it or felt he had anything in common with the Jewish race or religion: it is therefore quite possible to exaggerate the importance of this beyond all reality.

The first great defence raised by Old Christians against conversos was to exclude them from any part in public administration. This occurred as a result of the memorable disturbances at Toledo in 1449. As a result of the riots that year, the Old Christians held a court to determine whether the conversos should be allowed to continue holding public office. Pedro Sarmiento, a leader of the Old Christians, proposed a special statute (known as the *Sentencia-Estatuto*) which, despite the opposition of the bishop of Cuenca, was passed by the city council on 5 June 1449. In this it was resolved 'that no converso of Jewish descent may have or hold any office or benefice in the said city of Toledo, or in its territory and jurisdiction', and that the testimony of conversos against Old Christians was not to be accepted in the courts.[6] The immediate result of this was a bull issued by Pope Nicholas V on 24 September 1449 under the significant title *Humani generis inimicus*: in this he denounced the idea of excluding Christians from office simply because they came from a particular race. 'We decree and declare', the pope went on, 'that all Catholics are one body in Christ according to the teaching of our faith.' Another bull of the same date excommunicated Sarmiento and his colleagues for alleged rebellion against the Spanish crown. Other Spanish ecclesiastical authorities followed the pope in declaring that baptised converts were entitled to all the privileges of the Christian community. But the *Sentencia-Estatuto* represented powerful forces which could not easily be suppressed. The state of civil war then reigning in Castile made the crown all too willing to win friends by conciliation, and in 1450 the pope was asked by king Juan II to suspend his excommunication of those practising racialism. A year later, on 13 August 1451, the king formally gave his approval to the *Sentencia-Estatuto*. This meant a victory for the Old Christian party, a victory repeated once more when on 16 June 1468, in the year after the Toledo riots of 1467, king Henry IV confirmed in office in the city all holders of posts formerly held by conversos. The same king on 14 July of the same year conceded to the city of Ciudad Real the privilege of excluding conversos from all municipal office.[7]

The fact that two of the chief cities in Castile had succeeded in excluding conversos from public office meant that a new and dangerous turning point had been reached in the struggle between Old and New Christians. This was serious enough in its consequences for political stability in the kingdom, but a few conscientious clergy were also worried about the effect on the unity of the Christian body. It was after some deliberation, therefore, that on 12 May 1481 the archbishop of Toledo, Alonso Carrillo, condemned the existence in Toledo of guilds organized on racial lines, some of them excluding conversos and others excluding Old Christians. The archbishop stated:

Divisions bring great scandal and schism and divide the seamless garment of Christ, who, as the Good Shepherd, gave us a command to love one another in unity and obedience to Holy Mother Church, under one Pontiff and vicar of Christ, under one baptism, formed under the law into one body, so that whether Jew, Greek or Gentile we are regenerated by baptism and made into new men. From which it is obvious how culpable are those who, forgetting the purity of the law of the gospel, create different lineages, some calling themselves Old Christians and others calling themselves New Christians or conversos . . . what is evil is that in the city of Toledo, as in the other cities, towns and places of our see, there are many guilds and brother-hoods of which some under pretence of piety do not receive conversos and others do not receive Old Christians . . .[8]

The archbishop therefore by his authority dissolved the said guilds and forbade any similar racial associations under pain of excommunication. Unhappily his good intentions bore no fruit. Already by 1481, as we shall see later, the racial split between conversos and Old Christians had grown too wide for one prelate alone to heal. By constant propaganda and petty perse-cution the mood of the populace had been whipped into one of fury against the conversos. Several incidents contributed to this.

Since the conversos and Jews were the same thing to an anti-semite, it is not surprising if atrocity stories concerning Jews also served to discredit conversos. One of these stories concerned an alleged ritual murder performed by Jews on a Christian child at Sepúlveda, in the province of Segovia, in 1468. The converso bishop of Segovia, Juan Arias Dávila, is reported to have punished sixteen Jews for the crime, some of them being burnt and others hanged. Stories of this sort were legion at the time, similar cases being reported from all over the country as reasons for popular risings against Jews. Among the most famous of them was the case of the alleged ritual murder of a Christian infant at La Guardia in the province of Toledo, in 1491. Six conversos and as many Jews were said to have been implicated in this plot, for which a Christian child was apparently crucified and had its heart cut out in an attempt at creating a magical spell to destroy Christians and cause Judaism to triumph. Such at least was the plot pieced together from confessions extracted under torture by the Inquisition. The only odd thing, as Lea points out, was that 'no child had anywhere been missed and no remains were found on the spot where it was said to have been buried.'[9] Atrocity stories of this sort, common in Europe as a whole before and since – in England one need think only of the cases of St William of Norwich in 1144 and of St Hugh of Lincoln in 1255 – served to feed the most vicious kind of anti-semitism. If some Church authorities professed to give credit to them, there were nevertheless others in the highest quarters who condemned the deliberate fomenting of racial hatred. As early as 1247 the papacy denied emphatically that there was any truth in the legend of the ritual murder of Christian children by Jews. Occasionally – and too infrequently – Rome reiterated this view. It was not until the eighteenth century that the Jewish communities of Europe appealed to Cardinal Ganganelli (later pope as Clement XIV) to undertake an exhaustive historical enquiry into the origins of the ritual murder story. In 1759 the findings of the enquiry were issued. They showed that there had never at any time in European history been any factual evidence to show that the story was anything more than a popular myth.[10] But conclusions of this kind are invariably unpalatable to many, even among the learned. It is still possible for an allegedly serious historian of the period to believe in the truth of every one of the atrocities attributed to Jews in Spain at the time of the Inquisition.[11] Little wonder, then, that even more gullible members of a fifteenth-century public, resentful of a minority whom they, at the instigation of their masters, distrusted for every possible social and religious reason, should be moved to hatred at such depravity.

Anti-converso publicists exploited such incidents to the full. Events such as the discovery and immediate burning at Llerena (Extremadura) in September 1467 of two conversos for prac-tising Judaism, were visible proof of the religious insincerity of many New Christians. Preachers under Ferdinand and Isabella made the most of cases like this. Among them was Alonso de Hojeda, a Dominican prior of Seville, who devoted all his energies to making the crown aware of the reality of the danger from Jews and false converts. His opportunity came when queen Isabella arrived in Seville in July 1477 and stayed until October 1478. Historians are unanimous in citing Hojeda's preaching as one of the immediate influences on the queen in her final decision about the conversos. Soon after Isabella's departure from Seville, Hojeda uncovered evidence of a secret meeting of judaizing conversos in the city, and with this in hand he went to demand the institution of measures against the heretics. The evidence seems to have impressed the government, which asked for a report on the situation in Seville. The report, supported by the authority of Pedro González de Mendoza, archbishop of Seville, and that of Tomás de Torquemada, prior of a Dominican convent in Segovia, revealed that not only in Seville but throughout Andalucia and Castile the conversos were practising Jewish rites in secret. Faced with this situation, Ferdinand and Isabella consented to introduce the machinery of an Inquisition into Castile, and sent orders to Rome for the bull of institution to be obtained.

The Inquisition as such was not unknown in Spain. In 1238 a papal Inquisition directly subordinate to Rome and controlled by the Dominican order was instituted in the realms of the crown of Aragon, but this body had by the fifteenth century declined into complete inactivity. Castile, on the other hand, had never known the existence of an Inquisition, that is, of a body which concerned itself solely with rooting out heresy. The bishops and their church courts had so far sufficed to deal with the punishment of heretics. The argument used by Hojeda and others, however, was that the converso problem was of such great and grave dimensions that only the introduction of a full-time Inquisition would be adequate to meet the threat. Consequently, the bull which was finally issued by pope Sixtus IV on 1 November 1478 provided for the appointment of two or three priests over forty years of age as inquisitors: powers of appointment and dismissal were granted to the Spanish crown. After this, no further steps were taken for two years. This long interlude would seem to contradict Hojeda's argument about the urgency of the converso danger. What seems a likely explanation is that Ferdinand and Isabella favoured a cautious period of leniency before going on to severe measures, and that this policy may have been in part influenced by the large number of conversos in prominent positions at court. It was only on 27 September 1480, at Medina del Campo, that commissions as inquisitors in accordance with the papal bull were issued to the Dominicans Juan de San Martín and Miguel de Morillo, with Juan Ruiz de Medina as their assessor or adviser. With these appointments the Spanish Inquisition came into definitive existence.

The new body had clearly been set up as the result of agitation against the New Christians. Its immediate purpose, therefore, was to ensure religious orthodoxy in Spain. It is important to observe here that the Inquisition had authority only over baptized Christians, and the unbaptized were completely free from its disciplinary measures. This meant that Ferdinand and Isabella were not at the moment attempting to enforce unity of faith in the peninsula: they were merely attempting to solve the problem of social and racial dissidence which was aggravated above all by the doubtful orthodoxy of the conversos. This policy was all too obviously supported by Old Christians and by religious zealots, among whom conversos were prominent. Opposition to the new institution was inevitable. Immediately after their appointment the inquisitors were sent to work in Seville, where the spotlight had first been put on the converso danger. By mid-October 1480 operations had begun in Seville.

The first result was a mass exodus of conversos. In Seville and Córdoba and the towns of Andalucia, according to the chronicler Hernando del Pulgar, more than four thousand households took to flight, women and children included:

and since the absence of these people depopulated a large part of the country, the Queen was informed that commerce was declining; but setting little importance on the decline in her revenue, and prizing highly the purity (*limpieza*) of her lands, she said that the essential thing was to cleanse the country of that sin of heresy, for she understood it to be in God's service and her own. And the representations which were made to her about this matter did not alter her decision.[12]

Refugees who fled to the lands of neighbouring aristocrats, in the hope that feudal jurisdictions would protect them from the Inquisition, were speedily disillusioned when the nobles complied with an order to hand over all refugees within a fortnight, under pain of excommunication. Not all the conversos thought flight the best solution. In Seville the wealthy Diego de Susán, one of the city's leading citizens and father to a beautiful daughter Susanna, famous as the *fermosa fembra*, called together a group of converso colleagues, including prominent ecclesiastics and magistrates, for a meeting in the church of San

Salvador. With them, according to a contemporary source, were many other rich and powerful men from the towns of Utrera and Carmona. These said to one another, 'What do you think of them acting thus against us? Are we not the most propertied members of this city, and well loved by the people? Let us collect men together . . .' and thus between them they allotted the raising of arms, men, money and other necessities. 'And if they come to take us, we, together with armed men and the people will rise up and slay them and so be revenged on our enemies.[13]

The rising might well have succeeded but for the *fermosa fembra* who, anxious about the possible fate of her Old Christian lover, betrayed the plot to the authorities. All those implicated were arrested and the occasion was made the excuse for the arrest of the richest and most powerful conversos of Seville. With this prize catch the first *auto de fe* of the Spanish Inquisition was celebrated on 6 February 1481, when six people were burnt at the stake and the sermon at the ceremony was preached by Fray Alonso de Hojeda. Hojeda's triumph was short-lived, for within a few days the plague which was just beginning to ravage Seville numbered him among its first victims. According to Bernáldez:

A few days after this they burnt three of the richest leaders of the city, namely Diego de Susán, who was said to be worth ten million *maravedis* and was a chief rabbi, and who apparently died as a Christian; Manuel Sauli; and Bartolomé de Torralva. They also arrested Pedro Fernández Benadeba, who was one of the ringleaders and had in his house weapons to arm a hundred men, and Juan Fernández Abolasia, who had often been chief magistrate and was a great lawyer; and many other leading and very rich citizens, who were also burnt.[14]

When Susanna saw the result of her betrayal, she is said to have first retired to a convent, and then to have taken to the streets, remorse eating into her soul until she died in poverty and shame, her last wishes being that her skull should be placed over the door of her house as a warning and example to others.

The heretics brought to light by the establishment of an Inquisition at Seville justified the introduction of other tribunals throughout the country. The emergency, for it was seen as such, meant that more bulls would have to be obtained from Rome. Accordingly, a papal brief of 11 February 1482 appointed seven more inquisitors, all Dominican friars, among them being the well-known name of Tomás de Torquemada. New tribunals were set up at Córdoba in 1482, and at Ciudad Real and Jaén in 1483. The tribunal at Ciudad Real was only temporary, and was permanently transferred to Toledo in 1485. By 1492 the kingdom of Castile had tribunals at Avila, Córdoba, Jaén, Medina del Campo, Segovia, Sigüenza, Toledo and Valladolid; though not all these had a permanent existence, and the southern tribunals were far more active than those in the north. Opposition to the Inquisition inevitably took a violent form after the first despairing pleas and flights. In Toledo, one of the most important converso centres in the realm, a plot against the inquisitors was planned for the feast of Corpus Christi 1484: the outcome followed the pattern of Seville, with betrayal, arrest and execution. The despair of the conversos at this time is amply revealed by their tame subjection to arrest and execution during what a modern apologist for the Inquisition concedes was 'a period of imprisonments and trials whose like has perhaps never been equalled by any other tribunal.'[15] In the first eight years of life of the Seville tribunal alone, according to Bernáldez, 'more than seven hundred persons were burnt and over five thousand punished.'[16]

The machinery of the Inquisition was regulated in accordance with the needs of the administration. Isabella was at this time engaged in reforming the councils which controlled central government in Castile, so that when in 1480 at the Cortes of Toledo it was decided to confirm the existence of four councils (Council of Castile, Council of Hacienda or Finance, Council of State and Council of Aragon) it seemed natural to follow this up with a separate council for the increasingly important affairs of the Inquisition. Accordingly in 1483 the *Consejo de la Suprema y General Inquisición* (or *Suprema*, for short) came into existence. The new council consisted initially of three ecclesiastical members, and a fourth member as president of the council, with the title (this came into existence slightly later) of Inquisitor General. The first Inquisitor General was Fray Tomás de Torquemada. By 1483, then, the Inquisition had taken firm root in Castile, and had been given its essential administrative organization. The problem now was whether the Castilian Inquisition should be extended to the kingdom of Aragon.

Resistance to the introduction of the Inquisition into Castile had been meagre and abortive. Popular opinion had been prepared for it and racial rivalry welcomed it. Opposition to the methods of the tribunal did of course continue to exist for some time, but this usually took the form of peaceful and constitutional attempts to achieve reform. In the realms of Aragon the story was quite different. The mediaeval Inquisition had existed in Aragon since 1238 but had become almost defunct by the fifteenth century. As part of his new, vigorous policy Ferdinand took steps in 1481 and 1482 to assert royal control over the appointment and payment of inquisitors. His aim was to resurrect the old papal Inquisition but also to subject it to his own control so as to come into line with practice in Castile. In Aragon, therefore, the new Inquisition was simply a continuance of the old tribunal, with the difference that the crown now controlled appointments and salaries, so that the tribunal became effectively more dependent on Ferdinand than on the pope.

The first activites of this reformed tribunal, with its main centres in the cities of Barcelona, Saragossa and Valencia, were directed against the conversos, who took alarm at developments and prepared for mass emigration. But differences with the pope, supplemented no doubt by pressure on Rome from conversos, brought activities to a temporary stop. On 18 April 1482 Sixtus IV issued what Lea calls 'the most extraordinary bull in the history of the Inquisition'. In this remarkable bull the pope protested:

that in Aragon, Valencia, Majorca and Catalonia the Inquisition has for some time been moved not by zeal for the faith and the salvation of souls, but by lust for wealth, and that many true and faithful Christians, on the testimony of enemies, rivals, slaves and other lower and even less proper persons, have without any legitimate proof been thrust into secular prisons, tortured and condemned as relapsed heretics, deprived of their goods and property and handed over to the secular arm to be executed, to the peril of souls, setting a pernicious example, and causing disgust to many.[17]

Accordingly, in future episcopal officers should act with the inquisitors: the names and testimony of accusers should be given to the accused, who should be allowed counsel; episcopal gaols should be the only ones used; and appeals should be allowed to Rome. The bull was extraordinary because, in Lea's words, 'for the first time heresy was declared to be, like any other crime, entitled to a fair trial and simple justice.'[18] Apart from this, there is little doubt that the pope welcomed the chance to assert once more his authority over an Inquisition that had once been papal and had now slipped entirely into the hands of the king of Aragon. So favourable was the bull to converso claims that their influence in obtaining it cannot be doubted. The pope's intentions, however, may freely be doubted, since he had issued no comparable bull protesting against the horrors occurring simultaneously in Andalucia; and it is probable that converso money alone had helped to secure the bull for Aragon. Ferdinand was outraged by the papal action and pretended to disbelieve in the authenticity of the bull on the grounds that no sensible pontiff would have issued such a document. On 13 May 1482 he wrote to the Pope:

Things have been told me, Holy Father which, if true, would seem to merit the greatest astonishment. It is said that Your Holiness has granted the *conversos* a general pardon for all the errors and crimes they have committed . . . To these rumours, however, we have given no credence, because they seem to be things which would in no way have been conceded by Your Holiness, who have a duty to the Inquisition. But if by chance concessions have been made through the persistent and cunning persuasion of the said *conversos*, I intend never to let them take effect. Take care therefore not to let the matter go further, and to revoke any concessions and entrust us with the care of this question[91]

Before this resolution, Sixtus IV wavered, and in October 1482 announced that he had suspended the bull. The way lay completely open to Ferdinand. Papal co-operation was definitively secured by the bull of 17 October 1483, which appointed Torquemada as Inquisitor General of Aragon, Valencia and Catalonia, thus uniting the Inquisition of the Spanish crown under a single head. The new tribunal came directly under the control of the crown and was the only institution whose authority ran in all the territories of Spain, a fact of great importance for future occasions when the ruler of Castile wished to interfere in other provinces where his sovereign authority was not recognized. This was not the end of papal interference, however, and the next half century or so witnessed several attempts by

Rome to interfere in questions of jurisdiction and to reform abuses which might give the Inquisition a bad name. Besides this, the conversos in Spain never gave up their struggle to modify the practices of the tribunal, which they rightly considered a threat, not just to judaizers, but to the whole race of New Christians. Because of their representations to Rome, papal intervention was continued on their behalf, and thus led to several minor quarrels between crown and papacy.

Resistance to the introduction of the Inquisition into Castile had proved to be a broken reed, but in the realms of Aragon the situation was quite different. As we have seen, Aragon and Castile had not been united by the marriage of the Catholic monarchs, and each kingdom preserved its individual administration and liberties. The Aragonese, even more than the Castilians, prided themselves on the constitutional liberties (*fueros*) of the kingdoms and on their representative assemblies which were more independent and powerful than those of Castile. It was in the province of Aragon that the oath of allegiance made by the Cortes to its king took the form, 'We, who are as good as you, take an oath to you who are no better than we, as prince and heir of our kingdom, on condition that you preserve our *fueros* and liberties, and if you do not, we do not.' It was clearly dangerous to introduce a new tribunal without any reference to the Cortes who were so vigilant in guarding their constitutional rights. The resurrection of the old papal Inquisition by Ferdinand, and the sequence of events leading up to the quarrel with Sixtus IV, seems not to have provoked any concern for the *fueros* in Aragon, because the king was doing no more than revive an institution which had existed in Aragon for over two centuries. But the appointment of Torquemada was a different matter. Here was a Castilian inquisitor, the head of a Castilian tribunal, whose authority was now being extended over Aragon when in fact a papal Inquisition already existed there. The opposition was, as usual, led by the intractable Catalans.

When a meeting of the Cortes of the crown of Aragon was called at Tarazona on 15 January 1484, to approve the new Inquisition, the Catalans refused to send their deputies, claiming that it was illegal for them to be summoned outside the principality of Catalonia. They also claimed the right to an inquisitor of their own, and refused to accept an Inquisitor General, namely Torquemada. This claim was helped by the fact that Barcelona's own inquisitor, Juan Comte, had an independent papal commission, which the pope refused to revoke. For two years Ferdinand's efforts to enforce his claims were unsuccessful. Finally, however, in February 1486 the new pope Innocent VIII revoked all independent papal commissions granted in the kingdom of Aragon, and appointed Ferdinand's nominees to the Catalan tribunals, with Torquemada as the special inquisitor for Barcelona. Despite this the municipality of Barcelona held out and it was not until one and a half years later, in June 1487, that Torquemada's representative, Alonso de Espina, was finally allowed entrance into the city. The occasion was a significant one: officials, clergy and nobility came out to greet him, but the deputies and magistrates boycotted his arrival. In the division of parties the deputies represented the interests of the commercial classes who stood to lose most by the methods of the Inquisition. The previous years had seen mass flights of conversos which threatened the economic stability of the city: the depletion in their ranks is shown by the very few victims present at the first *autos de fe* held in Barcelona in 1488 and 1489. 'Foreign realms are growing rich and glorious through the depopulation of this country, which is becoming desolated', complained the councillors of Barcelona. But Ferdinand remained inflexible. 'No cause nor interest, however great and firm it may be, will make us suspend the Inquisition', he wrote in reply to them.[20] This answer, reflecting exactly the sentiments of Isabella, illustrates the unswerving adherence of the Catholic monarchs to a dogmatic ideal on which they refused ever to compromise.

In Valencia opposition was based similarly on the *fueros*. The Cortes at Tarazona in 1484 had approved the introduction of the new Inquisition, so that the crown would now legally make appointments of inquisitors in Aragon and Valencia. Torquemada went ahead in Valencia, but the four estates of the realm, assembled in their own Cortes, protested energetically against the alleged violation of their privileges and liberties, and the local authorities refused to allow the first two inquisitors in Valencia, Juan de Epila and Martin Iñigo, to commence their activities. The opening of a tribunal in Valencia city was forbidden on the grounds that, by the *fueros*, only native Valencians could hold office in the kingdom. This opposition was eventually broken down by Ferdinand, and the inquisitors began their work in November 1484. Even then, however, passive resistance continued, particularly on the part of the Valencian nobility, and Ferdinand found it necessary in August 1485 to endow the tribunal with power to arrest and imprison anyone who obstructed the work of the Inquisition, no matter how high his position.

In the province of Aragon developments took a far more serious turn. We have seen that not only were many of the most prominent officials of the kingdom conversos, but many conversos also played an important financial role in the capital city of Saragossa. Regardless of inevitable opposition, on 4 May 1484 Torquemada appointed the first two inquisitors for Aragon, Gaspar Juglar and Pedro Arbués de Epila. According to Lea, the inquisitors set to work immediately, holding *autos de fe* on 10 May and 3 June 1484. These dates, however, are not only excessively early, they also sin against the inquisitorial rule which allowed a term of grace, usually about a month, to elapse before taking action against heretics. It is therefore more likely that the *autos* in question were held in 1485.[21] This activity of the new tribunal deeply disturbed not only conversos but all those whose loyalty was to the *fueros* of Aragon. As the chronicler of Aragon, Jerónimo de Zurita, reported:

> Those newly converted from the Jewish race, and many other leaders and gentry, claimed that the procedure was against the liberties of the realm, because for this offence (of heresy) their goods were confiscated and they were not given the names of witnesses who testified against them.

> As a result (continued Zurita) the conversos had all the kingdom on their side, including persons of the highest consideration, among them Old Christians and gentry.[22]

When public opposition grew so great that there was a move to summon the four estates of the realm, Ferdinand hastily sent a circular letter to the chief nobles and deputies, justifying his position:

> There is no intention of infringing the *fueros* but rather of enforcing their observance. It is not to be imagined that vassals so Catholic as those of Aragon would have demanded, or that kings so Catholic would have granted, *fueros* and liberties adverse to the faith and favourable to heresy. If the old inquisitors had acted conscientiously

43

in accordance with the canons there would have been no cause for bringing in the new ones, but they were without conscience and corrupted with bribes.

If there are so few heretics as is now asserted, there should not be such dread of the Inquisition. It is not to be impeded in sequestrating and confiscating and other necessary acts, for be assured that no cause or interest, however great, shall be allowed to interfere with its proceeding in future as it is now doing.[23]

Whatever the motives, whether personal dread or constitutional opposition, resistance continued. The most remarkable case of resistance in the whole of Spain occurred in 1484 at the city of Teruel, a hundred miles to the south of Saragossa. In that year the tribunal of Saragossa sent two inquisitors to the city to establish a tribunal there, but the magistrates refused them permission to enter the city gates. The inquisitors thereupon withdrew to the neighbouring town of Cella, from which they issued an excommunication and interdict against the city and its magistrates. The clergy of Teruel promptly obtained papal letters releasing the city from these censures. The Inquisition thereupon in October 1484 decreed that all the public offices in Teruel were confiscated to the crown and their present holders deprived of them; this was followed by an appeal to the king to carry out the decree. Ferdinand replied with an order in February 1485 to all his officials in Aragon, asking them to raise arms and help the inquisitors. The response to this was not adequate, so Ferdinand also called on troops from the borders of Castile to help in the enterprise. Faced with such massive coercion the city was easily reduced to obedience, and with its submission in the spring of 1485 the Inquisition seemed to have triumphed everywhere in Aragon. The reasons for Teruel's resistance seem to have lain almost exclusively in the great influence exercised there by conversos, so that here there was little pretence of defending the *fueros* of Aragon. By 1485, indeed, the *fueros* were a dead issue.

But converso opposition had by no means been destroyed. On the one hand it was growing in strength with the passive support of Old Christians who resented the introduction of the new tribunal into Aragon, and on the other it was becoming more desperate because of the obvious failure of resistance as shown by the example of Teruel. In the highest converso circles the idea of the assassination of an inquisitor gained currency, and was supported by people as eminent as Gabriel Sánchez, treasurer of the king, and Sancho de Paternoy, treasurer of the kingdom of Aragon. The climax came on the night of 15 September 1485, as the inquisitor Pedro Arbués was kneeling in prayer before the high altar of Saragossa cathedral. Beneath his gown the inquisitor wore a coat of mail and on his head a steel cap, because of warnings about threats against his life. On the night in question eight conspirators hired by conversos entered the cathedral by the chapter door and stole up behind the inquisitor; after verifying that this was indeed Arbués, one of them stabbed him in the back with a stroke that went through his neck and proved to be his death wound. As Arbués staggered away, two of the others also inflicted wounds on him. The murderers made their escape and the canons of the cathedral rushed in to find the inquisitor dying: Arbués lingered for twenty-four hours and died on 17 September. The shock of this murder led to developments the conversos should certainly have foreseen. When it was discovered that the assassins were judaizers the whole mood of the city of Saragossa, and with it that of Aragon, changed. Arbués was declared to be a saint,* miracles were worked with his blood, mobs roamed the streets in search of conversos, and a national assembly voted to suspend the *fueros* while the search for the assassins went on. In this atmosphere the inquisitors came into their own. *Autos* of the reformed Inquisition were held on 28 December 1485, and the murderers of Arbués expiated their crime in successive *autos de fe* lasting from 30 June 1486 to 15 December the same year. One of them had his hands cut off and nailed to the door of the House of Deputies, after which he was dragged to the market-place, beheaded and quartered, and the pieces of his body suspended in the streets of the city. Another committed suicide in his cell the day before his ordeal, by breaking a glass lamp and swallowing the fragments; he too suffered the same punishment, which was inflicted on his dead body.

More than these initial measures was needed in order to uproot the whole conspiracy, which involved so many and such eminent people that individuals were being punished for it as

---

* He was popularly venerated as *el Santo martyr*, and was assigned a feast day in Spain in the sixteenth century. But a reluctant Rome did not canonize him until 1867.

45

late as 1492. The heads that now rolled came from the highest families in Aragon. Whether they were judaizers or not, members of the leading converso houses had connived at the murder and were sooner or later destroyed by the Inquisition, which remained in full control of all the judicial measures taken. A study of the list of victims [24] shows the constant appearance of the great names of Santa Fe, Santangel, Caballería, and Sánchez. Francisco de Santa Fe, son of the famous converso Jerónimo and a counsellor of the governor of Aragon, committed suicide by jumping from a tower and his remains were burnt in the *auto* of 15 December 1486. Sancho Paternoy was tortured and condemned to perpetual imprisonment. Luis de Santangel, who had been personally knighted by Juan II for his military prowess, was beheaded and burnt in the market-place of Saragossa on 8 August 1487; his cousin Luis, whose money loans made possible the voyages of Columbus, was made to do penance in July 1491. Altogether, over fifteen members of the Santangel family were punished by the Inquisition before 1499; and between 1486 and 1503 fourteen members of the Sánchez family suffered a similar fate. This immense sweep of conversos into the nets of the tribunal was effective in destroying forever the political and social grip of New Christians on the Aragonese administration. Not for the first time a cause triumphed through one useful martyrdom. For the conversos one murder, cheaply achieved at a total cost of six hundred gold florins (which included the wages of the assassins), turned out to be an act of mass suicide which annihilated all opposition to the Inquisition for the next hundred years.

In Majorca, where the old Inquisition had already begun activities against judaizers in 1478, the new tribunal was introduced without incident in 1488, and began operations immediately. The inquisitors, Pedro Pérez de Munebrega and Sancho Martín, found enough work to keep them occupied in the hundreds of cases that filled the years 1488 to 1491. Politically, the island was undisturbed, and no outbreaks against the tribunal occurred until a generation later under Charles V when a rising led by the converso bishop of Elna in 1518 led to the temporary expulsion of the inquisitors from the city of Palma. The acceptance by Majorcans of the activities of the tribunal is all the more unusual since conversos formed a considerable part of the population, thanks to the riots of 1391 in Palma, the preaching of Saint Vincent Ferrer in 1413 and 1414, and the final forcible conversion of the Jews in 1435. The large number of conversos in the *autos de fe* between 1488 and 1499 – 347 in all, excluding the hundreds who were pardoned for confessing voluntarily – proves that here also existed a minority problem of important dimensions.

The Spanish Inquisition was thus established everywhere in Spain several years before the final decision to expel the Jews. The period between the two events is of considerable importance in the history of both Castile and Aragon, for it revealed the extent to which coercion was being employed in the cause of religious orthodoxy. During these years conversos and Jews suffered side by side for reasons ostensibly religious but more emphatically racial and economic. At the very time that conversos were going into exile and being burnt at the stake for heresy, their Jewish colleagues were being expelled from diocese after diocese throughout southern Spain. The whole period between 1480 and 1492 constituted an exercise in racial and class conflict without parallel in the history of Spain. The Jews had been reduced in number by continuous oppression and persecution, until expulsion seemed no more than the logical way to dispose of those that remained: the conversos were eliminated by systematic campaigns carried on in the name of orthodoxy, their fate being worse simply because they were baptized. The fate of the two communities must be kept in mind together if we are to have any idea of the magnitude of the antisemitic measures of those years. The number of refugees fleeing abroad was so great that for every judaizer burnt, tens and hundreds were burnt in effigy as fugitives. This disproportion between those who escaped and those who were caught is shown in the figures for punishments meted out by the Inquisition. In the first two years of the tribunal at Ciudad Real, fifty-two victims were burnt alive but two hundred and twenty had to be condemned to death in their absence. In the Barcelona *auto de fe* of 10 June 1491, three persons were burnt alive but one hundred and thirty-nine were condemned *in absentia*. In Palma de Majorca, the same process was repeated when the *auto* of 11 May 1493 witnessed only three burnings in person but forty-seven burnings of the effigies of absent fugitives. The coming of the Inquisition had, in fact, been preceded by rumblings which gave a clear warning to all those who had reason to fear it. It was therefore not surprising that the total of victims actually punished in the first few years of the tribunal's existence, came to a much lower figure than one would have expected from the alleged size and gravity of the danger.

The Catholic monarchs had now brought into existence the machinery necessary for a solution of the converso problem. After 1492 this machinery was applied to the total Jewish population of the Spanish crown, since the only religions permitted in Spain after this date were Catholicism and Islam. The subsequent history of the Inquisition is therefore connected above all with the racial and religious problems arising from the continued presence of Jews in Spain. In the next few chapters, however, we shall be concerned less with the fate of the conversos than with the general impact made by the new tribunal on Spanish society. This is not simply because excessive attention to the history of the conversos would divert us from our central theme, but more obviously because the Inquisition came to concern itself with other matters ranging far wider than the confines of the Jewish question. We must also remember in this context not to associate the Inquisition exclusively with the problem of religious intolerance. As we have seen, the circumstances giving rise to the tribunal may be traced back to social conflicts which reflect more than the forces of religion. The Inquisition was founded to repress heresy and to deal with the problem caused by the place of Jews in society. Essentially, however, the problem was caused not by the Jews but by the feudal classes who, in alliance with the common people, disputed the key role played in the towns by the middle sections of society among whom the Jews and conversos were the most distinctive and flourishing. On a broad view, the Inquisition should therefore be represented as reflecting the interests of class more than of religion. The religious motive was obviously central, yet despite the almost fanatical Catholicism of the Catholic monarchs, at the beginning they seem to have had no plans for bringing about religious uniformity in Spain through the Inquisition. Only very gradually, with the elimination of the Jews in 1492 and of the Muslim minority nine years later, did this policy of uniformity begin to take shape.

CHAPTER FOUR

A MINORITY OPPOSITION

There were differing opinions.

Juan de Mariana, S. J., HISTORIA GENERAL DE ESPAÑA

'WHAT we cannot doubt', writes a modern Spanish apologist for the Inquisition, 'is that in the fifteenth and sixteenth centuries the immense majority of the Spanish people, with their kings, magistrates and bishops leading them, gave their decisive support to the proceedings of the Inquisition'.[1] This is a fact that no reputable historian would care to deny. Even the great Llorente, last secretary and first historian of the tribunal, was staggered by the lack of evidence for any opposition to it in Spain. As he declared in 1811 in a discourse read to the Royal Academy of History, meeting in Madrid at the height of the Peninsular War:

> If in investigating what a nation thought about a certain institution we were to be guided solely by the testimony of public writers, there is no doubt that the Spanish people had as much love as hate for the Inquisition ... You will find hardly a book printed in Spain from the time of Charles the Fifth to our own days in which the Inquisition is not cited with praise.[2]

The interpolation of 'hate' in this quotation satisfied Llorente's own prejudices, but he produced virtually no evidence to justify it. A modern liberal historian is no less lost in his attempts to search for evidence of massive popular opposition to the tribunal. How is it, one may ask, that so terrible a tribunal managed to consolidate its sway over the Spanish people without arousing hostility and hatred? The question is totally misplaced. As we have seen in preceding chapters, the Inquisition was not an institution imposed on the nation against its will.

It was a tribunal whose existence was based entirely on popular support, and which grew out of the bitter social and class struggles of the fifteenth century. As such, it represented the interests of the vast majority of the people – the Old Christians – and was directed only against the interests of a small but powerful minority within the citadel of Christianity. This popular support, of course, arose not only out of conscious struggle against the conversos, but also out of support for the interests of the landed and militant Old Christian nobility. Popular agitation, fomented by the upper classes, became the basis of the Inquisition's power.

This is to speak of Castile as a whole. What initial opposition there was in Aragon came from different circumstances, notably the struggle for the *fueros*. But although the mass of opinion favoured the Inquisition, the position was not the same in those circles of the upper and middle classes which were dominated by conversos. Here, in these upper reaches, there existed a considerable body of opinion which, in the first two decades after the introduction of the Inquisition, was opposed to the methods and policy behind the zeal for orthodoxy.

Whether they were true Catholics or not, conversos were bound to feel some anxiety at the tendency of the Inquisition to be more concerned with race than with religion. Anyone of converso descent became automatically suspect, no matter how well based his Catholicism. It was therefore to their interest to be concerned about the proportion of secret judaizers among true Christians. Yet were the judaizers wholly to blame? Had they ever been properly catechized after their baptism by force? One of the first to raise these questions was the royal secretary Hernando del Pulgar, himself a converso, who denounced the resort to coercion at a time when evangelization had not even been attempted. Tens of thousands of converso children in Andalucia, he informed the archbishop of Seville,

had never been out of their homes or heard and learned any other doctrine but that which they had seen their parents practise at home. To burn all these would be not only cruel but difficult to carry out.

I do not say this, my lord, in favour of the evildoers, but to find a solution, which it seems to me would be to put in that province outstanding persons who by their exemplary life and teaching of doctrine would convert some and bring back others. Of course (the inquisitors) Diego de Merlo and doctor Medina are good men; but I know very well that they will not produce such good Christians with their fire as the bishops Pablo (de Santa Maria) and Alonso (de Cartagena) did with water.[3]

What Pulgar objected to in particular was the infliction of capital punishment on judaizers, although he agreed that heresy should be repressed. His principal authority for this position was Saint Augustine, who had advocated the use of force but not the death penalty against the Donatist heretics of north Africa in the fifth century. The testimony of the liberal and humane secretary is important evidence that the temper of contemporaries was not entirely in favour of bloody measures, and that the more extreme actions of the Inquisition were not necessarily in conformity with the standards of the age.

That Pulgar was speaking not only for himself but for a respectable body of opinion is vouched for by the famous sixteenth-century historian Juan de Mariana. After describing the more controversial procedures of the Inquisition, the Jesuit goes on to say:

At the time there were differing opinions. Some felt that those who sinned in this way should not suffer the death penalty; but apart from this they admitted that it was just to inflict any other kind of punishment. Among others sharing this opinion, was Hernando del Pulgar, a person of acute and elegant genius.[4]

There was an opposing opinion, according to Mariana, but surprisingly he nowhere describes it as a majority one, and qualifies it only as 'better, and more correct.' We may conjecture that the position represented by Pulgar was widely held in higher circles, and was not one that could be ignored. From another source we have direct evidence that many people considered the conversos as individuals who had never been properly converted, and who therefore did not merit recrimination. At the same time these people opposed the expulsion of the Jews in 1492. The Sicilian inquisitor Luis de Páramo wrote that many learned Spaniards, both before and after 1492, thought the expulsion wrong in principle, as well as harmful to the Church, for two main reasons: firstly, because those who had been baptized by force had not received the sacrament properly and therefore remained essentially pagan;[5] secondly, because the expulsion was an implicit invitation to annihilate the Jews, which would be contrary to Scripture. The first reason was, of course, of paramount importance, for if Jews had been forced into conversion their baptism was invalid and the Inquisition had no jurisdiction over them. The standard reply to this argument was simple: the mere fact that the Jews had *chosen* baptism as an alternative to death or exile meant that they had exercised the right of free choice: there was therefore no compulsion, and the sacrament was valid. Against such die-hard reasoning no liberal theology could prevail, and conversos in subsequent centuries continued to be persecuted and burnt for failing to observe properly a religion they had never chosen and in which they had never been adequately instructed.

Among the examples of those who disliked the way in which the hapless conversos were treated, the case of Fray José de Sigüenza stands out. This sixteenth-century historian of the Order of Saint Jerome – the Jeronimites – lamented that there had been no other prelates in Spain like the saintly Hernando de Talavera, archbishop of Granada, confessor to Queen Isabella, and a converso by origin. In his treatment of New Christians, says Fray José, Talavera

would not allow anyone to harm them in word or deed, or burden them with new taxes and impositions, for he detested the evil custom prevalent in Spain of treating members of the sects worse after their conversion than before it . . . so that many refused to accept a Faith in whose believers they saw so little charity and so much haughtiness.

And if (continues Fray José) there had been more prelates who walked in this path, there would not have been so many lost souls stubborn in the sects of Moses and Mahommed within Spain, nor so many heretics in other nations.[6]

Testimony as powerful as this, penned a full century after the protests of Pulgar, bears witness to the continued existence in Spain of a responsible body of opinion which condemned not only the practices of the Inquisition but also the atmosphere reigning in a society which had lost its conscience. The voices quoted above were not crying in the wilderness. Others at the time, and later, as we shall see, were protesting against details of procedure followed by the tribunal, and the injustices in its administration. At times the protests cut so deep as to strike at the very basis of the Inquisition. These dissentient voices abhorred the racial persecution, the methods of coercion and dishonesty, the abdication of Christian responsibility and charity. The fact that men like these existed in an age where heresy was regarded as the worst of all social crimes, is a tribute to the pluralist society that had once existed in Spain. At the same time, it makes nonsense of the claims that the excesses committed in this period, whether by the Inquisition or by other bodies, can be excused because of the standards of the age. The few who differed are proof that no uniform standards existed in that age.

The new tribunal had to suffer some degree of opposition before it could settle down to a tranquil and secure existence. In the initial period this opposition was invariably promoted by conversos. Unable to secure support in Spain they turned to Rome. Thus a bull issued by Sixtus IV on 2 August 1483, and almost certainly obtained by converso money, ordered greater leniency to be exercised in the tribunal of Seville, and revoked all appeal cases to Rome. Only eleven days later, however, the pope withdrew the bull, after pressure from the Spanish rulers. Sixtus died in 1484, to be succeeded by Innocent VIII, a pontiff who followed his policy of intervening in favour of the conversos while taking care not to anger the Catholic monarchs. The bulls issued by Innocent on 11 February and 15 July 1485, asking for more mercy and leniency and for greater use of the practice of secret reconciliation,[7] are typical of the efforts made by the Holy See to avoid lasting infamy falling on the tribunal's victims. Yet even if we see the hand of the conversos in all these attempts to mitigate the worst aspects of inquisitorial procedure, it is impossible to maintain that conversos alone constituted the opposition. The testimony of Juan de Mariana, which might seem extraordinary were it not confirmed by other sources, shows that a great number of contemporaries were disturbed by the novel practices now introduced into the country. According to Mariana, inquisitorial procedure.

at its inception appeared very oppressive to Spaniards. What caused the most surprise was that children paid for the crimes of their parents, and that accusers were not named or made known, nor confronted by the accused, nor was there publication of witnesses: all of which was contrary to the practice used of old in other tribunals. Besides this it appeared an innovation that sins of that sort should be punished by death. And what was most serious was that because of these secret investigations, they were deprived of the liberty to hear and talk freely, since in all the cities, towns and villages there were persons placed to give information of what went on. This was considered by some the most wretched slavery and equal to death.[8]

So severe a verdict would appear to leave nothing to be said, yet it is worth noting that Mariana himself appears not to have agreed with the tenor of the passage, which he presents only as an opinion held by Pulgar and others. The contrary opinion, which he describes as 'better and more correct', as we have already seen, approved of the Inquisition all along the line. Two points in particular are worth noting about the passage above. Nowhere does Mariana give the impression that conversos alone objected to the tribunal. On the contrary, the specific points quoted, on innovations in judicial procedure, on the death sentence, and on the secret police system, were questions which could have been raised by any Old Christian, as indeed they were in several Cortes of the next few years. Secondly, Mariana admits that these harsh measures were a deviation from the normal charitable procedure of the Church; but, he says, it was held 'that at times the ancient customs of the Church should be changed in conformity with the needs of the times'.

The complaints outlined by Mariana had been at the root of opposition by both conversos and Old Christians in Aragon, and were to remain a matter of contention for many years. The one issue that perhaps aroused the most hostility from the very beginning was that victims were compelled to wear penitential garments known as *sanbenitos*. The practice was humiliating for those concerned, and brought ill-fame on the regions where it existed. Mariana says specifically that the usage 'at its inception appeared very oppressive to Spaniards'. In Andalucia, according to Bernáldez, victims were allowed to cease wearing them 'so that the disrepute of the territory should not grow'.[9] Of the system of police informers we shall treat more when we study the existence of 'familiars' in the Inquisition. What is not usually realized is that before 1492 the Jews themselves were asked to spy on their converso brethren. At Toledo in 1485 the inquisitors of the province collected the rabbis and made them swear to pronounce, within their synagogues, major anathemas on those Jews who did not denounce judaizers.[10] In view of the hatred in which Jews usually held apostate members of their own race, we may presume that this system produced some fruit.

In a tribunal as large as the Inquisition, governed by fallible men, abuses were no doubt inevitable. The historian, however, is obliged not to excuse abuses but to put them on record. Even before the death of Ferdinand in January 1516 the failings of the new tribunal had aroused a formidable tide of opposition throughout Spain. In Castile, where the Inquisition had been accepted almost without a murmur, the first rumblings of discontent made themselves heard only in 1499. In that year the inquisitor of Córdoba had been transferred to the city of Avila after an investigation into wholesale frauds and extortions committed under his direction. He was replaced by someone who was to prove to be even more nefarious. Diego Rodríguez Lucero became inquisitor of Córdoba on 7 September 1499. As early as 1501 he came into conflict with the municipal authorities, when one of the latter's principal officials was dismissed from office and exiled by the Inquisition for an indiscreet quarrel with employees of the tribunal. This success emboldened Lucero to go even further. From now on his career consisted in attempts to arrest leading citizens on trifling and often non-existent pretexts, in order to seize their property which would come to the tribunal in the form of confiscations. His actions were protected against government exposure by the complicity of a secretary of the king, Juan Roiz de Calcena, who was responsible for conducting royal correspondence in inquisitorial affairs. Prominent members of leading Old Christian families in Córdoba soon came into Lucero's net, and the fear among all classes in the city grew so great that an atmosphere of terror very quickly engulfed the whole community. Not content with this, Lucero invented stories of a vast conspiracy covering Spain in the interests of subverting Christianity, and used this myth as a justification for his extreme measures. A relatively mild summary of events is given by an annalist of Córdoba, who says that

to gain credit as a zealous minister of the faith and to gain higher dignities, he began to treat the accused in prison with extreme rigour, forcing them to declare their accomplices, which resulted in the denunciation of so great a number of people, both conversos and Old Christians, that the city was scandalised and almost burst into rioting. . . .

In view of this the Marquis of Priego and the Count of Cabra wrote to the archbishop of Seville Fray Diego Deza, the Inquisitor General, and the town council and cathedral chapter nominated deputies to make representations to him about the excesses of Lucero.[11]

It was easier to protest than to gain a remedy. Deza refused to take any action, and Ferdinand was reluctant to act for political reasons.[12] The bishop and chapter of Córdoba appealed to the pope, denouncing the greed of the inquisitors. Meanwhile Lucero pursued his course undaunted. A horrific story recounted by Lea tells how a judaizer who had been preaching his heresy was arrested by Lucero. Witnesses were made to denounce those who had attended his sermons, and these, to the number of 107, were burnt alive together in a single *auto de fe*. The inquisitor then reached out to the eighty years old Jeronimite archbishop of Granada, Hernando de Talavera, and denounced him as a judaizer. Although of converso descent, Talavera was so renowned for his liberality and sanctity that no one believed the charge. Nevertheless, in 1506 Lucero arrested the whole of Talavera's household, his nephew (the dean of Granada cathedral), sister, nieces and servants, as a prelude to arresting the archbishop himself. The relentless persecution to which Talavera was subjected illustrates how personal and political considerations now dominated the Inquisition under Lucero and Deza. He was ultimately acquitted of all charges by a papal sentence in May 1507, but the acquittal came too late to benefit the old man. Walking barefoot and bareheaded through the streets of Granada in the procession on Ascension Day, 13 May, he was seized by a violent fever which the following day ended his life. This great and holy man, whose care for his flock, regardless of race, had left him no time to care for himself, died in perfect poverty, and his household, for which he had not provided, had to resort to the charity of the bishop of Málaga. Nearly a century later, Fray José de Sigüenza claimed that his like had not since been seen in Spain.

On 16 July the same year Gonzalo de Ayora, captain general

and chronicler, wrote a letter of protest to the king's secretary Miguel de Almazan.

The government had failed to exercise effective control over its ministers. As for the Inquisition, the method adopted was to place so much confidence in the archbishop of Seville and in Lucero . . . that they were able to defame the whole kingdom, to destroy, without God or justice, a great part of it, slaying and robbing and violating maids and wives to the great dishonour of the Christian religion . . .

The damages which the wicked officials of the Inquisition have wrought in my land are so many and so great that no reasonable person on hearing of them would not grieve.[13]

The redress so urgently demanded began with the resignation of Deza under pressure, and the appointment on 5 June 1507 of Francisco Ximénez de Cisneros, Cardinal archbishop of Toledo, as the new Inquisitor General. In May 1508 the Suprema eventually voted to arrest Lucero, who was taken in chains to Burgos, while his victims in the prison of Córdoba were all released. The ex-inquisitor received no punishment for his sins, but was allowed to retire to Seville, where he died in peace.

While Lucero's case is important as involving a prominent inquisitor and causing wide social and political discontent, it is certain that he was not the only official of the tribunal who abused his duties. At the same time as the troubles in Córdoba, complaints were raised in Llerena (Extremadura) against the activities of the new inquisitor, a man named Bravo, who had for a time been an assistant of Lucero in Córdoba. So many wealthy prisoners were thrown into the cells by Bravo, despite the protests of one of his colleagues, that the relatives of the condemned finally gathered enough courage to petition the crown:

We the relatives and friends of the prisoners in the cells of the Inquisition of Llerena kiss the royal hands of Your Highness and testify that the inquisitors of that province, together with their officials, have persecuted and persecute both the prisoners and ourselves with great hatred and enmity, and have carried out many irregularities in the procedure of imprisonment and trial, and have maltreated not only the said prisoners but their wives and children and property.[14]

There is no record of any censure of Bravo's policy, and it appears likely that he was allowed to pursue his career un-

57

checked. Lucero's malign influence also seems to have haunted the tribunal at Jaén, where a professional 'witness' who had formerly served the inquisitor now extended his activities. The man's name was Diego de Algeciras, and for a reasonable pittance he was ready to perjure himself in testifying to the judaizing activities of any number of conversos. Thanks to his assistance, the richest conversos of the city were soon in gaol on suspicion of heresy. Those who still remained free petitioned the crown to restore jurisdiction over heresy to the bishop of Jaén, whose mercy they trusted more than the abuses of the officials of the Inquisition.[15]

In extenuation it should be emphasized that the majority of abuses probably originated not with the inquisitors themselves but with their subordinate officials, who were sometimes not merely venal and greedy for wealth, but turned out to be simply sadists. Lea notes that among the more notorious officials at Jaén was the notary, who on one occasion locked a young girl of fifteen in a room, stripped her naked, and whipped her until she agreed to testify against her mother. Such cases were very frequent. Just as frequent were the cases of fraud. A deposition drawn up by witnesses at Toledo, and dated 26 September 1487, asserts that the receiver of confiscated goods in that tribunal, Juan de Uría, had defrauded sums amounting to 1,500,000 *maravedis*, enough to set himself up in comfort.[16] There were opportunities for lining one's pockets even at the bottom of the ladder. In 1588 the inquisitor from Madrid who carried out the inspection of the tribunal at Córdoba, reported that both the door-keeper and the messenger of the tribunal were criminals and profiteers, and that this was well known throughout the city, although apparently not to the inquisitors of Córdoba.[17] Extenuation, however, does not alter the obvious fact that such abuses would never have been allowed to go on for as long as they invariably did, had it not been for the system of secrecy which the Inquisition adopted as its cardinal rule, and which prevented the exposure of evils until it was too late.

In Aragon the demand for reforms continued to exist, though taken up this time not by the conversos but by the Old Christians, basing themselves on the excessive jurisdiction exercised by the tribunal. The Cortes, as always, proved to be an ardent defender of the *fueros*. Meeting together at Monzón in

1510, the representatives of Aragon, Catalonia and Valencia raised the question of reform in jurisdiction. No further steps were taken until their next meeting at Monzón in 1512, when a comprehensive list of reforms was drawn up: to this list Ferdinand put his signature, thus agreeing to the first of the many *Concordias* made between the Inquisition and the individual provinces of Spain. Among other things the *Concordia* of 1512 stipulated that the number of familiars in the kingdom should be limited; that the Inquisition should not be exempt from local taxes; that officials of the tribunal committing crimes should be tried by a secular court; that in cases of confiscation, property which had formerly belonged to the condemned should not be included in the confiscation; and that trade with conversos should not be prohibited, since this depressed commerce. Moreover, the tribunal was not to exercise jurisdiction over usury, bigamy, blasphemy and witchcraft unless heresy were involved. The fact that pressure had to be put on the king through the Cortes proves how serious were some of the objections raised in Aragon against inquisitorial procedure. Yet the demands made in 1512 are relatively mild when compared with some of those made at a later date.

At the death of Ferdinand on 23 January 1516 the crown passed to his grandson Charles, who was at the time in Flanders. Ferdinand had since the death of Isabella on 26 November 1504 been king of Aragon only, and Castile had been under the rule of their daughter Juana the Mad, widow since 1506 of Philip of Austria, of the House of Habsburg. The death of Ferdinand would normally have meant the acceptance of Juana as queen, but her mental dislocation made her obviously unfitted to rule, so that her son Charles was everywhere accepted as rightful sovereign.

While awaiting the arrival of Charles in Spain, Ximénez maintained control of the Inquisition. In his will the Catholic King had called upon his successor to preserve the Inquisition. This Charles had every intention of doing. But the new reign aroused hopes of reform, particularly in converso hearts, and Ximénez was greatly alarmed by a rumour that Charles intended to allow the publication of the names of witnesses in inquisitorial trials. In a letter which the great and now aging Cardinal wrote to Charles, apparently in March 1517, he showed himself in an unusually conservative light. The Inquisition, he said, was so perfect a tribunal 'that there will never be any need for reform and it would be sinful to introduce changes'.[18] The publication of witnesses' names would lead inevitably to their murder, as had happened recently in Talavera de la Reina when an accused converso, on learning the name of his denouncer, went out to waylay him and assassinated him. Ximénez was not, however, unalterably opposed to reforms, as his own life and career had demonstrated. During his tenure of the post of Inquisitor General, he had taken care to dismiss the more notorious inquisitors, including the secretary of the Suprema. Of the royal secretary Calcena and others, he wrote to Charles in December 1576 advising him that they should have nothing further to do with the Inquisition, in view of their excesses. Lea's very fair verdict is that 'we may feel assured that he showed no mercy to those who sought to coin into money the blood of the conversos.'[19]

Whatever Ximénez's views may have been, many contemporaries thought that some reform in the judicial procedure of the Inquisition was essential, even if they did not question its actual existence. The arrival of the seventeen year old king from Flanders set off a train of requests and demands which constituted the last chapter in the struggle to subject the Inquisition to the rule of law. Consequently when Charles, after his arrival in Spain in September 1517, held the first Cortes of his reign at Valladolid in February 1518, the deputies presented a petition in which clause forty asked

> that Your Highness provide that the office of the Holy Inquisition proceed in such a way as to maintain justice, and that the wicked be punished and the innocent not suffer.

They asked moreover that the forms of law be observed, and that the inquisitors be chosen from reputable and learned men. The petition is negative evidence, but is nevertheless enough to show that a substantial body of opinion, not necessarily under converso influence, felt that Spaniards would benefit from stricter control over the men and methods of the Inquisition. The main result of this very general petition was the series of instructions for the Inquisition drawn up principally on the initiative of Jean le Sauvage, chancellor of the king, a man who was accused of being in the pay of the conversos. The preamble to these proposed instructions claims that

accused people have not been able to defend themselves fully, many innocent and guiltless have suffered death, harm, oppression, injury and infamy . . . and many of our vassals have absented themselves from these realms; and (as events have shown) in general these our realms have received and receive great ill and harm; and have been and are notorious for this throughout the world.

The proposed reforms, therefore, included provisions that prisoners be placed in open, public prisons, be able to receive visitors, be assigned counsel, be presented with an accusation on arrest, and be given the names of witnesses; in addition, goods of the accused should not be taken and sold before their actual condemnation, nor should the salaries of inquisitors be payable out of confiscations. Prisoners should be allowed recourse to mass and the sacraments while awaiting trial, and care should be taken not to let those condemned to perpetual prison die of hunger. If torture were used, it should be in moderation, and there should be no 'new inventions of torture as have been used until now'.[20] Each of these clauses points to the existence of evils which the new pragmatic was supposed to remedy. Whether the document was inspired by conversos or not is obviously irrelevant. The important thing was that serious abuses had crept into the practice of the Inquisition, and that a concern for justice demanded some reform.

Had the instructions ever been approved, a totally different tribunal would have come into existence. The burden of secrecy would have been completely lifted, and opportunities for abuses would have correspondingly diminished. Happily for those who supported the Inquisition, the new Inquisitor General appointed by Charles on the death of Ximénez, Cardinal Adrian of Utrecht, bishop of Tortosa, firmly opposed any innovation. Shortly after this, early in July 1518, Sauvage died. With him collapsed any hope of fundamental alterations in the structure of the Inquisition. Adrian, who as a Netherlander appears not to have had any close knowledge of Spanish problems, even reversed some of the reforms of Ximénez, by reappointing Calcena to a post of authority as secretary to the Suprema.

61

Meanwhile Charles had gone to Aragon, where he accepted the allegiance of the kingdom in the Cortes which opened at Saragossa in May 1518. Surprisingly, when these Cortes offered to advance him a large sum of money in exchange for Charles' agreement to a list of thirty-one articles which were substantially the same as those drawn up by Sauvage, the king agreed. It soon became clear that he had no intention of observing the agreement, for a subsequent message to the Spanish ambassador at Rome asked him to secure from the pope revocation of the articles and a dispensation from his oath to observe them. However, the Cortes had already taken the step of having Charles' signature to the articles authenticated by Juan Prat, the notary of the Cortes. All the relevant papers were then sent to Rome in the hands of Diego de las Casas, a converso from Seville. After the dissolution of the Cortes in January 1519, the Inquisition stepped in to arrest Prat on the charge of having falsified the articles drawn up at the Cortes. The accusation was obviously false, but both ecclesiastical and secular authorities in Castile acted as though it were true. The new chancellor, Mercurino Gattinara, urgently drew up papers which he sent to Rome in April, claiming that these were genuine and that the official copy was a forgery. By now a serious constitutional quarrel had arisen inside Aragon, and the deputies and nobility of the realm, meeting in conference in May, sent a request to Charles for the release of Prat, and threatening not to grant any money until their demands were met. They summoned the Cortes and refused to disperse until justice had been done.

At this stage pope Leo X intervened in favour of the Aragonese. In July 1519 he issued three briefs, one to Charles, one to the Inquisitor General, and one to the tribunal of Saragossa, reducing the powers of the Inquisition to the bounds of ordinary canon law, and revoking all special privileges granted by his predecessors. Charles and his officials refused to allow the publication of the briefs in Spain, and instead a firm protest was sent to Rome. The pope now shifted his position and suspended the briefs without revoking them. At this the Aragonese immediately discontinued payment of any grants to the crown. Finally, in December 1520 the pope confirmed the *Concordia* of 1518, but in terms which did not specify whether it was Prat's or Gattinara's version that was the correct one.

A compromise was eventually reached in 1521, when Cardinal Adrian accepted the Aragonese version for the time being, and released Prat. The victory of the Aragonese was an unsubstantial one. The Inquisition at no time afterwards admitted the validity of the *Concordias* of 1512 and 1518, so that the struggles of these years were after all in vain.

At the Castilian Cortes of Coruña in 1520, the requests made at Valladolid for a reform in the procedure of the Inquisition were repeated, but to no avail. Later that same year, while Charles was away in Flanders, another plan for reform was presented to him, but this and subsequent proposals were in vain. On his return to Spain a Cortes was held at Valladolid in 1523. Again the old suggestions for reform were brought up, fortified by a request that the salaries of inquisitors should be paid by the crown and not be drawn from confiscations. Failure was again the result. In 1525 the Cortes which met at Toledo complained of abuses committed by both inquisitors and familiars, but they achieved nothing beyond a promise that wrongs would be righted if they really existed. In 1526 in Granada the king was presented with a memorial demonstrating the evils of the secret procedure of the Inquisition, and asking for prisoners to be kept in public gaols instead of the secret cells of the tribunal.[21] To this there is no recorded reply. Almost annually such requests had been presented to the crown, and as regularly refused. Quite obviously a persistent stream of opposition was in continuous existence, dedicated not so much to the suppression of the Inquisition as to the cure of abuses. Against a stubborn Charles, however, no impact could be made. In April 1520 the king observed to a correspondent that 'in the Cortes of Aragon and Catalonia the Holy Office has been criticized and attacked by some people who do not care much for its preservation'.[22] The reference to Aragon should not divert us from the fact that, as we have seen, just as frequent criticism had been raised in the realm of Castile. Throughout Spain, then, the organs of constitutional government became the last channels of protest available to opponents of the Holy Office.

From 1519 to 1521 the energies of the peninsula were occupied in the famous revolt of the *Comuneros*, a confusing and complex struggle waged partly by town oligarchies against the royal authorities who had the support of the nobility, and partly by rival factions against each other in the great cities. Among the more important demands of the rebels was one asking for the removal of Charles' foreign advisers. The emphasis placed on broad issues like this, and the apparent indifference of the *Comuneros* to the position of the Holy Office, led Lea to conclude that 'the *Comuneros* had no grievance against the Inquisition'.[23] Such a conclusion is borne out by the situation in Valencia, where the rebellion took the form of social revolution waged by brotherhoods or *Germanías* against the aristocracy. The insurgents actually fortified the position and functions of the Inquisition by initiating wholesale and forcible conversions of the Moorish population. In Castile, however, several indications point to the fact that the converso population joined the *Comunero* side in the hope of bringing about reforms in the Inquisition. There is an impressive array of accusations against the conversos as fomentors of the rebellion. The Marquis of Mondéjar and the Constable of Castile both informed Charles V in 1521 that conversos hostile to the Holy Office were the chief culprits; the Constable claimed explicitly that 'the root cause of the revolution in these realms has been the conversos'. The Inquisition of Seville wrote in the same vein to the Emperor in April that year. A generation later the archbishop of Toledo, Siliceo, could claim that 'it is common knowledge in Spain that the *Comunidades* were incited by descendants of Jews'. All this might well be antisemitic fantasy but for the fact that several of the *Comunero* leaders were of converso origin, and that the heart of the movement was Toledo, ancient centre of Spanish Jewry. In Toledo, Segovia and Valladolid prominent *Comuneros* were of converso origin. Political discussions in *Comunero* circles frequently touched on the Inquisition. And when proposals were drawn up for the pacification of Toledo one of the articles stipulated that the salaries of the Inquisition should not be paid out of confiscations.[24]

Among the more important protests against the Inquisition in the years after the *Comunidades*, should be mentioned the long memorial drawn up on 5 August 1533 and read to Charles at the Aragonese Cortes held at Monzón.[25] The sixteen articles of this protest included complaints that 'some inquisitors of the Holy Office, in the voice and name of the Inquisition, have arrested and imprisoned people for private offences in no way touching the Holy Office'; that inquisitors were taking part in secular business; that they had extended their jurisdiction illegitimately by prosecuting cases of sodomy, usury, and bigamy, questions which had nothing to do with heresy; that the inquisitors of Aragon, Catalonia and Valencia had an excessive number of familiars, whose identity was kept concealed, thus provoking numerous abuses. As for the Moors, said the protest, addressing itself to the Inquisitor General, 'Your Reverence knows well the way in which they were "converted", and the little or no teaching or instruction in our Holy Catholic Faith which has been given them, and the lack of churches in the places where they live. Yet despite this lack of teaching and instruction, they are being proceeded against as heretics'. Worse still, the Inquisition was illegitimately seizing the land they had confiscated from the Moorish converts. To all these complaints Alonso Manrique, the Inquisitor General, gave a firm, negative reply. The protests were shelved.

Complaints along these lines were to play an important part in future controversies over the Inquisition. Inquisitorial jurisdiction in moral matters, for instance, was considered then, as later, a wrongful extension of its powers. But sweeping appeals like the protest of 1533 were growing fewer as the position of the Holy Office became stronger. Not only did the existence of the Inquisition become almost wholly unquestioned, but toleration of its attendant abuses became more widespread and pronounced. As papal and royal favour confirmed it in its position as one of the key institutions of the realm, it grew to overwhelm all opposition and criticism.

By the end of the reign of Charles V, the tribunal was invulnerable. This is hardly surprising once we concede that no firm opposition to it was ever brought into play. In nearly all cases it is possible to discover not mass opposition, but spasmodic attempts by religious and racial minorities, or by certain social classes, to hinder and disarm a tribunal whose interests were directly antagonistic to their own. This lack of profound opposition, together with the ready support of the Old Christian nobility and the lower classes in general, guaranteed the triumph of the Inquisition. The military victory of the forces of Charles V over the *Comuneros* at Villalar in 1520 provided the necessary political security which, involving as it did a relative decline in the power of the Cortes, muted the principal platform of discontent. In Aragon, where the political and social scene differed somewhat, constitutional organs continued to voice their protest long afterwards. In part, this was a way of expressing dissatisfaction with a government which had its seat in Castile and which insisted on pursuing policies at variance with the interests of the ruling circles in Aragon. But, significantly enough, no matter how many times the buildings of a local tribunal might be burnt down, or its officials maltreated and murdered, we have no evidence that a cry was ever raised for the actual abolition of the Inquisition.

The Inquisition was not the imposition of a sinister tyranny on an unwilling people. It was an institution brought into being by a particular socio-religious situation, impelled and inspired by a decisively Old Christian ideology, and controlled by men whose outlook reflected the mentality of the mass of Spaniards. It was popular as misconceptions are popular. And to this the exceptions were a few lonely intellectuals, and others whose race alone was sufficient to put them outside the pale of the new society being erected on a basis of triumphant and militant conservatism.

CHAPTER FIVE

'SILENCE HAS BEEN IMPOSED'

> It was a sad state when virtuous men, because of their great achievements, had to undergo hostility, accusations and injuries from those who should have been their defenders.
>
> *Juan de Mariana S. J.*, HISTORIA GENERAL DE ESPAÑA

'WE live in such difficult times that it is dangerous either to speak or to be silent', protested the great Spanish humanist Juan Luis Vives to Erasmus in 1534.[1] The ill wind of controversy was tearing down all the hopes of liberals in Europe, and Christian humanism was being forced to choose between an old world it disliked and a new one it mistrusted. Those who were not wise enough to conform went to the wall. In writing to Erasmus, Vives was only informing him of what the former knew was bound to happen. That year the English statesman and saint, Sir Thomas More, was taken into custody for denying royal supremacy over the Church: while the hope of humanists in Spain, doctor Juan de Vergara, was condemned to confinement in the cells of the Inquisition. The problem faced by these two men was a European one, intimately related to the political and religious issues that had been provoked by the revolt of Martin Luther. It was the reaction to this revolt, in Spain as in other countries, that led to a narrowing of intellectual frontiers until little room remained for the humanists and Spain withdrew into the confines of the 'closed' society.

Yet the reaction had been preceded by a dawn full of promise. At the beginning of the sixteenth century the great centres of humanism were in Italy and in northern Europe, where the name of Erasmus held sway. In 1509 a talented Renaissance prince ascended the throne of England, and Erasmus greeted in him the beginning of triumphs for the New Learning. The

67

Spanish peninsula was no less open to all that was best and learned in Europe. Native genius mingled with imported erudition to produce the beginnings of a vigorous cultural Renaissance. The wellsprings of this new learning were in Italy. It was there that the young Andalucian Antonio de Nebrija went in 1463 to complete his university education at Bologna, returning ten years later to the halls of his own Salamanca, from which he was subsequently transferred to become the brightest luminary of Ximénez's new university at Alcalá de Henares. And it was from Italy that Peter Martyr of Anghiera came in 1487 to educate the young nobles of Spain, preceded only the year before by Lucio Marineo Siculo, who joined the ranks of the illustrious professors at Salamanca. The learning they promoted was diffused throughout the realm by the introduction of the printing press, first set up at Valencia in 1474. No limit was set to the import of foreign literature, and a law of 1480 allowed books to be introduced freely into the realm without paying any duty. If the triumphs of Spanish humanism have often been exaggerated, this is partly the result of the extravagant enthusiasm shown by contemporaries, one of whom claimed that

> while it was a most rare occurrence to meet with a person of illustrious birth before the present reign who had even studied Latin in his youth, there were now to be seen numbers every day who sought to shed the lustre of letters over the martial glory inherited from their ancestors.[2]

And Erasmus, flattered by the attention he was receiving in a country he never knew, gave his opinion that

> liberal studies in Spain were in the course of a few years brought to so flourishing a condition as to excite the admiration of, and serve as a model to, the most cultivated nations of Europe.[3]

The reign of the Catholic monarchs was a worthy predecessor to the Spanish cultural and scientific achievements of the early sixteenth century. Even if nobility were the most prized quality in Spain, yet, says a contemporary, 'no Spaniard was accounted noble who held learning in indifference'.[4]

In this rich atmosphere it was not surprising to find reform in the air. With the appointment of Ximénez as archbishop of Toledo in 1495, the architect of reform under the Catholic monarchs assumed the chief position in the state. A lean and austere man, renowned for the holiness of his life and the severity of his discipline, Ximénez had already begun that reform of lax standards in Spanish monasticism which cleansed and purified the Church in the peninsula long before the cry against abuses was raised in Germany. As Inquisitor General from 1507 onwards, the archbishop also distinguished himself in upholding the norms of conduct in the Holy Office. Years before the protest against preaching indulgences had been made by Luther, Ximénez banned their preaching within Spain on the grounds that they took out money to Rome. But probably his greatest achievement was the foundation of the University of Alcalá in 1508. Alcalá represented all that was best in the native humanism of Spain. Its first chancellor, Pedro de Lerma, had studied at Paris. Nebrija was, as Erasmus wrote to Luis Vives in 1521, its 'principal ornament'. Among its brilliant professors were the converso brothers Juan and Francisco de Vergara, of whom the latter was described by Marineo Siculo as the greatest classical scholar in Spain. The breadth of the university syllabus, particularly in its faculty of theology, set it apart from the other centres of learning in Spain, and very soon its popularity rivalled that of Salamanca. Over and above this was the task which Ximénez set the professors of the university – to produce a critical edition of the Bible which would remain a classic of contemporary scholarship. The great Polyglot Bible which resulted from this enterprise consisted of six volumes, with the Hebrew, Chaldean and Greek originals of the Bible printed in columns parallel to the Latin Vulgate. The Complutensian Polyglot was finally published in 1522.

Meanwhile the influence of Desiderius Erasmus, dominant in European humanism, began to penetrate the open frontiers of Spain. In 1516 the name of Erasmus was first traced by a Spanish pen, and in 1517 Cardinal Ximénez unsuccessfully invited the famous Dutch scholar to come to Spain. By 1524 a number of intellectuals in the peninsula had rallied to the doctrines of Erasmus, to whom Vives wrote in June 1524, 'Our Spaniards are also interesting themselves in your works'. The wit and satire directed by Erasmus against ecclesiastical abuses, and particularly against lax standards in the mendicant orders, found a ready hearing in a country where the highest church officials had themselves led the movement in favour of reform. The presence of prominent intellectuals and literary men in the entourage of Charles V ensured protection for Erasmist doctrines at the court. Finally, the two principal prelates in the Church – the archbishop of Toledo, Alonso de Fonseca, successor to Ximénez, and Alonso Manrique, the Inquisitor General – were enthusiastic followers of Erasmus. The triumph of Erasmism was confirmed with the translation undertaken in 1524 of Erasmus' *Enchiridion* by Alonso Fernández, archdeacon of Alcor. Published towards the end of 1526, it was greeted by immediate and widespread enthusiasm in the peninsula. As the translator himself wrote to Erasmus in 1527:

At the Emperor's court, in the cities, in the churches, in the convents, even in the inns and on the highways, everyone has the *Enchiridion* of Erasmus in Spanish. Till then it had been read in Latin by a minority of Latinists, and even these did not fully understand it. Now it is read in Spanish by people of every sort, and those who had formerly never heard of Erasmus have learned of his existence through this single book.[5]

But the picture was not as entirely happy as this. In 1517, the year after the accession of Charles to the Spanish throne, Martin Luther made public in Germany his defiance of papal authority. Soon the name of Luther became identified with the most virulent heresy that had yet plagued Christendom. In Spain the leaders of the Church took comfort in the thought that many of the reforms demanded by the Lutherans had already been put into effect by Cardinal Ximénez. Nor need the Spanish Church fear the writings of liberal Catholics such as Erasmus, for Ximénez himself had invited him to Spain, and the translation of his *Enchiridion* had been issued with a dedication to, and under the auspices of, the Inquisitor General Manrique. When, therefore, some of the mendicant orders, who had long been chafing under the criticisms of Erasmus, pressed for a great national debate, finally held at Valladolid in March 1527, to decide whether Erasmus' works were heretical or not, it was no surprise that the conference, although it broke up without coming to a decision, was seen to set the seal on the triumph of Erasmism in Spain. This victory was crowned by a personal letter from Charles V to Erasmus on 13 December the same year, asking him not to worry over controversy in Spain:

as though, so long as we are here, one could make a decision contrary to Erasmus, whose Christian piety is well known to us . . . Take courage and be assured that we shall always hold your honour and repute in the greatest esteem.[6]

With the crown, the Inquisition, and the Spanish Church on his side, Erasmus's position was impregnable in Spain, where he enjoyed a popularity greater than in any other country in Europe. This promising start to what might have been a great cultural epoch was shattered by two distinct developments within Spain – the growth of illuminism, and the discovery of Protestants – and by the Europe-wide limitations imposed on free thought by political events.

The illuminists or *alumbrados* were a mystical sect not very different from similar sects which had arisen in other times and places in Europe. Their importance in this period was that the criticisms they levelled against excessive formalism in religion were dangerously appealing to all those – whether liberals, Erasmists or Lutherans – who shared their critical view of the established Church. Moreover, their extremely subjective view of religious practice – the passive surrender of the will to God, leading to direct communication with the divine being – appeared to deny the efficacy of grace, the sacraments, and good works in the spiritual life. Although illuminism proved to be a perversion of true mysticism, at times it resembled it so exactly as to mislead the authorities as well as individuals. Its beginnings may be traced to some Franciscan friars of converso origin who attracted public notice in 1512. Despite some scandals and doubts, no steps were taken to repress the movement, which grew undisturbed until the early 1520s. The advent of Lutheranism produced the first setback suffered by the illuminists. On 2 April 1525 the Inquisition banned the reading of Lutheran books throughout Spain, and then on 23 September it condemned those quasi-Lutheran beliefs which could be detected in the teaching of the *alumbrados*. Faced by this impasse, the illuminists turned to exploit Erasmism for their own purposes. Erasmist literature became their reading, and the *Enchiridion* their manual. In the events of the next few years, it sometimes became extremely difficult to distinguish Erasmists from illuminists, so closely did the two schools touch.

The turn of the tide came in 1529. In that year the Erasmist

Inquisitor General Manrique fell into disgrace and was confined to his see of Seville. At the same moment the protecting hand of the Emperor was withdrawn, for Charles left Spain that year for Italy and took with him some of the most prominent and influential Erasmists. Instantly the strong conservative forces which had bided their time after the defeat at Valladolid, came into action. Their first victim was an *hidalgo* of Old Christian origin, Diego de Uceda, who was chamberlain to a high official in the Order of Calatrava. A deeply religious Catholic, Uceda was also an Erasmist who shared the Dutchman's scepticism about superstition and miracles. Journeying in February 1528 from Burgos to his native city of Córdoba, he fell in with a travelling companion to whom he talked too earnestly and freely about religion, particularly about Luther. He was denounced to the Inquisition by his companion, arrested, tortured and condemned despite all the evidence that he was blameless in his religious beliefs and practices. He finally abjured his 'errors' at the *auto de fe* held at Toledo on 22 July 1529.[7]

It was in this same year also that the Holy Office arrested a leading woman illuminist or *beata*, Francisca Hernández, whose activities had so far been tolerated, but whose sexual and theological liberties were now becoming notorious. Her arrest had such wide implications that some attention must be paid to the circumstances. A woman of considerable qualities, not the least of which was her physical attraction, Hernández had been under observation by the Inquisition from as early as 1519. The circle she gathered round her in Valladolid consisted of *alumbrados* as well as those who, without being illuminists, regarded her as a truly spiritual woman. Among the former was a curate of Navarrete who proclaimed himself divinely inspired and sinless, and who therefore indulged in intimate physical relations with Hernández to show that no sin lay in it. Among the latter was Bernadino de Tovar, a brother of the great Erasmist Juan de Vergara. Hernández's influence was strongly suspect to the Inquisition, which arrested her in 1519 and again in 1525. Among those arrested with her as illuminists in 1525 was a certain Maria Cazalla, sister to bishop Juan Cazalla, himself an adept in the new kind of mysticism. The names of all these people are of key importance in events of the next few years. When Hernández was arrested for the third time and put on trial at Toledo in 1530, the complex net of relationships between all the members of her circle was finally undone. Not surprisingly, she compromised all those who had once been her spiritual (and sometimes physical) companions. Maria Cazalla was again arrested in April 1532, imprisoned and tortured, and accused of the various heresies of Lutheranism, illuminism, and Erasmism. Her trial dragged on until December 1534, when she was made to abjure, pay a fine, and promise not to associate again with illuminists. Her brother the bishop had opportunely died in 1530. The Inquisition had not yet finished with their family, however, for from them sprang the circle of Protestants which alarmed Valladolid two decades later. Among Francisca Hernández's other admirers, as we have seen, was Bernadino de Tovar. Although Tovar was an Erasmist, he was not immune to the *beata's* attractions, despite the repeated warnings of Juan de Vergara. It was no doubt this knowledge of Vergara's hostility that moved Hernández, at her trial in 1530, to denounce Vergara as a Lutheran, a claim which was supported by several of her disciples. Tovar was already in prison. He was followed there by his brother on 24 June 1530.

The arrest and trial of Vergara changed the whole climate of opinion in Spain.[8] This eminent humanist, who had been secretary to Ximénez and later to his successor in the see of Toledo, Alonso de Fonseca, was one of the foremost Greek and Latin scholars in Spain. He had collaborated in the Polyglot Bible, had held the chair of philosophy at Alcalá, and had proposed offering the chair of rhetoric there to Vives. Arrested in 1530, tried and imprisoned, Vergara was obliged to abjure his errors in an *auto* at Toledo on 21 December 1535, and to pay a fine of 1,500 ducats. After this he was confined to a monastery, from which he emerged in 1537. Because of his eminence, he was one of the few victims of the Inquisition allowed, even after his disgrace, to resume his old position in society; and we encounter him once more in 1547 at the centre of the great controversy carried on at Toledo over the proposed statutes to exclude conversos from office in the cathedral.

The arrest of Vergara was followed speedily by several others. Among these was Alonso de Virués, a Benedictine abbot and preacher to the Emperor Charles V. He was the first of several eminent preachers of the Emperor to be suspected of heresy, presumably because of the international contacts he had made, particularly in Germany. Arrested in 1533 and confined in prison by the Inquisition of Seville for four long years, he pleaded in vain that Erasmus had never been condemned as unorthodox. Finally in 1537 he was made to abjure his errors and was condemned to confinement in a monastery for two years, and banned from preaching for another year. Charles V, however, made strenuous efforts to save Virués, and in May 1538 obtained from the pope a bull anulling the sentence. Virués was restored to favour and appointed in 1542 as bishop of the Canary Islands, where he died in 1545.

The good fortune of these men in their return to favour was not shared by subsequent victims of the Inquisition. As the frontiers of academic freedom closed in, the chances of an untroubled old age became less likely. In 1530 Mateo Pascual, a professor at the University of Acalá and a distinguished Erasmist, was accused of doubting the doctrine of purgatory. He was tried by the Inquisition, sentenced to the confiscation of all his goods and retired abroad to Rome to end his days in peace.[9] Another outstanding victim, sometimes connected with the origins of Protestantism in Spain, was Juan de Valdés, also of the University of Alcalá, who in the fateful year 1529 published his theological study *Diálogo de Doctrina Christiana*, which was immediately attacked by the Inquisition despite the testimony of Vergara and others. The controversy over the book took so dangerous a turn that in 1530 Valdés fled to Italy, just in time to avoid the trial that was opened against him. His treatise was thereafter distinguished by its appearance in every Index of prohibited books issued by the Inquisition.[10]

One other significant case is that of Pedro de Lerma. Former chancellor of Alcalá university, former dean of the theological faculty at the Sorbonne, canon of Burgos cathedral, this eminent scholar fell under the influence of Erasmus and publicised this in his sermons. He was denounced to the Inquisition, imprisoned and finally in 1537 was made to abjure publicly, in the towns where he had preached, eleven propositions he was accused of having taught. In shame and resentment the old man shook the dust of Spain off his feet and fled to Paris where he resumed his position as dean of the faculty, dying there in August 1541. According to his nephew Francisco Enzinas, famous in the history of European Protestantism as Dryander, people in Lerma's home city of Burgos were so afraid of the possible consequences of this event that those who had sent their sons to study abroad recalled them at once.[11] Such a reaction from those who were not directly concerned in the struggle now being waged against the Erasmists, shows that the broader issues at stake were being all too well understood by educated Spaniards. Erasmism and the new humanism were being identified with the German heresy, and for some the only protection was dissociation.

The 1530s were in a way the end of the road. In December 1533 Rodrigo Manrique, son of the Inquisitor General, wrote bitterly from Paris to Luis Vives, on the subject of Vergara's imprisonment:

You are right. Our country is a land of pride and envy; you may add: of barbarism. For now it is clear that down there one cannot possess any culture without being suspected of heresy, error and Judaism. Thus silence has been imposed on the learned. As for those who take refuge in erudition, they have been filled, as you say, with great terror . . . At Alcalá they are trying to uproot the study of Greek completely.[12]

Faced by this wave of reaction, the mild goodwill of the humanists was powerless. Erasmus saw his friends in Spain being silenced one by one. His last surviving letter to that country is dated December 1533: beyond that lay silence. Three years later he died, still highly respected in the Catholic world, so much so that in 1535 the pope had offered him a cardinal's hat. But in Spain his cause was snuffed out, and the last hopes vanished with the death of Alonso Manrique in 1538.

By now the great fear of Spanish ecclesiastics was the Protestant menace. The Erasmist propositions so widely and freely held a decade before were now identified with the new German heresy, and it was the task of the Inquisition to root them out. Despite all official fears, however, and despite the ban on Lutheran books, there was at first no substance to the threat. In the period up to 1558 there were no more than thirty-nine cases of alleged Lutheranism among Spaniards brought before the Inquisition,[13] and even of this number a high proportion consisted merely of people who uttered propositions savouring of Lutheranism, without being actual heretics. Moreover, there

75

was absolutely no evidence of any organization among such people, so that the immediate danger was small. But the tradition of Erasmism was still strong, and it was this which provided the essential link between the 1530s and the 1550s, for the men who emerged as Protestants in the 1550s were those who had profited and learnt from the liberal atmosphere that had prevailed in the Erasmist period, particularly at Alcalá and Seville. What is particularly striking is the great number of people from Alcalá who came under the hammer of the Inquisition. The demise of that great university's liberal traditions meant the end of an epoch in Spanish culture.

Yet the new heterodoxy was slow to develop. Men like Juan de Valdés, who is usually taken as a forerunner of Protestantism in Spain, but who in fact died a Catholic, were Erasmists who never perceptibly sympathised with Lutheranism. Bataillon has shown how the Protestant stream which derived from Erasmist illuminism between 1535 and 1555 adopted the doctrine of *justification by faith alone* without ever stepping outside Catholic dogma.[14] Progress towards heresy was therefore far from rapid. What impetus there was came from prominent individuals, particularly in the south. Of these one of the most important was Juan Gil, or Egidio, the Aragonese founder of the Protestant community in Seville.[15] Canon and preacher of the cathedral of Seville, he was sufficiently esteemed by the Emperor to be nominated to the vacant see of Tortosa in 1550. Subsequently, however, he suffered a brief trial on suspicion of heresy, escaped with a light punishment, and died peacefuly in 1556. Not until after his death did investigation show to what extent his doctrines had corrupted those placed in his pastoral care, and his bones were dug up and burnt in 1560 to obliterate his memory. After Egidio's death the leadership of the Protestant community fell upon Constantino Ponce de la Fuente, canon of the cathedral and formerly a confessor and chaplain to Charles V. The Seville group totalled one hundred and twenty seven persons, including the prior and members of the Jeronimite monastery of San Isidro, and several members of the Jeronimite nunnery of Santa Paula. The Seville Protestants managed to exist in some security until the late 1550s, when suspicions were aroused, leading to the flight of several members of San Isidro: among these exiles were Cipriano de Valera and Cassiodoro de

Reina, whose names form no part of Spanish history but who were glories of the European Reformation.

Meanwhile in northern Castile another significant circle of Protestants had come into existence.[16] The founder was an Italian, Carlos de Seso, who had been converted to Protestantism by reading Juan de Valdés. His missionary zeal soon converted an influential and distinguished circle centred on Valladolid which, however, never exceeded fifty-five persons in number. The most eminent of all the converts was Doctor Agustín Cazalla, who in 1542 at the age of thirty-two had been appointed chaplain to Charles V and had journeyed with him to Germany in 1543, as well as accompanying prince Philip there in 1548. Cazalla had been converted by his brother Pedro, parish priest of Pedrosa, near Valladolid, and with him the whole Cazalla family fell into heresy.

The striking thing among members of these two groups was how much they had in common. Egidio and Constantino were both men from Alcalá university, and so was Cazalla, who graduated from there in 1530 on the same day as another young man named Diego Laínez. In the graduation lists that year, Laínez came second to Cazalla's first. The more discerning judgment of history and of the Church was to reverse these positions. In this generation of Alcalá alumni the seeds of liberalism had been sown too deeply to be eradicated, and even Laínez was to identify himself with a more liberal form of Catholicism than that which crushed his erstwhile colleagues in Spain. More startling than the common inheritance of Alcalá is the fact that in both Seville and Valladolid former royal chaplains were at the heart of the heresy. Finally, it is significant that some of the most prominent converts came from New Christian families, leaving us with the possibility that some connection can be established between the heterodoxy of conversos and that of the Protestants.[17] The Cazalla family was of converso origin, and so was Constantino, while Cassiodoro came from the other great racial minority, the Moriscos.

The storm broke over Spanish Protestantism in 1557. In October that year Don Juan Ponce de León, of the family of the Duke of Arcos, was arrested together with others for introducing heretical literature from Geneva. His chief accomplice was Julián Hernández, a man who had spent a considerable time in the Reformed churches of Paris, Scotland and Frankfurt, and who devoted himself to smuggling Protestant literature into his native country. By the following August Constantino had also been arrested, and the Seville group was split open. By 1558 carelessness had led also to the destruction of the Valladolid circle by the Inquisition. All those responsible were arrested and the situation was treated as a great emergency. The discovery within Spain, among reputable people, of the same evil that was tearing the Holy Roman Empire in two, alarmed political and ecclesiastical authorities alike, and the Holy Office dealt with the menace as though it were one of monumental proportions. In fact, as we know, at no time was Protestantism ever a threat to the Church in Spain: the group in Valladolid and its locality did not exceed fifty-five members, and those in Seville were not over one hundred and twenty-seven in number.

The Emperor Charles V, now in retirement at his isolated monastery of Yuste in Extremadura after the long years spent in preserving his lands against the Lutheran contagion, saw in the presence of heretics within Spain the possibilities of a new conflict like that which had split Germany. For him there would be only one answer to the situation – ruthless suppression. The letter which he sent on 25 May 1558 to his daughter Juana, then acting as regent in Spain because of the absence of Philip II in the Netherlands, deserves to be quoted at length, not only because it shows the disillusionment of the former patron of Erasmus, but also because it marks the beginning of the tough policy which now characterized the Spanish authorities.

I am very satisfied with what you say you have written to the king (he said) informing him of what is happening about the people imprisoned as Lutherans, more of whom are being daily discovered. But believe me, my daughter, this business has caused and still causes me more anxiety and pain than I can express, for while the king and I were abroad these realms remained in perfect peace, free from this calamity, but now that I have returned here to rest and recuperate and serve Our Lord, this great outrage and treachery, implicating such notable persons, occurs in my presence and in yours. You know that because of this I suffered and went through great trials and expenses in Germany, and lost so much of my good health. Were it not for the conviction I have that you and the members of your Councils will find a radical cure to this unfortunate situation, punishing the guilty thoroughly to prevent them spreading, I do not know whether I could restrain myself leaving here to settle the matter. Since this affair is more important for the service of Our Lord and the good and preservation of these realms than any other, and since it is only in its beginnings, with such small forces that they can be easily put down, it is necessary to place the greatest stress and weight on a quick remedy and exemplary punishment. I do not know whether it will be enough in these cases to follow the usual practice, by which according to common law all those who beg for mercy and have their confession accepted are pardoned with a light penance if it is a first offence. Such people, if set free, are at liberty to commit the same offence, particularly if they are educated persons.

One can imagine the evil consequences, for it is clear that they cannot act without armed organisation and leaders, and so it must be seen whether they can be proceeded against as creators of sedition, upheaval, riots and disturbance in the state; they would then be guilty of rebellion and could not expect any mercy. In this connection I cannot omit to mention what was and is the custom in Flanders, and more particularly Hungary. I wanted to introduce an Inquisition to punish the heresies that some people had caught from neighbouring Germany and England and even France. Everyone opposed this on the grounds that there were no Jews among them. Finally an order was issued declaring that all people of whatever state and condition who came under certain specified categories were to be *ipso facto* burnt and their goods confiscated. Necessity obliged me to act in this way. I do not know what the king my son has done since then, but I think that the same reason will have made him continue as I did, because I advised and begged him to be very severe in dealing with these people.

Believe me, my daughter, if so great an evil is not suppressed and remedied without distinction of persons from the very beginning, I cannot promise that the king or anyone else will be in a position to do it afterwards.[18]

This letter really marks the turning point in Spain. From now on, thanks to the fears of Charles and the policy which was laid down for the Inquisitor General Valdés, heterodoxy was treated as a threat to the state and the religious establishment. Writing to the pope on 9 September the same year, Valdés affirmed that 'these errors and heresies of Luther and his brood which have begun to be preached and sown in Spain, are in the way of sedition and riot.'[19]

Sedition and riot, armed organization and leaders–how far from the dreams of Cazalla and Constantino! Yet once again well-meaning men were prey to the tensions gripping Europe, and the result was a series of *autos de fe* which burnt out Protestantism in Spain. The first holocaust was held at Valladolid on Trinity Sunday, 29th May 1559. Of the thirty victims, fourteen were burnt, including Cazalla and a brother and sister of his. The only one to die unrepentant in his faith was Herrezuelo, a lawyer from Toro. All the rest died repentant after professing conversion, chief among them being Agustín Cazalla, who blessed the Holy Office and wept aloud for his sins. The next burning at Valladolid was held on 8 October. Of the thirty victims, twenty-six were Protestants, and of these twelve were burnt at the stake. Only Carlos de Seso and one other maintained their faith to the end. This ceremony was presided over by Philip II. It was now the turn of Seville. The first great *auto* there was held on Sunday, 24 September 1559.[20] Of the seventy-six victims present, nineteen were burnt as Lutherans, one of them in effigy only.* This was followed by the *auto* held on Sunday, 22 December 1560.[21] Of the total of fifty-four victims on this occasion, fourteen were burnt in person and three in effigy; in all, forty of the victims were Protestants. Egidio and Constantino were two of those burnt in effigy, while those actually burnt included two English sailors, William Brook and Nicholas Burton, and a native of Seville, Leonor Gómez, together with her three young daughters. This *auto de fe* was followed by one two years later, on 26 April 1562, and by another on 28 October: the whole of that year saw eighty-eight cases of Protestantism punished, including eighteen who were burnt in person, prominent among the latter being the prior of San Isidro and four of his priests.

With these burnings native Protestantism was almost totally extinguished in Spain. Nearly all subsequent condemnations for 'Lutheranism' (a term which covered any and every kind of Protestantism) were directed principally against foreign traders and sailors unwary enough to fall into the hands of the Inquisition. The disappearance of this heresy from Spain is attested by the figures methodically drawn up by Schäfer for each of the tribunals in the peninsula.[22] In Barcelona between 1552 and 1578 there were fifty-one alleged Lutherans burnt in person or

---

* Dead and absent victims were represented at *autos* by figures or effigies which were burnt in their stead: hence the need to talk of others being burnt in person.

in effigy, but all of them were of French origin. In the tribunal of Calahorra (later transferred to Logroño) there were sixty-eight cases of suspected Lutheranism among the Navarrese and Basque natives, out of a total of 310 cases in the years 1540-99. These high figures, however, can be attributed almost entirely to the proximity of the region to the French frontier. Nearly all the cases arising at Valencia from 1554 to 1598 involved foreigners, eight of whom were burnt either in person or in effigy. The exceptions were two Spaniards who after being punished on suspicion of Lutheranism in 1567 and 1573, were burnt in effigy in 1575 and 1576 for the same crime. Between 1545 and 1598 Saragossa saw only seventeen cases of suspected Protestantism among Spaniards; the only serious ones were the burning of a native Lutheran in 1585, and the burning of another in effigy in 1595. Córdoba had six cases of suspected Lutheranism between 1558 and 1567. Cuenca had seven between 1556 and 1585. Granada burnt a heretic in 1574 but otherwise had only twenty cases between 1565 and 1599. Llerena had about seventeen cases between 1556 and 1591. Murcia had about nineteen from 1560 to 1597. Santiago had a single case, one of self-denunciation, in 1582. Toledo, heart and centre of heterodoxy in Spain, had forty-five cases of native Spaniards between 1555 and 1596, and over 110 cases of foreign heretics. Thus if we exclude Valladolid and Seville, the total number of Spaniards tried for suspected Lutheranism by the Inquisition in the second half of the sixteenth century, comes to a total of about two hundred. This total is, however, quite misleading. It includes the extraordinary high number from Navarre, which was in a special position; and it does not indicate that the vast majority of cases were not heretics so much as ordinary people who in an unguarded moment uttered oaths or statements which savoured of heresy. Less than half a dozen people were actually burnt for heresy in these years. Protestantism never developed into a real threat in Spain, and was never accepted by any considerable section of the population. Consequently Spaniards remained in ignorance of what the new heresy was, and were taught to regard it only as a sinister threat to their country and a direct blasphemy of God.

Emergency precautions were nevertheless not relaxed by the authorities, for the German heresy was now too great a political menace to be treated lightly, and censorship and restriction of free movement marked the policy about to be adopted in Spain. In 1563 the Council of Trent closed its final session, and with this the Catholic Counter-Reformation reached a position of no compromise in the European struggle. Catholic Europe, and with it Catholic Spain, turned to the attack.

How far had the Inquisition served to protect Spain from the inroads of foreign contagion? It had certainly allowed the old orthodoxy to maintain its Reconquest mentality and racialist views. A recent Spanish study on the Inquisition affirms clearly and unequivocally that illuminism and even Lutheranism owed their Spanish origins to conversos,[23] and that these doctrines were therefore aberrations produced by non-Spanish minorities. This implies that the Inquisition was defending the purity of the Spanish race. Yet this was precisely the argument used in the sixteenth century by antisemites. As archbishop Siliceo of Toledo claimed in 1547:

> It is said, and it is considered true, that the principal heretics of Germany, who have destroyed all that nation and have introduced great heresies, are descendants of Jews.[24]

The opinion was common in Spain. Thus the struggle against Luther in 1559 was just a continuation of the struggle against the Jews in 1480. One crusade overlapped another. So did fact and fancy. There is no doubt that converso heterodoxy played an important part in the religious problems of Spain. Illuminism itself began among some Franciscans of Jewish origins, notably Fray Juan de Cazalla. Eminent Erasmists like Vergara were of converso origin, and so were others suspected of Lutheranism, such as Doctor Agustín de Cazalla, and Doctor Andrés de Laguna who in 1550 became physician to the pope. But the systematic identification of conversos with the principal heresies of the day could not possibly be substantiated. That it was seriously believed at the time is proof that the Inquisition, essentially an instrument of the ruling class, was still seen to be performing an important function in preserving the religious and racial unity of Spain.

The repercussions that followed from the case of Pedro de Lerma made it clear that the frontiers were closing around Spain. The freedom which had distinguished Renaissance academic life was being exchanged for conformity, lip-service, and silence. The split among European universities in 1530, when half of them for political reasons supported Henry VIII's argument on the nullity of his marriage with Catherine of Aragon, and the other half for the same reasons opposed it, was perhaps the first great crack in the life of international letters.[25] Universities, like individuals, had to bow under political pressures and choose national causes. For Spain the decision was made by Philip II, king since the abdication in 1556 of his father Charles who died at Yuste in September 1558. In September 1559 he returned from the Netherlands to the peninsula, never to leave it again. On 22 November 1559 he issued an order to all Spaniards studying or teaching abroad to return within four months, the only exceptions to this being those at particular named colleges at Bologna, Rome, Naples and Coimbra: no Spaniards were in future to be allowed abroad to study except to these colleges. At home a strict check was imposed by the Inquisition on any divergence from orthodoxy in the universities. This was carried out in two main ways: by censorship of all books used for reading and study, and by disciplinary action against rashly outspoken professors. Bishops were encouraged to inspect all libraries in their diocese, and at Salamanca university a score of the staff went carefully through the library to weed out any dangerous books.

The control of professors initiated a number of prosecutions which have given the Inquisition a notoriety not easily effaced from its history. The difficulties experienced at this period by certain academics of the University of Salamanca, have been explained away as the result of factions within the university and particularly as a result of the character of León de Castro, a petty, venomous and irresponsible retired professor of grammar whose campaign against more liberal spirits led to the imprisonment of several of his distinguished colleagues. Whatever the responsibility of León de Castro, and it is undeniably great, the fact remains that the Inquisition lent a ready ear to his outpourings and proceeded to prosecute some of the most prominent intellects of Spain.

Events began in December 1571, when Castro and a Dominican colleague, Bartolomé de Medina, laid before a representative of the Inquisition of Valladolid some articles of

accusation against three professors at the university of Salamanca. The three in question were Fray Luis de León, of the
Order of St. Augustine; Gaspar de Grajal; and Martin
Martínez de Cantalapiedra. The general accusations against
them said that they had taken heretical liberties with their study
of Scripture and theology. Fray Luis in particular bore the brunt
of the attack. Famous as a theologian and immortalized as one of
Spain's finest poets, at the age of thirty-four he was elected to a
chair at Salamanca and thereby aroused the hostility of his
rivals, who slandered him because of his Jewish descent and
accused him of uttering dangerous theological propositions.
Among other things it was said that he had questioned the
accuracy of the Vulgate translation of the Bible; had preferred
the Hebrew text to the Latin; had translated the Song of Songs
as a profane love song instead of a divine canticle; and had held
that scholastic theology harmed the study of Scripture. Grajal
was arrested on similar charges on 22 March 1572. Five days
later Luis de León and Martínez were taken into custody. Blind
belief in the justice of their cause and in the benevolence of the
Holy Office cheered the prisoners, but they were soon disillusioned. For Fray Luis it was to be the beginning of an imprisonment that lasted four years, eight months and nineteen
days. Cut off completely from the outside world in the cells of
the tribunal at Valladolid, his only consolation was the permission he received to read and write in his cell, out of which
emerged his classic devotional treatise *De los Nombres de Christo*.
From the first he was aware of a campaign against himself. On
18 April 1572 he wrote from his cell:

> I have great suspicions that false testimony has been laid against
> me, for I know that in the last two years people have said and still say
> many things about me that are transparent lies, and I know that I
> have many enemies.

He awaited justice, yet none was forthcoming, nor was there
any promise of an early trial. His constant appeals were of no
avail. A year later, on 7 March 1573, he was writing to the
inquisitors:

> It is now a year since I have been in this prison, and in all this time
> you have not deigned to publish the names of witnesses in my case,
> nor have I been given any opportunity of a full defence.

He was finally sentenced to a reprimand which involved retraction of the several propositions he was said to have held. In prison he had suffered despair, fever, and humiliation. Release from the cells came in mid-December 1576. Weary but undefeated, he greeted his freedom with characteristic restraint:

> Aqui la envidia y mentira
> Me tuvieron encerrado.
> Dichoso el humilde estado
> del sabio que se retira
> y de aqueste mundo malvado,
> y con pobre mesa y casa,
> en el campo deleitoso,
> con solo Diós se compasa,
> y a solas su vida pasa
> ni envidiado ni envidioso.*

Restored once more to his rostrum at the university, he is said to have begun his first lecture with the words, 'As I was saying last time . . . ' But for his enemies this was not the last time. In 1582 he was summoned to a second trial for having uttered rash propositions. The Inquisitor General, Gaspar de Quiroga, intervened on his behalf and in 1584 he escaped with a warning to avoid controversial issues in future.[26]

Less fortunate than Fray Luis were his other colleagues at the university. Gaspar de Grajal, who had been arrested five days before, was thrown into the cells of the Inquisition; there his health gave way, and he died before judgment could be passed on him. A colleague from the University of Osuna, Alonso Gudiel, who was professor of scripture there, was also arrested in the same month on the basis of Castro's accusations. Before this case had been dealt with, he also died in prison, in April 1573. The only one to outlast his treatment was Cantalapiedra, who had been professor of Hebrew at Salamanca and whose whole life had been dedicated to the study of Holy Scripture. His term of imprisonment in a Valladolid cell exceeded even that of Luis de León. It lasted for over five years, from March 1572 to May 1577, and despite his constant appeals for a quick decision

* Here envy and lies held me in prison. Happy the humble state of the scholar who retires from this malicious world and there in the pleasant countryside, with modest table and dwelling, governs his life with God alone, and passes his days all by himself, neither envied nor envying.

there was no hurry to bring him to trial. Eventually he was liberated but never regained his academic post. 'I have laboured to interpret scripture before the whole world', he told the inquisitors in 1577, 'but my only reward has been the destruction of my life, my honour, my health and my possessions'.[27] The bitter lesson he drew from this was drawn by many other contemporaries: 'it is better to walk carefully and remain prudent (*sapere ad sobrietatem*)'. It was a prudence that severely compromised academic life in every country where the established order silenced speculation.

The work of León de Castro was not yet over. The great Hebrew scholar and humanist Benito Arias Montano was working at the time on what was intended to be the crowning glory of Philip II's reign, the Royal Polyglot Bible which he published in Antwerp. In 1575, writing from Rome to the bishop of Cuenca, Montano complained of

> a great rumour which a certain León de Castro of Salamanca has raised in that university, to criticise and discredit the greatest work of letters that has ever been published in the world, the Royal Bible which His Majesty has for the benefit of Christendom ordered to be printed in Antwerp under my direction.[28]

León de Castro was not the only culprit: there were others, wrote Montano in 1579, men of letters who seek to find and note some error in my writings, making extraordinary efforts to do so.[29]

The free play given by the authorities to such people prejudiced the development of individual initiative, and despite the moderate policy of Inquisitor General Quiroga there was always the fear that some passing slip might be censured by the weighty apparatus of the Holy Office. In the case of Francisco Sánchez, 'el Brocense', one of the principal men of letters of his time and a professor of grammar at Salamanca, the fault lay as much with the victim as with his judges. He was denounced in 1584 on charges of loose and presumptuous opinions on theological matters, and summoned before the tribunal of Valladolid. Although the tribunal voted for his arrest and the sequestration of his goods, the Suprema altered this sentence to one of grave reprimand only. Brocense's turbulent and intemperate mind was not put off by this narrow escape, and he returned to the

The Virgin of the Catholic Monarchs, by an unknown painter.
Kneeling behind Ferdinand is Torquemada, first Inquisitor General
of Spain

A penitent in a *sanbenito*   A relapsed heretic due for the stake

Penitents in the procession to an *auto de fe*

fray, disputing theology with theologians, and casting contempt on Aquinas and the Dominicans. In 1593, therefore, at the age of eighty, this excitable old man found himself in trouble once more. Reports of his speeches were relayed to the tribunal of Valladolid, and in 1596 the Inquisition began proceedings against him. But no action was taken until 1600, when he was suddenly seized and put under house arrest, and his papers sequestrated. Among the charges raised against him was that 'he always subjects his understanding to obedience to the faith; but that in matters which are not of faith he has no wish to subject his understanding'.[30] Aged, in ill health, and humiliated by his treatment, Sánchez died at the beginning of December 1600. Because of the scandal hanging over his name, he was denied funeral honours by the University of Salamanca.

It is true that these were among the few prominent intellectuals to be directly censured by the Inquisition, and that the circumstances were special ones, involving the vicious slanders of León de Castro and others. Yet it is peculiarly significant that three of the victims, Luis de León, Gaspar de Grajal, and Alonso Gudiel were all conversos by origin, that Arias Montano was probably one, and that some of the witnesses appearing before the Inquisition claimed that Cantalapiedra was also one. In an academic atmosphere where the Inquisition seemed willing to prosecute scholars because they happened to be of Jewish origin, the chances of freedom being preserved were not very great. The importance of these prosecutions lay not in the small number of victims so much as in the wide repercussions felt by others. One example was sufficient to silence many. When Fray Luis de León heard of the arrest of his colleague Grajal he wrote indignantly to a friend in Granada, 'This fate of the master has scandalized everyone and given just cause for keeping silent out of fear'. On another occasion, said Fray Luis, he had been lecturing about the fraternal correction of heretics, when:

> those students who were furthest from the rostrum signalled that I should speak louder, because my voice was hoarse and they could not hear well. Whereupon I said, 'I am hoarse, and it's better to speak low like this so that the inquisitors don't hear us'.
> I don't know if this offended anyone.[31]

Fray Luis' own fate inspired a strong reaction in the eminent Jesuit historian Mariana. Commenting in a famous passage on the prosecution of Fray Luis and his colleagues, he said that the case:

caused anxiety to many until they should know the outcome. There was dissatisfaction that persons illustrious for their learning and reputation had to defend themselves in prison from so serious a threat to their fame and good name. It was a sad state when virtuous men, because of their great achievements, had to undergo hostility, accusations and injuries from those who should have been their defenders . . . The case in question depressed the spirits of many who observed the plight of another, seeing how much affliction threatened those who spoke freely what they thought. In this way, many passed over to the other camp, or trimmed their sails to the wind. What else was there to do? The greatest of follies is to exert oneself in vain, and to weary oneself without winning anything but hatred. Those who agreed with current ideas did so with even greater eagerness, and entertained opinions that were approved of and were the least dangerous, without any great concern for the truth.[32]

To build so great a volume of discontent on the prosecution of a a handful of academics, indicates that what lay at stake in the case of Luis de León and his colleagues was far more than elementary justice and their individual reputations. The issues extended beyond Salamanca to the whole intellectual world of post-Renaissance and Erasmist Spain. Proceedings such as those against the Salamanca professors stand out only because of their infrequency, and there is no evidence of any systematic persecution of academics. But it is certain that the spirit of individual and free enquiry was, not only in Spain but in the whole of post-Reformation Europe, being subordinated to the political and religious establishment. In this situation liberalism vanished from the academic world.

The most obvious guide to this development is the eradication of Erasmism from the peninsula. The first official Index of forbidden books issued in Spain, in 1551, included the *Colloquies* of Erasmus. This list was simply a re-issue of an Index drawn up by the University of Louvain in the Netherlands. While Louvain was debating whether to condemn Erasmus more fully, the Roman Inquisition under Paul IV came out in 1559 with a general condemnation of all the works of Erasmus. The Jesuits protested strongly against this measure, among the most vociferous being the Dutchman St Peter Canisius. Diego Laínez for his part said openly to the pope that the Index was something 'which restricted many spirits and pleased few, particularly outside Italy'.[33] The enlightened opposition of the Jesuits to any restriction on liberal writers came to nothing. The Index of prohibited books issued by the Spanish Inquisition in 1559 listed sixteen works by Erasmus, including the *Enchiridion*. Spain was following the lead of Rome. From this time the name of Erasmus was slowly and methodically obliterated from the memory of Spain. The Spanish Index of 1612 banned completely all works of Erasmus in Spanish, and classified the author in the category of *auctores damnati*. When the famous theologian Martín de Azpilcueta quoted at about this time from the works of Erasmus, he cited the author as *quidam*, 'someone': so completely did the greatest humanist of the century become an 'unperson' in Spain. Knowledge of his writings did not fade so quickly. It remained in the stream of thought that stretched as far as Cervantes, but when individuals cited the forgotten name (it was Francisco Sánchez who in 1595 declared in a lecture, 'Whoever speaks ill of Erasmus is either a friar or an ass!') they were called to answer before the Inquisition.

The most effective protection that the Spanish government could give its people was to erect a *cordon sanitaire* of censorship around the country, to prevent the entry of all dangerous doctrines. Nowhere was such censorship practised so thoroughly as in Spain. Reversing their early liberal policy, the Catholic monarchs on 8 July 1502 issued a pragmatic by which licences were made obligatory for the printing of books inside Spain as well as for the introduction of foreign books. Within Spain licences could be granted only by the presidents of the *Audiencias* of Valladolid and Granada, and by the six prelates of Toledo, Seville, Granada, Burgos, Salamanca and Zamora. There were no existing guides to heretical books, so the Inquisition had at first to rely on foreign direction. It was a papal order that provoked the first ban on Lutheran books in Spain, issued by Cardinal Adrian of Utrecht on 7 April 1521 in his capacity as Inquisitor General. By the 1540s the Inquisition had a rough unofficial Index of its own, which included among other things Protestant translations of the Bible. But the first printed Index to be used in Spain, issued by Inquisitor General Valdés in September 1547, was no more than a reprint of the Index compiled by the University of Louvain in 1546, with a special appendix devoted to Spanish books.[34] A slightly enlarged version of this was issued by Louvain in 1550, and this was issued the following year, again with a Spanish appendix, by the Inquisition.[35] Whereas, however, in 1547 the Index had been sent to all the local tribunals in Spain, in 1551 a different procedure was adopted, each tribunal being allowed to publish its own version. As a result we know of at least five Indices issued in 1551-2, by the tribunals of Toledo, Valladolid, Valencia, Granada and Seville.[36] All these Indices differed slightly in their contents. What they shared in common was a relative liberality which laid the ban only on works considered from the Catholic viewpoint as extreme. The writings of Bullinger, Bucer, Servet, Zwingli and others were not surprisingly of this number, as were unlicensed translations of the Bible.

This mildness did not continue for long. Censorship began in earnest with the decree issued on 7 September 1558 by the regent Doña Juana, in the name of Philip II.[37] This measure banned the introduction of all foreign books in Spanish translation, obliged printers to seek licences from the Council of Castile (which had in 1544 been granted control over such licences), and laid down a strict procedure for the operation of censorship. Contravention of any of these points would be punished by death and confiscation. At the same time the Inquisition was allowed to issue licences when printing for its own purpose, thus giving it perfect freedom and full armament for the battle now under way. According to the new rules, manuscripts were to be checked and censored both before and after publication, and all booksellers were to keep by them a copy of the Index of prohibited books. So thorough and effective was the decree of 1558 that it remained in force in Spain until the end of the *ancien régime*. The censorship organized by the Inquisition existed side by side with this censorship of the state, and was expressed mainly in the edition of Indices of heretical works. Inquisitorial censorship graded the books on its Indices according to the extent of their error: some authors had only a few words or a few lines deleted from their books, others had all their works condemned *in toto*. To carry out the task of censorship faithfully some of the most brilliant minds in Spain were called in to help with the work. Modern judgment on their labours must be tempered by the fact that they did their work honestly and fairly according to the principles by which they lived.

When so much effort was spent on protecting the people of Spain from foreign contagion, it is instructive to discover the principles on which the Spanish censors acted. The opinion of Jerónimo de Zurita, chronicler of Aragon and a secretary of the Inquisition in the sixteenth century, is of some interest. He divides harmful works into two categories, those in Latin and those in the vernacular. Harmful books in the first category may be kept by instructed persons, but should not be used in schools. Of those in the second category, some such as Boccaccio should be carefully expurgated. As for Spanish books in the second category, some are books of romance and chivalry, and 'since they are without imagination or learning and it is a waste of time to read them, it is better to prohibit them, except for the first four books of *Amadis*'. Others in this class are books on love, of which some, such as the *Celestina*, are serious and good, while others are of such poor quality that they should be banned. Also in this class are works of poetry, again including both good and bad: the bad should be expurgated or eliminated.[33] The interesting criterion employed by Zurita was obviously that of literary merit. At the same time it is clear that he was not discussing the fate of heretical works. Literary merit, as we shall see later, was to be the principal will-o'-the-wisp guiding the several censors, both clerical and secular, who were employed by the Spanish authorities. A modern supporter of censorship might well see in this criterion the only sane and possible way, and indeed apologists of the Inquisition have pointed to Zurita's opinions as reflecting the zeal of the Holy Office for the purity of literature: but in practice these principles never attained their desired end. Objectionable good literature was in fact suppressed or expurgated, and unobjectionable bad literature allowed to pass unhindered.

The Indices themselves were drawn up on certain principles which were usually printed in the introduction to each Index. Books were forbidden if they fell into any of the following categories – all books by heresiarchs; all religious books written by those condemned by the Inquisition; all books on Jews and Moors with an anti-Catholic bias; all heretical translations of the Bible; all vernacular translations of the Bible, even by Catholics; all devotional works in the vulgar tongue; all controversial works between Catholics and heretics; all books on magic; all verse using Scriptural quotations 'profanely'; all books printed since 1515 without details of author and publisher; all anti-Catholic books; all pictures and figures disrespectful to religion. These categories allowed little room for dissent. The date 1515 was no doubt chosen because it excluded all the anonymous literature of the Erasmist-Protestant period. But often the date varied. The Valladolid Index of 1551 forbade the use in schools and universities of any text-books written after 1510, while that of Toledo in the same year adopted 1525 as its dividing line.

The Spanish Index was controlled only by the Spanish authorities, and had no connection with that of Rome, which had also begun in the sixteenth century to draw up its own list of prohibited books. While Spain often had on its list works which Rome had prohibited, there was no rule that one Index should follow the lead of the other, and several authors were astonished to find that Spain had forbidden books of theirs which circulated freely in Italy. Alternatively, Rome would ban books which circulated freely in Spain. There was one other important difference between the two. The Roman Index was exclusively a prohibitory one, that is, it banned books without regard to the number of errors in it, and without specifying whether a book could be published if it were expurgated. The Spanish Index, on the other hand, both expurgated and prohibited books, so that some works could circulate if the relevant passages cited in the Index were excised. In this respect the Spanish system was more liberal. When the Indices clashed, reasons were invariably political. One of the more famous cases illustrating this concerns the Italian Cardinal Boronio, whose works were put on the Spanish Index in retaliation against Roman censorship of Spanish authors who defended the rights of the crown over the Spanish church. Writing to a friend in June 1594, the Cardinal protested that the pope had praised his writings, which had nevertheless been put on the Spanish banned list:

I have heard of the incredible audacity of the Inquisitors of Spain who, at their pleasure and without saying why, place whomever they wish on their Index of prohibited books. There are complaints of this throughout the world.[39]

Pardonable anger, but undoubted exaggeration. Apart from a few liberal spirits, and apart from intellectuals who would resent any kind of restraint on their writings, there were few complaints. Censorship of some kind had long been practised in Europe, and the new restrictions, harsh as they were, merely convinced many that prudence must be exercised in a time of crisis.

The principal Indices of the Spanish Inquisition in the sixteenth century were, apart from the first one of 1547, published in 1551, 1554, 1559, 1583 and 1584. Those of 1551, 1554 and 1559 were issued under Inquisitor General Fernando Valdés. They came out during the high-tide of heresy in Europe, and were consequently directed against heretical works and translations of the Bible in particular. The anxiety over heretical versions of the Bible and New Testament is reflected in a general censure issued by Valdés in 1554, condemning 67 editions of the scriptures issued in Lyon, Antwerp, Paris and other places. The Index issued in 1554 was a purely expurgatory one, devoted to censoring the texts of Bibles. It was not until 17 August 1559 that the first native Spanish Index came out, still partly based on the Louvain one of 1550, but containing for the first time a prohibited list reflecting Spanish tastes. As we have seen, sixteen of Erasmus' works appeared in this Index. Other items included Stephen Gardiner's *De vera obedientia*, the Catechism of archbishop Carranza of Toledo, Josephus' history of the Jews in a Spanish translation, the *Novelas* of Boccaccio in Spanish, and the first and second parts of the *Lazarillo de Tormes*. Among the eminent Spaniards to suffer were the Blessed Juan de Avila, Fray Luis de Granada, and St Francis Borgia. Of these the case of Luis de Granada is the most remarkable. His devotional book the *Libro de la Oración*, first published in 1554, became so popular in Spain that it went through 23 editions by 1559. But in that year it was put on the Index, principally at the instance of the famous theologian Melchor Cano, who had been among the first to smell heresy in the Catechism of the archbishop of Toledo. It was in vain that Fray Luis tried to get the ban rescinded. Finding no help in Spain he succeeded in getting the *Libro* approved by the Council of Trent and by the pope. Such approval was not enough for the Spanish authorities, and it was only when Fray Luis accepted certain 'corrections' in his text that his book was again allowed free circulation.[40] The prohibition of the *Obras del Christiano* of Borgia is as startling, but perhaps more explicable in view of the anti-Jesuit feeling prevalent in the Spanish Church in the sixteenth century. Despite the renowned sanctity of the author, and his eminent position as General of the Society of Jesus until his death in 1572, the book remained on the Index until 1583, when Quiroga's Index prohibited it only if in Spanish or any other vulgar tongue. This of course changed very little, and the book remained on the Index despite the subsequent canonization of its author.

The fruits of a systematic operation of censorship were revealed in the two great Indices issued in 1583 and 1584 by Inquisitor General Gaspar de Quiroga. The first of these was an Index of prohibited books, and the second simply of books to be expurgated, after which they were allowed to be read. The Index of 1583 excluded from reading in Spain not only Erasmus and all the heresiarchs, but some of the most eminent Catholic writers in Europe. One interesting touch of the 1583 list is the prohibition of the *opera omnia* of Henry VIII of England, presumably since he was regarded as an heresiarch. Under the category of 'Latin works', the authors prohibited included Boccaccio (the *Decameron*), Dryander, Rabelais (*opera omnia*), George Buchanan, William of Ockham (of whom only a few works were banned, particularly his writings against pope John XXII), William Tyndal, Savonarola, Hugh Latimer, Zwingli, Jean Bodin, John Foxe, Hus, a Lasco, John of Leyden, Juan Luis Vives (some of his annotations of St Augustine, which required expurgation), Marsiglio of Padua, Melanchthon, Servet, Peter Abelard, Dante (the *Monarchia*) and Thomas Cranmer. Two stalwarts of English Catholicism made their appearance in the persons of Thomas More (*vir alias pius et catholicus*, as the Index conceded), whose *Utopia* was forbidden until expurgated; and Reginald Pole, whose *Pro ecclesiasticae unitatis defensione* was forbidden until expurgated of words against papal supremacy. The works in Spanish on the list included Ovid's *Art of Love*, if in Spanish or other vulgar tongue; Gil Vicente's *Amadis de Gaula*; translations of Machiavelli's *Discourses*; Luis de Granada's *Guia de Peccadores*, if printed before 1561, since all subsequent editions were expurgated; and the first two parts of the *Lazarillo de Tormes*, if printed before 1573, since later editions had been corrected. In addition to the list of

Spanish, details were also given of books forbidden in Portuguese, German and Flemish.

This summary is enough to show that the Inquisition had at last succeeded in drawing up a comprehensive list of foreign, and sometimes native, works which might injure the faith of Spaniards if allowed into the peninsula. It did not matter if the prohibited authors included men whose Catholicism was never in doubt. The point was to defend peninsular Catholics from the eccentricities of foreign Catholics who undermined the citadel of orthodoxy. The sixteenth century closed with the descent of a curtain of censorship over the frontiers of Spain.

The Indices of the seventeenth century were those of 1612 (with an appendix in 1614), 1632 and 1640. That of 1612, issued under Cardinal Bernardo de Sandoval y Rojas as Inquisitor General, was a complete departure from previous ones. Instead of publishing separate volumes for prohibited and expurgated books, as was done in 1583-4, the Cardinal published both together in an *Index librorum prohibitorum et expurgatorum*. The enormous volume resulting from this plan departed in another way from previous practice. Instead of dividing the material simply into Latin and vernacular books, it was now proposed to divide the material into three classes. Into the first class went authors who were completely prohibited; into the second went books that were prohibited, regardless of author; and into the third went books not bearing the names of their authors. For example, all heresiarchs would go into the first class, whereas Dante's *Monarchia* would go into the second. Even this classification, however, was not strictly adhered to. Though Erasmus fell into the first class, and all his works without exception were banned in Spanish translations, yet several of his Latin works which were clearly beyond suspicion were permitted. Also in class one were Edmund Grindal, François Hotman, Rabelais, Buchanan, William Camden (with several exceptions allowed), Henry VIII (but allowing his book on the Sacraments, written against Luther), Hugo Grotius, Machiavelli, Philippe de Marnix, Richard Taverner, Sebastian of Munster, and Thomas Cartwright, among many others. Class two prohibited the *Relations* of Antonio Pérez, Arias Montano's commentaries on Habakkuk, Ovid's *Art of Love* in Spanish, Gil Vicente's *Amadis*, Castiglione's *Cortigiano* (unless expurgated),

D*

95

Dante's *Monarchia*, Petrarch's *Remedi del l'una e l'altra fortuna* (unless expurgated), Boccaccio's *Novelle* (except post-1578 editions, which had been expurgated), Bodin's *Republic*, Ariosto's *Orlando Furioso* (unless expurgated), William of Orange's *Apologia* and many other works.

The Index of 1632 was published under Cardinal Antonio Zapata as Inquisitor General. That of 1640 came out under Antonio de Sotomayor, titular archishop of Damascus and Inquisitor General. The latter Index is of considerable interest and importance. Similar to the 1612 compilation in scope and classification, it offered a general survey of the intellectual advances of the seventeenth century, and in so doing demonstrated the peculiar prejudices of the Spanish Inquisition. The greatest names of the philosophical and scientific world appeared in its pages, but with very disparate attention. Francis Bacon, described as *Anglus, Philosophus, Calvinianus*, appeared in class one, and all his works were banned save the *Sapientia veterum*, published at London in 1617. Curiously enough the compilers of the Index also condemned a certain Francis Verulam, *seu de Verulamio, Anglus, et Angliae Cancellarii, Londiniensis, Philosoph. Calvinianus*, whose *Instauratio magna*, published at London in 1620, was ordered to be expurgated. Others in the first class included Althusius, Hooker, Philippe du Plessis Mornay, and John Selden (one of whose books was expurgated). Johann Kepler and Tycho Brahe received special treatment. As heretics they were *auctores damnati* and therefore appeared in class one. But virtually all their works were permitted in Spain after very minor expurgations. Some were allowed without any expurgations but with the proviso that a note on the book should state it was by a condemned author. Into this category fell Kepler's *Astronomia nova* of 1609, his *Epitome Astronomiae Copernicanae* of 1618, and his *Chilias logarithmorum*, published at Marburg in 1624. This tolerance of men of science is an important factor which we shall discuss in the course of this book. In class two of the Index there were prohibitions of Apuleius' *Golden Ass*, which was banned in any vulgar tongue; of Guicciardini's *History of Italy* (the 1621 edition); and of all the unexpurgated works of Gil Vicente, with 16 specifically named exceptions. Others appearing in class one were Petrarch, who suffered some expurgations; Lucio Marineo Siculo, who underwent the same; and Juan de Mariana, who had to endure expurgations in seven works of his as well as in his *De mutatione monetae* and his *Tractatus de Morte et Immortalitate*. Finally, Cervantes lost by expurgation a sentence in book 2, chapter 36, of his *Quixote*, which concerned works of charity. This Index, by its wide range of prohibitions and its appearance at a critical moment in European history, may rightly be considered the most important ever issued by the Inquisition. Any judgment on the effect of the Holy Office upon intellectual life in Spain must take into account the writings which were by the 1640 list considered dangerous for circulation in the country.

With these Indices ends the first great period in the censorship organized by the Spanish Inquisition. The second period is occupied with other enemies and other books than those marked out for attention in the sixteenth and seventeenth centuries. The procedure adopted by the Inquisition sheds some light on the effectiveness of its work. All public and private libraries and bookshops within Spain were subject to its inspection. Lists of all the booksellers in a city were given to the inquisitors, who would make periodic visits to these shops to check the books on sale.[41] Private libraries were also thoroughly checked wherever possible: that these could not be cleansed satisfactorily is shown by the case of Don Joseph Antonio de Salas, a knight of the Order of Calatrava, whose library was offered for sale to the public on his death in 1651. It was then found that among the 2,424 volumes in the collection 'there were', to quote the censor, 'many books prohibited or unexpurgated or worthy of examination, either because they were by heretical authors or were newly published abroad by unknown writers'.[42] There were in fact 250 prohibited works in the library, a proportion of one in ten. This case shows that foreign books were smuggled regularly and often successfully into Spain, despite the death penalty attached to this crime. Any suspicious books were immediately seized by the inquisitors, but many managed to filter through. Among the most famous of the earlier book smugglers was Julián Hernández, who kept the Protestant community at Seville supplied with books, and perished both for this and for his beliefs in the *auto de fe* of 22 December 1560. The account of the *auto* says expressly of Hernández that 'he brought from

Germany to these realms many heretical books'. Seaports were inevitably the centres of inquisitorial scrutiny, and foreign sailors were especially vulnerable if they happened to be carrying with them while ashore their favourite devotional work. Unguarded stretches of sea coast made smuggling of literature fairly easy, as the Holy Office was quite aware. Unfortunately, attempts to prevent foreign literature entering Spain led to unpleasant incidents, thanks to Spaniards claiming the right to inspect foreign ships in territorial waters. When a merchant ship entered port it had to be visited by health and customs officials, but in addition to these there was also the representative of the Inquisition, who was entitled to examine on board all books and any packages which might contain books.

Literature collected during searches made by officials of the Inquisition was sent to the nearest tribunal for further judgment: there it remained until disposed of. Thus in December 1634 the tribunal of Saragossa had in its keeping 116 copies of the Bible, 55 copies of various works by Erasmus, and 83 volumes of the works of Francisco de Quevedo.[43] In earlier periods, when excessive zeal was predominant, books of this sort were consigned to the flames. Torquemada in his day had organized a book-burning in his monastery of St Stephen in Salamanca. The tradition was carried on by Cardinal Ximénez, who was reported during his conversion campaign among the Granada Moors in 1500 to have burnt in the public square of Vivarrambla over 1,005,000 volumes including unique works of Moorish culture. His successors found this a convenient way of destroying the last relics of heresy in Spain, and the Inquisition organized periodic book-burnings in subsequent years. But later generations of Spaniards sometimes preferred to keep forbidden books in a safe place until their destruction could no longer be avoided. The monastery of the Escorial was used regularly by the Suprema to store prohibited works, and in 1585 the prior reported that its library possessed 'many prohibited books sent at different times by His Majesty, and kept there by licence from the late Don Gaspar de Quiroga'. Half a century later the practice was still being carried on, for in 1639 the Escorial possessed a total of 932 prohibited books, including John Foxe's *Book of Martyrs*.[44] Laudable as this may have been, it was not practised everywhere, with the result that a great number of

98

books condemned by the Inquisition were all but wiped out of existence.

The preceding summary is obviously too brief to give a reader any idea of the magnitude of the task involved in censoring the whole body of a nation's literature. The thoroughness of the house-clearing staggers the imagination. All book shipments into the country, all bookshops and public and private libraries, were rigorously examined and expurgated or confiscated. The labour involved was immense. One censor reported to the Inquisition that to expurgate a private library in Madrid worth 18,000 ducats he had laboured eight hours daily for four months.[45] It was not in the interest of people to evade censorship, because of the heavy penalties involved, particularly the extreme one of death for illegal printing. Authors therefore submitted their manuscripts for examination, and importers of books took care to have their cargo passed by the Inquisition. Individuals suffered for negligence in these matters. A university professor was sentenced at Logroño in 1645 to four years' confinement and perpetual deprivation of the right to teach, for having expounded from a prohibited book. The often petty nature of such prosecutions indicates that the inquisitors had so thoroughly achieved their ends as to be left only with cases of minor importance to prosecute.

What effect did the restriction of free thought and writing have on Spaniards? To such a question there can be no clear answer. Mere citation of the many people who suffered from censorship is no proof that the Inquisition retarded the cultural growth of Spain. Moreover, the few famous writers who were censored by the tribunal did not thereupon cease their creative activity. It is a potent argument in favour of protagonists of the Inquisition that the years of its greatest activity were also the years of Spain's cultural greatness. In the words of Menéndez Pelayo, 'Never was there more written in Spain, or better written, than in the two golden centuries of the Inquisition'.[46] Those centuries were certainly golden. They were the age of Spain's greatest geographical, cultural and military expansion. Fresh from the triumphs at Granada and Oran, the Spanish aristocracy began to build an empire greater and vaster than those of Greece and Rome. What place did the Holy Office fill in this picture?

It is certain that the Inquisition in no way constricted or restrained the great cultural achievements of the sixteenth and seventeenth centuries, *provided* they kept within the limits of orthodoxy and the native traditions of Spain. There are famous instances of individuals who had difficulties with the tribunal. Not all cases were grave, so it is as well to recall a few of them. One of the gravest in its effects, though not in its character, was the suspicion cast on Nebrija by the inquisitor Diego Deza in 1504, for daring to correct alleged errors in the Vulgate for the Polyglot Bible. Nebrija was saved, of course, by Ximénez, who later when Inquisitor General assured him full protection. Yet the threat was enough to make the great humanist fear oppression:

Must I reject as false what appears to me in every way as clear, true and evident as light and truth itself? What does this sort of slavery mean? What unjust domination when one is prevented from saying what one thinks, although to do so involves no slight or insult to religion![47]

This may well appear as excessive protest over little persecution. The important point, however, is that even a small slight to intellectual liberty could be construed as a major threat. There were no doubt many others in the position of Nebrija, though not all would have had such illustrious protection, and many, as Juan de Mariana observed, decided to conform to hard times. It is difficult to envisage what the attitude of contemporaries to the Index may have been. The possibility is that several accepted the censorship as something necessary to faith, that others bore with it for lack of choice, and that only a small proportion felt themselves aggrieved as Nebrija had been. In academic circles the restrictions were serious and often humiliating, but outside these confines creative writers had little to fear. Góngora, for instance, had some difficulty with the censor in 1627, but appears never to have considered it worthy of protest.[48] This failure to protest could be explained by the fact that he died that year. Cervantes is a more controversial example, since, quite apart from the line[49] excised from his *Quixote* in 1632, critics have seen in his work oblique criticisms of the Inquisition.

The greatest and least of Spanish writers were liable to correction in the texts of their works. Saint Teresa of Avila, whose autobiography was denounced to the Inquisition in 1565, and whose works were described by the tribunal of Seville as 'superstitious and novel doctrine, like that of the illuminists of Extremadura', submitted at all times to the Holy Office. On one occasion, she remarks in her *Life*,

> people came to me in great alarm, saying that these were difficult times, that some charge might be raised against me, and that I might have to appear before the inquisitors. But this merely amused me and made me laugh. I never had any fear on that score.[50]

The attitude of Saint Teresa is important. Firmly orthodox, completely obedient, and deliberately wary of theology, she could afford to laugh at others' fears. All artists who concerned themselves with creation and contemplation, and avoided speculation, had nothing to fear from the Holy Office. It was only the minority, the speculative controversialists who flourished in the backwash of Erasmism, who suffered from official censorship. It was these of whom a learned Dominican at Salamanca complained in 1571 when he claimed that 'in this university there is great play about novelty, and little about the antiquity of our religion and faith.'[51] But even if the pursuers of novelty were often rash and mistaken, it seems undeniable that the pressure placed on them and on their colleagues was a threat to academic freedom and therefore to knowledge itself. Why search out a dangerous new truth if the old one was safer? It was in such a situation that the humanist Núñez wrote to Jerónimo de Zurita in 1566, complaining of the difficulties facing learning and letters, and

> the dangers present in them, for when a humanist corrects an error in Cicero he has to correct the same error in Scripture. This and other similar problems drive me insane, and often take away from me any wish to carry on.[52]

What lay at stake under the Inquisition, then, was not the future of creative literature and art, which attained their greatest glory in this period of imperial greatness, but the fate of speculative and experimental science. The extinction of Erasmism in Spain meant a closing not only of geographical but also of intellectual frontiers in the Spanish academic world. Academic discipline became restricted and static, and the most important speculative and experimental writings of contemporary Europe could be obtained in Spain only through unofficial channels and smuggling. Yet the decline of Spanish universities, which we shall comment on later, did not mean the end of cultural freedom in the peninsula. On the contrary, by withdrawing into itself Spain grew to discover and develop the riches of its native genius, and the century after the crisis of the Counter-Reformation witnessed the greatest glory and triumph of Spanish art and letters.

In this lay the strange contradiction of the closed society. Under Habsburg rule the armies of Spain dominated Europe, its ships covered the Atlantic and Pacific Oceans, its language was the master tongue from the Carpathians to the Philippines. Spanish names, among them the jurist and theologian Francisco de Vitoria (1480-1546), the theologian Francisco Suárez (1548-1617), the dramatist Lope de Vega (1562-1635), the novelist Miguel de Cervantes (1547-1616), the painters El Greco (1541-1614) and Diego de Velázquez (1599-1660), stand out in the cultural history of the sixteenth and seventeenth centuries. But within the strict confines of the peninsula (united after 1580, when Philip II had sent his forces into Portugal) the fear of racial and theological impurity, and the undisputed supremacy of the feudalistic classes, brought into existence a society dominated by values whose narrowness contrasted oddly with the extensive triumphs of Spanish imperialism. Whether such a society could for long hold on to an empire which its early militant spirit had created, was a question of more than passing importance. Already in 1570 the Inquisition had been introduced into Lima, capital of Peru, to be followed by the foundation of a tribunal at Mexico City in 1571 and Cartagena de Indias in 1610. In the savage atmosphere of Central America the inquisitors found it best to show indulgence not only to moral sins but also to theological ones. Yet the brutal persecution of conversos which constituted one of the chief activities of the American Inquisition, shows that already the values of Spain had been exported to the Indies.[53] It was now the task of the Inquisition to defend Spain overseas as well as at home. It was imperative above all to protect the good name of Spain. The struggle by a minority in Spain and America, led by the Dominican friar Bartolomé de las Casas, to win adequate guarantees for the Indian population, had provoked bitter controversy in the first half of the sixteenth century. The fiercest polemics were raised by Las Casas' account of the Spanish settlement in his *Brevísima Relación de la destruición de las Indias,** which gave gruesome statistics to illustrate the rapacity of the invaders. The *Brevísima Relación* instantly became part of the arsenal of anti-Spanish propaganda in Europe. Not surprisingly, therefore, the Inquisition after a century of indecision prohibited the account. Giving its reasons for the prohibition, which was dated 3 June 1660,[54] the tribunal of Saragossa said:

> This book contains a narrative of very terrible and savage events, whose like does not exist in the histories of other nations, committed, says the author, by Spanish soldiers, settlers in the Indies, and ministers of the Catholic King. It is advisable to seize these narratives as injurious to the Spanish nation, since even if they were true it would have sufficed to make a representation to His Catholic Majesty and not to publish them throughout the world, so giving the initiative to enemies of Spain and to heretics!

Even if they were true: in that lay the ultimate achievement of the policy of censorship. Las Casas at the time had been given complete freedom to publicise his case throughout the Hispanic world, and the Holy Office had taken care to remain neutral between him and his opponent Juan Ginés de Sepúlveda. But now that, over a century later, Las Casas was being used to denigrate Spain, the truth or falsity of his case was subordinated to the need to protect his country against adverse criticism. In this way the Inquisition became the guardian not only of the ideology but also of the reputation of the closed society.

There should be no need to stress that other countries besides Spain suffered the heavy hand of restriction, suppression and censorship in the dark years at the end of the sixteenth century, when freedom and humanism were snuffed out all over Europe and brave men like Edmund Campion, scholar and saint, paid with their lives for preferring truth. But nowhere was the imposition of orthodoxy so effective and complete as in the one country where an institution of international dimensions devoted its entire resources to the task.

* Brief account of the destruction of the Indies.

CHAPTER SIX

THE END OF MORISCO SPAIN

Los dos ríos de Granada,
uno llanto y otro sangre.

Lorca, BALADILLA DE LOS TRES RÍOS

MOORISH Spain, the Spain of the invaders from north Africa, remained in places under Muslim control for some seven centuries. Consequently, the peoples who thus entered Spanish history were no less a part of its structure than the Christian and Jewish population. They intermarried with them, and exchanged ideas and languages, so that the three religions were recognized as part of one empire. The Reconquest changed all this. The Christian advance took Saragossa in 1187, Córdoba in 1236, Valencia in 1238, and Seville in 1248; finally, after a long interval, Granada fell in 1492. The end of Moorish power meant that the Moors ceased to exist as a nation, and became no more than a minority within a Christian country. This lesser status, however, they never accepted. In the great Granada rebellion of 1568 the Morisco leader Aben Humeya proclaimed, 'We are no band of thieves, but a kingdom'.[1] It was an illusion which the Moorish remnant refused to give up, and led eventually to the expulsion of their race in 1609.

The capitulation of Granada included in its terms an agreement by Ferdinand and Isabella that the Moors were to be regarded as free subjects of the crown, with the free exercise of their own religion. This was reaffirmed in a solemn promise given by the sovereigns. Thus twelve years after the foundation of the Inquisition the Catholic monarchs showed no anxiety to achieve the unity of faith so often cited as a cornerstone of their policy. Meanwhile evangelization of the Moors was begun under the initiative of Hernando de Talavera as first archbishop of

Granada. His gentle methods and good example led to a significant number of voluntary conversions. The slow pace inevitable in such a policy irritated Cardinal Ximénez, who in 1499, on the invitation of Ferdinand and Isabella, began a campaign to coerce the Moorish population into the true faith. As a result of his endeavours it is reported that on 18 December 1499 about three thousand Moors were baptized by him and a leading mosque in Granada was converted into a church. Converts were encouraged to surrender their Islamic books, several thousands of which were destroyed by Ximénez in a public bonfire. A few rare works on medicine were kept aside for the University of Alcalá. These events, so clearly contrary to the accord of 1492, led inevitably to disturbances and a momentary uprising in Granada city.

Ximénez immediately denounced the uprising as rebellion, and claimed that by this the Moors had forfeited all their rights under the terms of capitulation. They should therefore be given the choice between baptism and expulsion. The government agreed with his arguments, and Ximénez then began the mass baptism of the population of Granada, most of whom preferred this fate to the more hazardous one of deportation to Africa. The speed with which the baptisms were carried out meant that there was no time in which to instruct the Moors in the fundamentals of their new religion, so that inevitably most of the new converts became Christian only in name. Those who refused the choice between baptism and deportation took to the mountain ranges of the Alpujarras where they began armed rebellion. This was put down methodically and brutally by the royal forces, so that by 1501 it was officially assumed that the kingdom of Granada had become a realm of Christian Moors – the Moriscos. Those Moors who wished to emigrate to Africa could do so on payment of a sum of money, but converts were not allowed to go. Ferdinand granted the Moriscos legal equality with Christians but at the same time disarmed the population, for fear of further risings. The success of the Granada campaign and the conversion of the Alpujarra population made it all the more intolerable that there should still exist in Castile scattered communities of Moors. There could be only one solution. Ten years after the expulsion of the Jews, Isabella on 12 February 1502 issued a royal order giving all remaining Moors in the realms of Castile the choice between baptism and expulsion. The majority of the native Moorish communities, the *Mudéjares*, chose to stay and be baptized. How free such a choice was is illustrated by the fact that emigration was made literally impossible. The historian Galíndez de Carvajal says that although Moors were technically allowed to leave if they chose, in practice the authorities would not allow them to go and instead forced them to accept baptism. Under such conditions the mass of the remaining Moorish population of Castile came into the Christian fold. With this the history of the Moriscos in Castile begins.

In the crown of Aragon, over which Ferdinand ruled, there was no comparable pressure on the Moors. The principal reason for this was the great power of the landed nobility and the authority of the Cortes. On the estates of the nobles the Moors formed a plentiful, cheap and productive source of labour, from which the expression arose 'Mientras más Moros más ganancia'.* Whether to placate his nobility or in pursuit of a moderate policy, Ferdinand repeatedly warned the inquisitors of Aragon not to persecute the Moorish population or resort to forced conversions. The Moors therefore continued to lead an independent existence until the outbreak in 1520 of the revolt of the *Comuneros*. Simultaneously with the uprisings in Castile, Valencia experienced disturbances of its own. Here the rebels, grouped into *Germanías* or brotherhoods, organized an urban revolution directed against the local aristocracy. Valencia had the largest Moorish population of any province in Spain. The Moors were almost exclusively a rural community and were subjected to the big landowners of the realm. The *Germanía* leaders saw that the simplest way to destroy the power of the nobles in the countryside would be to free their Moorish vassals, and this they did by baptizing them. The years 1520-2 in Valencia thus witnessed the forcible baptism of thousands of Moors. The defeat of the rebels by royal troops should in theory have allowed the Moors to revert to Islam, since forced baptisms were universally regarded as invalid. But the authorities were not so eager to lose their new converts. The Inquisition in particular was concerned to hold the Moors to the letter of their baptism. To the argument that the conversions had taken place

* 'More Moors, more profit'.

under compulsion, the standard answer was once again given, that to *choose* baptism as an alternative to death meant the exercise of free choice, which rendered the sacrament of baptism valid.[2] The Inquisition was therefore ordered to proceed on the assumption that all properly executed baptisms were valid. The task now was to save the Moriscos from relapsing into their old faith.

The fact that Castile and Valencia had large new Morisco communities made it incongruous that the Moors should still be tolerated in the province of Aragon. Charles V finally on 13 September 1525 issued orders that Moors were no longer to be tolerated in Spain except as slaves, and measures for their conversion were to be set on foot. This was followed on 25 November by a decree for the expulsion of all Moors from Valencia by 31 December, and from Catalonia and Aragon by 31 January 1526. The unfortunate Moors came forward in their thousands to accept a religion which they neither believed nor loved nor ever intended to practise.

By 1526 Morisco Spain was a reality. Within a few years it had become a problem of major dimensions. For the Inquisition the primary problem lay in the fact that the Moriscos had been converted by force and had therefore never been more than perfunctorily catechized. No proper missionary work among the population was undertaken and many parishes lacked clergy completely. In Valencia many Moriscos spoke only Arabic and knew no 'cristianesch'; but even those who spoke Valencian considered Arabic their mother tongue. In addition to the widespread ignorance of Christianity, therefore, there existed a language problem. The Spanish priests spoke no Arabic and most of them were like the bishop of Orihuela, who considered it the duty of the Moriscos, as subjects of the Spanish crown, to learn the Spanish tongue. In their communities the Moriscos still retained all the practices of their old faith as well as the traditional social customs which set them apart from the Christian population. This distinctive existence made it impossible to assimilate them into the body of a religiously united Spain. The important fact, however, is that it was the Christians who made such assimilation impossible. Wherever the Reconquest triumphed the Moors were relegated to a position of servitude. In 1568 the Moriscos of Granada under Aben Humeya initiated the Second Rebellion of the Alpujarras, a ferocious and desperate attempt to win justice for their people. The Spanish ambassador to France, writing to the secretary of Philip II, saw nothing but justice in their demands. The Moriscos are in revolt, but it is the Old Christians who drive them to despair. These many years they have suffered injustice, murder, robbery and rapine: in one parish the Moriscos ask for their priest to be removed, 'for all our children are being born with blue eyes like his'.[3] In Valencia the situation was, if anything, worse. The Moriscos there were little more than a rural proletariat, tilling the land which was their only source of wealth, and excluded from the life of the towns, so that they never grew into Spanish urban society, never became priests, soldiers, doctors, or lawyers, landlords or tax-farmers.[4] This situation in Valencia has aptly been compared to a colonial regime, or to the southern states of the United States, where the Moriscos, like the negroes, formed a depressed mass hated by the (Old Christian) proletariat of the towns, and despised – but exploited, and therefore defended – by the (Old Christian) colonial aristocracy.[5]

In all this the Inquisition played a key role. Immediately after the measures of 1525-6, it began a profitable series of *autos de fe* in Valencia, and protests in subsequent years show that the tribunal was taking seriously its duty to keep in their faith those who had been unwillingly thrust into it. There was one brake on the unchecked zeal of the Inquisition. In January 1526 the leaders of the Moriscos succeeded in obtaining from the crown and Inquisitor General Manrique a secret *concordia* or agreement that if they all submitted to baptism they should be free for forty years from any prosecution by the Holy Office, since it would be impossible for them to shed all their old customs at once. In 1528 this *concordia* was made public, and in that same year the Cortes of Aragon meeting at Monzón asked Charles to prevent the Inquisition prosecuting Moriscos until they had been instructed in the faith. Their request was timely, for the guarantee was no more lasting than the one granted to the Moors of Granada. The Holy Office interpreted the *concordia* to mean that it could bring to trial those converts who had slipped back into their Moorish rites and customs, and the figures for victims in these years show that inquisitorial rigour was unabated. From 1528 to 1530 there were one hundred and six cases of heresy cited before the Inquisition of Valencia. In 1531 there were fifty-eight trials for heresy, and about forty-five people were burnt for the same crime that year. From 1532 to 1540 the number of people tried for heresy came to 441.[6] These figures would include several Jewish conversos, but the majority were certainly cases of Moriscos.

The date 1526 was fateful in the history of the Andalucian Moriscos, for in that year the Inquisition of Jaén transferred its residence to Granada. This move was accompanied by the issue of regulations forbidding the Moriscos to use the Arab language or Moorish clothes or even Moorish names. Morisco money offered to Charles brought about the suspension of these rules. But the removal of one burden was balanced by the imposition of another in the form of the Inquisition, whose measures the Moriscos spent the next generation in trying to modify. Finally in 1567 an edict on the lines of that of 1526 was published in Granada by the authorities. By this measure all the rites, customs, and language of the Moriscos were forbidden under penalty. Books in Arabic were destroyed and Moorish clothes were forbidden. The list of prohibitions amounted to the suppression of every national characteristic of the Moriscos. So extreme an edict reaped its own deserts. In an atmosphere of mounting anger and despair the Morisco population at the end of 1568 burst into a revolt which set the whole region of the Alpujarras aflame and kept the best generals of Philip II at bay for the next two years.

In Aragon the only effective opposition to such treatment came from the lords of the Moriscos. The protests they raised against the Inquisition in the Cortes held at Monzón in 1533 included, as we have seen, claims that the tribunal was seizing land confiscated from its victims, to the detriment of the actual feudal owners of the land. Similar complaints were raised in the Cortes of 1537 and 1542. In 1546 the pope intervened and decreed that for a minimum period of ten years the Inquisition should not confiscate any property from the Moriscos. But only the year after this we find the Cortes of Valencia stating that the tribunal was disregarding such injunctions. It was after great difficulty that finally in 1571 the Inquisition showed itself open to compromise. The resulting *concordia* was embodied in a decree of October 1571 by which, in return for an annual payment of

2,500 ducats to the Inquisition, the tribunal agreed not to confiscate or sequestrate the property of Moriscos on trial for heresy. Monetary fines could be levied, but with a limit of ten ducats only. The agreement benefited all sides: the Inquisition, since it brought in a regular annual revenue; the Moriscos, since it protected property for members of their families; and the lords of the Moriscos, since it preserved lands they had leased to their Morisco dependents.

The principal problem facing both church and government was that of converting the Moriscos. Criticisms were frequently made that the Inquisition was prosecuting Moriscos for heresy when in fact they had never been catechized and were ignorant of Christianity. The criticism is not wholly true. In the years after 1526 the Valencian clergy made several serious efforts to evangelize their nominal converts. The Inquisitor General Manrique made an attempt in 1534 to educate Morisco children in the faith, and also establish a number of rectories to help priests catechize the population. The revenues of former mosques, now converted into churches, were devoted to this purpose. Juan de Ribera, the saintly prelate who became archbishop of Valencia in 1568, initiated a financial scheme to increase the stipends of priests and make work among the Moriscos more congenial to the clergy. He also helped to found a collegiate seminary and a college for Morisco boys and girls. For the forty-three years that he held this see, Ribera made every effort to travel round his bishopric and attend to the needs of Moriscos. The bishop of Segorbe was another who made attempts to win his flock from Moorish ways. If, therefore, the Moriscos had initially been forced into the faith without instruction, there was no lack of subsequent effort to make good the deficiency. Unfortunately, failure was to be expected from the very start. As long as the Moriscos remained a depressed minority and continued to be despised for their social position and race, there was no hope of them entering the Christian community voluntarily. In Lea's words, 'they were Christians as regards duties and responsibilities, but they remained Moors in respect to liabilities and inequality before the law'.[7] It was not the Inquisition that was to blame for this. The fault lay with the nobility of Valencia. When, for example, in 1561 the inquisitor Miranda named members of the rich Morisco family of

Abenamir as familiars of the Inquisition, the Duke of Segorbe, their overlord, ordered them to give up the appointment since his protection was sufficient for them. It was in the noble interest to keep their Morisco servants strictly subordinated, and to prevent them enjoying the social privileges which wealth might win for them. As a result, the Moriscos were subjected to heavy feudal taxation which they would not have had to pay had their official status as Christians been respected. In 1608 a Jesuit priest complained that one of the chief obstacles to effective conversion in Valencia was the tyranny of the lords. This was certainly recognized at the time, but the crown continued to support the nobility, and legislation under Charles V and Philip II reinforced the state of virtual serfdom in which most Moriscos lived, by forbidding any to change their domicile or lord, or to move from one province to another, under pain of death. Last, but not least, of the many burdens imposed on them was the racialist cult of *limpieza de sangre* or purity of blood, by which descendants of Moors and Jews were forbidden to hold any public office, secular or ecclesiastical, in the kingdom. This practice became almost universal in Spain from the mid-sixteenth century onwards, and in 1552 the Inquisition decided that no descendants of the two races should be appointed as familiars. It had already been a rule that candidates of Jewish blood were not allowed into the priesthood: in 1573 the pope extended this to cover Moriscos. Shut off in this way from public office in a very office-conscious age, the Moriscos became relegated to the rank of second-class citizens, condemned to live perpetually on the outer fringes of Spanish society.

The servitude in which Moriscos were kept by their lords was a clear contravention of the *concordia* of 1528, when Charles had guaranteed them all the liberties of Christians if they changed their religion. The king, however, never felt himself strong enough to enforce the *concordia* against his own nobility. It was left to the pope to intervene. A brief dated July 1531 and addressed to Manrique ordered the Inquisitor General to excommunicate lords who taxed their Morisco vassals more than their Old Christian vassals. Subsequently in 1534 Manrique gave instructions to commissioners to find out whether the New Christians were being treated the same as Old Christians. This brief intervention of the Inquisition on behalf of the Moriscos seems to have borne no fruit. The fact was that the tribunal acted against nobles only when they tried to protect their vassals against the Holy Office. Several distinguished peers suffered on this account. The most famous case is that of Sancho de Córdoba, Admiral of Aragon, who was made to abjure his errors, fined two thousand ducats, and confined by the Inquisition, for protecting Moriscos against the tribunal. In 1571 the Grand Master of the Order of Montesa was among those who appeared in an *auto de fe* for the same crime. Apart from cases like these, the Inquisition continued its activity principally against heresy among the Moriscos, who undoubtedly thought of the tribunal as an instrument of persecution. One of the methods of coercion used was to persuade poorer Moriscos to denounce richer ones and thereby profit from the percentage of confiscations or fines granted to delators. Faced with Christianity of such a merciless nature they resorted inevitably to rebellion or flight. In the Cortes at Monzón in 1542 it was stated categorically that Moriscos had been fleeing abroad and joining the Turks, 'because of the fear they have of the Inquisition'.[8] They turned to their friends abroad, to the Muslim kingdoms in north Africa and the near East, and to the Barbary pirates. The constant threat from Turkish expansion, and the repeated descents made on Spanish coasts by marauders, made official tolerance of the Moriscos even less likely. In 1579 in Andalucia and in 1586 in Valencia, Moriscos were forbidden to live near the sea coasts because of the easy routes available for escape as well as for invasion.

By the end of the sixteenth century the Morisco problem seemed to be insoluble. We have seen that this insolubility consisted largely in the unwillingness of certain interests to allow any sane solution to what was essentially a social problem. The two alternative solutions offered at the time differ so startlingly that it is worth looking briefly at them. The conservative point of view was expressed by Martin de Salvatierra, bishop of Segorbe, who in 1587 presented a memorial to Philip II in favour of the expulsion of the Moriscos.[9] The point of view was one now shared by many people, including Juan de Ribera. It was the view of those who thought that if the Moriscos were unwilling to be good Christians and also second-class citizens they had no place in Spanish society. The opposite opinion was expressed in an undated and unsigned memoir presented to the Inquisitor General, in which the most liberal and courageous measures were proposed. Taxation of the Moriscos should be just and equitable, and the tax payable to the Inquisition (by the *concordia* of 1571) should be abolished. With the remaining taxes colleges should be built to educate the children in the faith, and orphanages should be set up. Priests ministering to them should be made to learn Arabic. All offices and professions, including the priesthood, should be opened to them; and marriage with Old Christians should be permitted and encouraged.[10] A solution along these lines would have satisfied elementary justice and broken down the social and racial barriers which made the Morisco a virtual outcast. Instead the official establishment offered a settlement on no terms but theirs. The Inquisition shares equal responsibility with the nobility and the crown for the course events now took.

Once the Moriscos came to be regarded as impossible to assimilate, the whole question took on a different light. Their numbers seemed to threaten all the achievements of the Reconquest. Between Alicante and Valencia on one side and Saragossa on the other, a vast body of 200,000 Moorish souls advanced into the flesh of Christian Spain.[11] The threat came not only from the existence of this body but from its rate of growth, shown all too clearly in the total population of the province of Valencia, which increased from 64,075 households in 1563 to 96,731 in 1609, an overall increase of fifty per cent in one generation. What was terrifying, however, was that among the Morisco population the increase had been nearly seventy per cent, whereas among the Old Christians it was under forty-five per cent.[12] The problem did not exist in Valencia alone. The dispersal of Granada's Moriscos after the Alpujarra rebellion had led to their drift into Castile, and to a dangerous increase in the Morisco population of Toledo, where they flourished alarmingly. A report in 1596 claimed that there were twenty thousand Moriscos in Andalucia and Toledo with an income of over twenty thousand ducats a year. The old fear that native Moors might aid an invasion of Spain by Turkish forces now gained a hold on the popular mind. The most serious crisis suffered by the Spanish monarchy in this century was the Alpujarra rising, which was crushed only one year before the naval victory over the Turks at

Lepanto in 1571. Lepanto did not end the fears of invasion. In 1580 at Seville a Morisco conspiracy abetting invasion from Morocco was discovered. In 1602 they were plotting with Henry IV of France. And in 1608 the Valencian Moriscos asked for help from Morocco. The threat was powerful and terrifying. 'Fear entered into the heart of Spain'.[13]

The Morisco expulsions of 1609-14 are not our direct concern here. The operation, ordered on 9 April 1609, took place with all the armed and naval forces of Spain standing by. Expulsions commenced in Valencia, which contained half the Moriscos in the peninsula and was therefore potentially the most dangerous province. About 275,000 Moriscos were expelled from Spain out of a resident total of nearly 300,000.[14]

The consequences for the economy were disastrous, above all in Valencia, which lost the quarter of its population on which the economy had depended. Its agriculture floundered as the production of wheat and sugar-cane declined and collapsed. The entire labour force disappeared: 'who will make our shoes for us?' cried archbishop Ribera. The allotments formerly tilled by the Moriscos were seized and incorporated into large holdings, and the rural nobility, who had been hostile to the idea of expulsion, now contented themselves with the gain of land. Perhaps the most important result was the ruin and decline of the bourgeoisie. These, like all the churches, monasteries and municipalities of Valencia, had been largely a rentier class, living off the ground-rent from land held by Moriscos. After the expulsion, this income had to be claimed from the nobility who had seized the land and refused to pay out at the old rates of interest. In an aristocratic society, the crown supported the noble classes and lowered the rates of interest. Those who had savings in Valencia city were forced to resort to the savings bank, which consequently went bankrupt in 1613, spelling the ruin of all those who carried on commerce and finance.[15]

The Inquisition also faced a bleak future. In 1611 the tribunals of Valencia and Saragossa complained that the expulsion had resulted in their bankruptcy, since they were losing 7,500 ducats a year which they had formerly received from ground-rents. The tribunal of Valencia at the same time acknowledged receiving some compensation, but claimed that a sum of nearly 19,000 ducats was still payable to it by the government to make up for what it had lost.[16] A statement of revenue drawn up for the tribunal of Valencia just before the expulsion of the Moriscos shows that 42.7 per cent of its income derived directly from the Morisco population. A similar statement drawn up for the Inquisition of Saragossa in 1612 showed that since the expulsion its revenue had fallen by over 48 per cent.[17] In both cases the triumph of the Inquisition in bringing about the elimination of an entire nation of heretics, led ironically to its decline as the financial sources of its existence dried up.

The expulsion of the Moriscos was categorized by Cardinal Richelieu in his memoirs as the most barbarous act in human history. Cervantes, on the other hand, not necessarily speaking for himself, makes one of his Morisco characters applaud this heroic act of Philip III, 'to expel poisonous fruit from Spain, now clean and free of the fears in which our numbers held her'.[18] Both views were contemporary, therefore as tenable now as then. Our concern, however, is not with the morality of the act. The expulsion was the last stage in the creation of the closed society. As such, it was part of the process furthered inexorably by the Holy Office and by the machinery of Castilian government. Every stage of the Morisco problem was controlled and directed by the Inquisition, whose concurrence by itself made the expulsion possible. Within Valencia it was the ecclesiastics who favoured the expulsion and the nobility who opposed it. When the nobles heard of the 1609 decree 'they went in their numbers to assure the king and the Duke of Lerma that Valencia would be utterly ruined if the Moriscos were expelled, since they were the ones who did all the work'.[19] Boronat, the great historian of the Morisco question, glosses over the universal opposition of these nobles, and praises those few peers 'of pure blood and Christian heart' whose religion overrode their self-interest and made them support the expulsion. For the historian Florencio Janer the expulsion was the necessary excision of an 'enemy race' from the heart of Spain.[20] In these sentiments we can hear once again the echoes of the Reconquest. The tragedy of 1609 was the logical completion of the triumphant campaign against Granada in 1492. The defeat of the Moors ended now with their being driven into the sea. Thus behind the fate of Valencia loomed the shadow of Castile, Castile of the Reconquest and the

Inquisition, where the virtues of race and honour had been enshrined in the ideals of society. The expulsion of the Moriscos was a Castilian solution, proposed and executed by Castilians. It is even possible that the powerful hand of the Castilian guild of sheep-owners, the Mesta, lay behind the blow struck against agriculture by the expulsion.[21] What is certain is that the last hostile minority had finally been eliminated from the body of the closed society, with results that led to the temporary decline of the province of Valencia and the collapse of the agrarian economy of half of Spain.

CHAPTER SEVEN

RACE PURITY AND RACIALISM

Yo soy un hombre,
aunque de villana casta,
limpio de sangre y jamás
de hebrea o mora manchada.

Lope de Vega, PERIBÁÑEZ

THE lack of an effective middle class in mediaeval Spanish society, together with the absence of institutional feudalism, created a situation in which the highest and lowest classes could maintain social mobility without great fear of social distinction. One result was that the ideals of the nobility could filter down into the common people and exist in them with no less intensity than in the upper classes. Don Quixote is the ideal example of noble ideals assuming comic and reactionary proportions. With him, as with the genuine aristocracy, the concepts of honour, pride and *hidalguía* become the very foundations of action. These concepts of the nobility were given new life by the recovery of Granada, then by the discovery of America, and finally by the extension of Spanish power to Europe in the empire of Charles V. All classes of Spanish society shared in, and contributed to, these successes of the crown. In this way the notions of honour and pride permeated Spanish society and became identified with the social structure of the Reconquest. In the words of a distinguished historian, 'the common people looked upwards, wishing and hoping to climb, and let themselves be seduced by chivalric ideals: honour, dignity, glory, and the noble life'.[1] The consciousness of the normal division of society into upper and lower classes became blurred in a nation where honour became the *raison d'être* of every section of the population. In so far as this concept of honour was identified with the virtues of the Old Christian nobility, deference to honour became deference to the nobility. Honour was the patrimony of nobility, inherent in it and exclusive to it.

The noble virtues of honour and pride therefore dominated the forms of thought in sixteenth century Spain, and led to a stratification in social behaviour. The narrow concepts of the governing class became, for good or ill, the accepted code of conduct. The extreme deference paid to honour is shown in the writings of several contemporaries. In the *Manual de confesores* (1557) of Martín de Azpilcueta, for instance, the loss of honour is looked upon as equivalent to the loss of one's life.[2] The shame (*vergüenza*) of departure from the accepted social code, or the accepted official religion, made one correspondingly deserve to lose one's life. That individuals were infected by this outlook is shown by the remarkable case of Juan Díaz, a Spanish disciple and friend of the reformer Bucer, who was assassinated in Germany by his own brother Alfonso, a Catholic who feared that his brother's heresy would bring shame on his family and on all Spain.[3] The Inquisition in particular shared this attitude to the extent of trying to pursue Spanish heretics such as Miguel Servet even beyond the borders of Spain, for fear that their heresies would bring disgrace on the honour of the Spanish nation.

Within the country the social effects of 'honour' were perhaps more perverse. Secure in the traditions of the Reconquest, the Castilian nobility continued to regard their functions as essentially the same that they had always been. Their task was to fight and not to labour. *Hidalguía* would not permit a nobleman, even the lowest rank of nobleman, to labour or to trade. Trade, usury and work was the lot of the urban population and particularly of the middle classes. The logical result of this, in Spain as elsewhere in Europe, was that the noble concept of 'honour' also involved a disdain for manual labour and commerce, and in a country where 'honour' was the touchstone work and productivity became relegated to a dishonourable position, despite the efforts of statesmen and writers to denounce such an attitude as evil.

This very simplified picture presents a society which in ideals and structure is Old Christian. People like Sancho Panza were proud of the fact that, regardless of class, they were Old

St Dominic presiding at an auto de fe, by Berruguete. Several
unconnected incidents are here synthesized into one picture

Mercy and justice on the banner of the Inquisition

A contemporary Dutch print of the Valladolid *auto de fe* of 1559

SPAANSCHE INQUISITIE.

Christians and consequently were as good as the nobility. 'Though poor', says Sancho, 'I am an Old Christian, and owe nothing to anybody.'⁴ Spain, its traditions and its faith, belonged to the Old Christians. The heritage could not be shared, then, with those who were outside the picture. Jews and Moors must be relegated to despised positions in society. The Jews were the most dangerous minority, above all because their wealth and talents brought them into contact with the highest circles of the ruling class. This racial antagonism had fateful consequences. It made the concepts of honour and pride defensive, and led to the idea that the honour of one's faith and nation could be preserved by ensuring the purity of lineage from contamination by Jews. Yet what if the highest ranks of the nobility had been penetrated by Jewish blood? By the sixteenth century it was, as we have seen, notorious that the principal families of Aragon and Castile, and even perhaps the royal family, could trace their descent through conversos. Old Christian Spain would collapse if this process went on. A few zealous souls therefore considered that now was the time to stop the Jewish fifth column. With this we have the beginnings of a new stress on racial purity and the consequent rise of the cult of *limpieza de sangre* – purity of blood.

Racial discrimination through *limpieza* began in the fifteenth century. The university college of San Bartolomé in Salamanca has the distinction of being the first to introduce, through its foundation bulls granted by the pope in 1414 and 1418, rules forbidding any but those 'ex puro sanguine procedentes' from becoming members of the college. This innovation in a seat of learning spread rapidly during the century, and some colleges even directed that all officials and employees down to the water-carrier should be *limpios* (pure). These rules, however, had only a limited impact. More important was the form of antisemitism which tried to separate conversos and Jews as a whole from their Old Christian fellow-citizens, so leading on to serious 'racial' conflict in the towns. The most notable of the early cases concerns the town of Villena, to which in February 1446 the Castilian crown gave a royal privilege forbidding any conversos to live there. The next few years saw public attention concentrated mainly on the civil war in Toledo – and the promulgation of the celebrated statute against conversos. Its condemnation by the pope (typical of papal inconsistency when dealing with *limpieza*), by the archbishop of Toledo, and by public bodies, did little to check the racialist movement. In 1468, in reply to a request by Ciudad Real, Henry IV granted the city a privilege excluding all conversos from municipal office. In 1473 in Córdoba the formation of a confraternity excluding conversos led to massacres.

The principal impulse given to the spread of *limpieza* statutes was the founding of the Inquisition in 1480. The social antagonism of which Spaniards had always been aware was now heightened by the spectacle of thousands of judaizers being found guilty of heretical practices and herded to the stake. National security no less than religious purity seemed to depend on the exclusion of conversos from all positions of trust and importance. In 1483 a papal bull ordered that episcopal inquisitors should be Old Christians, and in the same year the military Order of Alcántara issued a statute excluding all descendants of Jews and Moors from its ranks. One by one the religious bodies of Spain began to insert conditions of *limpieza* into their statutes. The university college of Santa Cruz at Valladolid had a *limpieza* statute laid down for it by its founder in 1488. Other colleges did not hesitate to contradict the rules of their founders. That of San Ildefonso, founded by Ximénez in 1486, had no statutes against conversos, but after the Cardinal's death the college adopted one in 1519. When he founded the great monastery of St Thomas Aquinas at Avila, Torquemada applied to the pope in 1496 for a decree excluding all descendants of Jews. It was not until 1531 that any other Dominican foundation followed Torquemada's lead. The first cathedral chapter to adopt a *limpieza* statute was that of Badajoz in 1511. The cathedral chapter of Seville in 1515 adopted the same ruling, on the initiative of its archbishop the inquisitor Diego de Deza. The university of Seville, although it had been founded by a converso, in 1537 adopted a statute of *limpieza*, after someone had carefully blotted out of the original charter the clause making the university open to all.[5]

The Inquisition played a leading part in all these events. From the beginning it had been the rule, as set out in Torquemada's instructions issued at Seville in November 1484, that

the children and grandchildren of those condemned (by the Inquisition) may not hold or possess public offices, or posts, or honours, or be promoted to holy orders, or be judges, mayors, constables, magistrates, jurors, stewards, officials of weights and measures, merchants, notaries, public scriveners, lawyers, attorneys, secretaries, accountants, treasurers, physicians, surgeons, shopkeepers, brokers, changers, weight inspectors, collectors, tax-farmers, or holders of any other similar public office.[6]

This practice was upheld by the Catholic monarchs, who issued two decrees in 1501 forbidding the children of those condemned by the tribunal to hold any post of honour or to be notaries, scriveners, physicians or surgeons. Conversos were also excluded from academic life and the higher professions in Castile by a decree of the Inquisition in 1522 whereby the universities of Salamanca, Valladolid and Toledo were forbidden to grant degrees to descendants of Jews and of judaizers. Alcalá was excepted from this order, perhaps out of respect to its late founder, Ximénez. This one exception, however, was insignificant beside the fact that all the prominent institutions in both church and state, led primarily by the Inquisition, had combined to crush the life of a racial minority which had been forced into the Catholic fold against its will over a generation previously.

In this web of racial hatred and intolerance a few isolated voices attempted to convince the majority of their fellow Old Christians that antisemitism was wrong. One of the first attacks on the 1449 *Sentencia-Estatuto* was made by Alonso Díaz de Montalvo, who emphasized the common traditions and inheritance of Jews and Christians, and pointed out that a baptized Jew was no different from a baptized Gentile. The Mother of God and all the Apostles, he said, had been Jews. Those self-styled Christians who had drawn up the *Sentencia* were moved by material greed and were wolves disguised as sheep in the flock of Christ. It was the famous converso Alonso de Cartagena who in fact wrote the definitive refutation of the *Sentencia*, in the shape of his treatise *Defensorium Unitatis Christianae*, which was written in 1449-50. Turning the tables on the antisemites, the learned bishop of Burgos showed that the Catholic church was properly the home of the Jews, and that Gentiles were the outsiders who had been invited in. His moderate arguments were continued by the General of the Jeronimites, Alonso de Oropesa, who in 1465 completed his *Lumen ad revelationem gentium*, an argument which stressed the need of unity in the church, and outlined the rightful place held in it by Jews.[7]

The liberality of the Jeronimites makes it all the more tragic that theirs was the first religious order to adopt a statute of *limpieza*. The main reason for this was that several houses of the order turned out to be nests of judaizers. One of the more famous cases was that of Fray Garcia de Zapata, prior of the Jeronimite monastery of Toledo. When elevating the Host at mass he used to say to it, 'Up, little Peter, and let the people look at you', and when granting absolution in confession he always turned his back on the penitent. For these and other sins, the prior and two of his colleagues were burnt before the gates of the monastery. What finally determined the order, however, seems to have been the case of Fray Diego de Marchena, who was accepted into the monastery at Guadalupe although he had never been baptized. An *auto de fe* held by the Inquisition at Toledo in 1485 saw Marchena and fifty-two other persons perish in the flames for the heresy of practising Jewish rites.[8] Alarmed by the ill-fame which would fall on the order, a general meeting of the Jeronimites in 1486 accepted a statute excluding all descendants of Jews from the order. It was only forty years later, in 1525, that the Franciscans saw the need to follow suit. Soon after this the Dominicans began discriminating against conversos, and a *limpieza* statute was adopted by them in Aragon. All these measures were crowned by the definitive adoption of a statute by the cathedral chapter of Toledo in 1547.

The archbishop of Toledo had attempted unsuccessfully in 1539 to introduce a statute of *limpieza*. His successor in 1546, Juan Martínez Siliceo, did not mean to fail.[9] Born of humble peasant stock, Siliceo had struggled upwards to carve out a brilliant career for himself. He had studied for six years at the University of Paris and later taught there for three. Called home to teach at Salamanca, he soon attracted enough attention to be appointed tutor to Charles V's son, Philip, a post he held for ten years. When the see of Toledo fell vacant in 1546 he was appointed to it. The new archbishop was preoccupied with more than merely his freshly won dignity. He had been haunted all his life by the shadow of his humble origins, and drew his only pride from the fact that his parents had been Old Christians.

In his new post he felt in no mood to compromise with converso Christians whose racial antecedents were in his mind the principal threat to a secure and unsullied church. When therefore in September 1546 he discovered that the pope had just appointed a converso, doctor Fernando Jiménez, to a vacant canonry in the cathedral, and that the new incumbent's father had once been condemned by the Inquisition as a judaizer, he refused to accept the appointment. Siliceo wrote to the pope protesting against his candidate, and sounding a warning that the first church in Spain was now in danger of becoming a 'new synagogue'. The pope withdrew his man, but Siliceo thought this was not enough and proceeded to draw up a statute to exclude all conversos from office in the cathedral. A chapter meeting was hurriedly convoked on 23 July 1547 and with 10 dissentient votes against 24 the statute of *limpieza* was pushed through.

The voting figures show that not all the canons had been present at the meeting. An immediate protest was raised by the archdeacons of Guadalajara and Talavera, Pero González de Mendoza and Alvaro de Mendoza, both sons of the powerful Duke of Infantado, and both Old Christians. Condemning the injustice and impropriety of the statute, they criticized the archbishop for not calling all the dignitaries of the cathedral to his meeting, and also threatened to appeal to the pope. The controversy that followed gives us an invaluable summary of the views both of opponents and of supporters of the *limpieza* statutes. According to the explanatory document drawn up by Siliceo,[10] the policy of *limpieza* was now practised in Spain by the military orders, by university colleges, and by religious orders. The existence of a converso danger was proved by the fact that the Lutheran heretics of Germany were nearly all descendants of Jews. Nearer home, 'the archbishop has found that not only the majority but nearly all the parish priests of his archdiocese with a cure of souls . . . are descendants of Jews.'

Moreover, conversos were not content with controlling the wealth of Spain. They were now trying to dominate the church. The size of the danger was shown by the fact that in the last fifty years over fifty thousand conversos had been burnt and punished by the Inquisition yet they still continued to flourish. To emphasize this argument, the archbishop demonstrated that of the ten who had voted against the statute, no less than nine were of Jewish origin, five of them coming from the prolific converso family to which Fray Garcia de Zapata belonged. The opposition to the statute, however, was of greater significance than this might suggest. It is true that among the most hostile to the statute were the dean of the cathedral, Diego de Castilla, and the illustrious humanist Juan de Vergara, both conversos; but at least six other canons who shared their hostility were Old Christians. What distinguished these canons (two of whom were, as we know, of the noble house of Mendoza) and the dean was their irrefutably aristocratic lineage, in contrast to Siliceo, who was of humble origin. In the protest drawn up by the dissentient clergy[11] the complaint was made that, firstly, the statute was against canon law; secondly, it was against the laws of the kingdom; thirdly, it contradicted Holy Scripture; fourthly, it was against natural reason; and, fifthly, it defamed 'many noble and leading people of these realms'. The sting lay in the fifth article. As Siliceo and his opponents well knew, few members of the nobility had not been tainted with converso blood. By promoting a *limpieza* statute, therefore, the archbishop was obviously claiming for his own class a racial purity which the tainted nobility could not boast.

Despite all opposition, however, the statute was authoritatively confirmed and the pope ratified it in 1555. Philip II wavered at first in his attitude, but eventually in 1556 came down in favour. A letter written by the king at this time reveals his firm belief that 'all the heresies which have occurred in Germany and France have been sown by descendants of Jews, as we have seen and still see daily in Spain'.[12] When the judgments of the king of Spain and of the leader of the Spanish Church had been so clouded by antisemitic fantasies, it was not surprising to discover the same prejudices rooted in the heart of Spanish society.

Controversy over the question was not exhausted by Siliceo's success. The 1547 statute of Toledo was immediately condemned by the University of Alcalá as a source of 'discord sown by the devil'. In Rome pope Paul IV had approved the statute, but he did this out of policy and not principle. The same Paul IV in 1565 refused to approve a statute for the cathedral of Seville and condemned *limpieza* as contrary to canon law and ecclesiastical order. His successor Pius V, later canonized as a saint, was a consistent enemy of the statutes, and tried in vain to get a nominee of his who was not *limpio* elected as archdeacon of Toledo. The tide of controversy was stemmed by the Inquisition, which in 1572 tried to impose silence by forbidding any literature either in favour of or against the statutes. But as long as *limpieza* existed in practice and was officially upheld by Inquisition, Church and State, the dust could not be allowed to settle.

Torquemada's instructions to the Inquisition have shown us that the tribunal gave the first encouragement to *limpieza* by exluding from all public office anyone condemned for Jewish practices. Individual authorities extended this disability to any member of the family of those condemned. Soon public bodies began to exclude any conversos, even those who had had no brush with the Inquisition. It is at this stage that *limpieza* ceases to be a defensive mechanism against heresy and becomes openly racialist. Since the statutes clearly discriminated against orthodox Catholics simply because of their ancestry, the use of the word 'racialism' is inescapable.

With the success of the statutes it soon became necessary, when seeking public employment, to prove that one was not descended from any but Old Christians. Here difficulties arose. In theory the Inquisition visited the sins of fathers only up to the second generation, and this was supported by canon law. But the zeal for *limpieza* did not stop at this limitation. If it could be proved that an ancestor had either been made to do penance by the Inquisition or was a Moor or Jew, then his descendant was accounted of impure blood and correspondingly disabled from all public office. It was consequently of some importance for applicants for posts to draw up genealogical proofs of the purity of their lineage. By the end of the sixteenth century proofs of this sort were a compulsory requirement in the four chief military orders and in all the principal colleges and universities. The fraud, perjury, extortion and blackmail that came into existence because of the need to prove one's *limpieza*, reveal the moral evil conjured up by this question, which can be best studied in some cases of pretendants to posts in the Inquisition. By the 1560s all officials of the tribunal were required to be *limpios*, and therefore had to prove their purity before application for a post. The applicant had to submit his genealogy and, if married, that of his wife, to the officials of the Inquisition. The names and residences of parents and grandparents had to be included in the genealogy and if any signs of impure blood were found that was enough to disqualify the applicant. If no such evidence were found, the officials appointed commissioners who were to visit the localities concerned and take sworn statements from witnesses about the antecedents of the applicant. The commissioners were given authority to investigate archives and summon witnesses at will. The crucial role of the witnesses when all documentary evidence had proved inconclusive, was of course one of the chief paths open to abuse. A witness could be bribed to deny an applicant's converso origins or he could blackmail the applicant for the same purpose. Either way, it was the applicant who suffered. There were other ways of suffering. If an applicant was refused a post with the Inquisition the tribunal never gave any reason, with the result that the family of the accused soon became suspected of impurity even if this were not the case. Some applicants had to go through legal processes which lasted as long as two years, with all the attendant expenses, before a proper genealogy could be drawn up. Others resorted to perjury to gain posts, thus involving themselves and all their witnesses in heavy fines and infamy when the tribunal discovered their crime. Frequently, applicants would be disabled from employment simply by the malicious gossip of enemies, because 'common rumour' of impurity was sometimes allowed as evidence.[13] Genealogy became a social weapon, and in a society where the genealogical proof was one's only passport to a career in Church and State it may safely be said that racialism had been erected into the system of government.

The importance of the infamy that was attached to impurity cannot be exaggerated. The honour of a Spaniard lay in his religion and race. If either of these were impugned it would bring shame and disgrace upon both himself and his family and all his descendants. This view was followed by a writer of the time of Philip IV, Juan Escobar de Corro, who in his *Tractatus bipartitus de puritate et nobilitate probanda* equated the words 'purity' and 'honour', and considered death preferable to infamy. For Escobar the stain on an impure lineage was ineffaceable and perpetual.[14] Here was a racialist doctrine of original sin of the most repulsive kind, at least by Christian standards, for it meant that not even baptism was able to wash away the sins of one's fathers. The Inquisition made its own contribution to this attitude. Recalcitrant heretics were burnt in *autos de fe*, but lesser offenders were given punishments including, as has been said, the wearing of garments called *sanbenitos*, worn also by victims before they were burnt. Early in the sixteenth century the practice was begun of hanging up the *sanbenitos* of victims after the period for which the garment had to be worn. This practice was standardized by the official Instructions of 1561, which stipulated that

all the *sanbenitos* of the condemned, living or dead, present or absent, be placed in the churches where they used to live . . . in order that there may be perpetual memory of the infamy of the heretics and their descendants.[15]

The declared aim of displaying these *sanbenitos* was therefore to publish and perpetuate the infamy of condemned persons, so that from generation to generation whole families should be penalized for the sins of their ancestors. There is no doubt that the deliberate aim was perpetuation of infamy, for it became general practice to replace old and decaying *sanbenitos* with new ones bearing the same names of the offenders. These *sanbenitos* were widely hated not only by the families concerned but also by the districts on which they brought disrepute. The city of Logroño (Navarre) in 1570 successfully petitioned the Suprema to be allowed to remove from its churches the great number of *sanbenitos* belonging properly to churches in other regions.[16] The fear in this case was that so many garments would bring disrepute on the whole city and province. In the rising against the Spanish government in Sicily in 1516 the *sanbenitos* in the churches were torn down and never replaced. In the peninsula, however, the tribunal took every care to ensure that *sanbenitos* should be exposed ceaselessly, and this was everywhere practised diligently until the end of the eighteenth century. One of the obvious and particular uses of this system was that genealogical proofs could easily be tested against the evidence of the garments. As matters turned out, in the end it mattered not at all whether a man had been burnt or simply made to do penance in an *auto de fe*. Thanks to the *sanbenito*, his descendants still laboured under civil disability and public infamy.

The social consequences of the *limpieza* cult were so vast and so depressing that there were always a few Spaniards who did not shirk condemning it. The issue was not simply that a whole section of the population was excluded permanently from any active part in the life of the country. Something more than justice – morality itself – was at stake. The question lay at the heart of the long and bitter enmity between the Society of Jesus and the Spanish Inquisition. Saint Ignatius Loyola first encountered the hysteria of antisemitism when, as a student at Alcalá in 1527, he was suspected of Judaism because of his strict religious practices. This was the very year that the Cortes of Guipúzcoa made into law an earlier ordinance of 1483 forbidding conversos to enter that province. At this time Ignatius indignantly denied any knowledge of Judaism, since he was a noble from a province (Guipúzcoa) which had hardly known Jews. Some years later, however, he declared while dining with friends that he would have considered it a divine favour to be descended from Jews. When asked his reason for saying this, he protested, 'What! To be related to Christ Our Lord and to Our Lady the glorious Virgin Mary?' On another occasion a fellow Basque who was a friend of his had spat at the word 'Jew' when the saint mentioned it. On this, Ignatius took him aside and said, according to his biographer, ' "Now, Don Pedro de Zárate, be reasonable and listen to me" – And he gave him so many reasons that he all but persuaded him to become a Jew'.[17] These incidents show that Ignatius had so far escaped the influence of the atmosphere in Spain as to become a deep and sincere spiritual Semite.

Like its founder, the Society of Jesus refused to associate itself with racialism. When in 1551 the Jesuits opened a college at Alcalá without the permission of archbishop Siliceo, the latter issued an order forbidding any Jesuit to act as a priest without first being personally examined by him. It was no secret that the reason for this order was Siliceo's hostility to the presence of converso Christians in the college. Francisco Villanueva, rector of the college, wrote indignantly to Ignatius about this.

It is a great pity that there seems to be nobody willing to leave these poor people anywhere to stay on earth, and I would like to have the energy to become their defender, particularly since one encounters among them more virtue than among the Old Christians and *hidalgos*.[18]

Among Spanish Jesuits, however, there were inevitably those who took their race seriously. The first Provincial of the Jesuits in Spain, Antonio de Araoz, was one of these. He impressed upon Ignatius the fact that Siliceo had promised to visit the order with great favours if it would only adopt a statute of *limpieza*. He also warned that the good name of the Society in Spain would be harmed by the knowledge that there were New Christians in its ranks. Despite this Ignatius refused to change his attitude. All through the controversy in Spain about the statutes of *limpieza*, and up to his death in 1556, he would not allow his order to discriminate against conversos, and when conversos did apply to enter its ranks he advised them to join the Company in Italy rather than in Spain. When talking of the *limpieza* cult he would refer to it as 'the Spanish humour' – *el humor español*; or, more bitingly on one occasion, *humor de la corte y del Rey de España* – 'the humour of the Spanish king and his court'. Because of the opposition of the Jesuits, Siliceo conceived an ardent hatred of the order, and in this he was followed by other prominent members of the Spanish clergy and the Dominican-controlled Inquisition. All three Generals of the order after Loyola were firm in their opposition to the statutes. The immediate successor of Ignatius was Diego Laínez, General from 1558 to 1565. The fact that he was a converso aroused bitter opposition to his election from Philip II and the Spanish Church. In a letter to Araoz in 1560 Laínez denounced *limpieza* as *el humor o error nacional* (the national humour or error) and demanded total obedience from the Spanish Jesuits. His successor was a Spaniard of unimpeachable Old Christian blood – Francisco Borja, Duke of Gandia, famous to history as St Francis Borgia. Borgia's position was so well known that he was victimized to the extent of having some of his works put on the Index of prohibited books. On one of his visits to Spain the prime minister of Philip II, the Prince of Eboli, asked Borgia why his Company allowed conversos in its ranks. Borgia's retort was uncompromising:

Why does the king keep in his service *x* and *y*, who are conversos? If His Majesty disregards this in those he places in his household, why should I make an issue about admitting them into the service of that Lord for whom there is no distinction between persons, between Greek and Jew, or barbarian and Scythian?[19]

By the 1590s, however, the Jesuits in Spain found that recruits were falling off as the whispering campaign initiated by its enemies succeeded in presenting the Society as a party of Jews. Moreover by a process of selection the chief posts in the Spanish province were going to Jesuits who favoured the statutes. The result was the success of pressure for a modification to the constitution of the Society, and at the General Congregation held at Rome in December 1593 it was voted to exclude all conversos from membership. Against this dishonourable retreat the lone voice raised in protest was that of a Spaniard, Father Ribadeneira. Due almost exclusively to his singlehanded efforts to keep the Society to the path laid down by Loyola, a reaction to the vote of 1593 took place in the order. This led to a modificatory decree in February 1608, by which all conversos who had been Christians for five generations were allowed to enter the Society. The 1608 decree was nominally only a concession, but in practice it involved the complete reversal of the decision of 1593, since most conversos in Spain had in fact been Christians for five generations, thanks to the compulsory conversions of 1492.

Despite the silence imposed on controversy over *limpieza* by the Inquisition, the flow of printed works did not dry up. In 1575 Diego de Simancas, bishop of Zamora and later a bitter enemy of archbishop Carranza of Toledo, published his *Defensio Statuti Toletani*. This was one of the last great defences of the racialist doctrines of Siliceo. By the end of the sixteenth century a profound dismay at the consequences of *limpieza* had begun to penetrate the upper circles in society. The need to prove one's purity of blood in a society where the degree of racial admixture gave no guarantee against impure blood, threatened the security of the noblest families. Every time one changed employment or won promotion to a superior office, an exhaustive genealogical enquiry into every branch of the family was undertaken. The expenses were enormous, particularly in the case of those living abroad in America who had to have research into their ancestry carried out in Spain. We have the case of a Franciscan friar, Francisco Delgado, who had to have his genealogy verified in the Canary Islands in order to get a post in the Inquisition of Peru. His costs came to the prohibitive sum of 3,352 silver *reales*.[20] More iniquitous than the expense, however, was the uncertainty. Membership of the most exalted families was seldom protection against a diligent enquiry into genealogy, and for one member of the family to be refused a post because of suspicion of impurity meant an automatic and sometimes perpetual stigma on the rest of the family. The practice of *limpieza* therefore threatened to expose the entire nobility to shame and infamy.

It was a Dominican, Fray Agustín Salucio, who eventually broached the problem in a *Discurso* written in about 1599, at the beginning of the reign of Philip III. For the first time the reasons given for attacking *limpieza* were not the traditional ones of canon law and justice. Salucio pointed out that unless genealogical enquiries were limited to a century or so, investigations would show that nearly everyone in Spain had some trace of impure blood. The only people to benefit would be the lower classes, whose genealogies were untraceable and who therefore passed without question as Old Christians. The main preoccupation in Salucio was obviously not principle, but the fear that this cult which had been set in motion against a racial minority would backfire and undermine the whole honour and purity of the Spanish ruling classes. A similar preoccupation was shown by several noble representatives of Castile who managed to have a junta formed under Philip III to treat of this matter. The main complaint of these representatives was that 'in Spain we esteem a common person who is *limpio* more than a *hidalgo* who is not *limpio*'.[21] As a result, the memorial continued, there were now two sorts of nobility in Spain, 'a greater, which is that of *hidalguía*; and a lesser, which is that of *limpieza*, whose members we call Old Christians'. Irrational criteria of purity had also come into existence: swordsmen were reputed *limpios* and physicians were reputed Jews; people from León and Asturias were called Old Christians and those from Almagro conversos.

All this is so absurd that were we another nation we would call ourselves barbarians who governed themselves without reason, without law, and without God ...

Another evil effect is that because of rigorous genealogical proofs the State loses eminent subjects who have the talent to become great theologians and jurists but who do not follow these professions because they know they will not be admitted to any honours.

As a result, people of no rank and little learning had risen to high posts in the country, while true and learned nobility had been deprived of the chance to pursue their careers. Discrimination against Jewish blood, the memorial continued, would only make the conversos become more compact, defensive, and dangerous; whereas in France and Italy the lack of discrimination had allowed them to merge peacefully into the community. The natural consequence of *limpieza* proofs would be that those who were irrefutably *limpios* (and hence alone capable of holding office) would soon be a tiny minority in the country, with the great mass of the people against them, 'affronted, discontented and ripe for rebellion'.

By the reign of Philip IV (1623-65) it was realized that some change must be made in the method of applying the statutes. In February 1623 a *Junta de Reformación* drew up new rules for the practice of *limpieza*. One proof was enough when applying for office and no others were needed when promoted or changing one's job. Verbal evidence was not admitted if unsupported by more solid proof, and 'rumour' was disallowed. All literature purporting to list the descent of families from Jews, such as the notorious *Libro verde de Aragón*, was ordered to be publicly destroyed and burnt. Although these measures aroused much opposition, they also released a flood of anti-*limpieza* writings which take their stand with the other literature that makes this reign a time of intellectual crisis in Spanish history. That the problem was appreciated in the highest circles is shown by the report given by one member of the *Junta de Reformación*, who claimed that *limpieza* was

the cause and origin of a great multitude of sins, perjuries, falsehoods, disputes and lawsuits both civil and criminal. Many of our people, seeing that they are not admitted to the honours and offices of their native land, have absented themselves from these realms and gone to others, in despair at seeing themselves covered with infamy. So much so that I have been told of two eminent gentlemen of these realms who were among the greatest soldiers of our time and who declared on their deathbeds that since they were unable to gain entry into the orders of chivalry they had very often been tempted by the devil to kill themselves or to go over and serve the Turk, and that they knew of some who had done so.[22]

To question *limpieza* was to question the fundamentals of life as practised since the end of the fifteenth century. This ability to recognize the darker side of a social dogma was part of the *crise de conscience* and soul-searching that characterized the atmosphere of decline in seventeenth-century Spain. From the king downwards, it became imperative to confess one's errors as a way of finding out what had gone wrong in Spain and in the empire. 'Count', said Philip IV, writing to Olivares in about 1640, and referring to the tide of military defeat, 'these evil events have been caused by your sins and by mine in particular'. Writing to the Council of State the king said,

> I believe that God our Lord is angry and irate with me and with my realms on account of many sins and particularly on account of mine.[23]

In a world that was beginning to crumble the time had come to make a reckoning. But already it was too late, in the eyes of those who saw no reason for the calamities that were beginning to overwhelm Spain. Eighteen days before his death in 1645 Francisco de Quevedo could find no meaning in the whirl of events. Writing to his friend Francisco de Oviedo, he said:

> From all sides come very bad news of utter ruin, and the worst of it all is that everyone expected this would happen. Señor Don Francisco, I do not know whether the end is coming or whether it has already come. God only knows; for there are many things which seem to exist and have their being, and yet they are nothing but a word or a figure.[24]

It was in this mood of moral collapse that an inquisitor led the attack against the statutes of *limpieza*. The *Discurso de un Inquisidor*[25] drawn up under Philip IV has been attributed to Juan Roco Campofrío, inquisitor, and bishop successively of Zamora, Badajoz and Soria. According to the inquisitor, the proofs of *limpieza* were a source of moral and political scandal in the nation. The stigma of impurity had divided Spain into two halves, one of which was constantly warring against the other. The outrages and quarrels provoked by the statutes had been responsible for over ninety per cent of the civil and criminal trials in Spanish courts. The racialism of the statutes was wrong, for many conversos and Moriscos had been more virtuous than so-called Old Christians, and many of those brought to trial by the Inquisition had in fact been Old Christians and not Jews. The great danger, the inquisitor went on, was that the greater part of the population of Spain would soon be branded as impure, and the only remaining guarantee of Old Christian blood would be one's plebeian origin. The defection of the inquisitor from the traditional belief in *limpieza* represented only one, if perhaps the most important, of the many tracts written in this period against a cult that divided society against itself. In 1624 a fluent and bitter attack on the statutes was launched by a certain Francisco Murcia de la Llana, who condemned both the racialism and xenophobia of his contemporaries:

> Look into yourself (he addressed Spain) and consider that no other nation has these statutes, and that Judaism has flourished most where they have existed. Yet if any of your sons marries a Frenchwoman or a Genoan or an Italian you despise his wife as a foreigner. What ignorance! What overwhelming Spanish madness![16]

Another memorial, written at the end of the reign, probably by Portuguese converso financiers, appealed to past authorities both papal and Spanish to show that all converts should be free from discrimination and free to assume public office.[27] But this was the old line of reasoning. The more common basis of opposition was the social effect of *limpieza*. Despite the *crise de conscience* under Philip IV, no modifications were made to the statutes beyond the measures of 1623. The racial cult therefore continued to exist up to and beyond the end of the *ancien régime* and the Inquisition in Spain.

If *limpieza* owed much of its strength to the Inquisition, it also owed its decline to the same body. So thoroughly had the tribunal cleansed Spain of heretical conversos by the beginning of the eighteenth century that the Jewish question ceased, for all practical purposes, to exist. The disappearance of the Jewish menace meant that antisemitism degenerated into an irrational prejudice with no roots in actual conditions. The 'Jew' became a myth, a legend – no more. Judaizers were a curious rarity in the second half of the eighteenth century. Yet the official apparatus of *limpieza* continued to function, more and more obviously at variance with right reason. It was this irrational nature of the statutes no less than their pronounced social effect that first attracted the attention of the ministers of the crown. In 1751 José de Carvajal thought the treatise of Agustín Salucio so convincing that he ordered a copy of it to be made for himself;[28]

and the Count of Floridablanca considered the penalties for impurity unjust because they punish a man's most sacred action, that is, his conversion to our holy faith, with the same penalty as his greatest crime, that is, apostasy from it.[29]

But it needed more than reforming ministers to abolish *limpieza* which, being part of the social system more than a religious issue, survived the abolition of the Inquisition. Official recognition of its need ceased with a royal order of 31 January 1835 directed to the Economic Society of Madrid, but up to 1859 it was still necessary for entrance into the corps of officer cadets. The last official act was a law of 16 May 1865 abolishing proofs of purity for marriages and for certain government posts.

The main effect of *limpieza* was obviously to divide Spanish society into the 'ins' and 'outs'. Of this the most vicious example was the treatment meted out to the conversos of Palma de Majorca. As late as the mid-eighteenth century, 'although good Catholics, their sons were denied entrance to the higher ranks of the clergy, and their daughters to the religious orders. They were forced to live in a restricted area of the city, and the people calumniated them with the names *Hebreos, Judíos, Chuetas*. Guilds, army, navy and public offices were closed to them'.[30] Despite various efforts by the government and some clergy, discrimination continued up to the end of the nineteenth century. In 1858 they were still 'refused all public offices and admission to guilds and brotherhoods so that they were confined to trading. They were compelled to marry among themselves, for no one would contract alliance with them nor would the ecclesiastical authorities grant licences for mixed marriages'.[31] Happily this state of affairs was not common in peninsular Spain.

A less conspicuous but no less important result of *limpieza* was the perpetuation of the concept of 'honour' in its worst social sense. So far did purity of blood cease to have any connection with the Jewish problem that in 1788 we find Charles III's minister Aranda using the phrase *limpieza de sangre* in the sense of purity from any taint of servile office or trade, so that the synonymous term *limpieza de oficios* also came into existence by the end of the century.[32] Here we have the term used in a purely class context: the upper classes were pure, and the lower servile, the distinction being grounded on a racialist dogma whose origins had almost been forgotten. The net result was that the upper classes continued to maintain their (racial and class) purity by refusing to undertake any industry or employment that was beneath their 'honour' and dignity. In this way an essentially mediaeval social outlook was transmitted into the nineteenth century through the *limpieza* statutes. How mediaeval, is shown in the constitution of the military Order of Santiago, from which by statutes of the late sixteenth century not only Jews, Moors, heretics and their descendants were excluded, but also any 'trader or barterer or one holding vulgar and mechanical employment, such as silversmith, mason, innkeeper, painter . . . or other inferior employment, such as tailors and other such people who live by the work of their hands'.[33] Like the Order of Santiago, the aristocracy was based on a racial and economic exclusivism which was fated to give it a particularly retrogressive character in the history of modern Spain.

CHAPTER EIGHT

THE SPANISH INQUISITION:
ITS ORGANIZATION

We have corrected Thy work and have founded it upon miracle, mystery and authority.

Dostoevsky, THE BROTHERS KARAMAZOV

THE Spanish Inquisition, as we have seen, superseded entirely the mediaeval tribunal which had existed in the kingdom of Aragon since 1238. The new institution was in character and purpose of Castilian origin, and as such aroused substantial opposition in other parts of the peninsula. By the early sixteenth century, however, most of this opposition had been eliminated, and we are left with a centralized tribunal under Castilian control whose authority extended over all the realms of the Spanish crown. From its inception the Inquisition was meant by Ferdinand and Isabella to be under their control and not under that of the pope, as had been the case with the mediaeval tribunal. Sixtus IV was surprisingly co-operative, and his bull of institution of 1 November 1478 gave the Catholic monarchs power not only over appointments but also, tacitly, over confiscations. The inquisitors were to have the jurisdiction over heretics normally held by bishops, but were not given any jurisdiction over bishops themselves. Subsequently the pope saw his error in granting independence to a tribunal of this sort, and enshrined his protest in a brief of 29 January 1482. At the same time he refused to allow Ferdinand to extend his control over the old Inquisition in Aragon. Further conflict ensued with the bull issued by Sixtus on 18 April denouncing abuses in the procedure of the Inquisition. Ferdinand, however, held firm to his policy despite opposition at Rome and in Aragon, and his eventual victory was confirmed by the bull which on 17 October

1483 appointed Torquemada as chief inquisitor of the kingdom of Aragon. Earlier that year Torquemada had also received a bull of appointment as Inquisitor General of Castile. He was now therefore the only individual in the peninsula whose writ extended over all Spain, since even the crowns of Castile and Aragon were only personally and not politically united.

The Inquisition as it existed in 1483 and thereafter, was in every way an instrument of royal policy and remained politically subject to the crown. This, however, did not make it a secular tribunal. It was at one time a favourite claim of Catholic apologists that the Spanish Inquisition was no more than a secular tribunal, and that its excesses could be excused as the responsibility of Spaniards and not of the Church. The claim is quite inadmissible. Any authority and jurisdiction exercised by the inquisitors of Spain came directly or indirectly from Rome, without whom the tribunal would have ceased to exist. Bulls of appointment, canonical regulations, spheres of jurisdiction – all had to have the prior approval of Rome. The Inquisition was consequently an essentially ecclesiastical tribunal for which the Church of Rome assumed full responsibility.

The central organization of the new tribunal was in 1483 named the *Consejo de la Suprema y General Inquisición*, and this body was added to the four administrative councils whose existence had already been confirmed at the Cortes of Toledo in 1480. Although Torquemada was the first Inquisitor General, the real founder of the Inquisition was in fact Pedro González de Mendoza, archbishop of Seville and later Cardinal archbishop of Toledo. It was this prelate, famous as a patron of Columbus, who set on foot the negotiations with Rome leading to the establishment of the Inquisition. Yet above him towers the shadow of Torquemada. The great, austere and fanatical Dominican friar, who was prior of the convent of Santa Cruz at Segovia, left the indelible mark of his character on the tribunal he headed. Existing portraits of him give little hint of the man who was alleged to have refused the see of Seville and to have preferred the humble life of a friar. Nor is there much sign of his well-known asceticism in the full features painted by the contemporary artist. But history supplies what evidence is lacking in art. Torquemada did more than anyone else before or after him to establish the power and authority of the Inquisition in Spain, and in 1484 Sixtus IV praised him for having 'directed your zeal to those matters which contribute to the praise of God and the utility of the orthodox faith'.[1] By his severity in the prosecution of heretics he set the standard which made the tribunal a name of fear among the ungodly. Though of converso origin himself, he was the first to introduce a statute of *limpieza* into a Dominican monastery, his own foundation at Avila dedicated to St Thomas Aquinas. A modern visitor to the silent chapel and beautiful courtyards of this magnificent building will find no trace of the name, and virtually none of the memory, of its founder. Yet the walls of the monastery were built with money gathered from repentant heretics, and at the foot of the altar lies the marble tomb of prince Juan, son of Ferdinand and Isabella, whose death was said to be one of the occasions for the expulsion of the Jews. Here in stone lie testimonies to the achievement of the hammer of the Jews.

The importance of Torquemada suggests that the Dominicans were controlling the new Inquisition as they had controlled the old one. In fact, although the Dominicans continued to predominate in the new tribunal they were never given any explicit control of its organization. Consequently we often find laymen in inquisitorial posts usually reserved for ecclesiastics, and in the eighteenth century we even find the tribunal governed largely by Jesuits, who were notoriously the rivals of the Dominican order. Torquemada's importance is also misleading on another issue. Although the Inquisitor General may seem to have been a powerful individual, in practice his commission was often limited in authority, and renewable only after papal approval. Moreover the pope frequently granted equivalent powers to other clerics in Spain, as when in 1491 a second Inquisitor General of Castile and Aragon was appointed for a brief time, and in 1494, when four bishops in Spain were promoted to this post at the same time that Torquemada held it. This plural headship of the tribunal continued to exist for political reasons. When Torquemada died in 1498 he was succeeded by Diego Deza, who in 1505 became archbishop of Seville. It was not until 1504 that Deza became sole head of the Inquisition, because the bishops appointed under Torquemada continued to hold office up to that date. Queen Isabella died on 26 November 1504, and this led to a temporary separation of the kingdoms of Castile and

Aragon, because of Ferdinand's quarrels with his son-in-law, Philip I of Castile. As a result, Ferdinand asked the pope to appoint a separate Inquisitor for Aragon. This occurred in June 1507 when Ximénez was appointed to Castile and the bishop of Vich, Juan Enguera, to Aragon. The two posts remained separate until the death of Ximénez in 1518, when Charles I appointed Cardinal Adrian of Utrecht, bishop of Tortosa and since 1516 Inquisitor General of Aragon, as Inquisitor for Castile as well. After this the tribunal remained under one head alone.

The Spanish Inquisition was based essentially on the mediaeval one but was allowed to modify all previous practices to suit its own needs. This was obviously necessary in view of the special social circumstances which had brought it into being. Torquemada and his colleagues were allowed to draw up their own rules, regardless of the views of the crown or of Rome. The consequence was that several serious quarrels occurred between the tribunal and the two powers to whom it was theoretically subject. The first rules drawn up were those agreed upon in a council at Seville on 29 November 1484. Under Torquemada these rules were extended in 1485, 1488 and 1498, and his successor Diego Deza added some articles in 1500. All these regulations were known under the collective title of the *Instrucciones Antiguas*. Subsequent inquisitors added their own modifications, which were printed by Gaspar Isidro de Argüello at Madrid in 1627 and 1630 in a compendium called the *Instrucciones del Santo Oficio de la Inquisición, sumariamente, antiguas y nuevas*. This was followed by the comprehensive *Compilación de las Instrucciones del Oficio de la Santa Inquisición*, published at Madrid in 1667 by the Inquisitor General.[2] These rules as a whole illustrate how a powerful ecclesiastical body could legislate for itself and create its own rules of conduct without any particular reference to the laws of the community in which it existed. The autonomy of the tribunal was to be almost the only source of conflict in subsequent years when men had ceased to question the *raison d'être* of the Inquisition.

The Inquisition was governed at the top by an Inquisitor General in the Council, which was known briefly as the *Suprema*. All authority exercised by inquisitors was at one time held to be by direct delegation from the pope, but later this was modified to the opinion that it was the Inquisitor General himself who delegated the papal powers. Growth of the Inquisitor General's power was in this way parallel to the increasing authority of the *Suprema*, which had at first been merely a deliberative body but by 1605, according to the Venetian ambassador Contarini, had become absolute in all matters of faith and was not obliged, like the other Councils, to consult the king. The relationship between *Suprema* amd Inquisitor General was never satisfactorily settled because they usually acted in concert and did not dispute supremacy. But on certain occasions the *Suprema* was indubitably independent and not subject to the Inquisitor. All the members of the *Suprema* (their number was not fixed) were appointed by the king alone, and the *Suprema* itself more often than not issued orders without any need to have the vote of the Inquisitor General. When divisions arose in the Council a decision was taken by majority vote, in which the vote of the Inquisitor General counted no more than that of another. In general, however, no clear rules for procedure were ever adopted, and the authority of the Inquisitor General depended on circumstances and on his own character. One outstanding case, that of Fray Froilan Díaz, brought out clearly to what extent the Inquisitor General could be expected to overrule the opposition of the *Suprema*.

Froilan Díaz, a Dominican who had been confessor since 1698 to the king, Charles II (1665-1700), was arrested in 1700 after various palace intrigues, on the charge of having helped to cast a spell over the hapless king, known in Spanish history as *el Hechizado*, the bewitched. The prosecution was at the instance of the German queen and her friend Balthasar de Mendoza, bishop of Segovia, who had in 1699 been appointed Inquisitor General. Díaz, who was an ex-officio member of the *Suprema*, was imprisoned while an investigation was made by five theologians who found that in fact there was no basis for a serious charge against him. Accordingly in June 1700 all the members of the Council except Mendoza voted for Díaz's acquittal. Mendoza refused to accept the finding and ordered the arrest of the other members of the *Suprema* until they assented to the arrest of Díaz. At the same time he ordered the tribunal of Murcia to bring Díaz to trial. This the inquisitors did – and acquitted him. Mendoza thereupon ordered a retrial and kept

Díaz in prison. Opposition to the actions of the Inquisitor General was by now universal. There was consequently wide support for the new French king, Philip V, when he discovered that Mendoza was politically opposed to the Bourbon dynasty and confined him to his see of Segovia. Mendoza now made the mistake of appealing to Rome, an act which was unprecedented in the whole history of the Spanish Inquisition. The crown immediately stepped in to prevent any interference from Rome, and finally in 1704 Díaz was rehabilitated and reinstated in the *Suprema*, while Mendoza was replaced as Inquisitor General in March 1705.[3]

The case proved to be the last important one in which the Inquisitor General attempted to assert his supremacy. Thereafter the preoccupation of the tribunal with administrative routine and censorship, rather than with great matters of state, involved less opportunities for personal initiative, and authority came more and more to reside in the *Suprema* and the machinery it controlled. More obscure prelates were also chosen as Inquisitor General, a significant example being the choice of the bishop of Ceuta (North Africa) to succeed Mendoza in 1705.

The growth of the *Suprema*'s authority led to greater centralization in the Inquisition, a process hastened in the seventeenth century as the volume of heretics, and therefore of business, diminished in the provincial tribunals. In the early days, as the case of Lucero showed, local autonomy could be carried to scandalous extremes. This situation was later remedied by more conscientious *Supremas*. At first cases were referred by provincial tribunals to the *Suprema* only if agreement could not be reached, or if the latter made a special order summoning a case before it. In the early 1530s, when it was felt that the Barcelona tribunal was showing excessive severity in suppressing a witch-craze in Catalonia, all sentences passed by it were required to be confirmed by the *Suprema*. The Barcelona inquisitors do not seem to have accepted interference from the centre, for the Inquisitor General in 1566 was obliged to examine their records and to denounce the irregularities and cruelties in the tribunal. From this time onwards greater attention was paid by the *Suprema* to the procedure and sentences of local tribunals, who were required after 1632 to send in monthly reports of their activities. By the mid-seventeenth century all sentences were required to be submitted to the *Suprema* before being carried out. With this, the machinery of the Inquisition reached its most complete stage of centralization. In the eighteenth century business became so rare that the tribunals became mere appendages of the *Suprema*, which initiated and executed all prosecutions.

The supremacy of the Council extended in particular to finances, and all the tribunals were expected to pay sums on demand to the central administration. At other times, more fortunate tribunals were expected to contribute to the expense of the less fortunate ones. In all this, the standard procedure of ecclesiastical organization was followed. As we shall see, the Inquisition was by no means a wealthy concern, and for the greater part of its life had some difficulty in making ends meet. Its particular misfortune was that time brought an increase in the deadweight of administrative officials but a decrease in the volume of fines and confiscations, so that it would clearly be wrong to regard it as a profit-making organization.

The tribunals of the Inquisition in Spain were at first given no seats of residence, but were created whenever or wherever the need arose. As a result many of the original tribunals ceased to exist after they had cleansed the locality of the judaizers living in it. To this class of temporary tribunals belonged those established at Alcaraz, Avila, Balaguer, Barbastro, Burgos (later transferred to Valladolid), Calahorra (later transferred to Logroño), Calatayud, Ciudad Real (founded in 1483, and later transferred to Toledo in 1485), Daroca, Guadalupe, Huesca and Lérida (joint tribunals later incorporated in Saragossa), Medina del Campo, Orihuela, Osuna, Perpignan, Segovia, Sigüenza, Tarazona, Tarragona, Teruel, and Jérez de la Frontera.[4] These supplemented or were later merged into the more permanent tribunals, whose dates of foundation are as follows:

Kingdom of Castile

Seville	1480	Las Palmas	1505
Córdoba	1482	Llerena	1509
Toledo	1485	Santiago c.	1520
Valladolid	1485	Granada	1526
Cuenca c.	1500	Logroño	1570
Murcia c.	1500	Madrid c.	1640

Kingdom of Aragon

Saragossa	1484	Barcelona	1486
Valencia	1484	Palma de Majorca	1488

Some of these tribunals were founded late simply because other tribunals had been acting in the area before them. The tribunal of Logroño (kingdom of Navarre), for instance, had been preceded by that of Calahorra, which was established as early as 1493, so that in fact the Inquisition had already been active in the area for eighty years. Similarly, no need was felt for any organization in Madrid, which was amply catered for by the Toledo tribunal, until pressure of work at Toledo and the rapid growth of Madrid made another tribunal necessary. This provincial organization provided a network of inquisitors covering the entire kingdom, making the Inquisition the only body to have unlimited access to all parts of Spain, even to those regions where the king's writ was limited by local privileges. Portugal, for the period 1580-1640 when it came under the Spanish crown, did not have its Inquisition incorporated into that of Castile, and this tribunal therefore functioned independently for a while. But in 1586 Philip II managed to have the Cardinal Archduke of Austria, who was also governor of Portugal, nominated as head of the Portuguese Inquisition, so that for the next ten years and indeed after the departure of the Archduke, the Portuguese tribunal was closely subject to Spanish royal control. The development of the Portuguese Inquisition, however, does not concern us here.

Each tribunal, according to Torquemada's instructions of 1484, was to consist of two inquisitors, an assessor, an *alguacil* (constable) and a fiscal (prosecutor), with any other necessary subordinates. This establishment was bound to expand with the increase of business, especially confiscations, and with the greater number of people who had claims to live off the tribunal, such as gaolers, notaries, chaplains and so on. But the expansion that did take place was soon recognized as a serious abuse by crown and people alike. Complaints were directed principally against the number of familiars in the kingdom. The familiar, whose name has since acquired so sinister a ring, was a common feature of the mediaeval Inquisition, and was continued in the Spanish one. Essentially he was a lay servant of the Holy Office, ready at all times to perform duties in the service of the tribunal. In return he was allowed to bear arms to protect the inquisitors, and enjoyed a number of privileges in common with the other officials. To become a familiar was a high honour, and in the earlier decades of its history the Inquisition could boast of a high proportion of nobles and titled persons among its familiars. By the beginning of the sixteenth century the familiars were banded together in a brotherhood or *hermandad* known as the Congregation of St Peter Martyr, modelled directly on the associations founded by the mediaeval Inquisition after the murder of an inquisitor, St Peter Martyr, in Italy in 1252. In theory the *hermandad* was meant to include all members of the tribunals, but in practice the familiars formed the bulk of the membership.

Although familiars acquired notoriety in fact and in legend for the way in which they acted as a fifth column of informers and spies, in practice contemporaries seem to have been far more concerned about their increasing numbers and, because of the privileges behind which they sheltered, their resultant lawlessness. The exaggerated representation of familiars as a species of secret police has no foundation in fact. Certainly tongues would be controlled in the presence of a familiar. But even a brief survey of the records of the Inquisition shows that the majority of denunciations presented to the tribunal were made by ordinary people, neighbours, travelling-companions, acquaintances. The phenomenon is a commonplace of closed societies. There was no need to rely on a secret police system because the population as a whole had been taught to recognize the enemy within the gates. Familiars offended more by their numbers, and agreements had to be reached to put a ceiling on how many could be created. In the realm of Castile a *Concordia* was drawn up in March 1553 after half a century of disputes over whether familiars were to be free from civil prosecution for criminal acts. The Inquisition conceded that in all important civil cases the familiars were to come under the jurisdiction of the secular authorities. At the same time their numbers were limited. The very high ceiling figures adopted show that there had been real cause for complaint. The tribunal of Toledo was allowed 805 familiars, that of Granada 554, and that of Santiago 1,009. The figures were determined in proportion to population. *Concordias* similar to that issued in Castile in 1553 were granted to Valencia in 1554 and to the whole kingdom of Aragon in 1568. By these agreements the tribunal of Saragossa was allowed 1,215 familiars and that of Barcelona 905. What is surprising is that the number of familiars ran into such large figures. The office brought great privileges, but also cost much for that very reason. In 1641, for instance, the Inquisition tried to raise money by selling familiarships for 1,500 ducats each. Worse than the open selling of offices was the abuse by which familiars were appointed without any record being kept of their appointment, so that trouble frequently arose whenever thieves and murderers attempted to evade arrest by claiming ecclesiastical privilege as familiars: this was one of the points made by the Aragonese Cortes in 1530 and again in 1533. Blame for many difficulties caused in this way must be laid against the provincial tribunals and not against the *Suprema*, which tried in vain to limit the number and functions of the multitudinous officials employed by the Inquisition.

The sale of offices contributed greatly to the multiplication of familiars and other unsalaried or salaried officials. Philip II in 1595 noted the existence of venality of offices, which was unfortunately continued with royal approval in 1631, when offices were sold to pay for some of the expenses of the government. The abuse was perpetuated when a number of these offices were allowed to become hereditary. The net result of all this was the creation of a superfluous bureaucracy with no duties to fulfil and concerned only with the income or privileges attached to office. Here, of course, the Inquisition was not setting a new trend but simply following current developments in Church and State administration.

One remarkable feature of the Spanish Holy Office is, as we have said, that it was never a wealthy organization. Its finances rested principally on three bases: salaries, investments and confiscations. Salaries were by nature not income but expenditure, a point of some importance when we realize that the Inquisition was meant to pay its own way without direct help from the government. Consequently, the salaries were in fact drawn from fines and confiscations. That this would lead to greater zeal in exacting fines and confiscating property was the great fear of all those who in the early years of the tribunal petitioned the crown to pay the inquisitors a government salary and not to allow them to draw their wages from confiscations. As it was, the tribunal was left to fend for itself, which suggests that it was intended to be a temporary body only, or else more permanent provision for its needs would have been made. Of the salaries of the *Suprema* in its earlier years no details are available, but it is recorded that in the 1520s the total salaries of three members of the *Suprema* and ten subordinates came to just under three thousand ducats. This was at a time when a ducat would have bought 185 litres of wine or 220 kilos of bread. In the next century this situation had changed. By 1600 the general price level had risen by one hundred per cent and in some commodities such as wheat by two hundred per cent. A ducat now bought just over 13 litres of wine or 55 kilos of bread. The salaries of the *Suprema* barely managed to keep pace with this inflation. In 1629 the salary of the Inquisitor General was just over 3,870 ducats, and each of the members of the Council received half this amount; in all, the thirty-six persons attached to the *Suprema* received a total sum of 26,855 ducats. A century later, in 1743, these figures had roughly doubled: the Inquisitor General was receiving about 7,000 ducats and the total salaries of forty members of the *Suprema* came to 64,100 ducats. Over this later period, however, prices had not risen excessively, so that inquisitorial salaries at the beginning of the eighteenth century were fairly comfortable.[5]

In the provincial tribunals the position was comparatively less happy. An inquisitor in 1498 received a salary of 160 ducats, by 1541 this had become 267 ducats and by 1606 it was 800 ducats. His subordinates received fractions of this, according to the regulations of 1498. Fiscals (prosecutors) and notaries (secretaries) were meant to receive half the amount of an inquisitor. The only subordinate who at first actually received more than the inquisitor was the *alguacil*, who had to care for the prison out of a lump sum which covered his wages. According to Lea, the salaries of provincial tribunals remained the same from 1606 till the end of the eighteenth century.[6] This would certainly have caused extreme distress in the inflationary periods of the mid-seventeenth and mid-eighteenth centuries.

Investment was never undertaken on an adequate scale, and the Inquisition therefore failed to provide for itself in less fortunate times. In 1635, for example, the *Suprema* held various government securities (*juros*) and municipal bonds (*censos*) which brought in an annual revenue of about 26,237 ducats, but its current expenses turned this figure into a deficit of 12,966 ducats. In 1657 the *Suprema* could boast of an investment revenue of 50,000 ducats, yet in 1681 it was complaining of poverty, no doubt sincerely in view of the great deflation of 1680. These vicissitudes of fortune were typical of the tribunal's haphazard financial organization.

If we examine the finances of one tribunal, that of Seville, the deterioration in its position through the years becomes clear. In February 1600 it had an annual income (from *censos*, rented houses, and other sources) of 10,781 ducats; expenses for the past year came to 9,346 ducats. Figures for subsequent periods are:[7]

	Income	Expenditure
1630:	12,328 ducats	11,598 ducats
1699:	12,653	15,869
1726:	15,075	20,642

These figures do not reflect total income, because revenue from confiscations has not been included. But then there were few large confiscations except in the period 1721-2. Comparing the table with the figures for 1600, we can see that investment expanded by under fifty per cent, while direct expenditure increased by over two hundred per cent; this, of course, in addition to the fact that salaries as a whole remained fixed while prices rose catastrophically up to the year 1680.

Pausing for a moment, we can look at the financial structure of one tribunal in mid-career, to give us some indication of how expenses were organized. Taking the Inquisition of Córdoba in 1578, it should be remembered that this and other tribunals drew substantial income from canonries and other ecclesiastical offices. These offices had been granted first by pope Alexander VI in 1501, to supplement the declining income of tribunals.[8] The regular annual income of Córdoba, excluding that from confiscations, was:

Juros and *censos*	757,590 *maravedis*
Canonries in Córdoba, Jaén etc.	866,560
Penances, fines etc.	150,000
Total:	1,774,150 *maravedis*

In the same year, 1578, Córdoba's salaries came to a figure almost as high as its income. A large part of this bill went on the money which each tribunal set aside annually for the needs of the *Suprema*. The full list of salaries was as follows:

Consigned to the *Suprema*	313,200 *maravedis*
The three inquisitors	562,500
The fiscal	97,750
The three secretaries	205,250
The *alguacil*	67,750
Notary of sequestrations	57,750
Prison guard	61,250
Messenger	40,250
Porter	30,000
Receiver (treasurer)	97,750
Juez de bienes	30,000
Judicial officer	10,000
Advocate	10,000
Accountant	20,000
Procurator	8,000
Guard of perpetual prisons	6,000
Two chaplains	15,000
Two physicians	8,000
? Recorder	7,500
Timekeeper	5,000
Barber	2,000
Total	1,654,950 *maravedis*

In addition to these salaries came ordinary and extraordinary expenses, which amounted to 378,700 *maravedis* annually. The grand total of expenses was therefore 2,033,650 *maravedis*. This, on paper at least, left the tribunal in the red with a deficit of 259,500 *maravedis*. Once again, however, confiscations have not been included, and as we shall see the income from confiscations was often extremely high. Confiscations aside, the Córdoba tribunal was representative of most of its colleagues in having a regular deficit.

Year	Income	Expenditure
1642	94,639 *reales**	119,987 *reales*
1661	105,120	140,662
1726	81,397	90,507[9]

After the last crop of confiscations in the early 1720s the Inquisition faced a bleak financial future. An official account of its finances in 1731[10] shows that the *Suprema* and its sixteen Spanish tribunals had a joint total income of 145,798 ducats, and a total liability of 195,452 ducats, leaving a deficit of nearly 50,000 ducats. Some tribunals were more responsible than others for this deficit, the most culpable being the *Suprema* itself (including the tribunal of Madrid), followed in order by those of Toledo, Saragossa and Logroño. By the end of the eighteenth century some of the tribunals had improved their position by wise investment, but the forcible sale of all real estate owned by the Inquisition in 1799,[11] followed by the need to contribute to the military effort against Napoleon and the latter's confiscation in 1808 of all the property of the Holy Office, gave the final death-blow to its financial stability.

Perhaps the most important because the most controversial source of revenue was that from confiscations. Under canon law a heretic was punished not only in his person but in his goods, which were seized (sequestrated) and confiscated. If a heretic was unrepentant he was 'relaxed' to the secular arm and burnt; if repentant he was reconciled to the Church; in both cases, however, he suffered the loss of his property. The only exception to this rule was if the heretic had come forward to denounce himself and others voluntarily during the 'term of grace', the period of thirty or forty days grace given by the Inquisition before it started proceedings in a district. The penitent who thus came forward to be reconciled was freed from all imprisonment and confiscation.

The first to suffer confiscation by the Inquisition were the conversos, whose notorious wealth must have stirred many an orthodox spirit. As Hernando del Pulgar wrote sardonically of

* 1 *real* = 34 *maravedis*.

the citizens of Toledo during a time of civil disturbances: 'What great inquisitors of the faith they must be, to be finding heresies in the property of the peasants of the town of Fuensalida, which they rob and burn!'[12] From the very first, then, the inquisitors were associated with confiscation of property, and it became common practice to imply, as Pulgar did, that the search for heretics was really a search for property. The initial confiscations carried out by the Inquisition were very substantial indeed. Diego Susán, who led the plot in Seville in 1481 and was later burnt, was reputed to be worth nearly 30,000 ducats, and he was only one of 'many others, very prominent and very rich', to quote Bernáldez. In the words of a later chronicler of Seville, 'what was noticeable was the great number of prosecutions against moneyed men'.[13] In the years after this, great and wealthy converso families were ruined by even the slightest taint of heresy, for 'reconciliation' meant that all the culprit's property was confiscated and none of it was allowed to pass to his descendants, so that widows and children were often left without any provision. Whole families faced beggary and destitution because of the sins of one member only. These were the harsh fruits of heresy.

Confiscations were meant in the first place to finance the work of the Inquisition, and throughout its history confiscations were an important adjunct to revenue, with the result that the tribunal lucky enough to discover a nest of rich heretics stood to gain appeciably from its luck. Not all the perquisites, however, went to the Inquisition. Officially the tribunal had no control over confiscations, since it was strictly concerned only with the heresy from which confiscation followed as a legal penalty. All confiscated property therefore went technically to the crown. But the tribunal soon made it its task to gain control over as many sources of revenue as possible, especially the property of clerical heretics. It is reported that Ferdinand and Isabella divided all profits from confiscations into three sections, one for the war against the Moors, one for the Inquisition, and one for pious purposes, but this division seems never to have been formally practised. A contemporary was of the opinion that the Catholic monarchs had obtained the enormous sum of 10,000,000 ducats from confiscations, as a contribution to their struggle against the Moors of Granada.[14] If this were true, the sum must have covered all confiscations and not simply a third. One other interested party, the nobility, also received a share in the proceeds. This occurred only in cases where vassals had their goods forfeited for heresy, in which event the crown recognized that the feudal lords had a property in their vassals and granted them one third of any confiscations made within their estates. Those who benefited from this concession included the Dukes of Segorbe (in 1491), Béjar, and Infantado, and Ximénez himself. The practice, however, was not continued under Charles V.

In addition to the profits made at Seville, the Inquisition found that confiscations could be profitable elsewhere. During its brief one-year stay in the small city of Guadalupe in 1485, enough money was raised from confiscations by the tribunal to pay almost entirely for the building of a royal residence costing 7,286 ducats.[15] In most of the cases we have on record, the money from confiscated property seems to have been largely disposed of by the Inquisition. What will probably never be clear, however, is what proportion of money went to the crown and what to the tribunal. Generalizations cannot be made from available examples. In 1676, to take one instance, towards the end of the last great and fruitful campaign of the Inquisition against the Portuguese judaizers resident in Spain, the *Suprema* claimed that it had obtained from the royal treasury confiscations amounting to 772,748 ducats and 884,979 pesos. These sums are extremely large for the period, and suggest that the crown was receiving a high proportion of confiscations. Yet if we look at the value of property confiscated on Majorca after the alleged converso conspiracy of 1678 had been discovered, we find that the totals come to well over 2,500,000 ducats,[16] certainly the biggest single sum gathered in by the Inquisition in all the three centuries of its existence. Of this vast sum, however, it seems that the crown received under five per cent only. What happened to sums like these when they had been seized? Invariably judicial disputes arose over property. Debts of victims had to be paid, the expenses of officials and of court cases had to be met. The crown could claim a third, as had been customary. Some of the money was invested in *censos* and houses by the inquisitors. If we take the city of Lérida in 1487, the confiscations made there from converso property were assigned in part to the city council, to a religious order, to a hospital, and to various other needs, so that the Inquisition did not manage to control all the revenue available.[17] By a thousand different routes the money trickled out of the hands of the inquisitors. When the reason was not mismanagement, it was the sheer dishonesty of minor officials. Whatever the income from confiscations at any time, it is safe to assume that the tribunals did not grow appreciably wealthier, or at least did not keep up their temporary wealth for long periods.

Confiscations were decreed principally at *autos de fe*. A study of individual *autos* shows how income from this source could vary. Here we should note the difference between confiscations and sequestrations. The former was outright seizure, the latter was usually temporary seizure while the victim was in confinement. In practice, however, sequestrations were often lost altogether: their income was used to pay judicial costs and to finance the expense of keeping the prisoner for the weeks, months, or years of his confinement. A few figures should illustrate the role of income of this sort in the accounts of tribunals. In 1731 the Inquisition of Cuenca calculated that the sequestrations it had carried out on twenty-nine prisoners had brought in a total sum of 777,453 *reales*. This was only slightly less than the sequestrations collected by the Inquisition of Santiago between January 1703 and January 1704 – a sum of 961,440 *reales*. Alternatively, an *auto* held at Santiago on 18 October 1655 had only brought in a total of 96,033 *reales*.[18] One other set of figures will help us to compare the relative income of tribunals from confiscations. The following table gives the amount received from confiscations by eight tribunals in the mid-sixteenth century, a period when heretics were relatively few.[19]

Tribunal	Period	Income maravedis
Valladolid	March 1542-December 1543	193,494
Toledo	October 1542-December 1543	1,504,172
Llerena	June 1541-July 1542	1,841,260
Murcia	December 1535-43	4,072,778
Córdoba	July 1541-3	10,501,126
Seville	December 1541-December 1542	196,908
Granada	November 1541-October 1543	19,128,421
Cuenca	November 1535-December 1542	40,518,029

Those who suffered from confiscations were not only the humble. The middle years of the seventeenth century were among the cruellest for converso men of property in Spain. In a later chapter we shall see how the Inquisition helped to destroy the wealthiest financiers of Spain at a time when the Spanish crown could ill afford the sacrifice of such men. The fortunes taken over by the tribunal in these years mounted into millions of ducats. By the beginning of the eighteenth century the income from confiscations had almost dried up. Yet even after this the revenue from those confiscations that were held as capital investment by the Inquisition (rents, *censos* and *juros*) continued to bring in important sums of money. Actual confiscation all but disappeared. In the tribunal of Toledo the last sentence involving confiscation was issued in 1738. By 1745 all the tribunals of Spain had but a single receiver of confiscations between them, instead of having one each.

What essentially was the function of the Inquisition? After what we have seen of its origins and work, there is little need to repeat that it was established principally to eradicate heresy. The important detail, however, is that heretics were by definition those who had betrayed their baptism, so that the tribunal exercised jurisdiction only over those who had been baptized. Time and again victims accused of heresy by the Holy Office claimed that they were not baptized, so removing them immediately out of its power. In a case given by Lea, a woman on her way to be burned for judaizing claimed that she had not been baptized, and was promptly removed from the proceedings. Nevertheless there were no doubt several people in this category whom the tribunal claimed on a technicality. In the case of foreign Protestants accused by the Inquisition, the problem was a bit more complex. The Church recognized (and recognizes) any baptism if validly administered, even by a heretic. Properly baptized Protestants were thereby members of the Catholic Church and as such subject to the Inquisition. Foreign sailors unwary enough to clash with the Holy Office soon found themselves undergoing rigorous interrogation and torture for the heresy in which they had been born. This delimitation of jurisdiction to baptized persons alone meant that in its early years the Inquisition was powerless against the large Jewish and Muslim communities in the realm: there was therefore every reason for it to support the expulsions in 1492 and in the 1500s. By the mid-sixteenth century every soul in the peninsula was nominally Catholic, and the Inquisition had no further need to discriminate between the baptized and the unbaptized.

Quarrels of jurisdiction continued to plague the Holy Office long after its foundation. Before the organization of the papal Inquisition in the thirteenth century, the bishops of the Church had the principal jurisdiction over heretics. This episcopal power was not continued in the Spanish Inquisition, which claimed and maintained exclusive authority over all cases of heresy. Bishops still in theory retained their rights of jurisdiction, but in practice they seldom or never put the claim into effect. In January 1584 the *Suprema* informed the Bishop of Tortosa that the popes had given the Inquisition exclusive jurisdiction over heresy and had prohibited cognizance by others, but this claim was obviously false since in 1595 the pope, Clement VIII, informed the archbishop of Granada that the authority of inquisitors in cases of heresy did not exclude episcopal jurisdiction.[20] These opposing pretensions led to frequent serious quarrels between bishops and tribunals which were never satisfactorily settled. The implications for the Spanish Church were rather more serious, for the increase of inquisitorial power at the expense of the bishops paved the way for a new spiritual absolutism in the Church. How this absolutism operated is illustrated by the position of the religious orders and the Society of Jesus.

Most of the religious orders were by their constitution subject immediately to the papacy and were therefore generally free from episcopal jurisdiction. Since, however, the powers of the Inquisition derived from the papacy, the tribunal made every effort to bring the friars under their control in matters of faith. Some political rivalry entered into this question, because the first inquisitors, including Torquemada, were usually Dominicans and the Dominican order had won for itself a special position not only in the mediaeval Inquisition but also in the Spanish. Hostility between Dominicans and Franciscans led to the latter obtaining bulls from Rome to protect their privileges. Under Charles V the opposition crumbled. In 1525 the Emperor obtained two briefs from the pope subjecting all friars in Spain to the Inquisition and its officers. This did not last long, for in

1534 and subsequently the pope restored to the Franciscans and other orders all the privileges they had previously enjoyed. The struggle went on intermittently until the beginning of the seventeenth century, when papal briefs of 1592 and 1606 decided entirely in favour of the Inquisition.

We have seen that the Society of Jesus, although founded and controlled by Spaniards, was never welcome in the closed society of sixteenth century Spain. Siliceo, the archbishop of Toledo, showed particular hostility to the Jesuits, and the famous Dominican Melchor Cano led a vigorous series of campaigns in which he denounced the *Spiritual Exercises* of St Ignatius as heretical, and condemned the Society and all its works. Cano and Siliceo were only part of a wider campaign of persecution led by the court and the Inquisition, to discredit the Jesuit order.[21] One of the liberties questioned by the Inquisition was the Jesuit privilege of not having to denounce heretics to anyone but their own superior in the order. When in 1585 it was learned that the fathers of the Jesuit college at Monterey, in Galicia, had been concealing the heresies of some of their number instead of denouncing them to the Holy Office, the latter acted immediately by arresting the provincial of Castile and two fathers from Monterey. The Inquisition did not succeed in punishing its victims because the case was revoked to Rome in 1587, but the circumstances proved how correct it had been to claim exclusive jurisdiction over heresy, and this *cause célèbre* clinched its victory over the religious orders.

Only one class of people, the bishops, remained beyond inquisitorial jurisdiction. All others, from the highest nobles of the blood downwards, were liable to the authority of this tribunal which they unquestioningly supported for the greater part of its existence. Bishops could be tried only by Rome, a rule which had been upheld in the mediaeval Inquisition. In Spain, of course, the issue was of some importance, because of the high proportion of bishops who had converso blood. Among the earliest of those singled out for attack by the Inquisition was bishop Dávila of Segovia, who entered his see in 1461. He had refused to allow the Holy Office into his diocese and on being accused by the tribunal was summoned to Rome in 1490, in his eightieth year. Even more distinguished was Pedro de Aranda, bishop of Calahorra and in 1482 president of the Council of

Castile. He was summoned to Rome in 1493 and died there in disgrace in 1500. One of the most eminent converso bishops to suffer patent injustice was Hernando de Talavera, whose case we have already noted. But the most famous example of a clash between inquisitorial and episcopal authority, in a case which also involved royal and papal privileges, was that of Bartolomé de Carranza, archbishop of Toledo.

Bartolomé de Carranza y Miranda was born in 1503 in Navarre, of poor but *hidalgo* parents.[22] At the age of 12 he entered the University of Alcalá and at seventeen joined the Dominican order. He was sent to study at Valladolid where his intellectual gifts soon won him a chair in theology. In his early thirties he went to Rome to win his doctorate in the same subject, and returned to Spain famous. For a while he acted as a censor to the Inquisition, but refused all offers of promotion made to him. In 1542 he refused the wealthy see of Cuzco in America, and likewise rejected the post of royal confessor in 1548, and that of bishop of the Canaries in 1550. He was twice sent to the sessions of the Council of Trent as a Spanish representative in 1545 and 1551. He returned to Spain in 1553 and in the following year accompanied prince Philip on his matrimonial journey to the England of Mary Tudor. There the ardent Carranza distinguished himself by the zeal with which he crushed heretics and purified the universities of Oxford and Cambridge, winning for himself the title of the Black Friar. He stayed in England from July 1554 to July 1557, after which he went to join Philip in Flanders. It was in May 1557 that archbishop Siliceo of Toledo died. Philip immediately decided to give the post to Carranza, who refused the honour as he had refused all others. The king was adamant. Eventually Carranza said that he would accept only if ordered to do so. In this way the humble, devout and unambitious Dominican friar became the tenant of the most important see in the Catholic world after Rome.

Carranza was a parvenu in the ecclesiastical circles of Spain. His claims to Toledo were less than those of other distinguished prelates in Spain, notably Inquisitor General Valdés. Like Siliceo, he was a man of humble origins thrown into a rigidly aristocratic milieu. He had been nominated to the see while abroad without any effort by Philip to consult his Spanish advisers. Intellectually he was far inferior to his brother

Dominican, Melchor Cano, a brilliant theologian who had always been Carranza's bitterest rival in the order. These among other factors were enough to raise up a host of enemies for the new archbishop. Only the weapon of attack was lacking. This was supplied by Carranza himself in his *Commentaries on the Christian Catechism* which he published in 1558 at Antwerp.

The *Commentaries* in themselves are now considered thoroughly orthodox in doctrine. The Council of Trent examined and approved the work, and numerous other distinguished theologians in Spain agreed with this. But there is no doubt that Carranza was a bad stylist and a careless theologian. Phrases in his work were seized upon by hostile critics, notably Cano, and were denounced as heresy. The archbishop of Granada called the *Commentaries* 'reliable, trustworthy, pious and Catholic'; the bishop of Almería said the book 'contained no heresy and much excellent doctrine'. Yet Melchor Cano asserted that the work 'contains many propositions which are scandalous, rash and ill-sounding, others which savour of heresy, others which are erroneous, and even some which are heretical'. Led by Valdés, the Inquisition accepted Cano's opinion. Small wonder that pope Pius V claimed, 'The theologians of Spain want to make him a heretic although he is not one!' If there were no actual heresies in Carranza, why was he looked upon with suspicion by his enemies? It is not enough to say that personal enmity loomed large, though this is true. Both Valdés and Cano detested Carranza. Another mortal enemy was Pedro de Castro, bishop of Cuenca, who had entertained hopes of the see of Toledo, and his brother Rodrigo. Both these men, sons of the Count of Lemos, were aristocrats who resented the rise of men of humble birth to positions of influence. They were to play a key part in the eventual arrest and imprisonment of the archbishop.

Behind the personal enmities lay the fact that Carranza, for all his ardent Catholicism, was a liberal by Spanish standards. In 1530 as a student he had been twice denounced to the Inquisition for holding Erasmist views. At the Council of Trent he had supported the introduction of radical reforms in Church discipline. Later, during his imprisonment, his name was repeatedly linked with that of Reginald Pole, the Cardinal of England, another liberal who was looked upon in Spain as a heretic in Catholic clothing. What ruined Carranza was the Protestant crisis in Spain, which occurred at precisely the time of his elevation to the see of Toledo. Interrogation of Carlos de Seso and Pedro Cazalla resulted in detailed denunciations of the archbishop. On one occasion he was said to have told them he believed as they did; on another he was reported as saying, 'As for me, I don't believe in purgatory'. Preaching in London he was said to have used Lutheran terminology. The Inquisitor General carefully took note of all these testimonies. Still the Holy Office could not act against Carranza, for as a bishop he was answerable only to Rome. Valdés made urgent representations to Rome, and in January 1559 pope Paul IV sent letters empowering the Inquisition to act against bishops for a limited period of two years, but both the prisoner and the case were to be referred to Rome. Valdés received the brief on 8 April 1559. On 6 May the fiscal of the Inquisition drew up an indictment calling for the arrest of Carranza 'for having preached, written and dogmatized many heresies of Luther'. After much pressure Philip II gave his sanction on 26 June. On 6 August Carranza, expecting the blow to fall any day, was summoned to Valladolid by the government.

Fearing the import of the summons, Carranza set out but delayed the progress of his journey. On 16 August he was met by a Dominican colleague and friend from Alcalá who warned him that the Inquisition was searching to arrest him. Shaken by this, the archbishop continued his journey until four days later he reached the safety of Torrelaguna, just north of Madrid, where he met his friend Fray Pedro de Soto, who had come from Valladolid to warn him. But already it was too late. Carranza did not know that four days before his arrival the officials of the Inquisition had taken up their residence in Torrelaguna and were awaiting his coming. Carranza reached the little town on Sunday, 20 August. Very early in the morning of Tuesday, 22 August the inquisitor Diego Ramírez and Rodrigo Castro (who was a member of the *Suprema*), together with about ten armed familiars, made their way up to Carranza's bedroom and demanded, 'Open to the Holy Office!' The intruders were let in, and an official addressed the archbishop, 'Your Honour, I have been ordered to arrest Your Reverence in the name of the Holy Office'. Carranza said quietly, 'Do you have sufficient warrant for this?' The official then read the order signed by the *Suprema*.

Carranza protested, 'Do the inquisitors not know that they cannot be my judges, since by my dignity and consecration I am subject immediately to the pope and to no other?' This was the moment for the trump card to be played. Ramírez said, 'Your Reverence will be fully satisfied on that account', and showed him the papal brief. All that day the archbishop was kept under house arrest and in the evening a curfew was imposed on the town. No one was to venture into the streets after 9 p.m. and nobody was to look out of the windows. In the silence and darkness that midnight the inquisitors and their prey were spirited out of Torrelaguna. On the night of 28 August Carranza was shuffled into the cells of the Inquisition in Valladolid. In the words of Lea, he 'disappeared from human sight as completely as though swallowed by the earth'.

Carranza was allotted two rooms in the prison cells. Here he was kept for over seven years, completely out of touch with the world outside. During all his confinement he was not allowed any recourse to the sacraments. In human terms, the tragic story of the archbishop was just beginning. But politically the story was at an end. From now on Carranza ceased to matter as a human being and became a mere pawn in the struggle for jurisdiction between Rome and the Inquisition. He no longer counted in a controversy where the real issues had become the ambitions of individuals and the pretensions of ecclesiastical tribunals. Marañón observes that in this atmosphere of villainy there was at least one just man – doctor Martín de Azpilcueta, known as doctor Navarro, who sacrificed his career in Spain for the sake of defending the unfortunate archbishop faithfully and well at his trial.

The long negotiations between Rome and the Spanish authorities will not concern us here. Briefly, the papacy was concerned to claim its rights over Carranza and thereby to vindicate its unique control over bishops. Philip II saw the papal claim as interference in Spanish affairs and refused to allow the Inquisition to surrender its prisoner. Pope Pius IV in 1565 sent a special legation to negotiate in Madrid. Among the members of the legation were three prelates who later became popes as Gregory XIII, Urban VII and Sixtus V. These distinguished clerics failed to make the mission a success. As one of them wrote back to Rome:

Nobody dares to speak in favour of Carranza for fear of the Inquisition. No Spaniard would dare to absolve the archbishop, even if he were believed innocent, because this would mean opposing the Inquisition. The authority of the latter would not allow it to admit that it had imprisoned Carranza unjustly. The most ardent defenders of justice here consider that it is better for an innocent man to be condemned than for the Inquisition to suffer disgrace.[23]

With the accession of Pius V to the papal throne in 1566 a solution came into sight. Carranza from his prison cell managed to smuggle a message out to Rome in the form of a paper bearing in his handwriting the words, 'Lord, if it be thou, bid me come to thee upon the waters' (Matthew XIV, 28). This was exactly what Pius intended to do. In July 1566 he ordered the Spanish authorities to send Carranza and all relevant documentation to Rome, under penalty of excommunication. The aging archbishop reached Rome, and was placed in honourable confinement in the Castle of Sant' Angelo. This second imprisonment lasted nine years. Pius V died in 1572 without having decided the case. His successor Gregory XIII finally issued sentence in April 1576. The verdict was a compromise, made no doubt in order to placate Spain. The *Commentaries* were condemned and prohibited and Carranza was obliged to abjure a list of 'errors', after which he was told to retire to a monastery in Orvieto. Meanwhile the papacy was to administer the vacant and wealthy see of Toledo. The sentence satisfied Philip and the Inquisition, whose authority would have suffered by an acquittal. It satisfied Rome, which had vindicated its sole authority over bishops, and, in a sense, it satisfied Carranza who was not accused of any heresy, despite the prohibition of his *Commentaries*, which was to remain in all the editions of the Spanish Index except the last one in 1790. Justice had been replaced by political compromise. Everything had been taken into consideration except the frail old man who, eighteen days after the papal verdict had been read over him, contracted an illness from which he died at 3 a.m. on 2 May 1576.

CHAPTER NINE

THE SPANISH INQUISITION:
ITS PROCEDURE

'But I am not guilty', said K., 'it's a misunderstanding. And
if it comes to that, how can any man be called guilty? We are
all simply men here, one as much as the other'.

'That is true', said the priest, 'but that's how all guilty men
talk'.

Franz Kafka, THE TRIAL

THE procedure of the Inquisition was calculated to achieve the
greatest degree of efficiency with the least degree of publicity.
This practice of secrecy inevitably darkened knowledge, with
the result that misconceptions about the severity of the tribunal
became extremely common. Although in some respects we can
modify the picture of a cruel and merciless Inquisition, what
cannot be explained away is the atmosphere that prevailed
prior to arrest and condemnation. Mariana, as we have already
seen, chronicled the consternation among Spaniards when they
found that 'they were deprived of the liberty to hear and talk
freely, since in all the cities, towns and villages there were
persons placed to give information of what went on. This was
considered by some the most wretched slavery and equal to
death'. The passage refers specifically to the familiars and professional informers of the Inquisition. But the fear of denunciation, the weight of suspicion and hostility, was something
created within the community itself by its wholehearted support
of the antisemitic campaign. The whole community con-
ditioned itself into a state where denunciation of one's neighbour, often for the most trifling fault, was followed psycholo-
gically by denunciation of oneself. Official policy gave the
initial impetus to this devastating social espionage. We have

seen that in 1485 the inquisitors of Toledo collected the rabbis of the province and made them swear to pronounce in their synagogues major anathemas on any Jews who did not denounce secret judaizers among the conversos. One half of the Jewish community was therefore invited to spy on the other half, a task willingly performed by many Jews who resented the conversos for their apostasy and their social success.

The whole population was taught very clearly how to recognize the secret Jews in their midst. When the inquisitors began operations in a district they usually declared an initial 'term of grace' during which voluntary confessions would not be penalized. The 'term' was publicized by issuing an Edict of Grace calling on heretics to come forward and denounce themselves or others. A calendar month or in some cases forty days was the usual period allowed for this. Since reconciliation to the faith under the terms of grace involved no serious penalties such as confiscation of property, the early years of the Inquisition witnessed a vast number of voluntary denunciations. In Majorca for instance, the first Edict to be published brought in 337 conversos who denounced themselves. In Seville the Edict filled the prisons to overflowing. Self-denunciation became a mass phenomenon. While Edicts of Grace were regular practice in the early years of the Inquisition, they were replaced after about 1500 by Edicts of Faith, which omitted the 'term of grace' and instead threatened the penalty of excommunication against those who did not denounce heretics, whether themselves or others. Together with the Edict of Faith went a statement describing in detail the practices of heretics, especially judaizers, Muslims, Illuminists and Protestants. If anyone saw a neighbour practising the acts noted in the instruction, he was to denounce him to the Inquisition. Some of the paragraphs relating to judaizers would go as follows[1]:

If you know or have heard of anyone who keeps the Sabbath according to the law of Moses, putting on clean sheets and other new garments, and putting clean cloths on the table and clean sheets on the bed on feast-days in honour of the Sabbath, and using no lights from Friday evening onwards; or if they have purified the meat they are to eat by bleeding it in water; or have cut the throats of cattle or birds they are eating, uttering certain words and covering the blood with earth; or have eaten meat in Lent and on other days forbidden by Holy Mother Church; or have fasted the great fast, going bare-footed that day; or if they say Jewish prayers, at night begging for-giveness of each other, the parents placing their hands on the heads of their children without making the sign of the cross or saying any-thing but, 'Be blessed by God and by me'; or if they bless the table in the Jewish way; or if they recite the psalms without the *Gloria Patri*; or if any woman keeps forty days after childbirth without entering a church; or if they circumcise their children or give them Jewish names; or if after baptism they wash the place where the oil and chrism was put; or if anyone on his deathbed turns to the wall to die, and when he is dead they wash him with hot water, shaving the hair off all parts of his body . . .

In such cases and many others, the onlooker would know he was among heretics and would have to denounce them. The atmos-phere of denunciation and mutual recrimination created in this way would almost certainly have been 'equal to death' for those unhappy people for whom popular suspicion led inevitably to condemnation. Petty denunciations were the rule rather than the exception. For a neighbour to change sheets at the end of the week was sufficient proof to warrant denunciation. In about 1530 Aldonça de Vargas in the Canary Islands was reported to the Inquisition for having smiled when she heard mention of the Virgin Mary. In 1635 Pedro Ginesta, a man over eighty years old, was brought before the tribunal of Barcelona by an erstwhile comrade for having forgetfully eaten a meal of bacon and onions on a day of abstinence. 'The said prisoner', ran the indictment, 'being of a nation infected with heresy (i.e. from France), it is presumed that he has on many other occasions eaten flesh on forbidden days, after the manner of the sect of Luther'.[2] Denunciations based on suspicion therefore led to accusations based on conjecture. Some delations, of course, had nothing to do with heresy, as with Alonso de Jaén, who was prosecuted in 1530 for urinating against the walls of a church; or with Gonçales Ruiz, who said to his opponent during a game of cards, 'Even with God as your partner you won't win this game'.[3] The self-denunciations were almost without exception occasioned by the fear that if one did not confess one would be denounced: for people in this frame of mind the Edicts offered a welcome opportunity to unburden oneself of fear rather than of guilt. Lea cites the case of two husbands who in 1581 accused themselves of having asserted in conversation with their wives that fornication was no sin. The wives were summoned and confirmed the confessions. The only possible motive for the action taken by the husbands was fear that their wives would denounce them.[4] The case is not unusual. The records of the Inquisition are full of instances where neighbours denounced neighbours, friends denounced friends, and members of the same family denounced each other. Many of these cases would have arisen through sheer malice or hatred. But there were the others, more significant and terrible, where fear of denunciation alone became the spur to confession and counter-denunciation. The 'term of grace' had an important clause which set the seal on all this. To denounce oneself as a heretic was not enough to enable one to benefit from the terms of the Edict of Grace. It was also necessary to denounce all those accomplices who shared the error or had led one into it. The chain reaction set in process by this was highly effective in uprooting heresy. The price paid for such orthodoxy was a heavy one. It is possible to believe that only a small proportion of the population went about in perpetual fear of denunciation and that the orthodox majority breathed openly and freely. But the trivial nature of thousands of denunciations shows that even the majority might be, as they were, liable to prosecution. The equanimity with which Spaniards accepted the violation of their personal thoughts and consciences brings one back with a start to the experience of the twentieth century. Certainly there is some truth in Lea's assertion that 'the shadow of the Holy Office lay over the land'. The problem arose out of the Inquisition. But the tribunal itself was only a weapon in the hands of a society that had surrendered its liberty to the voluntary purpose of excising from the heart of Spain all those who refused to conform to a specific set of values.

If the Holy Office welcomed denunciations, it often knew when to distinguish between the false and the true. In 1637, when Felipe Leonart, a needlemaker of French origin living in Tarragona, was unanimously denounced by his wife, son and daughter-in-law for Lutheranism, the tribunal very quickly realized that the charges had been made out of sheer malice, and suspended the trial after rejecting the accusations.[5] False-witness was not very frequent, if we take the example of the tribunal of Toledo, in which the 1,172 trials that took place between 1575

and 1610 contained only eight cases of perjury. Perjurers themselves were not treated with any severity commensurate with the
ruin they brought upon their victims, though in some few cases
they suffered burning, scourging and the galleys, which may
have acted to dissuade false-witness for the future. More difficult
to deal with were cases of pathological self-denouncers such as
the French nun in a convent at Alcalá, Ursule de la Croix, who
confessed to heresy and eating meat on Fridays. She was
absolved for this, but confessed again to the same crimes. The
second time she was reconciled and given a very light penance.
When, however, she decided to denounce herself for the third
time in 1594, she was obligingly sent to the stake.[6] This for-
bearance by the Inquisition shows the relative leniency shown to
voluntary confession, although such confessions guaranteed
impunity only during the 'term of grace'.

The heavy reliance put upon denunciations raises the question of the trustworthiness of witnesses. In the Spanish Inquisition, unfortunately, witnesses were given more advantages than
in any secular judicial tribunal, because their names were concealed. This concealment provoked widespread hostility, clearly
expressed in the several Cortes held under Charles V, particularly that of Valladolid in February 1518. But the influence of
Ximénez was thrown heavily against allowing the publication
of witnesses' names, and the Inquisition retained its practice un-
altered. The concealment of names often meant that when a
charge was levelled against a prisoner it had to be phrased in general terms so that the accused would not know from the occasion
cited who the accuser might be. In other words, a prisoner would
be kept entirely in the dark about the reasons for his confinement,
and if accused in general terms of heresy he would have to rely
entirely on his memory to decide which occasion had led to his
arrest. The necessity for concealment was justified by cases in
which witnesses had been murdered in order to prevent them
testifying. This at least was the argument of Ximénez. But, as
a memorial from the city of Granada put it in 1526, the system
of secrecy was an open invitation to perjury and malicious
testimony.[7] This objection would not have been valid but for the
fact that all denunciations were taken seriously and that even if
a man were later exonerated the evil brought on him by a
slight and secret accusation was immense. When, for example,

Doctor Jorge Enríquez, physician to the Duke of Alva, died in 1622, secret witnesses claimed that his body had been buried according to Jewish rites. The consequence was that all Enríquez's family, relatives and household were thrown into prison and kept there for two years until their acquittal for lack of evidence.

Judicially, the courts of the Inquisition were no worse and no better than the secular courts of the day. Faults existing in the procedure of the Holy Office would be found no less in the royal courts where reforms were instituted by the famous Cortes of Toledo in 1480. The distinguishing feature of the Inquisition, its absolute secrecy, was the one which made it more open to abuses than any public tribunal. This secrecy was not, it seems, originally a part of the inquisitorial framework, and early records refer to public trials and to a public prison rather than a secret one. But by the beginning of the sixteenth century secrecy became the general rule and was enforced in all the business of the tribunal. Even the various Instructions of the Inquisition, although set down in print, were for restricted circulation only and not for the public eye. What this necessarily involved was general public ignorance of the methods and procedure of the Inquisition, an ignorance which in its earlier period helped the tribunal by creating reverential fear in the minds of evildoers, but which in its later period led to the rise of fear and hatred based on a highly imaginative idea of how the tribunal worked. The Inquisition was therefore largely to blame for the unfounded slanders cast upon it in the eighteenth century or even before. The natural outcome of this enforced ignorance is shown by the debates in the Cortes of Cadiz in 1813, on a projected decree to abolish the Inquisition. If the defenders of the tribunal relied on the argument of a mystical and mythical unity given to Spain by the Inquisition, its detractors relied almost completely on legendary misapprehensions about the entire structure and function of the institution.[8]

The outside world may have been kept uninformed, but internally the flow of information was almost impeccable. The administrative and secretarial apparatus of the tribunal took care to set down on paper even the most trifling business. Thanks to this, the Spanish Inquisition is one of the few early modern institutions about whose organization and procedure so vast a volume of documentation is available that wilful distortion of its history becomes impossible.

Before an arrest took place, the evidence in the case was presented to a number of theologians who acted as censors (*calificadores*) to determine whether the charges involved heresy. If the *calificadores* decided that there was sufficient proof of heresy, the prosecutor or *fiscal* drew up a demand for the arrest of the accused, who was then taken into custody. Such at least were the rules. But in numerous cases arrest preceded the examination by *calificadores*, so that all the preliminary safeguards against wrongful arrest were dispensed with. As a result, prisoners sat in inquisitorial gaols without any charge ever having been produced against them. This led the Cortes of Aragon in 1533 to protest against arbitrary arrest as well as arrest on trifling charges. Zeal of officials and inquisitors alike often outran discretion, and we have cases in the tribunal of Valladolid in 1699 when several suspects (including a girl aged 9 and a boy aged 14) had lain in prison for up to two years without any *calificación* having been made of the evidence against them. It should be noted, however, that when abuses like this came to the notice of the *Suprema* it invariably issued severe rebukes to the culprits.

Arrest was accompanied by immediate seizure of the goods held by the accused. An inventory was made of everything in the possession of the man or his family, and all this was held by officials of the Inquisition until the case had been decided. The inventories drawn up in this way are of great historical interest since they allow us to see in minute detail exactly how the household of a sixteenth or seventeenth century family was run. Every item in the house including pots and pans, spoons, rags, and old clothes, was carefully noted down in the presence of a notary. In some cases these items were valued at the time of the inventory, an important measure because of the frequent need to sell the items to pay for the upkeep of a prisoner or his dependants. If a prisoner's case went unheard or undecided for years on end the sequestration of his property involved real hardship for his dependants, deprived at one blow of their means of income and even of their own homes. For as long as the accused stayed in prison the costs of his upkeep were met out of his sequestrated property, which was as a rule sold piece by piece at a public auction. Initially no provision was made for relatives during sequestration and the government had to intervene to help. In July 1486 Ferdinand ordered the tribunal in Saragossa to support the needy children of an accused man, Juan Navarro, out of the latter's property while the case was being heard. Others were not so lucky. There were instances of a rich prisoner's children dying of hunger and of others begging in the streets. These evils were finally remedied in the Instructions of 1561, which allowed the support of dependants out of sequestrations. This concession, already in practice but not codified in the mid-sixteenth century, came too late to save two generations of conversos from destruction of their property. Even after 1561 accused persons sometimes found little security for their property against dishonest officials, or against arbitrary arrest and lengthy trials.

The arrested person was usually spirited away into the prisons of the Inquisition, there to await trial. Of the various grades of prison kept by the tribunal, the most rigorous was the 'secret prison', meant particularly for the lengthy confinement of prisoners and not for temporary detainees awaiting trial. The Inquisition was fortunate in its choice of residences. In some of the largest cities of Spain it was allowed the use of fortified castles with ancient and reliable prison cells. The tribunal of Saragossa resided in the Aljafería, that of Seville in the Triana (in 1627 it moved to a site within the city), and that of Córdoba in the Alcázar. In all these buildings the gaols were in a fairly good condition. This may explain why the secret prisons of the Inquisition were generally considered less harsh and more humane than either the royal prisons or ordinary ecclesiastical gaols. There is the case of a friar in Valladolid in 1629 who made some heretical statements simply in order to be transferred from the prison he was in to the milder one of the Inquisition. On another occasion, in 1675, a priest confined in the episcopal prison pretended to be a judaizer in order to be transferred to the inquisitorial prison. No better evidence could be cited for the superiority of inquisitorial gaols than that of Córdoba in 1820, when the prison authorities complained about the miserable and unhealthy state of the city prison and asked that the municipality transfer its prisoners to the prison of the Inquisition, which was 'safe, clean and spacious. At present it has twenty six cells, rooms which can hold two hundred prisoners at a time, a completely separate prison for women, and places for work'. On another occasion the authorities reported that 'the building of the Inquisition is separate from the rest of the city, isolated and exposed on all sides to the winds, spacious, supplied abundantly with water, with sewers well distributed and planned to serve the prisoners, and with the separation and ventilation necessary to good health. It would be a prison well suited to preserve the health of prisoners.'[9]

A more personal description of an inquisitorial prison is given by a Portuguese who entered the cells of the tribunal at Lisbon in 1802. The picture resembles any Spanish inquisitorial prison:

The gaoler who for greater diginity has the name of Alcaide, that is, keeper of the castle, addressed to me almost a little sermon, recommending me to behave in this respectable house with great propriety; stating also that I must not make any noise in my room, nor speak aloud, lest the other prisoners might happen to be in the neighbouring cells and hear me, with other instructions of a similar kind. He then took me to my cell, a small room 12 feet by 8, with a door to the passage; in this door were two iron grates, far from each other, and occupying the thickness of the wall, which was three feet, and outside of these grates there was besides a wooden door; in the upper part of this was an aperture that let into the cell a borrowed light from the passage, which passage received its light from the windows fronting a narrow yard, but having opposite, at a very short distance, very high walls; in this small room were a kind of wood frame without feet, whereon lay a straw mattress, which was to be my bed; a small water-pot; and another utensil for various purposes, which was only emptied every eight days, when I went to mass in the prisoners' private chapel. This was the only opportunity I had of taking fresh air during such a period, and they contrived several divisions in the chapel in such a manner that the prisoners could never see each other, or know how many were granted the favour of going to mass. The cell was arched above, and the floor was brick, the wall being formed of stone, and very thick. The place was consequently very cold in winter, and so damp that very frequently the grates were covered with drops of water like dew; and my clothes, during the winter, were in a state of perpetual moisture. Such was my abode for the period of nearly three years.[10]

The fact that the practice in inquisitorial prisons differed from tribunal to tribunal shows relative laxity, which is sometimes interpreted falsely to show how benevolent the Inquisition was. What is undeniable is that the gaols were not dens of horror. Prisoners were fed regularly and adequately from their own purse, on available food, particularly bread, meat and wine. One fortunate prisoner in Toledo in 1709 managed to order for himself in addition regular supplies of oil, vinegar, ice, eggs, chocolate and bacon.[11] The expenses of all paupers were paid for by the tribunal itself: at Las Palmas the money spent on the pauper Catalina de Candelaría during her six-month stay in 1662 came to 154 *reales*. One of those who could afford to pay for themselves, Isabel Perdomo, had to pay twenty-eight *reales* for her seven-week stay in the same prison in 1674.[12] Apart from food, prisoners in some tribunals were well cared for, this depending on their financial resources. One Juan de Abel, of Granada, was granted in his cell the use of 'a mattress, a quilt, two sheets, two pillows, a rug, a blanket', and other items.[13] Even paupers were given slippers, shirts and similar items. Besides this, some comforts were allowed, such as the use of writing paper, a concession exploited to the full by Luis de León, who spent his four years in prison at Valladolid composing his great devotional treatise *Los Nombres de Cristo*.

There was, however, another side to the picture. Prisoners were cut off strictly from all contact with the world outside and even within the prison were secluded from each other whenever possible. On finally leaving the gaol they were obliged to take an oath not to reveal anything they had seen or experienced in the cells. Small wonder if this absolute secrecy gave rise to the most blood-curdling legends about what went on inside. A rule of the Spanish and the Roman Inquisitions (though apparently not of the Portuguese Inquisition, as the extract above shows) was that detainees were denied all access to mass and the sacraments. One of the most notable sufferers in this respect was Carranza, whose trials must have been doubled by this heavy deprivation of spiritual comfort for the eighteen years of his imprisonment. To balance the fortunate few who were treated kindly there are records of those who did not fare so well. John Hill, an English sailor captured in 1574 and imprisoned by the Las Palmas tribunal, complained of having to sleep on the floor with fleas, of lack of bread and water, and of being left all but naked.[14] These were standard complaints which could have been made of any other prison, secular or ecclesiastical. Other common ordeals would include having to wear chains (which were not frequently used by the Inquisition) and being left interminably in unlit and unheated cells. In addition the Inquisition used two instruments to punish awkward prisoners: one was the *mordaza* or gag used to prevent prisoners talking or blaspheming; the other was the *pie de amigo*, an iron fork utilised to keep the head upright forcibly. Keeping in mind the general state of prisons in Europe as a whole down to relatively modern times, we may conclude with Lea 'that the secret prisons of the Inquisition were less intolerable places of abode than the episcopal and public gaols. The general policy respecting them was more humane and enlightened than that of other jurisdictions, whether in Spain of elsewhere'.[15]

The severities of prison life led to a regular death-rate which should be attributed not to torture (about which inquisitors were very careful) but to disease and relatively unhealthy conditions. As the Inquisitor General, Cardinal Adrian, observed in 1517, the prisons were meant for detention only and not for punishment. Inquisitors made it their special care to avoid cruelty, brutality and harsh treatment. The use of torture, therefore, was not looked on as an end in itself. The Instructions of 1561 laid down no rules for its use but urged that its application should be according to 'the conscience and will of the appointed judges, following law, reason and good conscience. Inquisitors should take great care that the sentence of torture is justified and follows precedent'.[16] At a time when the use of torture was universal in European criminal courts, the Spanish Inquisition followed a policy of mildness and circumspection which makes it compare favourably with other institutions. Torture was used only as a last resort and applied in only a minority of cases. Often the accused was merely placed *in conspectu tormentorum*, when the sight of the instruments of torture would provoke a confession.

Confessions gained under torture were never accepted as valid because they had obviously been obtained by pressure. It was therefore essential for the accused to ratify his confession the day after the ordeal. If he refused to do this, a legal pretext was invoked. As the rules forbade anyone to be tortured more than once, the end of every torture session was treated as a suspension only, and refusal to ratify the confession would be met with a threat to 'continue' the torture. Besides being compelled to confess their own heresies, victims were often also tortured *in caput alienum*, to confess knowledge of the crimes of others. Here again, however, the procedure was used far less in Spain then elsewhere in Christendom. Lea estimates that in the Toledo tribunal between 1575 and 1610 about 32 per cent of those whose offences were liable to the use of torture, were in fact tortured.[17] If we take this as an average it shows that the Inquisition relied less on extreme methods than some writers have made out. The lurid scenes of sadism conjured up by enemies of the Inquisition have their existence only in legend. By the mid-eighteenth century torture had virtually fallen out of use in the tribunal, and finally in 1816 the pope forbade its use in any of the Inquisitions subject to the Holy See.

'The popular impression', says Lea, 'that the inquisitorial torture-chamber was the scene of exceptional refinement in cruelty, of specially ingenious modes of inflicting agony, and of peculiar persistence in extorting confessions, is an error due to sensational writers who have exploited credulity'.[18] The error still persists, largely because loose and inaccurate comparisons are regularly made between the techniques of the Inquisition and those of modern totalitarian states. The prison, in such accounts, is represented as a place to which one was sent for the sole purpose of eliciting a fraudulent confession and inducing repentance. The confession would be obtained by torture or the threat of torture, and repentance would be achieved by an equivalent of brain-washing. All this is to give excessive credit to the inquisitors, who were at no time sophisticated enough even to approach the achievements of their modern counterparts. Their methods were honest, simple and straightforward, and there were no psychological refinements.

The torturers employed by the Inquisition were usually the public executioners who worked for the secular courts. Those required to be present at the proceedings were the inquisitors themselves, a representative of the bishop, and a secretary to record everything faithfully. Physicians were usually available in case of emergency. The basic rule to be observed was that the victim should suffer no danger to life or limb. In the vast majority of cases the rule was adhered to, but there are a few examples of victims who had their legs or arms broken because they persisted in refusing to confess. Even less in number are those victims who died as a result of torture. In such cases the inquisitor could comfort themselves that the victims died through their own obstinacy.

No distinctive tortures were used by the Inquisition: those most often employed were in common use in other secular and ecclesiastical tribunals and any complaints of novel tortures would certainly refer to rare exceptions. The three main ones were the *garrucha*, the *toca*, and the *potro*. The *garrucha* or pulley involved being hung by the wrists from a pulley on the ceiling, with heavy weights attached to the feet. The victim was raised slowly and then suddenly allowed to fall with a jerk. The effect was to stretch and perhaps dislocate the arms and legs. The *toca* or water torture was more complicated. The victim was tied down on a rack, his mouth was kept forcibly open and a *toca* or linen cloth was put down his throat to conduct water poured slowly from a jar. The severity of the torture varied with the number of jars of water used. The *potro*, which was the most common after the sixteenth century, involved being bound tightly on a rack by cords which were passed round the body and the limbs and were controlled by the executioner who tightened them by turns of the cords at the end. With each turn the cords bit into the body and travelled round the flesh. In all these tortures it was the rule to strip the victims first. Both men and women were divested of all their clothes and left completely naked except for minimal garments to cover their shame.

There seems to have been no age limit for victims, nor was there any limit on the torture. A victim would often have to undergo all the three tortures before he would confess. Less obdurate ones need only suffer one torture. While the Inquisition did not usually subject the very old and very young to torture, there are cases when tribunals apparently found this necessary. Women aged between seventy and ninety years are on record as having been put on the *potro*. In 1607 at Valencia a girl of thirteen was subjected to torture, but she seems to have been mildly treated since she overcame it without confessing.

The records of the Inquisition, exhaustive and thorough in other respects, are no less thorough in describing the procedure during torture. Every word, every gesture, was noted down by the secretary present at the torture. As a feat of reporting, these accounts are without parallel in their time. Here are extracts from the official accounts of three tortures carried out in the sixteenth century. In the first is a woman, accused in 1568 of not eating pork and of changing her linen on Saturdays.

She was ordered to be placed on the *potro*. She said, 'Señores, why will you not tell me what I have to say? Señor, put me on the ground – have I not said that I did it all?' She was told to tell it. She said 'I don't remember – take me away – I did what the witnesses say'. She was told to tell in detail what the witnesses said. She said, 'Señor, as I have told you, I do not know for certain. I have said that I did all that the witnesses say. Señores, release me, for I do not remember it'. She was told to tell it. She said, 'Señores, it does not help me to say that I did it and I have admitted that what I have done has brought me to this suffering – Señor, you know the truth – Señores, for God's sake have mercy on me. Oh, Señor, take these things from my arms – Señor release me, they are killing me'. She was tied on the *potro* with the cords, she was admonished to tell the truth and the *garrotes* were ordered to be tightened. She said, 'Señor, do you not see how these people are killing me? I did it – for God's sake let me go'.[19]

Foreign heretics were submitted to the same procedure. Here is the case of Jacob Petersen from Dunkirk, a sailor aged twenty years, who was examined by the tribunal of the Canaries in November 1597. He was stripped and bound and given three turns of the cord.

On being given these he said first, 'Oh God!' and then, 'There's no mercy'; after the turns he was admonished, and he said, 'I don't know what to say, oh dear God!' Then three more turns of the cord were ordered to be given, and after two of them he said, 'Oh God, oh God, there's no mercy, oh God help me, help me!'[20]

After three more turns he confessed. The next example concerns George van Hoflaquen, a merchant from Bruges, who was tortured by the same tribunal in December 1597 after the inquisitors disbelieved his claim to be a Catholic.

He was bound and admonished and said: 'Señor Inquisidor, what does your lordship want me to say', and that he had told the truth and was a Catholic. They ordered him to be given three turns of the cord and when these were given he was warned, and he said he had nothing to say. Then they ordered another three turns of the cord, and he was warned and said that it was true he was a Catholic and had always been and that if it were otherwise he would say so. He was admonished to tell the truth. He said he knew no more and if he did he would say so; when he made this reply, they ordered another three turns of the cord and when these were given he was admonished. He said if they wanted him to say he was a heretic he would say so because of the torture, but he had been and was a Catholic. He was then admonished to tell the truth. He said if he knew otherwise he would say so, and that it was true he was a Catholic. At this reply they ordered another three turns of the cord, and after this he was admonished. He said the truth was that he was a Catholic and 'what does your lordship want me to say'. He was admonished to tell the truth. He said that he had told the truth and that if he said anything else it would be with the pain of the torture, and that he had never been to the churches of the heretics and that he had heard many things about them in Melimburg, he had heard say that they were evil heretics and Catholics used to say this and he had no more to say. Then they ordered him removed from the seat and placed on the *burro* and before they removed him he said that he had now been made a heretic from the agonies he suffered and that the many times he had omitted to go to Catholic churches in these islands and in Bruges it had been through his own fault.[21]

While these examples give us some insight into the agony of victims who underwent torture, it should be remembered that the hundreds of cases of people who overcame it demonstrate the relative mildness of inquisitorial procedure. A comparison with the deliberate cruelty and mutilation practised in ordinary secular courts of the time shows the Inquisition in a more favourable light than its detractors have cared to admit. This in conjunction with the relatively high standard of prison conditions makes it clear that the tribunal as a whole had no interest in cruelty and that it attempted at all times to temper justice with merciful treatment.

CHAPTER TEN

THE SPANISH INQUISITION: TRIAL AND CONDEMNATION

Qué maldita canalla!
Muchos murieron quemados,
Y tanto gusto me daba
Verlos arder, que decía,
Atizándoles la llama:
'Perros herejes, ministro
Soy de la Inquisición Santa'.

Calderón, EL SITIO DE BREDA

SINCE the Inquisition usually arrested suspects only after the evidence against them seemed conclusive and had been approved by *calificadores*, the victim was naturally presumed guilty from the start and on him fell the onus of proving his own innocence. The sole task of the Inquisition was to obtain from its prisoner an admission of guilt and a penitential submission. If in the process of enquiry it was found that the evidence was false and the prisoner presumably innocent, he was immediately set free. The main task of the tribunal, however, was to act not as a court of justice but as a disciplinary body called into existence to meet a national emergency. In these circumstances, and considering the standards of justice prevailing at the time, the courts of the Inquisition were fully adequate for their task.

One of the peculiarities of inquisitorial procedure – and one which brought hardship and suffering to many – was the refusal to divulge reasons for arrest, so that prisoners went for days, months and even years without knowing why they were in the cells of the tribunal. Instead of accusing the prisoner, the inquisitors approached him and gave three warnings over a period of weeks, to search his conscience, confess the truth, and trust to the mercy of the tribunal. The third warning was accompanied by information that the prosecutor intended to present an accusation, and that it would be wisest to confess before the charges were laid. The effect of this enforced ignorance was to depress and break down a prisoner. If innocent, he remained bewildered about what to confess, or else confessed crimes the Inquisition was not accusing him of; if guilty, he was left to wonder how much of the truth the Inquisition really knew, and whether it was a trick to force him to confess.

When, after the three warnings, the prosecutor eventually read out the articles of accusation, the accused was required to answer the charges on the spot, with no time or advocate to help him think out his defence. Any reply made in these circumstances could hardly fail to be incriminating. Only after this was permission given to enlist legal help for the defence.

One important concession made by the Spanish Inquisition, and not made by the mediaeval one, was that the accused could have the services of an advocate and a solicitor. This concession was written into the Instructions of 1484 and was generally upheld, though later modifications to the rule sometimes rendered the use of a lawyer farcical. In the earlier years of the Inquisition, accused could choose their lawyers freely, but the growing caution of the Holy Office later confined the choice to special lawyers nominated by the tribunal, so that by the mid-sixteenth century the prisoners' advocates or *abogados de los presos* were recognized as officials of the Inquisition, dependant upon and working with the inquisitors. This new class of lawyers was obviously distrusted by some prisoners, for in 1559 we have the case of a prisoner in Valencia telling his cell-mate that:

though the inquisitor might give him an advocate he would give him no one good but a fellow who would do only what the inquisitor wanted, and if by chance he asked for an advocate or solicitor not of the Inquisition, they would not serve, for if they went contrary to the inquisitor's wishes he would get up some charge of false belief or want of respect and cast them into prison.[1]

This does not mean that many *abogados de los presos* did not do their duty conscientiously. But they were hindered by the restrictions of the tribunal and by the subtle and dangerous task of defending the prisoner while condemning his heresy. Some special cases exist where the accused were allowed counsel of their own choice: one such was Carranza, who chose among others the distinguished canonist Martín de Azpilcueta to defend him.

When a prisoner was finally accused he was given a copy of the evidence against him in order to help him prepare a defence. This publication of the evidence was by no means as helpful as it might seem. In the first place, as we have seen, the names of all witnesses were suppressed. Even more important, all evidence which might help to identify witnesses was also suppressed. This meant that the prisoner was often deprived of any knowledge of the complete case against him. The inquisitors were in this way free to use as evidence information which had not been communicated to the accused. While this helped to protect witnesses against identification and recrimination, it sometimes crippled the defence. On this question the practice of the *Suprema* was not at first decided, but the Instructions of 1561 finally stipulated that any evidence liable to betray a witness could be omitted, and that only evidence contained in the publication was to be used in the case. This last regulation preserved the forms of justice.

The accused had several avenues of defence short of proving the complete falsity of an accusation. He could call favourable witnesses; disable hostile witnesses by proving personal enmity; or object to his judges, a process known as recusation. Several extenuating circumstances such as drunkenness, insanity, extreme youth, and so on, could also be pleaded. All these expedients were resorted to regularly, not always with equal success. In the great majority of trials before the Spanish Inquisition, defence consisted solely in the resort to witnesses, since this was the only way to get at the unknown sources of evidence. The problem caused by anonymous witnesses was a serious one. We have the case of Diego de Uceda, who was accused in 1528 of Lutheranism on the basis of a chance talk with a stranger on the road from Burgos to Córdoba. The suppression of all details of time and place in the published evidence led Uceda to imagine that the accusation arose from a talk some nights later at Guadarrama, and all his energies were spent vainly on proving that this latter conversation had been innocuous, while the real evidence against him went uncontradicted. Uceda decided to call witnesses in his favour: he had to wait six months before they could all be traced, and even then their depositions did not help to contradict the evidence. The resort to favourable witnesses was thus an unreliable and lengthy procedure. Greater success could be had by disabling hostile witnesses. Felipe Leonart, whose case we have already noted,[2] had no difficulty in 1637 in proving that accusations by his family had been made out of malice. Similarly Gaspar Torralba of the village of Vayona, near Chinchón, gave in his defence in 1531 a list of 152 persons as his mortal enemies; most of the thirty-five witnesses against him happened to be on the list, and he was consequently let off lightly.[3] The disabling of witnesses, however, proved possible only when the accused had some idea of his possible denouncers. If, as in the case of Uceda, he had no idea at all, the evidence remained unshaken.

Recusation of judges called for considerable courage, and was therefore not resorted to except where the prisoner could prove their personal enmity. Carranza was one of the few who succeeded in having his judges changed for this reason, though in the event it was of little help to him. Extenuating circumstances were also infrequently adduced. For example, Pedro Ginesta, whom we have met already,[4] cited old age and a failing memory for having forgotten to fast and abstain on St Bartholomew's eve; thanks to this he was set free. Insanity was a more common excuse, difficult to disprove and therefore difficult to verify. The attitude of any tribunal of the period, whether secular or ecclesiastical, towards mental disease could hardly have been enlightened. But the Inquisition at least took extreme precautions and went to great lengths to establish the truth behind any acts of apparent madness. This is best illustrated in the inquisitorial attitude to witchcraft, which was treated as a form of insanity and very mildly punished.

There was no formal trial, in the sense of a single act carried out in a single room within a set period of time. The trial was composed instead of a series of audiences, at which the prosecution and defence made their respective depositions, and a series of interrogations, carried out by the inquisitors in the presence of a notary. When both prosecution and defence had completed their duties the case was held to be concluded, and the time arrived for sentence to be pronounced. For this it was necessary to form a *consulta de fe*, a body consisting of the inquisitors, one representative of the bishop, and a few graduates in theology or law, known as consultors. A vote on the case was taken by this body. According to the Instructions of 1561, if the inquisitors and the episcopal representative agreed, their vote prevailed even against a majority of consultors; but if they disagreed the case was to be referred to the *Suprema*. By the eighteenth century, however, centralization under the *Suprema* meant that few if any important decisions were made by provincial tribunals, and *consultas de fe* ceased to exist because all sentences were passed by the *Suprema* alone.

Such was the basic procedure. But it was of course open to abuse at every stage. The most important drawback from the prisoner's point of view was the impossibility of adequate defence. His advocate's role was limited to drawing up articles of defence which were presented to the judges: beyond this no argument or cross-examination was allowed. This meant that in reality the inquisitors were both judge and jury, both prosecution and defence, and the prisoner's fate depended entirely on the mood and character of the inquisitors. One other drawback that affected most prisoners was the interminable length of trials. The classic case is that of Carranza, but others suffered no less. There is the extreme case of a Mexican priest, Joseph Brunon de Vertiz, who was arrested in 1649, died in prison in 1656 before his trial had even begun, and was eventually tried posthumously, condemned, and burnt in effigy only in 1659. Another example is that of Gabriel Escobar, a cleric in minor orders, who was arrested by the Inquisition of Toledo in 1607 on a charge of Illuminism, and died in prison in 1622 before his trial had finished. These delays took a toll not only of the years and health of a prisoner but also of his sequestrated property, which was retained all this time to pay for any expenses incurred.

Condemnation invariably meant that the victim had to appear in an *auto de fe*. This ceremony was either private for lighter cases, the *auto particular*, or public for heavier offences, the *auto pública*; it is the latter which has become notorious as the *auto de fe*. The penalties enforced by the Inquisition were decreed at each of these ceremonies. As the range of punishment was infinite, it would be helpful to tabulate first the incidence of crimes punished by the Inquisition, and then the incidence of corresponding punishments. A representative sample may be taken from the cases recorded in two distinct periods by the tribunal of Toledo.[5]

Offences

	1575-1610	1648-1794
Judaizers	174	659
Moriscos	190	5
Fornication not considered sinful	264	3
Blasphemy	46	37
Witchcraft	18	100
Heresy	62	3
Solicitation in confession	52	68

In this table the rise in judaizers is really confined only to the second half of the seventeenth century, when Portuguese immigration aggravated the problem. On the face of it, the amusingly disparate figures for those who did not consider fornication wrong, points to a thorough moral reformation brought about by the Inquisition. But the decline more probably shows that the tribunal had ceased to bother about such petty crimes. In the same two periods the punishments meted out by Toledo are as follows:

Punishments

	1575-1610	1648-1794
Reconciliation	207	445
Sanbenito	186	183
Confiscation	185	417
Imprisonment	175	243
Exile from locality	167	566
Scourging	133	92
Galleys	91	98
Relaxation in person	15	8
Relaxation in effigy	18	63
Reprimand	56	467
Acquittals	51	6
Dismissed and suspended	128	104

The number of acquittals, small as they were, meant an improvement on the mediaeval tribunal, which as a rule never acquitted. Outright acquittal, however, meant admitting an error, so the more usual course was to dismiss or suspend the cases of innocent persons. Suspension was more to be feared than welcomed: it meant that the trial could at any time and under any provocation be renewed, and one remained ever thereafter technically under suspicion. From the sentence there was only a limited chance of appeal. In cases that ended in a public *auto de fe*, this was because the accused were not informed of their sentence until they were in the actual procession during the *auto*; by then it was too late to appeal. The delay in delivering a verdict would naturally heighten the suspense, fear and despair felt by prisoners. But when a man was sentenced to be relaxed he was always informed of his fate the night before the ceremony to give him time in which to prepare his soul for confession and repentance. Later in the history of the tribunal this information was given as much as three days in advance. In private *autos* there was much more opportunity to appeal after the sentence had been read out. In such cases the appeal always went to the *Suprema*, appeals to Rome not being encouraged.

The punishment decreed was, from the point of view of the Inquisition, a penance, and this penitential aspect of its procedure must be emphasized. The tribunal devoted its efforts not merely to finding its victims guilty, but to extracting penitential confessions from them. This means that the *auto de fe* was literally an act of faith. It was a public expression of penance for sin and hatred for heresy, and all those who were present in the act were granted an indulgence of forty days. The solemn religious mood of penance and piety that prevailed at an *auto* was responsible time and again for the last-minute conversion of stubborn heretics. There were the many who were converted simply out of fear of being burnt alive, but there were also those who went to their deaths with apparently sincere praises for their new-found faith on their lips. It is because of these that we must take seriously the psychological impact of the atmosphere of an *auto*.

A few words should be said about the less obvious punishments in the list above. Reconciliation, which was the fate of the majority of penitents, was in theory the return of a sinner to the bosom of the Church after due penance had been performed. In practice it was probably the most severe punishment inflicted by the Inquisition, second only in severity to the stake, for at the ceremony of reconciliation each penitent was condemned to one or other of the other punishments in the list, such as confiscation and imprisonment. Confiscation was carried out in virtually all cases, so that even if a prisoner escaped with a prison sentence of a few months he came out an orthodox Catholic indeed, but facing a life of beggary. An additional rule, frequently enforced, was that anyone backsliding after reconciliation was to be treated as a relapsed heretic and so was sent to the stake.

The *sanbenito*, a corrupt form of the words *saco bendito*, was a penitential garment used in the mediaeval Inquisition and taken over by the Spanish one. It was usually a yellow garment with one or two diagonal crosses imposed on it, and penitents were condemned to wear it as a mark of infamy for any period from a few months to life. Those who were to be relaxed at an *auto de fe* had to wear a black *sanbenito* on which were painted flames, demons and other decorative matter. Anyone condemned to wearing the ordinary *sanbenito* had to put it on whenever he went out of doors, a practice by no means popular in the first decades of the Inquisition. The order to wear a *sanbenito* for life should not be taken literally. As with sentences of perpetual imprisonment, the order was invariably commuted to a much shorter period at the discretion of the inquisitor. The chief criticism to be levelled against these garments is not the deliberate shame they were meant to cast on their wearers so much as the policy of perpetuating infamy by hanging them up in the local church *ad perpetuam rei memoriam.*

The imprisonment decreed by the Inquisition could be either for a short term of months and years, or for life, the latter usually being classified as 'perpetual and irremisible'. Neither sentence need involve actual confinement in a prison. By the Instructions of 1488 the inquisitors could at their discretion confine a man to his own house or to some other institution such as a convent or hospital, with the result that very many 'prisoners' served their sentences in moderate comfort. The main reason for this surprising concession was that the tribunals often lacked prison space when their cells were already full, and had to make do with alternatives. Prisoners made the most of this. In 1655 a report on the tribunal of Granada observed that prisoners were allowed out at all hours of the day without restriction, they wandered through the city and its suburbs and amused themselves at friends' houses, returning to their prison only at night; in this way they were given a comfortable lodging-house for which they paid no rent.[6] Another modification to the apparent stringency of inquisitorial decrees is that 'perpetual' imprisonment was almost never enforced. By the seventeenth century a 'perpetual' term rarely involved imprisonment for more than three years, if the prisoner was repentant, and 'irremisible' prison usually meant confinement for about eight years. Despite this the Inquisition continued to decree 'perpetual' sentences, probably because in canon law it was the custom to condemn heretics to life imprisonment. Incongruous sentences such as 'perpetual prison for one year' appear as a matter of course in inquisitorial decrees.

The galleys were a punishment unknown to the mediaeval Inquisition, and devised for the new one by Ferdinand, who thereby found a cheap source of labour without having to resort to open slavery. This punishment was perhaps the most indefensible of any operated by the Spanish Inquisition, but was not frequently used, and victims were never sentenced to any period over ten years, in contrast to secular tribunals which then and later condemned prisoners to the galleys for life. The galleys constituted an economical form of punishment. Tribunals were freed from the duty of maintaining penitents in their prisons, and the state was saved the need to hire rowers at some expense. By the mid-eighteenth century the tribunal had ceased to use the galleys as a punishment.

A more common form of physical punishment was scourging. The use of the lash as chastisement was very old in Christian tradition, but under the Inquisition the punishment became very much more than chastisement. The penitent was usually condemned to be 'whipped through the streets', in which case he had to appear stripped to the waist, often mounted on an ass, and was duly flogged through the streets with the specified amount of strokes by the public executioner. During this journey round the streets, passers-by and children would show their hatred of heresy by hurling stones at the victim. Women were flogged in the same way as men. Nor was there any limit on age, cases on record showing that girls in their teens and women of seventy or eighty were subjected to the same treatment. It was the general rule to prescribe no more than 200 lashes for the accused, and sentences of 100 lashes were very common.

These and other punishments were sometimes decreed separately, sometimes together. At the Granada *auto* on 30 May 1672 Alonso Ribero was sentenced to four years banishment from the locality, six years in the galleys and 100 strokes of the lash, for falsifying documents of the Inquisition; and Francisco de Alarcón was sentenced to five years banishment, five years in the galleys, 200 strokes of the lash, and a money fine, for blasphemy.[7] Other penalties in the canon need little explanation. Exile or banishment from the locality was a common sentence for bad influences. Confiscations were exacted whenever possible. Of the several unusual punishments which at one time or another made their appearance in the Inquisition it is worth noting the one dealt out in the Mexican Inquisition in December 1664 to a penitent who was smeared with honey, then covered with feathers and made to stand in the sun for four hours during an *auto de fe*.

The ultimate penalty was the stake. The execution of heretics was by the fifteenth century such a commonplace of Christendom that the Spanish Inquisition cannot be accused of any innovation in this respect. It had been the practice, hallowed by the mediaeval Inquisition, for Church courts to condemn a heretic and then hand him over, or 'relax' him, to the secular authorities. These were obliged to carry out the sentence of blood which the Holy Office was forbidden by law to carry out. In all this there was no pretence that the Inquisition was not the body directly and fully responsible for the deaths that occurred. It is consequently difficult to understand why apologists for the Inquisition have pretended that the tribunal bore no responsibility at all. Its responsibility was so absolute that contemporaries, like Hernando del Pulgar, were in no doubt that to mitigate the severity of the tribunal they must approach the Inquisitor General and not the secular authorities. Two classes of people alone qualified for the stake – unrepentant heretics and relapsed heretics. The latter class consisted of those who, after being pardoned for a first serious offence, had repeated the offence and were adjudged to have relapsed into heresy. Those who actually died at the stake were only a small proportion of the victims listed in the records as 'relaxed'. These unlucky few were always given the choice between repenting before the *auto de fe* reached its climax, in which case they were 'mercifully' strangled when the flames were lit; or remaining unrepentant, in which case they were roasted alive. The majority of those who were 'relaxed' were in fact burnt in effigy only, either because they had died or because they had saved themselves by flight. In the early years of the Inquisition the large number of victims burnt in effigy is a guide to the volume of refugees escaping from the tribunal.

The proportionately small number of those actually burnt is an effective argument against the legend of a bloodthirsty Inquisition. We shall examine the figures for this later. It is worth emphasizing that the Inquisition usually avoided the extremity of the stake whenever possible. Copious and extensive efforts were regularly made to try and convert stubborn heretics and when the impenitent subject was notified of his impending execution these efforts were redoubled. When one victim was condemned to relaxation in the Seville *auto* of 25 July 1720, 'during the three days prior to the auto all the learning and piety of Seville was enlisted in his conversion, while prayers for his soul were put up in all the churches'.[8] The relative frequency of burnings in the first savage years of the Inquisition disappeared in the eighteenth century, and in the 29 years of the reigns of Charles III and Charles IV only four people were burnt.[9]

The ceremony of an *auto de fe* has a literature all to itself. Among native Spaniards it began its career as a religious act of penitence and justice, and ended it as a public festivity rather like bullfighting or fireworks. To foreigners it always remained a thing of impressive horror and fear. Their journals and letters written while on tour in Spain reveal both amazement and disgust at a practice which was unknown in the rest of Europe. If reminded that the public execution of criminals in other countries was no better than the *auto de fe* they would no doubt have rejected any such comparison, since the one was motivated by 'fanaticism' and the other by 'justice'. Whatever the modern verdict, there is no doubt that *autos* were popular. Accounts, engravings and paintings show us that every function of this sort always had a maximum audience up to the beginning of the eighteenth century. Visitors would throng in from outlying districts when it was announced that an *auto* would be held, and the scene would invariably be set in the biggest square or public place available. The elaborate and impressive staging of the proceedings, depicted clearly in paintings of the period, made for heavy expense and because of this public *autos* were not very frequent. Their frequency depended entirely on the discretion of individual tribunals, which sometimes tried to hold *autos* at least annually. Prisoners were carefully preserved for this most solemn occasion. When enough prisoners had accumulated to make the holding of an *auto* worthwhile a date was fixed for the event and the inquisitors informed the authorities of the municipality and the cathedral. One calendar month before the *auto*, a procession consisting of familiars and notaries of the Inquisition would march through the streets of the town proclaiming the date of the ceremony. In the intervening month all the preparations would have to be made. Orders went out to carpenters and masons to prepare the scaffolding for the occasion, and furniture and decorations were made ready. The evening before the *auto* a special procession took place, known as the procession of the Green Cross, during which familiars and others carried the cross of the Holy Office to the site of the ceremony. All that night prayers and preparations were made, then early next morning mass was celebrated, breakfast was given to all who were to appear in the *auto* (including the condemned), and a procession began which led directly to the square where the *auto* would be held.

There is available a contemporary account of the *auto de fe* held at Toledo on Sunday, 12 February 1486, during which several hundred judaizers were reconciled to the Church. At this early epoch there was little or no emphasis on ceremonial, and the inquisitors were occupied solely with the task of reconciling large numbers of heretics quickly and efficiently.

All the reconciled went in procession, to the number of 750 persons, including both men and women. They went in procession from the church of St. Peter Martyr in the following way. The men were all together in a group, bareheaded and unshod, and since it was extremely cold they were told to wear soles under their feet which were otherwise bare; in their hands were unlit candles. The women were together in a group, their heads uncovered and their faces bare, unshod like the men and with candles. Among all these were many prominent men in high office. With the bitter cold and the dishonour and disgrace they suffered from the great number of spectators (since a great many people from outlying districts had come to see them), they went along howling loudly and weeping and tearing out their hair, no doubt more for the dishonour they were suffering than for any offence they had committed against God. Thus they went in tribulation through the streets along which the Corpus Christi procession goes, until they came to the cathedral. At the door of the church were two chaplains who made the sign of the cross on each one's forehead, saying, 'Receive the sign of the cross, which you denied and lost through being deceived'. Then they went into the church until they arrived at a scaffolding erected by the new gate, and on it were the father inquisitors. Nearby was another scaffolding on which stood an altar at which they said mass and delivered a sermon. After this a notary stood up and began to call each one by name, saying, 'Is *x* here?' The penitent raised his candle and said, 'Yes'. There in public they read all the things in which he had judaized. The same was done for the women. When this was over they were publicly allotted penance and ordered to go in procession for six Fridays, disciplining their body with scourges of hempcord, barebacked, unshod and bareheaded; and they were to fast for those six Fridays. It was also ordered that all the days of their life they were to hold no public office such as *alcalde, alguacil, regidor* or *jurado*, or be public scriveners or messengers, and that those who held these offices were to lose them. And that they were not to become moneychangers, shopkeepers, or grocers or hold any official post whatever. And they were not to wear silk or scarlet or coloured cloths or gold or silver or pearls or coral or any jewels. Nor could they stand as witnesses. And they were ordered that if they relapsed, that is if they fell into the same error again, and resorted to any of the forementioned things, they would be condemned to the fire. And when all this was over they went away at two o'clock in the afternoon.[10]

Two o'clock is the time of the midday meal in Spain. The inquisitors had therefore managed to get through 750 prisoners in one morning. This is a far cry from the dilatory pace, pomp and ceremony of later *autos* which went on well into the night and sometimes were continued the following day, as happened at Logroño in November 1610. The speed at Toledo in 1486 was probably a record, for after the 750 victims in February the tribunal managed to deal with 900 reconciliations on 2 April, 750 on 11 June, and 900 on 10 December, not to speak of two other *autos* on 16 and 17 August when twenty-seven people were burnt.

To contrast with the simplicity and efficiency of *autos* in the first years of the Inquisition a good example is the grandiose *auto* held on 30 June 1680 in the Plaza Mayor of Madrid in the presence of the king and his court. The narratives of the ceremony and the vast canvas of it painted by a contemporary artist give no hint that the splendour of the proceedings took place amid the ruins of Spanish power, at a time of universal misery brought on by bad harvests, deflation, and the spread of plague from the southern coasts of the peninsula.[11] A usefully summarized version of the contemporary narrative of the *auto* was published in London in 1748 and goes as follows.[12]

A Scaffold, fifty Feet in Length, was erected in the Square, which was raised to the same Height with the Balcony made for the King to sit in. At the End, and along the whole Breadth of the Scaffold, at the Right of the King's Balcony, an Amphitheatre was raised, to which they ascend by twenty-five or thirty Steps; and this was appointed for the Council of the Inquisition, and the other Councils of Spain. Above these Steps, and under a Canopy, the Grand Inquisitor's Rostrum was placed so that he was raised much higher than the King's Balcony. At the Left of the Scaffold and Balcony, a second Amphitheatre was erected of the same Extent with the former, for the Criminals to stand in.

A month after Proclamation had been made of the Act of Faith, the Ceremony opened with a Procession,* which proceeded from St. Mary's Church in the following order. The March was preceded by an Hundred Coal Merchants, all arm'd with Pikes and Muskets; these People furnishing the Wood with which the Criminals are burnt. They were followed by Dominicans, before whom a white Cross was carried. Then came the Duke of Medina-Celi, carrying the Standard of the Inquisition. Afterwards was brought forwards a green Cross covered with black Crepe; which was followed by several Grandees and other Persons of Quality, who were Familiars of the Inquisition.† The March was clos'd by Fifty Guards belonging to the Inquisition, clothed with black and white Garments and commanded by the Marquis of Povar, hereditary Protector of the Inquisition. The procession having marched in this Order before the Palace, proceeded afterwards to the Square, where the Standard

---

*This procession took place on the eve, 29 June.

† 'Several' is an understatement. The procession contained no less than 25 grandees, 37 nobles and 23 illustrious persons.

and the Green Cross were placed on the Scaffold, where none but the Dominicans stayed, the rest being retired. These Friars spent Part of the Night in singing of Psalms, and several Masses were celebrated on the Altar from Daybreak to Six in the Morning. An Hour after, the King and Queen of Spain, the Queen-Mother, and all the Ladies of Quality, appeared in the Balconies.

At Eight O'clock the Procession began, in like Manner as the Day before, with the Company of Coal Merchants, who placed themselves on the Left of the King's Balcony, his Guards standing on his Right (the rest of the Balconies and Scaffolds being fill'd by the Embassadors, the Nobility and Gentry). Afterwards came thirty Men, carrying Images made in Pasteboard, as big as Life. Some of these represented those who were dead in Prison, whose Bones were also brought in Trunks, with Flames painted round them; and the rest of the Figures represented those who having escaped the Hands of the Inquisition, were outlawed. These Figures were placed at one End of the Amphitheatre.

After these there came twelve Men and Women, with Ropes about their Necks and Torches in their Hands, with Pasteboard Caps three Feet high, on which their Crimes were written, or represented, in different Manners. These were followed by fifty others, having Torches also in their Hands and cloathed with a yellow Sanbenito or Great Coat without Sleeves, with a large St. Andrew's Cross, of a red Colour, before and behind. These were Criminals who (this being the first Time of their Imprisonment) had repented of their Crimes; these are usually condemned either to some Years Imprisonment or to wear the Sanbenito, which is looked upon to be the greatest Disgrace that can happen to a Family. Each of the Criminals were led by two Familiars of the Inquisition. Next came twenty more Criminals, of both Sexes, who had relapsed thrice into their former Errors and were condemn'd to the Flames. Those who had given some Tokens of Repentance were to be strangled before they were burnt; but for the rest, for having persisted obstinately in their Errors, were to be burnt alive. These wore Linen Sanbenitos, having Devils and Flames painted on them, and Caps after the same Manner: Five or six among them, who were more obstinate than the rest, were gagged to prevent their uttering any blasphemous Tenets. Such as were condemned to die were surrounded, besides the two Familiars, with four or five Monks, who were preparing them for Death as they went along.

These Criminals passed, in the Order above mentioned, under the King's Balcony; and after having walked round the scaffold were placed in the Amphitheatre that stood on the left, and each of them surrounded with the Familiars and Monks who attended them. Some of the Grandees, who were Familiars, seated themselves on two Benches which had been prepared for them at the lowest Part of the other Amphitheatre. The Officers of the supreme Council of the Inquisition, the Inquisitors, the Officers of all the other Councils, and several other Persons of Distinction, both Secular and Regular, all of them on Horseback, with great Solemnity arrived afterwards and placed themselves on the Amphitheatre towards the Right hand, on both Sides the Rostrum in which the Grand Inquisitor was to seat himself. He himself came last of all, in a purple Habit, accompanied by the President of the Council of Castile, when, being seated in his Place, the President withdrew.

They then began to celebrate Mass . . .

About Twelve O'clock they began to read the Sentence of the condemned Criminals. That of the Criminals who died in Prison, or were outlawed, was first read. Their Figures in Pasteboard were carried up into a little Scaffold and put into small Cages made for that Purpose. They then went on to read the Sentences to each Criminal, who thereupon were put into the said Cages one by one in order for all Men to know them. The whole Ceremony lasted till Nine at Night; and when they had finished the Celebration of the Mass the King withdrew and the Criminals who had been condemn'd to be burnt were delivered over to the Secular Arm, and being mounted upon Asses were carried through the Gate called Foncaral, and at Midnight near this Place were all executed.

In this particular *auto de fe* ten people abjured their errors *de levi* (because of a lesser crime) and one abjured *de vehementi* (because of a graver crime), abjuration being the procedure adopted for certain moral crimes and for a suspicion of heresy. The penitent swore to avoid his sin in the future, and if he swore *de vehementi* any relapse from his oath made him liable to the stake on the next occasion. Fifty-six were reconciled, two of whom were reconciled in effigy because they had died in the secret prisons. There were fifty-three relaxations, of which nineteen were in person, including a woman over seventy years old. The procedure at this *auto* represented the the fully developed practice of the Inquisition. It can be seen that the burning of victims was not a part of the principal ceremony and took place instead at a subsidiary one, often outside the city, where the pomp of the main procession was absent. The central features of the *auto* were the procession, the mass, the sermon at the mass, and the reconciliation of sinners. It would be wrong to suppose, as is commonly done, that the burnings were the centrepiece. Burnings may have been a spectacular component of many *autos* but they were the least necessary part of the proceedings and hundreds of *autos* took place without a single faggot being set alight. The phrase *auto de fe* conjures up visions of flames and fanaticism in the mind of the average Protestant reader. A literal translation of the phrase would bring us nearer to the essential truth.

The burning of a judaizer is described in detail in a contemporary narrative by an inquisitor of the *auto* held at Logroño on 24 August 1719. We enter the picture at the stage where the victim is already on the stake and a lighted torch is passed before his face to warn him of what awaits him if he does not repent. Around the judaizer are numbers of religious who

pressed the criminal with greater anxiety and zeal to convert himself. With perfect serenity he said, 'I will convert myself to the faith of Jesus Christ', words which he had not been heard to utter until then. This overjoyed all the religious who began to embrace him with tenderness and gave infinite thanks to God for having opened to them a door for his conversion ... And as he was making his confession of faith a learned religious of the Franciscan Order asked him, 'In what law do you die?' He turned and looked him in the eye and said, 'Father, I have already told you that I die in the faith of Jesus Christ'. This caused great pleasure and joy among all, and the Franciscan, who was kneeling down, arose and embraced the criminal. All the others did the same with great satisfaction, giving thanks for the infinite goodness of God ... At this moment the criminal saw the executioner, who had put his head out from behind the stake, and asked him, 'Why did you call me a dog before?' The executioner replied, 'Because you denied the faith of Jesus Christ; but now that you have confessed, we are brothers, and if I have offended you by what I said, I beg your pardon on my knees'. The criminal forgave him gladly, and the two embraced ... And desirous that the soul which had given so many signs of conversion should not be lost, I went round casually behind the stake to where the executioner was, and gave him the order to strangle him immediately because it was very important not to delay. This he did with great expedition.

When it was certain that he was dead, the executioner was ordered to set fire at the four corners of the pyre to the brushwood and charcoal that had been piled up. He did this at once, and it began to burn on all sides, the flames rising swiftly up the platform and burning the wood and clothing. When the cords binding the criminal has been burnt off he fell through the open trap-door into the pyre and his whole body was reduced to ashes.[13]

The ashes were scattered through the fields or on the river, and with this the heretic, whose conversion had brought him no temporal benefit, passed out of existence though not out of memory, for a *sanbenito* bearing his name would as a rule have been placed in the local church after his death. There was no age limit to victims meant for the stake: women in their eighties and boys in their teens were treated in the same way as any other heretics.

Because of the elaborate ceremony, *autos* often tended to be very costly. In itself this was a reason to dissuade tribunals from holding too many public *autos*. The private version was simpler and cheaper. The costs of a public *auto* varied enormously and it is difficult to say why this was so. A few examples will help. The *auto* held at Logroño on 18 October 1570 cost a total of 37,366 *maravedis*, most of which was spent not on the *auto* but on the east of celebration held after it. This profligate expenditure was criticized by the *Suprema* and the cost of an *auto* held the following year, on 27 December 1571, was cut down to 1,548 *maravedis*.[14] These costs may be compared with those of a larger tribunal, Seville, which in 1600 calculated that each of its *autos* cost over 300 ducats (112,500 *maravedis*).[15] Itemized accounts of the expense on *autos* in the mid-seventeenth century give us an idea of where the money went in a period of rapidly rising prices. First, the tribunal of Seville.[16]

Seville Auto de Fe of 30 January 1624

General expenses	28,076	*maravedis*
Benches, carpets etc.	36,552	
Cloth for *sanbenitos*	17,136	
Candles	23,366	
Advocates for criminals	26,520	
Building of scaffolding	264,724	
Total	396,374	*maravedis*

Seville Auto de Fe of 29 March 1648

General expenses	84,184	*maravedis*
Painting of effigies, and clothing	37,400	

Militia	10,200
Building of scaffolding	351,560
Meals for soldiers and effigy-bearers	21,148
Candles, shawls, hats	82,416
Bringing of accused from Córdoba	68,000
Meals	156,680
Total	811,588 *maravedis*

Even higher than these costs were those run by the tribunal of Córdoba for its *auto* on 3 May 1655.[17] The three largest items were:

Building of scaffolding	644,300 *maravedis*
Benches, cushions etc.	273,326
Meal for tribunal and its ministers	103,258

The total costs came to 2,139,590 *maravedis*, a staggering figure if those we have already cited are anything to go by. Beside this figure the sum of 4,000 ducats (1,500,000 *maravedis*) spent by the tribunal of Majorca on an *auto* in 1675 seems moderate by comparison.[18]

With expenses at this level, the whole business of holding an *auto* would often be a heavy burden, defrayed very seldom by extensive fines and confiscations. Despite this, *autos* were held with remarkable frequency. In the history of the Inquisition there were three main waves of repression, directed principally against conversos, and it was at these times that *autos* were the most frequent. The first wave was from about 1480 to 1490, the second from the 1650s to 1680, and the third from 1720 to 1725; the last two waves were directed mainly against immigrant conversos from Portugal. In between these peaks the local tribunals managed to hold regular *autos* of varying significance. Between 1549 and 1593, a slack period for heretics, the Inquisition of Granada held no less than fifteen *autos de fe*; between 1557 and 1568, another slack period, the tribunal of Murcia held ten *autos*, a rather high average; and in the nine years from 1693 to 1702 the tribunal of Córdoba held seven. Apart from the brief Protestant alarm, the sixteenth century was a period of relative calm, and fewer people were burnt in those years of Spanish greatness than in earlier and later epochs.

By the eighteenth century the lack of victims and the rising cost of public ceremonies meant that *autos de fe* gradually fell into disuse. The new Bourbon king, Philip V, was the first Spanish monarch to refuse to attend an *auto* which was held in 1701 to celebrate his accession to the throne. Later in 1720, however, he assisted at one. Philip's reign saw the end of mass persecution in Spain, and by the second half of the century only private *autos* were in use by the Inquisition. There is no need to attribute this to the growth of tolerance. The simple reason was that heretics had been successfully purged out of existence, so depriving the tribunal of combustible material for its fires.

CHAPTER ELEVEN

SPECIAL SPHERES OF JURISDICTION

Rampart of the Church, pillar of truth, guardian of the faith, treasure of religion, defence against heretics, light against the deceptions of the enemy, touchstone of pure doctrine.

Fray Luis de Granada (on the Inquisition), SERMÓN DE LAS CAÍDAS PÚBLICAS

THOUGH it was created to combat the dangers of heresy alone, the Spanish Inquisition did not long confine itself to this activity. By the beginning of the sixteenth century it had managed to obtain jurisdiction over nearly all crimes which had at one time or another been under the survey of Church courts. The reasons for this extension of inquisitorial powers are easier to explain than to excuse. Once the power of bishops over cases of heresy had been surrendered (in fact though not in theory) to the Holy Office, the episcopal courts began to lose the initiative, simply because the Inquisition extended the term 'heresy' to cover as many other crimes as possible. In this way a tribunal which might easily have been limited in power because its juris-diction extended only over heretics and cases of heresy, became in fact all-powerful because its authority was brought to bear on every aspect of the life of Spaniards.

Very early in its career the Inquisition took direct action against bigamists without the need to ask for special powers of jurisdiction. This was because all crimes against marriage were subject to punishment by both Church and State and were not the prerogative of episcopal courts. At first bigamy was found to occur in conjunction with other heretical practices and was therefore punished as one heresy among others: this occurred in the case of Dionis Ginot, an Aragonese notary, whose effigy was burnt at Saragossa in 1486 both for judaizing practices and for bigamy. But later recorded cases show that the Inquisition was punishing individuals for bigamy pure and simple, and this aroused protests in Catalonia. By the Catalan *Concordia* of 1512 (confirmed by the pope in 1516) it was laid down that bishops alone should try cases of bigamy, unless heresy were involved. This last clause provided the loophole through which the Inquisition slipped. It continued for the rest of its career to pursue bigamists despite the repeated protests of the Cortes of the crown of Aragon in the sixteenth century. The way in which the clause was utilized was quite simple. Since bigamy involved contravening the unique nature of marriage, the culprit was examined on his intentions and prosecuted for holding erroneous ideas about the sacrament of marriage. Erroneous ideas in religion meant heresy. Though several unhappy sinners consequently found themselves condemned as heretics, there were mitigating factors. They were never really penalized as serious heretics, and the punishment they received was usually lighter than they would have received from a secular court. The three young men punished for bigamy in the Granada *auto de fe* of 30 May 1672 were each sentenced to eight or ten years banishment from the region and four or five years in the galleys. Another typical sentence is that on Francisco Fernández, who was for his bigamy sentenced in the Toledo *auto* of 19 March 1721 to 200 lashes and five years in the galleys.[1]

The theological twist given to what might have been a simple moral crime, was the excuse for an unusual invasion of private life. Immorality came to be prosecuted by the Inquisition not because of the actual sin but because of the presumed mental error behind it. As a result a large number of cases brought before the tribunal involved little more than careless and often harmless statements about private morality. Fornication might be committed but it must not be believed in. Yñes de Castro, a widow who denounced herself in 1576 to the Las Palmas tribunal for having said that it was sometimes better to sleep with a virile man who was not her husband than to be married to a man who was decrepit, would have been proceeded against not for immoral intent but for heresy.[3] From this it was an easy step to interfere with private morality even where no heresy existed: Lea cites a case in 1784 where Josef Mas of Valencia was prosecuted for singing an improper song at a dance.

Among the earliest crimes punished by the tribunal was blasphemy. In this it followed the standard practice of the middle ages, by which blasphemy was considered an insult to God, punishable by both the secular and ecclesiastical authorities. The mediaeval Inquisition, however, claimed jurisdiction over cases of blasphemy only where some article of faith was contradicted, since this alone involved heresy. The obvious difficulty in deciding whether individual blasphemies constituted heresy or not, led to several abuses by the Inquisition and corresponding protests from the Cortes of Castile and Aragon in the sixteenth century. The Cortes at Madrid in 1534 asked specifically that cases of blasphemy should be reserved to the secular courts alone. The Inquisition managed to retain control over graver cases of blasphemy, despite all opposition. This did not mean that blasphemy was treated as a major crime, for the inquisitors clearly had a sense of proportion, and most offenders in this category escaped with nominal penalties only. There are several cases where the tribunal dismissed the accused because they understood the circumstances of the outbreak of impious language. In this as in other respects the inquisitors knew what human frailty involved.

The first real concession to the Inquisition of power over questions not connected with faith, was given by pope Julius II in his bull of 14 January 1505.[3] By this the Spanish Inquisition was allowed jurisdiction over cases of usury. This was only a repetition of the powers granted by the pope to the mediaeval Inquisition in 1258 and was therefore not unprecedented, particularly in view of the well-known fact that usury was officially considered a crime by the mediaeval Church. But this extension of jurisdiction in Spain assumed particular significance because the people who had been traditionally detested as usurers and who had inspired the foundation of the Inquisition, were the Jews. The new jurisdiction aroused the protests of the Cortes and of powerful conversos. In 1516 the pope therefore removed usury from the field covered by the Holy Office. But, as with all the other promises of 1516, nothing happened. The Inquisition continued to claim its right to prosecute cases of usury, a claim the Cortes at Monzón in 1533 could not understand, when they complained of the tribunal 'proceeding generally against usurers, although usury in itself does not constitute heresy'.[4] The long struggle over this question only ended in March 1554, when the *Suprema* forbade its tribunals to proceed any more against cases of usury.

The struggle over jurisdiction was as eagerly contested in another moral question – that of sodomy. Homosexuality in the middle ages was treated as the ultimate crime against morality, and the standard definitions of it refer to the 'abominable' or the 'unspeakable' crime. For all this, it was no less prevalent than at any other period in history. The usual punishment was burning alive or, in Spain, castration and stoning to death. Under Ferdinand and Isabella the punishment was changed to burning alive and confiscation of property. Since the old Inquisition had exercised jurisdiction over sodomy the Spanish tribunal seems to have begun to do so, but on 18 October 1509 the *Suprema* ordered that no action was to be taken against homosexuals except when heresy was involved.[5] Here a curious split in policy seems to have occurred, because although the tribunals of Castile never again exercised jurisdiction over sodomy the Inquisition in Aragon now officially adopted powers over this very crime. On 24 February 1524 the pope, Clement VII, issued a brief granting the Inquisition of the realms of Aragon jurisdiction over sodomy, irrespective of the presence or absence of heresy. From this time onwards the Aragonese inquisitors kept their new authority, which they never gave up, despite the typical complaints raised by the Cortes of Monzón in 1533. Aragon was rather unique in this matter, for not even the Roman Inquisition exercised jurisdiction over sodomy. The punishment for all adults over the age of 25 was burning, according to one description of the practice of the tribunal of Saragossa; minors were whipped and sent to the galleys. But the penalty of death was not rigorously enforced by the Inquisition. Even when sentence was passed, it was very often commuted. In this the humaneness and leniency of the Inquisition contrasts sharply with the invariable execution of accused by the secular courts. Special leniency was shown towards clergy who sinned in this matter, and they were as a rule not burnt except after the failure of repeated warnings.

Of all the minor activities of the Holy Office, control over clerical morals was perhaps the most difficult and trying, not only because immorality was always rearing its head among a celibate clergy but also because the task of keeping cases secret and so avoiding scandal was a necessary burden. Sexual lapses among the clergy were even more explicable in Spain than in other countries because of the exceptionally high proportion of priests and friars in the population. What the Inquisition was particularly concerned about, however, was not generally immorality but *de solicitatione ad libidinem in actu confessionis*,[6] or solicitation in the confessional. The confessional-box as we know it today did not come into use in the Church until the late sixteenth century, before which there was no physical barrier between a confessor and the penitent, so that occasions for sin could easily, as they often did, arise. The scandals that arose from the activities of errant clergy due to this, caused Inquisitor General Valdés in 1561 to obtain from Pius IV authority for the Inquisition to exercise control over cases of solicitation, which was interpreted as heresy because it misused the sacrament of penance. In this interpretation lay grave weaknesses. By showing concern over the theological and not the moral aspects of solicitation the Inquisition was forced later on to show leniency to confessors who could prove that any immoral acts of theirs had occurred either before or after the actual confession and so had not violated the sacred character of the confession itself. Besides this, quarrels over jurisdiction and the casuistry of moral theologians limited the effectiveness of inquisitorial action, so that the tribunal can in no sense be said to have succeeded as well here as elsewhere.

The prevalence of witchcraft and sorcery in mediaeval Europe could not for long escape the attention of the Church authorities and in the early fourteenth century pope John XXII issued a series of bulls condemning all traffic with demons and sorcerers. This definition covered not only pacts with the devil but also all the arts connected with astrology and other claims to foretell the future. In 1512 the Cortes of Aragon asked for the further prosecution of sorcery, and the Inquisition of Aragon thereupon assumed jurisdiction over this question, with full papal approval. Aragon was followed by the Inquisition of Castile, which included references to magic and divination in its definitions of heresy. The extensive prevalence of superstitious practices soon overcame any scruples the inquisitors had about whether sorcery could be construed as heresy, and by the mid-sixteenth century the Spanish Inquisition was uncompromising in its pursuit of any individuals who dealt in spells, charms, cures and other magic. The final approval for this campaign came from Sixtus V in his bull *Coeli et terrae* issued in 1585, which condemned all astrology, magic and demonology. The progressive attitude of the papacy and the Inquisition in this matter is worth stressing, because astrology was accepted throughout Europe, in even the most learned circles, as a legitimate science, and the drawing of horoscopes for royal children was a standard practice of the time. Even before the bull of 1585 was issued the Inquisition decided to take firm steps to remove astrology from the strongly favoured position it held at the University of Salamanca. The inquisitor sent to examine the teaching of astrology in the university found that so many lecturers were guilty of teaching the subject in a superstitious way that it would take an unbearable time to punish them all. A start was made with the banning of all astrological writings in the Quiroga Index of 1583. Once again, as Lea points out, 'delinquents were fortunate in having the Inquisition as a judge rather than the secular courts, which everywhere showed themselves merciless where sorcery was concerned'.[7] The sentences passed by the tribunal, varying from a reprimand and abjuration *de levi* to whipping and banishment, confirm this opinion and show that the Inquisition was prepared to be lenient to popular delusions so long as they did not involve active heresy. A typical verdict is that on the three young women, aged between twenty-three and twenty-six years, who were condemned in the Granada *auto de fe* of 30 May 1672 to 100 lashes each and from four to six years banishment from the locality.[8] Persecution could not hope to cure the problem, however, and the Spanish tribunals from 1780 to 1820, that is in their last period, had no less than a total of 469 cases of superstition and sorcery cited before them.[9]

The most shameful of all the crazes to sweep Europe and even America in the sixteenth and seventeenth centuries was the witch-hunt. The communal madness provoked by it led to the death of hundreds of thousands of innocent victims, above all in rural areas, where credulity and superstition had their strongest hold. The total number of so-called witches executed in the seventeenth century in Germany alone has been put as high as 100,000, a figure which is probably four times as great as the number of people burned by the Spanish Inquisition in all its history. For Great Britain alone the figure given is a total of 30,000 victims. Numbers of this sort are problematical. What is instructive is, with judicial murder of such dimensions before us, to compare the fate of witchcraft in Spain, a country which suffered no less from this invidious superstition.

Magic, sorcery and witchcraft had their origins in remote antiquity, but Christendom was not concerned with it on any appreciable scale before the late fifteenth century. It was only in 1484 that pope Innocent VIII issued his bull *Summis desiderantes* which first recognized witchcraft as a disease to be exterminated from the body of Christian Europe. The bull showed particular anxiety about the practice of witchcraft in northern Germany and deputized two German Dominicans, Kramer and Sprenger, to root out the superstition in the provinces of northern and central Germany. Two years later Kramer and Sprenger issued to the world their handbook on the treatment of witchcraft known as the *Malleus Maleficarum*, whose title may be loosely translated as *The Hammer of Witches*. In this superb compilation of case histories and methods of curing them, the Dominicans taught the faithful that far from witchcraft being a delusion it was a practice based on actual commerce with Satan and the powers of darkness, and that witches did in fact eat and devour human children, did in fact copulate with devils, did in fact fly through the air to their meetings or sabbaths, did in fact injure cattle, raise up storms, and conjure down lightning.[10] No book did more in its time to promote belief in a superstition it was allegedly fighting. The point of view of the *Malleus* was supported by the constant decrees issued by popes and bishops in the sixteenth century. When prelates by their condemnation of occult practices implicitly subscribed to the view that these practices had a basis in reality, the faithful could hardly fail to be misled. It is true that there was an important minority opinion in both Italy and Spain, where several bishops considered the talk of flying through the air and copulation with devils to be fantasies and delusions in no way worthy of severe punishment. But in Europe as a whole the witch-craze gained momentum, particularly after it gained the authoritative support of the Protestant reformers. Luther, Melanchthon,

Bullinger, Calvin and others gave their support to persecutions unheard of in Catholic Europe. Calvin in 1545 personally led a campaign in Geneva which executed thirty-one persons for witchcraft. In Great Britain the end of the sixteenth and the beginning of the seventeenth century saw the worst murders. In Scotland witchcraft was virtually unknown before the passing of an Act of Parliament against it in 1563. The preventive created the problem. In the next forty years at least 3,400 Scots were burnt for the crime. In England James I in 1604 passed a statute against witches. The result was the execution of thousands. Under the Commonwealth a witchhunter named Matthew Hopkins made it his business to go round purifying the country. 'The total number of witches executed as a result of Hopkins' activities cannot be estimated even in the vaguest figures. It certainly amounted to several hundreds. It may have run into thousands'.[11] Europe as a whole suffered greater catastrophes. From the fourteenth to the seventeenth centuries one authority 'reckons the victims . . . at millions, and half a million is thought to be a moderate estimate. In Alsace, 134 witches and wizards were burned in 1582 on one occasion, the executions taking place on the 15th, 19th, 24th, and 28th October. Nicholas Remy of Lorraine gathered the materials for his work on the worship of demons, published in 1595, from the trials of some nine hundred persons whom he had sentenced to death in the fifteen years preceding. In 1609, de l'Ancre and his associates are said to have condemned six hundred in the Basque country in four months. The efforts of the bishop of Bamberg from 1622 to 1633 resulted in six hundred executions; the bishop of Wurzburg in about the same period put nine hundred persons to death'.[12] The list is endless but the attention we have given to this phenomenon should serve to make the picture in Spain clearer.

The Spanish authorities at first followed traditional practice in showing severity to witches. The Bible itself commanded that witches should not live. In early cases that arose in Spain, women were consequently burnt. The Saragossa tribunal burnt one in 1498, another in 1499, and three in 1500. In 1507, according to Llorente, the tribunal of Calahorra burnt thirty women for witchcraft.[13] From this time cases of witches were regularly reported. the first such at Toledo being in 1513 and at

Cuenca in 1515. At Cuenca the popular fear was fed by stories of children being found bruised and murdered, 'wherefore it is suspected they were wounded or killed by *xorguinos* and *xorguinas*' (these being the popular words for wizards and witches).[14]

The Inquisition was first moved to take serious action by the outbreak of a witch-craze in Navarre in the late 1520s. A special meeting of inquisitors was called to Granada in 1526 to discuss the problem. Out of the deliberations some significant conclusions arose. Although a majority of the meeting considered the confessions of witches to be actually true, a minority led by the future Inquisitor General Valdés considered that the confessions were little more than delusions; and when it came to deciding on future action, the vast majority favoured a lenient policy, to include the sending of preachers to instruct the ignorant common people of Navarre. The meeting was an opportune one, for in these very years 1527-8 a savage campaign against witches was being carried on by the secular authorities in Navarre, resulting in mass executions by the over-zealous officials concerned. One of the Navarrese inquisitors took a leading part in the campaign and claimed to have been responsible for executing fifty witches whose evil arts could be seen everywhere at work in the valleys: children had been smothered, crops had withered, and acorns had shrivelled up. Views like this continued to prevail and the efforts of the Inquisition to initiate a saner policy did not immediately succeed. It was only in 1530 that the *Suprema* sent a circular letter to all tribunals calling for restraint in their activity against witches.

A curious *cause célèbre* of the period must be noted here. It concerns a famous magician and physician of Cuenca called Eugenio Torralba, who began his strange career during his medical studies at Rome at the beginning of the sixteenth century. While in Rome he met a Dominican friar who offered to introduce him to the occult through a good spirit whose name was Zequiel. The good spirit took to Torralba so well that he soon became permanently attached to him and showed him great secrets of knowledge, science and prophecy. In 1519 Torralba returned to Spain, a simple task since he dispensed with ordinary methods of travel and was merely borne through the air by Zequiel. On at least one occasion, when Torralba in 1520 made a lightning visit to a friendly prelate in Rome who knew that Torralba should at that moment have been in Valladolid, the good doctor came near to giving himself away. In 1525 he became physician to the Queen Mother of Portugal. It was in 1527 that he betrayed himself. Learning through Zequiel that Rome was about to be sacked by the imperial troops on 6 May 1527, he asked the spirit to carry him there to witness the horrifying scene. He left Valladolid at 11 p.m. on the night of the 5 May, and was back by 3 p.m. the next day to tell his friends what he had witnessed. Suspicions were immediately aroused by his knowledge of events that nobody in Spain knew of until very much later. In 1528 the Inquisition of Cuenca ordered his arrest, and on 6 March 1531 Torralba was sentenced to wear a *sanbenito* and be confined in prison for a few years.[15] The punishment was extremely mild for one whose fame as a sorcerer had been so great.

Although cases of witchcraft occurred all over Spain the most intensive epidemics were limited to the mountainous regions near the Pyrenees, both in Navarre and Catalonia, where they assumed monstrous proportions, inculpating whole villages and communities. So vast a problem could not be solved by persecution, and in 1538 the inquisitor Valdeolitas was sent to Navarre with instructions to ignore the general demand of capital punishment for witches, and to explain to the population that phenomena such as the blighting of crops were not caused by witches but by the weather. He was told not to put full credence in the *Malleus Maleficarum*, which was written by a fallible human who could have been misled. Together with this attempt to reduce the panic to a rational basis, the Inquisition was obliged to dispute jurisdiction over prisoners with the secular authorities. Only after 1576 did the *Suprema* manage to secure effective, though not exclusive, control over cases of witchcraft. This victory for inquisitorial jurisdiction was reflected in the treatment of cases after this date. Joana Izquierda, tried before the Toledo tribunal in 1591, confessed to taking part in the ritual murder of a number of children. Sixteen witnesses testified that the children had in fact died suddenly, and that Izquierda was reputed to be a witch. What would in any other European country have earned Izquierda the death sentence, in Spain earned her nothing more than abjuration *de levi* and two hundred lashes.

The next great witch scare occurred in Navarre in 1610, and led to the only retrograde step taken by the Inquisition in this matter. The emotion aroused by the scare swept along with it the inquisitors of Logroño, one of whom, Alonso de Salazar Frias, we shall meet later. A great *auto de fe* was held in the city on Sunday, 7 November 1610, and so lengthy were the proceedings that the ceremony had to be continued into the following day. Of the fifty-three prisoners who took part in the *auto*, twenty-nine were accused of witchcraft and of these five were burnt in effigy and six in person.[16] This extreme measure produced a reaction in the *Suprema*, which in March the next year deputized Alonso de Salazar Frias to visit the relevant districts of Navarre, carrying with him an edict of grace to invite the inhabitants to repudiate their errors. Salazar's mission was to be an epoch-making one. He began work in May 1611 and ended his labours in January 1612 but only on 24 March did he eventually present his report to the *Suprema*. The contents of the report are of profound importance for the history of witchcraft in Spain. During the time of his mission, Salazar declared, he reconciled 1,802 persons: of these, 1,384 were children between the ages of 9 and 12 in the case of girls, and between 9 and 14 in the case of boys; of the others, 'several were old and even senile, over the age of 70 and 80'.[17] After close examination of all the confessions and evidence about murders, witch-sabbaths, and sexual intercourse with devils, Salazar came to his astounding conclusion:

Considering the above with all the Christian attention in my power, I have not found even indications from which to infer that a single act of witchcraft has really occurred. Moreover, my experience leads to the conviction that, of those availing themselves of the edict of grace, three-quarters and more have accused themselves and their accomplices falsely. I further believe that they would freely come to the Inquisition to revoke their confessions if they thought that they would be received kindly without punishment, for I fear that my efforts to induce this have not been properly made known, and I further fear that in my absence the commissioners . . . do not act with due fidelity but with increasing zeal are discovering every hour more witches and sabbaths, in the same way as before.

I also feel certain that under present conditions there is no need of fresh edicts or the prolongation of those existing, but rather that, in the diseased state of the public mind, every agitation of the matter is harmful and increases the evil. I deduce the importance of silence and reserve from the experience that *there were neither witches nor bewitched until they were talked and written about.* This impressed me recently at Olagüe, near Pamplona, where those who confessed stated that the matter started there after Fray Domingo de Sardo came there to preach about these things. So when I went to Valderro, near Roncesvalles, to reconcile some who had confessed, when about to return the *alcades* begged me to go to the Valle de Ahescoa, two leagues distant, not that any witchcraft had been discovered there but only that it might be honoured equally with the other. I only sent there the edict of grace, and eight days after its publication I learned that already there were boys confessing.[18]

This enlightened report stands as a monument to the triumph of reason over superstition. Salazar's system of intelligent enquiry was paralleled by efforts made elsewhere in Europe to get at the truth about witchcraft. It was the eminent physician Harvey who a few years after this disproved the reality of witchcraft to his own satisfaction by dissecting a toad which a reputed witch had claimed to be her demon familiar. On finding that the animal was a common toad and no more Harvey was confirmed in his belief that witches were simply old women suffering from delusions. Yet the belief in witchcraft still had a hold on eminent intellectuals, scientists and divines in Europe, and the toll in lives had not yet come to an end. Only in Spain was the picture different. There the *Suprema* fully supported Salazar's argument, which was confirmed by the speedy disappearance of witchcraft in the districts which the inquisitor had visited. As a result on 31 August 1614 the *Suprema* issued authoritative instructions which were to remain the principal guide to the future policy of the Inquisition. Drawn up in thirty-two articles, the instructions adopted Salazar's scepticism towards the claims of witches, and advised caution and leniency in all investigations. Belated justice was done to the victims of the Logroño *auto* of 1610: their *sanbenitos* were not to be exposed, and no stigma was to attach to them or to their descendants. Although the Inquisition was still obliged to follow European opinion and regard witchcraft as a crime, in practice all testimony to such a crime was rejected as delusion, so that Spain was saved from the ravages of popular witch-hysteria and witch-burnings at a time when it was prevalent all over Europe.

This does not mean that cases of witchcraft disappeared completely. In the Madrid *auto* of 4 July 1632, for instance, no less than eleven of the 44 accused were punished for this crime.[19] But burnings disappeared altogether, and in time accusations of witchcraft also did. There were no cases of witchcraft in the Valladolid tribunal after 1641 and none in the Toledo tribunal after 1648. In their place we get only minor cases of superstition, spells and sorcery: Toledo had 216 such cases in the seventeenth and eighteenth centuries, and Cuenca had 134. They were petty offences. Serious cases of diabolic possession and the usage of witchcraft became infrequent and eventually extinct. The Inquisition can justly take the credit for having stamped out of Spain a superstition which in other countries claimed more victims than any epidemic of religious fanaticism. It is particularly notable that the tribunals of New Castile never in their history burnt a single person for the crime of witchcraft. So rational and beneficial a tribunal may well be expected to have adopted an equally sane attitude in other more mundane matters. That this was not so is clear from the fate meted out to foreigners in Spain.

The foreigners who gave most trouble to the Inquisition were generally traders. While the Spanish authorities welcomed merchants freely, they were anxious to prevent any intercourse between foreign heretics and possible native ones. In addition they took exceptional care to protect the native population from any contact with foreign heresy. Foreign sailors and travellers were therefore obliged to restrain their tongues within the realm and to avoid being found with any illicit publications such as Protestant Bibles. Even when they kept to these rules, however, foreigners were sometimes arrested and thrown into the prisons of the Inquisition. This happened so frequently that Protestant powers trading to Spain made it their primary concern to secure guarantees for their traders before they would proceed any farther with commercial negotiations. England, being a market for Spanish raw materials, secured easier terms than might have been expected. In 1576 the Alba-Cobham agreement settled the position of the Inquisition *vis-à-vis* English sailors. The tribunal was allowed to act against sailors only on the basis of what they did *after* arriving in a Spanish port. Any confiscation was to be confined to the goods of the accused alone, and was not to include the ship and cargo, since these did not usually belong to him. Despite the outbreak of hostilities between England and Spain over the Dutch question, the agreement of 1576 continued to hold good for at least two decades after.[20] When peace eventually came under James I, the agreement was incorporated into the treaty of 1604 which ended hostilities. The guarantee was again renewed after the war of 1624-1630 in article nineteen of the peace treaty of 1630, which promised security to English sailors 'so long as they gave no scandal to others'. The proviso was not to Cromwell's liking. In 1653 he proposed to Spain a treaty of alliance which would have given Englishmen virtual immunity from the Inquisition. The relevant articles would have allowed English subjects to hold religious services openly, to use Bibles freely, to be immune from confiscation of property, and to have some Spanish soil set apart for the burial of English dead. So great was his prestige that the Council of State was quite ready to concede the articles,[21] but the proposal was rejected because of the firm opposition of the *Suprema*, which refused to allow any compromise.

All properly baptized persons, being *ipso facto* Christians and members of the Catholic Church, came under the jurisdiction of the Inquisition. Foreign heretics therefore appeared from time to time in *autos* held in Spain. The burning of Protestants at Seville in the mid-1500s shows a gradual increase in the number of foreigners seized, a natural phenomenon in an international seaport. Of those appearing in the Seville *auto* of April 1562, twenty-one were foreigners and nearly all Frenchmen. The *auto* of 19 April 1564 saw six Flemings relaxed in person, and two other foreigners who abjured *de vehementi*. That of 13 May 1565 saw four foreigners relaxed in effigy, seven reconciled, and three who abjured *de vehementi*. One Scottish Protestant was relaxed at the Toledo *auto* of 9 June 1591, and another, master of the ship *Mary of Grace*, at the *auto* of 19 June 1594. The harvest reaped by the Inquisition was by now greater from foreign Protestants than from natives. In Barcelona from 1552 to 1578 the only relaxations of Protestants were of fifty-one French people. Santiago in the same period punished over forty foreign Protestants. These figures were typical of the rest of Spain. The details given by Schäfer show that up to 1600 the cases of alleged Lutheranism cited before the tribunals of the peninsula come to 1,995, of which 1,640 cases concerned foreigners. 'Harvest' is the right word to use when we come to the plight of foreign merchants whose countries were hostile to Spain. Their crews were arrested, their ships seized and their cargoes confiscated. Of the two Englishmen relaxed at the great Seville *auto* of 12 December 1560, one, Nicholas Burton, was a ship's master whose cargo had been confiscated and whose losses, when added to the other confiscations levied at the *auto*, made up the grand total of £50,000. Such at least was the report, and it certainly pointed to some profit having been made by the Inquisition.[22]

Generalizing from the fact that by the end of the seventeenth century Protestantism made no appearance in the records of *autos de fe*, Lea supposes that the number of foreigners in Spain also diminished and that 'the Inquisition had succeeded in its efforts to limit intercourse between Spain and its neighbours and to isolate it from European civilization'.[23] This is quite a wrong conclusion. In the first place it was not the Inquisition alone that was responsible for Spanish isolation. In the second place, immigration increased as Spain declined. The second half of the seventeenth century saw the greatest volume of French immigration into Castile. Andalucia and the Cadiz hinterland was another focus of foreign traders; and Catalonia absorbed a stream of Frenchmen from across the Pyrenees. The decline in prosecution of foreigners and foreign heretics can be attributed partly to the fact that most of the foreign settlers were Catholics, and partly to the adoption of a more realistic policy by the Inquisition. From 1640 onwards isolation was beginning to crumble, and as the seventeenth century drew to its end there was a greater readiness to compromise with the tenets of the world outside. It is significant that after the long war of the Spanish Succession from 1702 to 1714, when thousands of heretical (Huguenot, English and German) troops had been captured by Spanish forces on Spanish territory, not a single fire was lit by the Inquisition to burn out any heresy that might have entered the country.

The fate of foreigners who fell into the hands of the Holy Office may best be examined in the well documented history of the tribunal in the Canary Islands. The Canaries were a regular port of call for Englishmen not only for direct trade (in wines) but also because they were a convenient halt before the long voyage across the Atlantic to Spanish America and the South

Seas. Between 1586 and 1596 in particular English traders and sailors were subjected to severe persecution by the Spanish authorities, then at war with England. An *auto de fe* held at Las Palmas on 22 July 1587 included for the first time fourteen English seamen, one of whom, George Gaspar of London, was relaxed in person, being the only Englishman ever to suffer death in this tribunal. The next public *auto*, on 1 May 1591, included the burning of the effigies of four English seamen, two of whom had been reconciled in the previous *auto*. The *auto de fe* of 21 December 1597, apparently the last in which Englishmen appeared,[24] included eleven English sailors. This is not, of course, the total number of Englishmen who were captured by the Inquisition. The lists show that from 1574 to 1624 at least forty-four Englishmen were detained in the cells of the Inquisition.[25] And these were only a proportion of the sailors of all nations who hazarded their safety in Spanish ports. The English sailors were particularly vulnerable to the Inquisition because many of them were old enough to have been baptized in the true faith under Queen Mary, and young enough to have conformed without difficulty to the Elizabethan settlement. They were consequently apostates and heretics, and as such not readily forgivable by the tribunal.

Soon, however, a more realistic attitude towards foreigners began to be shown by the Inquisition. When war broke out again in 1624 between England and Spain the resident English were left unmolested, thanks to the inquisitors in the Canaries. Commercial reasons were the main motive behind the anxiety of the authorities not to persecute foreigners unnecessarily, and this moderate attitude seems to have encouraged the traders, for by 1654 the number of Dutch and English residents in Tenerife alone was put at 1500.[26] This happy state of affairs was almost immediately shattered by Cromwell's clumsy aggression against Hispaniola in 1655. The Spanish authorities undertook reprisals against the community of English merchants in the peninsula, who, forewarned of the Hispaniola expedition, got out of the country before the blow fell. Reports from tardy officials in charge of the reprisals were pathetic. In Tenerife the confiscations 'in this island, in Canary, and in La Palma are of small consideration'. In the port of Santa Maria 'there was one Englishman, no more'. In Cadiz only the English Catholics remained. In San Lucar 'they were so forewarned that nothing considerable remains', and 'the majority of them and the richest have sold everything and left with the English fleet'.[27] They eventually came back, as they always did. By that time Protestant merchants had little to fear from the wrath of the Inquisition, which had grown to respect the existence of *bona fide* trading communities where religion counted far less than the annual profit. To this extent the Holy Office was moving out of an intolerant age into a more liberal one.

CHAPTER TWELVE

THE LAST DAYS OF THE CONVERSOS

> The greatest crime held against them was not the sins they had committed but the profits they had acquired.
>
> *Menasseh ben Israel*, ESPERANÇA DE ISRAEL (1650)

WE have seen that the converso community in Spain suffered waves of persecution that eventually died away by about 1730. This recrudescence of persecution shows clearly that they were unable as a body to become assimilated into society. This perennial weakness of the Jewish community contributed to the isolation and destruction of the conversos. More than this, it was a destruction they brought on themselves. The papers of the Inquisition show abundantly that the judaizers were unable to restrain their contempt for the official religion and in a hundred different ways, by phrases and acts which were classified broadly as 'blasphemous', they made obvious their religious hostility and so invited recrimination. The pressures which impelled them to express their feelings in this way can readily be understood in modern times, when racial and religious minorities refuse to accept the demands of an ideologically 'united' state where only one way of life and thought is tolerated. In both cases, however, the repression that follows is inevitable.

The large number of judaizing cases that occurred in the early 1500s marked the end of the generation of Spanish Jews who had some acquaintance with the Mosaic law as taught before 1492. Anyone punished for judaizing in 1532 at the age of fifty years would have been ten years old in 1492, probably just old enough to know the law of Moses and to speak Hebrew. This generation would perhaps have disappeared from the scene by the mid-sixteenth century, so accounting for the absence of persecution in that period. The new generation of children

An eighteenth-century print, by Picart, showing the burning of victims after an *auto de fe*

The tortures of the Inquisition, depicted in another print by Picart

The great *auto de fe* of 1680, held in the Plaza Mayor at Madrid before King Charles II. Detail from the contemporary canvas by Francisco Rizi

would be brought up in quite a different way from their fathers. Even if the parents were judaizers the children would be kept ignorant of Judaism at least up to the age of reason, for fear that a childish indiscretion might betray the whole family. When in 1527 in the town of Atienza, in Guadalajara province, the community of judaizers held a secret memorial service over one of their family the children could not understand the Hebrew prayers made by their elders.[1] Necessary dissimulation meant that most children were brought up as orthodox Christians, and even circumcision was dispensed with, usually for younger children who preferred to run around naked. Prayer books ceased to be used, ceremonies were modified, dogmas were dropped. Native Judaism decayed swiftly and within a generation whole communities had become Catholic in practice, remaining Jewish only in so far as they revered the history of their fathers. Master Salucio, whom we have encountered writing against the *limpieza* statutes, affirmed in the early seventeenth century that judaizers had almost totally disappeared from the realm, 'and although there are signs that some remain, it is undeniable that in general there is no fear or suspicion of them'.[2]

Except for some well organized and secret groups of conversos, native judaizers disappeared from Spain, and with them all the great heritage of Spanish Judaism. It was at this stage that the cycle of persecution reasserted itself. Of the refugees who fled from Spain before and during 1492, a great number went to Portugal, perhaps as many as 120,000 in all, swelling the Jewish community in Portugal to about a fifth of the country's total population. Portugal did not yet have an Inquisition so that the trials now suffered by the Spanish exiles who had gone there were caused by the crown, the clergy and the populace. The permission which had been granted to Jews to reside in Portugal (at the price of nearly a ducat a head) was limited to six months only, after which they were offered the same alternatives of conversion or expulsion. When the time was up the richer Jews bought themselves further toleration but the poorer were not so lucky and many went into exile again, over the sea and across to Africa. The final imposition of conversion on the Jews in Portugal was modified in 1497 by the promise not to persecute conversos for a period of twenty years. Although the crown benefited from tolerating this wealthy minority, communal hatreds were soon stirred and in 1506 Lisbon witnessed the first great massacre of New Christians. Despite such outbreaks, there was little official persecution until about 1530, so that the conversos in Portugal were flourishing undisturbed at precisely the time that their generation was being rooted out in Spain. In 1532 King João III determined to introduce an Inquisition on the Spanish model. The institution of this tribunal was delayed only by the powerful support commanded at Rome by the wealthy New Christians.[3] Eventually in 1540 the Portuguese Inquisition celebrated its first *auto de fe*. But its powers were still not fully defined, thanks to the vacillation of Rome and the enormous bribes offered periodically by the conversos. Only on 16 July 1547 did the pope issue the bull which finally settled the structure of an independent Portuguese Inquisition.

The introduction of a native Inquisition does not by itself explain what we are concerned with – the mass emigration of Portuguese New Christians back into Spain, which for many of them had been the land of their birth. In the three tribunals of the Portuguese Inquisition at Lisbon, Evora and Coimbra there were between 1547 and 1580 only thirty-four *autos de fe*, with 169 relaxations in person, fifty-one in effigy, and 1,998 penitents.[4] This activity, for a country with so large a percentage of Jewish descendants, is obviously restricted when compared to the activity of Spanish tribunals, and indicates that political conditions and political pressure had weakened the hands of the Portuguese inquisitors. The great change occurred only in 1580, when Philip II annexed Portugal and introduced an inquisitorial rigour which would have been possible only in a conquered country. In 1586 the Cardinal Archduke Albert of Austria, who was also governor of Portugal, was named Inquisitor General of the country, with the result that within nineteen years (1581-1600) the three Portuguese tribunals witnessed fifty *autos de fe*, in forty-five of which there was a total of 162 relaxations in person, fifty-nine in effigy, and 2,979 penitents.[5] Small wonder that by the end of the reign of Philip II the Spanish Inquisition was alarmed to discover within Spain the existence of a new threat, this time from the Portuguese who had fled from their own Inquisition.

The new trend is shown by the increase in judaizers at *autos de fe.* The *auto* at Toledo on 9 June 1591, at which the king was present, included twenty-seven judaizers, of whom one was relaxed in person and two in effigy; that at Granada on 27 May 1593 included over seventy-five judaizers; and one at Seville in 1595 included eighty-nine judaizers.[6] As the new century advanced, the preponderance of Portuguese judaizers became clear and undeniable. To take a few examples at random: in the *auto* at Córdoba on 2 December 1625, thirty-nine of the forty-five judaizers penanced were Portuguese, and the four relaxations were all of Portuguese; another *auto* there on 21 December 1627 included fifty-eight judaizers, all of them Portuguese, and Portuguese figured in all the eighteen relaxations, of which five were in person; an *auto* at Madrid on 4 July 1632 showed that seventeen of the forty-four victims were Portuguese, and similarly one at Cuenca on 29 June 1654 showed that eighteen out of fifty-seven were of the same nation; finally, the Córdoba *auto* of 3 May 1655 showed that three out of five judaizers relaxed were Portuguese, also seven out of nine penanced, and that almost all the forty-three reconciled were of the same nationality.[7] The ebb of Castilian Jewry was replaced by a floodtide of Portuguese New Christians who fed the flames and coffers of the Spanish monarchy.

The immigrants brought a new perspective into the life of the Inquisition, which now found that it had to struggle against the royal wish to tolerate such wealthy subjects as the Portuguese. Just after 1602 the Portuguese offered Philip III a gift of 1,860,000 ducats (not to mention enormous gifts to the royal ministers) if the crown would issue a general pardon to judaizers of their nation for all past offences. That the conversos could afford so great a sum is clear from their own admission that they were worth eighty million ducats all told. Royal penury gave way before such a magnificent offer, and application was made to Rome. The papal decree for a pardon was issued on 23 August 1604 and published on 16 January 1605; on the latter date the three Portuguese tribunals released a total of 410 prisoners.[8] By this astonishing agreement the Spanish crown revealed its own financial bankruptcy and its willingness to jettison religious ideals when the profits from a bribe exceeded those from confiscations.

This did not mean any more than a temporary respite in the

work of the Inquisition, which resumed activity in both Portugal and Spain as soon as the terms of the pardon had been worked off. In Portugal particularly the Inquisition resumed work with a thoroughness it had not shown in the old days, and when in 1628 the prelates of Portugal proposed new measures to be enforced against the New Christians, these paid Philip III another handsome sum, probably well over 80,000 ducats, to allow them to leave for Spain. The emigrants, however, left not only for Spain but also for foreign lands of the dispersion, so swelling the numbers of the communities in France, Holland and England. That such emigration was a grave loss to Spain was perfectly obvious to everyone, and it formed the basic problem discussed with the royal minsters by the Portuguese resident in Spain under Philip IV. A memorandum sent to the king by the New Christian merchants claimed that they were the financial mainstay of the crown, since their contribution lay in

sending to the East Indies countless ships laden with merchandise, whose customs duties maintain the navy and enrich the kingdom; supporting Brazil and producing the machinery to obtain sugar for all Europe; maintaining the trade to Angola, Cabo Verde and other colonies from which Your Majesty has obtained so many duties; delivering slaves to the Indies for their service, and journeying and trading from Spain to all the world. Finally, the New Christians are today in Portugal and Castile those who maintain commerce, the farming of the revenues to Your Majesty, and the agreements to supply money outside the realm.[9]

Because of emigration, they claimed, the advantages of their services were being lost and Rouen, Bordeaux, Nantes and Florence were benefiting from it. The Spanish authorities were susceptible to this kind of argument, and to stories that the commercial powers, particularly Holland and, after Cromwell's day, England, were controlled by Jews. The Portuguese merchants must therefore be retained in the peninsula. This became easier after the first state bankruptcy of Philip IV's reign, in 1626: the losses suffered by the Genoese bankers created a vacuum into which Portuguese financiers moved, not without great protests from contemporaries. One of these, the writer Pellicer de Ossau, in 1640 put his objections in this way:

It was thought that the evils brought about by the Genoese financiers could be cured by resorting to the Portuguese, for since they were at the time subjects of the crown to make use of them would also benefit the crown. But this was only to go from bad to worse. For since most of the Portuguese merchants were Jews, fear of the Inquisition made them establish their main trading houses in Flanders and cities of the north, keeping only a few connections in Spain. The result was that far from Spain benefiting, most of the profits went to the Dutch and other heretics.[10]

The Count Duke of Olivares, prime minister of Philip IV, saw matters in quite a different light. He ignored any protests which might interrupt his plans to use Jewish finance to restore the fortunes of the monarchy, and the years of his ministry in Spain were those when converso bankers flourished most.[11] It is significant that the only period in Habsburg Spain when discussions were undertaken by the government with a view to limiting the extreme racialism of *limpieza* and curbing the authority of the Inquisition, was under Olivares. In 1634 and again in 1641 he opened negotiations with the exiled Jews in Africa and the Levant, to persuade them to return to Spain under guarantees which would reverse the evil consequences of their expulsion. The inspiration for such a radical and certainly unpopular policy is difficult to find, and it seems to have contributed eventually to the downfall of Olivares. With him went the end of all hopes to found a truly united Spain: united not in the narrow sense demanding expulsion of all racial and religious minorities, but in the broader sense envisaged in the Union of Arms – a commonwealth of equals, without the provincialism of *fueros* or the sectarianism of race.

1628 is the most important date in the history of the Portuguese financiers. In that year Philip IV granted them freedom to trade and settle without restriction, hoping thereby to win back from foreigners a section of the Indies trade. Thanks to this, the New Christians extended their influence to the principal trading channels of Spain and America. However successful they may have been in business, they could nevertheless not escape the consequences of their racial origin, and several of them had to suffer the rigours of the Inquisition. From the 1630s to the 1680s some of the wealthiest men in Spain were ruined in fame and fortune by the Inquisition. The logic of this persecution is difficult to follow. It is true that by eliminating prominent financiers the crown may have rid itself of creditors and the Inquisition may have gained considerable sequestrations. But the sum total of this policy involved depriving the monarchy of precisely the sources of internal and external credit it required in order to shore up a crumbling financial structure.

Of the several great and small financiers who fell prey to the Inquisition, there will be space to deal with only a few. It is important to remember that after 1640, when Portugal revolted successfully against the Spanish crown, the Portuguese in Spain began to be looked upon as a fifth column in the realm. The unhappy financiers found that in addition to being despised as Jews they were detested as coming from a nation of rebels. With the fall of Olivares in 1643 their last protector had gone. But already before this date a number of them had suffered the tender mercies of the tribunal. We shall deal with these first.

In 1636 the Inquisition brought the financier Manuel Fernández Pinto to trial for judaizing. On one occasion during his career he had lent Philip IV the sum of 100,000 ducats. Now the tribunal extorted from him the enormous sum of 300,000 ducats in confiscations.[12] Even more prominent than Pinto was Juan Núñez Saravía,[13] whom we first meet as contributor with nine other Portuguese financiers to a loan of 2,159,438 ducats made to Philip IV in 1627. In 1630 Saravía was denounced to the Inquisition as a judaizer and protector of judaizers. No action was taken by the tribunal, which continued to accumulate evidence from France and America showing that besides his religious errors Saravía was also guilty of exporting bullion to his co-religionaries abroad and importing base money in its place. Early in 1632 Saravía and his brother Enrique were arrested, and after the usual delays of the Inquisition Juan was finally in 1636 put to mild torture under which he admitted nothing. He was condemned to abjure *de vehementi* and fined 20,000 ducats, appearing with his brother and other judaizers in the Toledo *auto* of 13 December 1637. From men of Saravía's standing the tribunal could expect to make large profits, and besides the fine on Juan it is estimated that his brother Enrique was condemned to confiscations which mounted to over 300,000 ducats. Juan Saravía was no doubt ruined by a case which had destroyed his good name and obliged him to fritter away five years in an inquisitorial prison, for he never makes any further appearance in the number of bankers who served the crown.

After 1640, as we have observed, the Portuguese financiers in Spain were in a difficult position, without a native country and without official support, particularly after the fall of Olivares. The wealthier among them were eliminated one by one. In 1641 a probable relative of Saravía called Diego de Saravía was tried by the Inquisition and suffered the confiscation of 250,000 ducats in gold, silver, and coin.[14] In 1646 the aged financier Manuel Enrique was arrested and condemned, and in 1647 another financier not named in the records was tried at Toledo. The records bring out the close connections between victims. In 1646, for instance, the property of the wealthy financier Esteban Luis Diamante was sequestrated by the Inquisition. Diamante was a colleague in the banking firm of his brothers-in-law Gaspar and Alfonso Rodríguez Pasarino, of whom the latter was in prison accused of judaizing while the former had saved himself by flight. Alfonso had a daughter named Violante who was married to the eminent banker Simon de Fonseca Piña, an astute and wealthy businessman who seems never to have come into conflict with the Holy Office. The property confiscated from the Pasarinos on this occasion probably exceeded 100,000 ducats.[15]

Apart from the wealthy few, there were whole families of ordinary conversos living in Madrid who suffered from the renewal of persecution. The 1650s saw the beginning of wholesale arrests and trials which constituted nothing less than a reign of terror for the Portuguese converso minority in Spain. A contemporary living in Madrid in mid-century supplies us with a dramatic account of facts and rumours about arrests. 'Since last Saturday the Inquisition in Madrid has imprisoned seventeen Portuguese families . . . In the street of the Peromostenses they are hurriedly building a prison big enough to hold all the people that fall every day into the trap. It is said for certain that there is not a Portuguese of high or low degree in Madrid who does not judaize' (18 September 1655). 'On Monday the 13th at midnight the Inquisition seized fourteen Portuguese traders and financiers, in particular two tobacconists. These people sprout like mushrooms' (15 September 1655). 'There is not a single seller of tobacco in Madrid whom the Inquisition hasn't arrested. The other day they took away two entire families, both parents and children. Many others are fleeing to France' (23

October 1655). 'No one trusts the Portuguese financiers any more. They are falling bankrupt and fleeing from the Inquisition. I have been assured that after the *auto* at Cuenca over two hundred families took to flight during the night. That is what fear can do' (22 August 1654). 'In Seville at the beginning of April four wealthy Portuguese merchants were seized at night by the Inquisition' (17 May 1655). 'The Cardosos have fled to Amsterdam, taking 200,000 ducats in wool and 250,000 in gold. It is said this was because the Inquisition wished to arrest them, and so they are in search of a land where one lives in greater freedom than in Spain' (2 June 1655). The wealthy Cardoso brothers, who administered taxes in several provinces, fled because a blackmailer had threatened to testify that they were judaizers unless they paid for silence. Faced with the possibility of having to prove their case against false testimony, 'they preferred to fly from punishment rather than remain in gaol until the truth was established' (29 May 1655). The diarist thought it a serious matter that lying witnesses should be able to ruin the lives of prominent men like these.

The fact is that if it is the practice in the Holy Office, as they say it is, not to punish false witnesses because no one would denounce if they did so, then that is terrible and even inhuman, to leave the life, honour and property of one who may be innocent to the mercy of his enemies. Every day we see many people like this emerging from their travails after great sufferings and years of prison.

The condemnation of judaizers and the flight of wealthy fugitives brought about precisely the situation Olivares had attempted to avoid: bankruptcies among the trading classes of Madrid and other cities, leading to a collapse of confidence in some leading financiers and a consequent contraction in the size of the group of bankers on whom the crown could ultimately rely. Heads continued to roll. 'There has been an *auto* at Cuenca. Brito abjured *de vehementi*; he was condemned to the *sanbenito*, banishment and to pay 6,000 ducats. Montesinos met the same fate, but the fine was higher: 10,000 ducats. Blandon, 4,000. El Pelado, 300 . . . All were from Madrid and had lived years there; very rich men' (8 January 1656). Brito was the financier Francisco Díaz Méndez Brito, who was made to do penance here once, and again later in 1651 found himself imprisoned by the Inquisition. Montesinos was the banker and merchant

Fernando de Montesinos Téllez, a prominent financier who at the age of 66 was imprisoned together with his wife Serafina de Almeida in 1654, by the Inquisition of Cuenca. Serafina was a cousin of the Cortizos family, whom we shall meet presently. Fernando was a man of enormous fortune. His assets at the time of his arrest amounted to 213,721,195 *maravedis* or 567,256 ducats; of this sum a substantial part was tied up in Amsterdam, so that his effective assets were put conservatively at 474,096 ducats. His household goods alone, worth 10,000 ducats, were a testimony to his affluence.[16] Yet the Inquisition penalized the couple only and left the fortune undisturbed. Fernando and Serafina were fined a total of 8,000 ducats. After this 'he went to Amsterdam to live there freely, terrified of being burnt if he returned. He left his sons behind, having given them all his property. It is said that they will send the property over there bit by bit, and then one day do the same as he' (22 November 1656). Montesinos apparently therefore returned to the open practice of Judaism in Amsterdam. But his sons, far from following his example, continued the family's financial services to the crown. The great deflation of 1680 began their ruin as bankers, and by the beginning of the eighteenth century they had gone into liquidation.

The liberal attitude of the Inquisition towards Montesinos' fortune was not dictated by unselfishness. The fact was that so many wealthy financiers were appearing before the tribunal that the government took alarm at the possible threat to the financial stability of Spain. On 7 September 1654 the Council of Finance (Hacienda) came to an agreement with the Inquisition that the latter was to attend only to the personal property of those accused, and that money which was involved in official contracts was to be dealt with by the former. The agreement had the virtue of differentiating between a financier and his firm. As a result we find that the imprisonment of principals such as Fernando Montesinos did not automatically lead to the dissolution of their business.

The *auto de fe* held at Cuenca on 29 June 1654 included among its victims the financier Francisco Coello, administrator of taxes in Málaga.[17] In 1658 Francisco López Pereira, administrator of taxes in Granada, who had once before been tried by the Inquisition of Coimbra in 1651, made another appearance before the tribunal in Spain but had his case suspended. Diego Gómez de Salazar, administrator of the tobacco monopoly in Castile, and a fervent judaizer, was reconciled in the *auto* held at Valladolid on 30 October 1664, and almost all his family suffered condemnation in due course. This list of cases could be prolonged much further. What transpires from the evidence is not only that some of the more important Portuguese financiers were condemned for judaizing, but also that converso finance played a key part in the Spanish economy. Among the most prominent families of converso financiers was that of Cortizos. Manuel Cortizos de Villasante was born in Valladolid of Portuguese parents. His astuteness and financial dealings raised him to the highest ranks in the kingdom, and he had become by the end of his life a knight of the Order of Calatrava, lord of Arrifana, a member of the Council of Finance, and secretary of the Contaduria Mayor de Cuentas, the principal department of the royal treasury. All this occurred at a time when the statutes of *limpieza* were still in full force. Suddenly, after his death in 1650, it was discovered that he had been a secret judaizer and had been buried according to Jewish rites. The discovery would normally have led to the ruin of his family. But their rank and attainments saved them from disaster, and up to the war of the Spanish Succession the Cortizos continued to be prominent in the public service of the crown.

Under Charles II the elimination of financiers went on steadily. In November 1669 Luis Márquez Cardoso, an administrator of the tobacco state monopoly, was reconciled together with his wife in an *auto* at Toledo. They came from a wealthy family which held a position in society comparable to that of the Cortizos. Perhaps the greatest financier of his reign, Francisco Báez Eminente, who controlled the customs duties of Cadiz, Andalucia and Castile, was condemned by the Inquisition in about 1691.[18] This did not affect the house of Eminente, which under his son Juan Francisco Eminente continued to render important services to the royal treasury. Philip V testified in the next century that the Eminentes had served the Habsburgs 'for a period of over forty years, with credit, industry and zeal that were well known'.[19] Another distinguished financier, Simon Ruiz Pesoa, who had supported the monarchy through difficult times, was arrested and his property sequestrated in 1691.[20]

Francisco del Castillo, also a leading Portuguese financier and a native of Ecija, was arrested in Seville in 1694 and his property sequestrated. These cases show that the reigns of the last two Habsburgs were fatal to converso finance in Spain.

Judaizers were the main preoccupation of the Inquisition in the latter half of the seventeenth century, but the intensity of the persecution died away after about 1680, when the last great numbers occur. In the Granada *auto de fe* of 30 May 1672, there were seventy-nine judaizers out of ninety victims, fifty-seven of them being Portuguese; the great Madrid *auto* of 30 June 1680 included 104 judaizers, of whom nearly all were of Portuguese origin; and Córdoba *auto* of 29 September 1684 included thirty-four judaizers among the forty-eight penitents.[21] *Autos de fe* after the 1680s show a definite decline from these numbers, indicating that the first generation of Portuguese conversos had been wiped out as surely as the native conversos had been at the beginning of the century.

A special exception to this decline of persecution must be noted in Majorca, where the burnings erupted only in the second half of the century. Cut off as it was from the mainland, Majorca followed a slightly different development from the rest of Spain. The mediaeval Inquisition had existed there since 1232 and the new tribunal was introduced only in 1488. Even before this, the island suffered from a Jewish problem which paralleled that on the mainland. The great massacres of 1391 were repeated here in riots at Palma in August 1391, and Saint Vincent Ferrer extended his proselytizing activities to the island in 1413. By about 1435 it was reckoned that the whole Jewish population had embraced Christianity, but as in Spain it was found necessary to introduce the Inquisition to root out the doubtful cases. The first *autos de fe* showed the existence of a real problem: in 1489 there were fifty-three relaxations of conversos, most of whom were burnt in effigy as fugitives. On 26 March 1490, after no less than 424 conversos had responded to the terms of clemency offered in an edict of grace, eighty-six conversos were reconciled; and on 31 May 1490 there were thirty-six relaxations and fifty-six reconciliations. Up to September 1531 every person relaxed in the Majorcan Inquisition was Jewish, and the total number of relaxations to that date was 535.[22] By the 1530s the same phenonemon that we have noted for peninsular Spain occurred: the number of converso victims declined sharply and a whole generation of judaizers ceased to exist. Now, however, the Morisco problem took its place, aggravated by the fact that Morisco refugees from Valencia often chose to flee to the Balearic islands. Mass reconciliations of Moriscos occurred in Majorca from the 1530s and the first nine relaxations took place in the *auto* of 10 July 1535. Between 1530 and 1645 there were ninety-nine Moriscos reconciled in Majorca, twenty-seven of them in 1613 alone.[23] The corresponding absence of judaizers is shown by the fact that between 1535 and 1645 only ten people were relaxed, and of these seven were Moriscos. The absence of judaizers at this particular period when they proliferated in Spain, is evidence that the Portuguese emigrants did not make their way to the Balearics in any numbers.

After a lull of well over a century, the storm burst eventually over the converso descendants – the Chuetas – in 1675, when a young man of nineteen years, Alonso López, was burned in the *auto* of 13 January held in La Palma.[24] With him were burnt the effigies of six Portuguese judaizers, indicating that persecution in the Spanish peninsula had at last driven this race out into the Mediterranean. Repercussions from this case led in 1677 to a general arrest of conversos and by 1678 the Inquisition had arrested 237 of them on the charge of complicity in what seems to have been a genuine plot to assert their political and human rights. Now followed two great waves of devastation in 1679 and 1691. In the spring of the former year no less than five *autos de fe* were held in Majorca, with a total of 221 reconciliations. As we have seen, the confiscations made at these *autos* reached a record total of well over 2,500,000 ducats. Crushed by these events the conversos waited ten years before they could stir again. In 1688 some of them led by Onofre Cortes and Rafael Valls attempted to recoup all in a plot which fell through and led directly to the four *autos de fe* held in 1691, at which thirty-seven prisoners were relaxed in person; those reconciled or burnt in effigy increased this figure to a total of eighty-six converso victims. After this great suppression the conversos of Majorca made no further attempt to improve their position. They remained a depressed community subjected to calumny and discrimination, and continued like this into modern times.

Throughout Spain, then, the seventeenth century closed with

a holocaust of conversos. The eighteenth opened with a new dynasty and a new outlook on religion. Philip V seemed to mark the change to a new era by refusing to attend an *auto de fe* held in his honour at the beginning of the reign. With the elimination first of the native judaizers and then of the Portuguese immigrants, it appeared that the converso problem had at last been solved. All this was delusion. Philip V grew to learn that he must live according to the customs of his subjects, and did not after this refuse to attend *autos*. The change of dynasty involved very little change in religious practices, and the persistence of judaizers in Spain was treated with as great severity as in the preceding century. A final wave of repression occurred in the early 1720s. Why it came so late, in a period when several people were beginning to consider persecution unjust, is difficult to say. It is possible that the breakdown of order in the war of the Spanish Succession led to conversos taking greater liberties. One historian claims that the fall of Gibraltar to the English in 1704 gave the Jews a channel of entry into Spain,[25] although it would be more likely that it gave conversos a way *out* of Spain in order to go to London, by now the centre of the wealthiest and most aristocratic Jewish families of Europe. A notable feature of the judaizers of the 1720s is that the majority were Portuguese. Perhaps most of these were of the second generation of immigrants from Portugal, but there may have been some few fresh immigrants who had crossed into Spain in the wake of the Portuguese forces during the war of the Succession.

One of the more famous victims of the persecution in the 1720s was Doctor Diego Zapata, a well-known physician who was born in Murcia in the 1660s, of Portuguese parents. A judaizer from his earliest days, Zapata gave proof of his brilliance during his studies at Valencia and Alcalá. In the early 1690s he was suspected of judaism and imprisoned briefly by the Inquisition of Cuenca, but his case was suspended for lack of evidence. This did not disturb his career. At the turn of the century he became prominent as physician to the Cardinals Portocarrero and Borja and others of similar rank. Later he was inscribed as a member of the progressive Royal Medical Society of Seville. But his activities as a Jew aroused attention and after arrest and torture he eventually appeared in the *auto* held at Cuenca on 14 January 1725, when he abjured *de vehementi*, was condemned to a year in prison and ten years banishment and the loss of half his property.[26] Zapata is important not merely in Jewish history, but also in the history of Spanish thought. He was only one among the many Jewish doctors who were victims of racialism, but among them he was distinguished by his growing hostility to the established medical dogmas of the time. His posthumously published *Ocaso de las formas aristotélicas (Sunset of the Aristotelian forms)*, which appeared in 1745, was a sustained attack on the scholasticism and devotion to Galen which still marked orthodox medicine in Spain.

The judaizers of this period were as severely punished as in earlier times. We fortunately have detailed accounts of all the *autos de fe* carried out at this time, and from them we can arrive at a fairly accurate picture of the toll in lives. Although there were several important *autos* in 1720 in Madrid, Majorca, Granada and Seville the real wave of repression broke out in 1721 and stretched into the late 1720s. The peak years were 1722-3. Over the period 1721 to 1727, according to Lea, sixty-four of the *autos* that took place condemned a total of 824 judaizers, with over 100 other victims.[27] If we take only the judaizing victims in Castile, it is possible to draw up a representative table for the years 1721-5. The number of relaxations (both in person and in effigy) is given in parentheses but is included in the total figures.[28]

	1721	1722	1723	1724	1725
Madrid	14 (5)	11		20 (9)	
Granada	48 (20)	48	108 (12)	38 (21)	27 (7)
Seville	38 (7)	82 (11)	35 (2)	41 (1)	10 (3)
Cuenca	31 (5)	18 (3)	1	8 (6)	10 (8)
Murcia		63 (1)	18 (1)	7 (2)	4
Córdoba	27	13 (4)	25 (8)	34 (8)	
Valladolid		14 (3)	2	5 (4)	5
Toledo		44 (11)	6 (1)		5 (1)
Llerena		17	11 (1)		14

Total: 902 (165)

From this table we can see that within these five years, in nine of the tribunals of Castile, over 900 judaizers were condemned to punishments ranging from burning at the stake for over 160 persons, to the more ordinary penalties of reconciliation and confiscation. To these figures we must add those for the other tribunals of the peninsula. In the years after 1725 the number of *autos* and of victims declined rapidly, and by mid-century the converso community had ceased to be a major religious issue. With this last great persecution the practice of Judaism in Spain crumbled and decayed. Cases were rare in the later eighteenth century, the last one to occur at Toledo being in 1756. Among more than five thousand cases coming before the tribunals between 1780 and 1820 when the Inquisition was suppressed, there were only sixteen cases of judaizing, and of these ten were of foreigners, while the remaining six were prosecuted only on suspicion.[29] The Jews had been to all appearances eliminated from Spain, the last prosecution of their race being the case of Manuel Santiago Vivar at Córdoba in 1818.

The presence of the Jew continued to be felt long after this date. So long as the doctrines of *limpieza* existed in Spain, racial distinction remained an obsession. It was the task of nineteenth century liberals to wipe out the shame of racialism from their country's statute books. The Cortes of Cadiz in 1811 abolished *limpieza* in several fields but the reactionary regime of Ferdinand VII in 1824 reinforced all the old regulations. Not until well into the nineteenth century were Spaniards allowed to take office in their own country regardless of their distant racial antecedents, and the liberal constitutions of the period made it their duty to set this down in writing. It was only under Isabella II in 1865 that *limpieza* was eventually made unnecessary for entry into offices of state.

All this did not mean a relaxation of antisemitism. When in 1797 the finance minister Pedro Varela resurrected the long-forgotten plans of Olivares and attempted to bring the Jews back into Spain, his suggestions were firmly rejected by Charles IV. As late as 1802 the crown was issuing threats against those of its subjects who were shielding Jews from the Inquisition. In 1804 a French Jewish merchant of Bayonne was molested by the tribunal, whereupon the indignant French ambassador intervened to say 'that the exercise of international rights ought not to depend on an arbitrary distinction about the religion in which a man was born and the religious principles he professed'.[30] The struggle continued into the opening decades of the twentieth century, where it merged into problems that are part of contemporary history.

To the new generation of Spaniards, Jews were the dark stain on the history of their country. Their shadow was everywhere present, yet they themselves were extinct. The only surviving memory of them was in the *sanbenitos* which foreign travellers report having seen hung in churches in the peninsula up to well into the nineteenth century. But if the Inquisition could claim to have rid Spain of the Jewish menace it was still partly to blame for the bitter legacy of antisemitism in the country. The political right-wing in nineteenth century Spain adopted the Jew as its prototype enemy, sometimes distinct from and sometimes identified with the freemason. The Jew, who had now become a myth and no more, became identified in certain minds with all that was hostile to the tradition represented by the Inquisition. To be a Jew meant not being a Catholic, therefore not to be a Catholic meant being a Jew: the result of this popular reasoning meant that 'Jews and freemasons', 'Jews and Protestants', and 'Jews and foreigners', became self-explanatory identifications. In the constant struggle waged by the right-wing to preserve Catholic Spain, all that was hostile and sinister became personified in the Jew who was on the other side. But this is a matter of myth, not of history, and does not concern us directly. The aberrations of the nineteenth century found their last heyday in the racist literature circulated in Spain during the Second World War. Gradually but firmly this antisemitic legend is being rejected in modern Spain.

Speculation and curiosity still hang around the issue of Jewish survivals in the nineteenth century. The question was put at its most dramatic by George Borrow during his indefatigable travels with the Bible round western Spain. In 1836 he was riding by night on his ass through Old Castile, when about two leagues before Talavera he fell into conversation with a figure making the same journey on foot. Hardly had a few words been exchanged than

> the man walked on about ten paces, in the same manner as he had previously done; all of a sudden he turned, and taking the bridle of the *burra* gently in his hand, stopped her. I had now a full view of his face and figure, and those huge features and Herculean form still occasionally revisit me in my dreams. I see him standing in the

moonshine, staring me in the face with his deep calm eyes. At last he said—

'Are you then *one of us*?'[31]

In this way, in the middle of the nineteenth century, Borrow came upon one of the few remaining communities of secret Jews in Spain. The incident has been fiercely attacked by writers of all shades of opinion, and there is little doubt that the speeches Borrow puts into the mouth of his new friend Abarbanel verge on fantasy. Yet there seems no reason to doubt that Borrow did meet Spaniards, as he later met an ex-inquisitor, who testified to their personal experience of secret judaizers in the country. Several other travellers bear witness to the same phenomenon. The obvious difficulty is that it is impossible to locate or estimate the number of judaizers living underground. Popular exaggeration would have affected Borrow as much as anyone else. One of his predecessors, Joseph Townsend, reports in 1787 after travelling through the country:

Even to the present day both Mahometans and Jews are thought to be numerous in Spain, the former among the mountains, the latter in all great cities. Their principal disguise is more than common zeal in external conformity to all the precepts of the Church; and the most apparently bigoted, not only of the clergy, but of the inquisitors themselves, are by some persons suspected to be Jews.[32]

Once again, to follow up this enquiry would lead us nowhere. To some extent the existence of crypto-Judaism may be part of the arsenal of antisemitic propaganda, but it seems reasonable to believe that Borrow at least based his conclusions on genuine talks with genuine Jews. Whatever the truth of the matter, the fact remains that Judaism continued to be an issue in Spain long after the last heretic had died at the stake. On the one hand, there was a legacy of suspicion and fear based on antisemitism – the willingness to blame the secret and concealed enemy for all the evils of policy and history. On the other, there was a distinct atmosphere of racialism which has persisted into modern times. On both counts the Inquisition had some part to play and some responsibility to bear in the tragedy of a hunted people.

CHAPTER THIRTEEN

POLITICAL CONFLICT

> There is no vassal free of its power whom it does not treat
> as an immediate subordinate, subjecting him to its mandates,
> censures, fines and prisons; no casual offence or light incivility to
> its servants which it does not avenge and punish as a crime
> against religion.
>
> Report of the Royal Councils, 1696

THE temporal privileges of the Inquisition were quite naturally
subjected to criticism and hostility throughout its career. Since
it possessed remarkable ecclesiastical and political powers the
tribunal came regularly into direct conflict not only with the
government but also with Rome. These quarrels can usually be
described as one concerning jurisdiction, but occasionally certain transcendent principles would be at stake, so elevating a
simple issue of jurisdiction into something much greater. With
Rome the difference can be traced back to the very beginning,
simply because the Inquisition derived its authority from the
pope and was consequently governed by papal regulations.
Complaints against the tribunal could be best dealt with if taken
directly to the fount of authority, the pope. As we have seen,
the conversos did their best both in Castile and in Aragon to
obtain papal decrees to modify the rigour of the Holy Office.
This was a legitimate procedure, since the constitution of the
tribunal allowed appeals to Rome, and Rome was eager to
maintain its rights in the matter, not only to preserve control
over the courts of the Inquisition but also to preserve possible
sources of revenue, since the conversos paid liberally for any
bulls granted by the pope. But the Spanish monarchs, supported
by the inquisitors, refused to take cognizance of papal letters
which openly contradicted the verdict of their courts. Ferdi-

nand's famous letter to Sixtus IV in May 1482 illustrates the firmness of the Spanish attitude. The vacillation of Rome before Spanish claims, and the contradictory policies followed by successive popes, made it possible in the end for the inquisitors to have things their own way. As early as 2 August 1483 Sixtus IV granted to the conversos a bull which revoked to Rome all cases of appeal, but only eleven days later he suspended this, claiming he had been misled. When his successor Innocent VIII tried to pursue a similar policy of issuing papal letters to appellants from Spain, Ferdinand stepped in and issued on 15 December 1484 a pragmatic decreeing death and confiscation for anyone making use of papal letters without royal permission.[1]

Papal policy continued to be intransigent well after this date, and the persistence of jurisdictional conflict is shown by Ferdinand's next decree of 31 August 1509, which in effect renewed the penalties of the 1484 decree. Under Charles V the papacy became more cautious, and Clement VII in 1524 and 1525 renewed the permission it had regularly (in 1483, 1486, 1502, 1507, 1518 and 1523) granted to the Inquisitor General to exercise appellate jurisdiction in place of the pope and to hear appeals which would normally have been directed to the Holy See. This did not mean that Rome had given up the right to hear appeals, and when papal letters again began to be issued Charles V in 1537 reinforced the decree of 1509. On occasion Charles wrote to the pope himself, as in his letter of 4 May 1527 demanding the revocation of a papal brief issued to Luis Alvárez de San Pedro, 'imprisoned by the Holy Office'.[2] This firmness on his part assured a period of tranquillity in relations between Spain and Rome (without of course considering the military differences between the two, and the tragic sack of Rome by imperial troops in 1527), and in 1548 the pope again confirmed his unwillingness to interfere with the independent jurisdiction of the Spanish Inquisition. But under Philip II, and with the accession in 1555 of the bizarre pope Paul IV to the see of Peter, conflicts between the two broke out with increased ferocity. Although Rome did occasionally refer appeals back to Spain,[3] the Inquisition was more usually employed rejecting the claims made by holders of papal letters. This situation continued throughout the seventeenth century. But the Inquisition was not unduly concerned by difficulties with Rome, and even before the end of the sixteenth century we find the secretary of the *Suprema* asserting complacently that the Holy See had abandoned its claim to ultimate jurisdiction over cases tried by the tribunal. Under Philip V the new Bourbon dynasty tolerated no interference by Rome, and so continued the tradition of Philip II. Hostility under Philip V was aggravated by the exigencies of the international situation and by the papal support given to the Archduke Charles, Habsburg pretender to the throne of Spain. In 1705 papal decrees were forbidden in Spain and all appeals to Rome prohibited. This assertion of 'regalism' was supported by most of the bishops and also by the advocate-general Melchor de Macanaz, whom we shall encounter presently, in a famous memorandum in 1713. With the advent of the Bourbons and their new extension of power over the western Mediterranean, in both Spain and Italy, a declining papacy had little opportunity to assert its old jurisdictional claims.

In its relations with the crown the Inquisition was not quite so fortunate. From the beginning the tribunal was so closely allied with and so dependent on the crown that later historians came to regard it as a secular tribunal more than an ecclesiastical one. This argument was adopted especially by Catholic apologists who hoped to disembarrass the Church of an unattractive chapter in ecclesiastical history. There is a *prima facie* case for the argument. The crown had absolute powers of appointment and dismissal of inquisitors, power which Ferdinand employed whenever he felt it necessary. In questions of administration, although decisions were in practice left to inquisitors, the king was kept carefully informed. A letter from Ferdinand to Torquemada, dated 22 July 1486, even shows the king laying down regulations for sixteen detailed and minor points such as the salaries of doorkeepers in the Inquisition; for any other question, he tells Torquemada, 'see to it yourself and do as you think fit'.[4] That the king did exercise control over the Inquisition is shown by the protests of the earlier Cortes of the sixteenth century, which all went to the crown for redress and reform. Ultimately, of course, control rested on the fact that the tribunal was financially dependent on the crown. As we have seen, the Inquisition was never given a financial basis of its own. Most confiscations, for instance, in theory went directly to the king and only indirectly to the tribunal; and for all additional salaries the inquisitors and their employees had to resort to the royal treasury.

Royal control of the Holy Office would have made it an exceptionally useful tool for executing royal policy, but, as Lea shows conclusively,[5] the tribunal was almost never used to further any specific aims of the crown. Now and then it carried out minor functions, and occasionally it became involved in cases of political intrigue, but up to the end of the eighteenth century it was never an instrument of royal despotism. The kings of Spain were wise enough to see that the Inquisition would be more effective and more respected if its autonomy were guaranteed, and if it were not moulded into a docile administrative tool. But one fact remained a threat to non-Castilians and a temptation to the king – that over all the Spanish realms, half of which rejoiced in provincial liberties (*fueros*) which freed them effectively from royal control, the only tribunal to exercise unquestioned authority was the Inquisition, and because of this the crown was obliged to make use of it when all other methods of coercion failed. In 1507, for example, Ferdinand was pursuing one of the members of the Borgia family who had escaped into Navarre and assumed high office under the d'Albret rulers. Failing to secure his victim by any other means, Ferdinand persuaded the Inquisition to initiate proceedings against him for blasphemy, atheism and materialism. But death in battle cheated both the Holy Office and the king of Aragon of their prey.[6] What is surprising is that instances like this are extremely rare in the history of the tribunal. It might have been expected that Charles V would use the Inquisition to prosecute several of the malcontents in the war of the *Comuneros*, but there is no evidence of it acting directly in this matter. For concrete examples of intervention we have to fall back exclusively on periods of disaffection in the *fuero* provinces, when the Holy Office would have been the first convenient weapon to hand. When the revolution of 1640 broke out in Catalonia, for example, it was the Inquisitor General himself who suggested that his tribunal begin proceedings against the rebels.[7] During the war of the Spanish Succession from 1702 to 1714, when once again the provinces of Aragon broke away from Castilian tutelage, it was the Inquisition that threatened ecclesiastical censures against those guilty of treacherous opinions.

An inquisitorial edict of 1706 ordered penitents to denounce confessors who told them in the confessional that Philip V was not rightful king of Spain.[8] These measures were in the realm of threat rather than action. The tribunal rarely took any action which could even remotely be described as political, and it would consequently be quite false to regard it as an instrument of state. Philip II is said to have claimed on one occasion that 'twenty clerics of the Inquisition keep my realms in peace'.[9] This flattering claim, repeated often by the Inquisition itself, certainly referred to nothing more than religious peace, and there was no possible ground on which the tribunal could maintain that it had helped to keep the people of Spain subservient to the crown.

The most important cases in which the Inquisition took part in political events concerned intrigues rather than matters of state, and in each case the intrigue revolved round one particular person. The trial and arrest of Carranza may be viewed in this way, although in his case there were concrete charges of heresy. The first great political case involving the Inquisition was that of Antonio Pérez.

In all its ramifications the history of Antonio Pérez concerns matters of personal, national and international intrigue and rivalry. The story has been told repeatedly, and at last definitively by Gregorio Marañón.[10] In 1571 Pérez became secretary of state to Philip II: two years later his patron and the chief minister of Philip, Ruy Gómez, Prince of Eboli, died. Pérez thereby obtained one of the most powerful posts in the monarchy and also inherited leadership of the court faction formerly led by Ruy Gómez. A contemporary observed that Pérez 'climbed so high that His Majesty would not do anything save what the said Antonio Pérez marked out for him. Whenever His Majesty even went out in his coach, Antonio Pérez went with him. When the pope, my lord Don Juan of Austria, or other lords required anything of the king, they had recourse to Antonio Pérez and by his means obtained what they solicited of His Majesty'. Another said, 'Great men worshipped him; ministers admitted his superiority; the king loved him'.[11] Philip depended for advice and policy almost entirely on this brilliant and sinister young man of converso origin whose success enabled him to live as a great lord and whose charm led him into an intimate and still mysterious liaison with the Princess of Eboli, the beautiful one-eyed widow of Ruy Gómez. Ambition eventually led to Pérez's ruin. At the centre of the monarchy he held the king's secrets and controlled the money offered by pretendants to favours. His long hand stretched as far as Flanders, where at that moment the king's half-brother, the famous Don Juan of Austria, was acting both as governor and as pacifier of rebellion. While claiming to sympathize with Don Juan's moderate policy, and keeping up a correspondence with his secretary Juan de Escobedo, to whom he entrusted several state secrets, Pérez also seems to have opened up negotiations with the Dutch rebels in order to promote his own interests. Eventually rivalry with Escobedo and distrust of Don Juan led Pérez to adopt a hostile attitude towards the two, and he began to influence Philip surreptitiously against his half-brother. Philip's secret jealousy of the martial victor of Lepanto needed no encouragement. Suspicious of the way his plans for Flanders were being blocked by Madrid, Don Juan sent Escobedo to Spain in 1577 to make enquiries. On arriving at the court it became clear to Escobedo that Pérez had been playing a double game with his master and with the king. He began to look around for evidence to condemn the royal secretary. But Pérez had already managed to convince Philip that Escobedo was the malign influence in the affairs of Flanders and in the end he persuaded the king that the only solution was to eliminate Don Juan's secretary. Reasons of state supplied Philip with the necesary moral justification for judicial murder, and he gave his approval to any action Pérez might take. First poison was tried, but this failed. Then on the night of Easter Monday, 31 March 1578, hired assassins came up to Escobedo as he rode with a few friends through the narrow, dark streets of Madrid, and ran him through the body.

Popular rumour instantly pointed to Pérez as the assassin, and Escobedo's family, aided by Pérez's rival in the secretariat of state, Mateo Vázquez, demanded justice for the murdered man. Despite all the rumours, it is interesting to note that Cardinal Gaspar Quiroga, archbishop of Toledo and Inquisitor General, 'did not hesitate to face public opinion by showing an ostentatious liking for Pérez and his group. On the day after the imprisonment of Pérez and La Eboli, when all Madrid singled them out as responsible for the crime, Don Gaspar visited

Antonio's wife and children, and offered money to them, as also to the Princess's children'.[12] The imprisonment did not occur immediately. Philip was torn between covering up for Pérez, which would mean that he had approved of the murder, and punishing Pérez, a course which was even more dangerous because of what the latter was capable of revealing. At this juncture Don Juan died and his state papers were sent to Spain. On reading them Philip discovered that Pérez had deceived him and that his brother and Escobedo were guiltless of the imputations cast against them. Disillusion on the king's part grew into dislike and then into hatred. He encouraged Mateo Vázquez in his attacks on Pérez, and then in 1579 summoned Cardinal Granvelle from abroad to become his chief minister. Pérez sensed the change in Philip's attitude, and prepared for flight. But on the night of 28 July 1579, the very day that Granvelle reached Madrid, Pérez and the Princess of Eboli were arrested.

It was not until June 1584 that the charges against Pérez were drawn up by the prosecutor. In these he was accused of selling posts, receiving bribes, and betraying state secrets. The Escobedo affair was left aside as though it were irrelevant, a sure sign of the king's intervention. The investigation that followed led to Pérez being sentenced to two years' imprisonment and an enormous fine. He was still subjected to mild treatment, however, principally because he had in his possession state papers which incriminated the king. His refusal to surrender the papers led to firmer treatment by the government, and in 1588 an accusation of murder was presented against him. After two years of rigorous imprisonment, in February 1590 he was put to the torture and ordered to state the reasons which had made him advise the king to have Escobedo eliminated. His statement under torture produced an implicit confession of responsibility for Escobedo's death, but gave no concrete reasons for his advice to the king which had led to the assassination. Philip could now ease his conscience with the consideration that Pérez had misled him and therefore bore the sole guilt for the murder. All this time the Cardinal Inquisitor had continued to protect the secretary. He sent Pérez advice, guided the tactics of his defence, kept him informed of proceedings in the royal Council, and knew of and perhaps assisted in his plans of escape to Aragon. Escape had now become necessary since all hope was lost after

Pérez's confession. In April 1590, with the help of several highly placed friends, Pérez escaped from prison in Madrid and rode across country to the borders of Aragon.

There he was protected from the king's hand by the *fueros*. Once he had set foot in Aragon the crown of Castile was powerless to touch him. There was only one course open to Philip – to use the Inquisition to get at Pérez. And it was Quiroga, as Inquisitor General, who was forced to set in motion what Marañón calls the 'last and cruellest prosecution against his former friend'. Safe in Aragon, Pérez was lodged for his own security by the Aragonese authorities in the Justiciar's prison at Saragossa. From this vantage point he began a campaign to win over Aragon to his cause. In Madrid, meanwhile, sentence of death was pronounced against him. Philip's recourse to the Inquisition encountered some difficulty at first, because it was necessary to find Pérez guilty of heresy before charges could be preferred against him. But the royal confessor, Father Chaves, who had seventeen years before taken part in the prosecution of Carranza, and who had repeatedly given Philip his spiritual approval for acts carried out in the name of *raison d'état*, now managed to find evidence of heresy in some of the more innocuous expletives used by Pérez. Of one sentence where Pérez wagered his word against God's nose, Chaves noted: 'This proposition ... is suspect of the Badian heresy which says that God is corporal and has human members'. Such nonsense was supported by other testimony, which ruled that Pérez's assumed intention to escape abroad from prison, in so far as it included a plan to escape across the Protestant state of Béarn, involved heresy because it implied consorting with heretics. Armed with these fabricated accusations, the Inquisition proceeded to move against Pérez.

On 24 May 1591 the inquisitors in Saragossa had Pérez transferred from the Justiciar's prison to their own in the Aljafería, after the Justiciar had been induced to sign a warrant for the removal. By now, however, Pérez's propaganda against the king had made him a popular hero in Saragossa, and no sooner had the news of the inquisitorial action been made known than a vast mob thronged the streets calling for Pérez's release and threatening the authorities. In the ensuing tumult the viceroy of Aragon, the Marquis of Almenara, received wounds from which he died a fortnight later. But Pérez was victoriously returned to the Justiciar's prison by the mob, which 'went all the way calling out, "Liberty!" And he cried out with them'.[13] The May riots were to be repeated in September, when once again the Inquisition claimed jurisdiction over the prisoner and tried to remove him to the Aljafería. After this occasion, when Pérez was set free by the rebels in Saragossa, the whole political situation changed. The Inquisition had failed in its immediate purpose and a viceroy had been murdered by rebels harbouring a fugitive. Philip therefore resorted to armed force. In October 1591 Castilian troops entered Aragon, crushed a rebel army raised in defence of the *fueros*, subdued Saragossa, and executed the Justiciar and other Aragonese nobles. Pérez fled abroad to Béarn, attempted an unsuccessful invasion in 1592, and then went into exile in France and England, still maintaining his campaign against Philip II. What always remained transparently obvious was that there was no truth in the charge of heresy levelled by the Inquisition against Pérez, so much so that in 1607 pope Paul V issued a brief absolving Pérez from these alleged charges. In 1611, the year of Pérez's death in Paris, the papal nuncio there certified that he had lived and died a Catholic.[14]

There is little evidence of the Inquisition being used for political purposes in the seventeenth century. The one outstanding case of Jerónimo de Villanueva, who enjoyed power and influence under Olivares and fell soon after his master, was based on legitimate charges arising out of the illuminism of the nuns of the convent of San Plácido.[15] The prolonged persecution of Fray Froilan Díaz, whom we have discussed already, concerned obscure issues which were neither religious nor political. It is only when we come to the reign of Philip V that we encounter a case which has been described as the last successful prosecution achieved by the Inquisition.[16] This was the case of Melchor de Macanaz.

Macanaz, the first great reformer and the most prolific political writer of Bourbon Spain,[17] has suffered unduly from being classified by Menéndez Pelayo among the great heretics of Spanish history. Entering the royal service in the early 1700s, this energetic and opinionated legist devoted his career to extending and establishing royal power in the peninsula. His opportunity came in 1707 when, as a result of the so-called rebellion of the realms of Aragon, Valencia and Catalonia against Philip V, the crown decided to take the step that Philip II had preferred not to take in 1591, and abolished the *fueros* of Aragon. Encouraged by this, Macanaz, in his capacity as a minister first in Valencia and then in Aragon, proceeded to enforce the royal authority against all local opposition, basing his actions on a theory most conveniently described as 'regalism', which believed in the untrammelled supremacy of the crown. When later in 1713 Macanaz was appointed advocate general of the crown, he was asked by Philip V to draw up a comment-ary on the negotiations then being pursued for resuming diplo-matic relations with the papacy. Relations had been broken off in 1709, because of papal support for the Habsburg pretender during the war of the Spanish Succession. Macanaz obediently wrote a memorandum which was issued to the other members of the Council of Castile in December 1713. This famous docu-ment[18] has been condemned by Menéndez Pelayo as regalist and schismatic. The contents leave no doubt that this is true. It denied Rome any fiscal rights in Spain, no appeals were to go to Rome save through the government, no nuncios were to be allowed if they claimed jurisdiction, ecclesiastical tribunals were to be deprived of all temporal power, and the Church could freely be taxed by the crown. If the memorandum was derogatory to Rome, however, this was only in the Spanish tradition, and there was little novelty in it. Perhaps half, and probably more than half, of the Spanish bishops at this period supported the regalist position. In 1709 the bishop of Córdoba and viceroy of Aragon, Francisco de Solis, had actually pub-lished a schismatic tract entitled *On the abuses of the Roman Court concerning the regal rights of His Catholic Majesty, and the jurisdiction of bishops*.[19] Despite such support for Macanaz, the Inquisition chose to attack him. The Inquisitor General, Cardinal Giudice, had long borne a grudge against Macanaz, who prevented him gaining the archbishopric of Toledo on the death of the previous holder.[20] He now on 31 July 1714 issued a con-demnation of the memorandum. This was followed by a decree of the *Suprema* and by denunciations from the Universities of Salamanca and Alcalá.[21] The king was unwilling to tolerate such pressure on one of his principal ministers and ordered the resignation of Giudice as well as the suspension of all censures against Macanaz. The action of the Inquisition justified any proposals to curb its power. Philip thereupon asked Macanaz and a colleague to examine the archives of the Inquisition with a view to reforming the tribunal and subordinating it completely to the crown. The report which these two drew up in November 1714 was never acted upon, because the tide of political favour was running against Macanaz. The Italian faction at court, led by Giudice and Alberoni, gained a signal victory with the marriage of Philip V to Elizabeth Farnese in December 1714. After this it was only a matter of time before the enemies of the Italians were overthrown, and on 7 February 1715 Macanaz was finally dismissed from power. Ten days later Cardinal Giudice arrived in Madrid to find himself restored to favour and influence. Philip V consented half-heartedly to a reissue of the inquisitorial condemnation of Macanaz, and with this hanging over his head Macanaz was sent hurrying into exile. Like Antonio Pérez, he suffered an inquisitorial sentence which was transparently political in inspiration, and which continued to be the chief barrier against any return to Spain. Between these two men, however, there was an important difference. Pérez played the traitor to his country and wrote scurrilous pamphlets from abroad against the king and the Inquisition. But Macanaz never raised his voice against Spain, and continued to be a fervent supporter of the existence of the Inquisition,[22] claiming that any evils in it arose simply because it was not under royal control. As he wrote from exile to the king's secretary Grimaldo in 1722, his aim in all his writings on the tribunal was 'so that Spain may emerge from the error in which fear of the Inquisition keeps it, since the king has no control over anything the inquisitors do'.[23] Clearly, then, he believed that subjection to the crown would eliminate popular dread of the Inquisition. How valid this reasoning was is highly debatable, but it is interesting to find a supporter of the tribunal admit that it inspired fear in Spain. His other writings on the subject show their tenor by their titles: the two most important are his *The Spanish Inquisition has no superior but God and the King*,[24] and his lengthy and unimaginative *Critical defence of the Inquisition*.[25]

Macanaz's regalist position on the Inquisition was not of course anything new. The question of control over the Inquisition had existed from the very beginning, and was aggravated whenever jurisdictional disputes arose, as they frequently did. Under Ferdinand the Catholic, royal control over the tribunal was unquestioned, and the king successfully disputed control with the pope. Subsequent monarchs did not depart fundamentally from this practice, and although for long periods the Inquisitor General rather than the crown seems to have exercised supreme control over the Inquisition, in the last resort it was the crown that decided questions such as the appointment of officials. This was simply because the crown never lost hold of the vital privilege of appointing and dismissing the Inquisitor General himself. In theory the appointment of the Inquisitor General was always in papal hands and his authority derived directly from the papal delegation of power, so that the king had on the face of things no power to dismiss a papal nominee. But in practice the bull of appointment was invariably given to a person approved by the crown. When it came to dismissing inquisitors, the king tended to choose methods which would not contradict papal authority. Since canon law required a bishop to reside in his see, and the duties of an Inquisitor General made prolonged absences necessary, the two functions could be considered incompatible if no dispensation for non-residence were given. Under Philip III this incompatibility was used as an excuse to be rid first of Inquisitor General Portocarrero in 1599, and then of his immediate successor Fernando Niño de Guevara in 1601.[26] Failing this method, the king could get rid of an Inquisitor General by appealing to the pope, or by putting pressure on him to resign: these courses were necessary when the Inquisitor held no see or else, like Sotomayor in 1632, held a see *in partibus infidelium.*

The Inquisition, as we have seen, was financially dependent on the crown and consequently limited in the initiatives it might care to take. But even before the end of the sixteenth century there were signs that the Inquisition was tending to achieve financial autonomy. This became possible principally through concealment from the crown of the amount brought in by confiscations. In 1560 and 1561 instructions were circulated to inquisitors telling them to suppress all statements of confiscations when making reports to the king, and to inform the *Suprema* only.[27] Not that confiscations were the only source of revenue at

243

this or any other time. But the great rise in the numbers of judaizers prosecuted, particularly after the Portuguese immigration from the end of the sixteenth century onwards, gave confiscations a special importance. How far they increased either the wealth or the freedom of the Inquisition is a matter for conjecture. All that seems probable is that the tribunal had less need to resort to the royal treasury because it had a flourishing income of its own. This relative autonomy, which existed only in the seventeenth century, was destroyed under Philip V, who in 1703 ordered strict control to be exercised over the salaries and expenses of the tribunals, with the result that up to the abolition of the Inquisition it became necessary to obtain a special order countersigned by the *Suprema* to obtain any grant.

The crown also had occasion to intervene in jurisdictional disputes, which proliferated at a local level and regularly came up for discussion at government level. In the majority of cases, these disputes over jurisdiction amounted to little more than an effort by the Inquisition to enforce the privileges which it had gained for itself and its officials, and the struggle revolved most often around the familiars of the tribunal. Since familiars were invariably laymen it was inevitable that criminal and other cases involving them should be claimed by the secular courts. Conflicts arose regularly over this, and it was only in 1518 that Charles V decreed that the cognizance by secular courts of criminal cases concerning familiars and other officials and servants of the Inquisition, was contrary to its privileges. After this ruling the tribunal did not hesitate to protect even the humblest of its employees from the justice of the civil courts, a position which led to further friction and quarrels.

One solution which the Inquisition agreed to was a voluntary limitation of the number of familiars. The *Concordia* of Castile in 1553 was devoted largely to defining the number of familiars and the jurisdiction of the civil courts: in all serious crimes secular justice was to hold good and the Inquisition was limited to the cognizances of petty offences only. Although this *Concordia* remained in force until the end of the Inquisition, it was only partly successful, for disputes continued as before, and neither the secular nor the inquisitorial courts were concerned to observe its stipulation. In the *fuero* provinces the concession of new *Concordias* became more frequent because they were even less observed than in Castile. Although Valencia received a *Concordia* in 1554, by which the number of familiars was reduced and jurisdiction defined, it was found necessary in 1568 to issue a new one reinforcing the clauses of the earlier *Concordia* and adding new rules. Even this was insufficient, to judge by a report of the Council of Aragon on 21 July 1632, which claimed that no peace or safety could be expected in Valencia unless there was a reform in the selection of familiars, since nearly all the crimes committed involved familiars who were sure to escape with impunity, relying as they did on the intervention of their protectors the inquisitors.[28] In Aragon the struggle was even more pronounced because of the great pride taken in their constitutional liberties by the aristocracy of the realm. Here the question of familiars was not resolved till the *Concordia* of 1568, which was the same as that issued in Valencia the same year. As in Valencia, however, the *Concordia* was not enough to pacify the province, and disputes continued as before. It was only after 1646, when the Cortes of Aragon had passed as law measures which restricted the jurisdiction of the Inquisition, that some satisfaction was gained by the secular tribunals of the realm. In Catalonia the situation was comparable, and often worse because of the prevalence of lawlessness and banditry. The temper of the Catalans is revealed in the reception given to the *Concordia* of 1568 when it was proposed for Catalonia. The deputies of Barcelona rejected it out of hand, claiming that it was contrary to their *fueros* and that they were ready to oppose it with their lives. Small wonder that in February 1569 the inquisitors there reported gloomily that the people would not be content until they had driven the Inquisition from the land.[29] Instead of the *Concordia* of 1568 the Catalans now and later based their claims on that of 1512, which the Inquisition had never fully accepted. In this impasse no real agreement was ever reached, despite temporary compromises such as the *Concordia* of 1630 which was named after Inquisitor General Zapata.

The jurisdictional conflicts in the realm were taken seriously by ministers of the crown, and several times in the course of the seventeenth century the Council of Castile urged the king to take action, notably in proceedings in 1620, 1622, 1631 and 1639, when the inquisitors were accused of 'enjoying the privilege of afflicting the soul with censures, life with adversity, and honour with exposure'.[30] It is significant that most of these protests occurred in the reign of Philip IV, and under Olivares, at the very time that an inquisitor had taken it upon himself to question the wisdom of the statutes of *limpieza*. This questioning of the role of the Inquisition was typical of the crisis of conscience prevalent in the mid-seventeenth century. Reformers began to fear that the liberty granted to the Inquisition threatened the proper exercise of royal power. In 1696 under Charles II a famous junta was convoked at which there were present two members each from the Councils of State, of Castile, of Aragon, of Italy, of the Indies, and of the military orders. The report drawn up eventually by this Council on 12 May[31] is the first great regalist attack on the Inquisition before the writings of Macanaz, who could not fail to have been influenced by it. The report begins with an attack on the jurisdictional excesses of the tribunal:

There is no vassal free of its power whom it does not treat as an immediate subordinate, subjecting him to its mandates, censures, fines and prisons; no casual offence or light incivility to its servants which it does not avenge and punish as a crime against religion; not satisfied with exempting the persons and property of its officials from all public taxes and contributions, it even wishes to claim the immunity of not having criminals arrested in its houses; in the style of its letters it uses and affects ways to decrease respect for the royal judges and even respect for the authority of superior magistrates . . .

It then goes on to prove that precedent fully favours complete royal authority over the Inquisition in all matters not pertaining to faith. Although the report was not acted upon, the attitude of Philip V in the subsequent reign made it clear that he wished to subject the tribunal more closely to royal control, and the regalism which was propagated so enthusiastically by Macanaz and others came to be the official policy of the state with regard to the Inquisition. What consequences this had in the later development of the Inquisition we shall soon see.

'Not everyone knows': a comment on the Inquisition by Goya

'For opening his mouth in dissent': a penitent in *sanbenito*, sketched by Goya

A masterpiece of satire: Goya's *Auto de fé*

CHAPTER FOURTEEN

IN DEFENCE OF THE ANCIEN REGIME

> De aquí la perpetuación del odio, no sólo contra la Inqui-
> sición, sino contra la religión misma.
>
> *Jovellanos,* REPRESENTACIÓN A CARLOS IV

IF from its inception the Inquisition had represented the social
and political interests of Reconquest Spain, this did not cease to
be true with the final elimination of Judaism from the peninsula
in the 1720s. The case of Melchor de Macanaz showed that the
tribunal continued as before to identify itself with a clearly out-
dated order of things and that it was in the last resort an enemy
of royal power. But its usefulness as the guardian of the closed
society had not declined, and in this lay its chief justification in
the eyes of the crown, particularly during the Spanish cultural
revolution of the eighteenth century. The Inquisition continued
to maintain its power so long as it would serve the policy of the
governing class in Spain. Now that racial minorities had ceased
to exist and heterodoxy had been wiped out, it only remained to
consolidate the achievements of the past two centuries – to
preserve the purity of Spanish ideas just as the *limpieza* of race
had been preserved. To do this the only remaining weapon, the
only remaining field of inquisitorial activity, was censorship.
The eighteenth century was to witness a curiously inconsistent
relationship between this problem of censorship and the position of the governing class in Spain.

The new Bourbon dynasty which dates from 1700 is frequently
credited with bringing new ways of thought and action into
Spain. That this was not the case is easily proved by the heavy
incidence of persecution during the 1720s, and by Philip V's
unwavering support of the Inquisition's religious policy. The
spectacular failure of Macanaz's campaign to subject the tri-

I 247

bunal to royal control gave it an added lease of life and protected the closed society for another generation. What is surprising is that the first great effort to keep foreign influences out of Spanish territory in the eighteenth century came not from the Inquisition but from the French government. The instructions drawn up by the French government in 1701 for the Marquis de Louville, tutor to Philip V at the beginning of his reign, emphasized that he must 'prevent with all his power the progress of Jansenism, particularly in Naples and the Netherlands, ... (and) prevent any increase in the authority of the pope in Spain'.[1] True to this injunction the first Bourbon maintained a religious policy which, while it saw the extension of some royal rights over the Church, altered nothing fundamental in the position of the Church and the Inquisition in Spain. Despite the change of dynasty in 1700 there was remarkably little discontinuity between the social regime of the last Habsburg and that of the first Bourbon, a fact which helps to explain the undisturbed isolation in which the closed society remained until the middle of the eighteenth century. The dominating position of the noble classes and the consequent imposition of their political system continued to be felt throughout the peninsula. The great lords still controlled the land, their holdings at the end of the eighteenth century being estimated at over half the surface of Spain, while in the peninsula as a whole one estimate is that they exercised direct jurisdiction at the end of the century over fifteen cities, 2,286 towns and over 6,000 villages.[2] In 1710 it was believed that in Castile alone the nobility controlled 500 of the 700 cities and large towns.[3] At the same period Macanaz in Valencia estimated that of the 560 townships in the province 527 were controlled by nobles, and even in the thirty-three under royal control not all the taxation went to the government.[4] These figures are set in focus by the fact that less then eight per cent of the population consisted of nobles.

This stress on the predominance of the nobility is not misplaced. It was their monopoly of power that sustained the closed society, and their abdication of power that led to the opening of Spain's frontiers to Europe. At a time of crisis, as when under Philip IV the aristocracy failed to live up to its status by not aiding the crown in its struggle against revolution in both Catalonia and Portugal, the collapse of the noble estate involved the collapse of confidence in the whole structure of society – and in the Inquisition. Antonio de Mendoza, secretary to one of the royal Councils under Philip IV, observed that 'the Inquisition is trampled under foot and its ministers are discredited, and very many express their discontent openly every day, blaming it on their indisposition'. What was most serious, however, was that 'the nobles, who are today considered safe in blood and in religion, speak disdainfully of it, while those who are suspect in both dare to vent their anger and hate on it'.[5] As it happened, the crisis under Philip IV led to no structural changes in Spanish society. The reverse was true under Philip V. Under him during the war of the Spanish Succession the flower of the ancient nobility of Spain was eliminated: grandees and nobles deserted to the enemy, were exiled, and imprisoned, and in this way the political power of an effete aristocracy was wiped out. For the rest of his reign the king relied on a new noble class that originated in the ranks of the people and owed its position not to hereditary wealth but to royal confidence, and this state of affairs become normal under Bourbon rule. But the old cultural outlook prevailed, just as the old wealth and social preponderance of the aristocracy in Church and State remained undisturbed. Philip V introduced an administrative revolution but was unable to revolutionize the cultural priorities built into the mentality of Spain.

Because of this the Inquisition continued to be the unchallenged guardian of the closed society, and change was slow in coming. Just over a decade after it had condemned Melchor de Macanaz the tribunal reached out against a man who was to become the chief minister of Spain, Joseph del Campillo, an official who, like Macanaz, had risen through the humblest ranks of the royal service. Hearing that the Inquisition of Logroño was about to proceed against him, Campillo in July 1726 wrote to the inquisitor there, protesting against allegations 'that I read prohibited books, communicate with heretics, and hold unorthodox opinions'.[6] Whatever the truth about Campillo (and there is little reason to doubt his orthodoxy) this minor incident of 1726 was a sign of the coming great schism between the ministers of the crown and the tribunal of the Holy Office.

The forerunner and herald of this schism was a Benedictine

monk named Benito Jerónimo Feijóo, who taught theology at Oviedo, spent his spare time reading books (particularly foreign ones), and from 1726 onwards began to publish a series of volumes covering nearly every aspect of human knowledge, under the title of *Teatro crítico universal*. Long before his death in 1764 Feijóo had published nine volumes of the *Teatro crítico*, which were followed by five volumes of *Cartas eruditas*. In 1750 he obtained from Ferdinand VI the official recognition not given him in the previous reign, and his writings were now declared to enjoy royal favour. In the undermining of the closed society Feijóo was to play a pioneer role.

In its culture, as in other important aspects, the state of Spain at the beginning of the eighteenth century is still relatively unknown. It has been maintained that in poetry, prose and the theatre, Spanish literary production was virtually non-existent.[7] The truth seems to be that there were still in existence remnants of a great tradition, which modern scholarship is gradually uncovering. But in the sciences, as Feijóo pointed out, 'while abroad there is progress in physics, anatomy, botany, geography and natural history, we break each other's heads and drown our halls with howls over whether Being is univocal or analogical'.[8] The reason for this decadence, he said, was not merely ignorance and the 'preoccupation against all novelty that exists in Spain'. It was also a false notion of national pride which was nothing less than a hypocritical defence of ignorance.[9] Against this obscurantism of his time Feijóo proposed a completely new attitude. Science should no longer be speculative and bound in by abstract principles. It should be based on experiment, the new highway to the Indies, 'that of *observation* and *experience*'. 'I want experience', he wrote, 'to be preferred to all ratiocination'.[10] Slowly the doctrines of Feijóo were imbibed and accepted by the embryonic intelligentsia in Spain. His medical formulations influenced the Royal Medical Society of Seville, a body which was formed in 1697 and was in 1700 denounced by the University of Seville as being influenced by 'Cartesian doctrines originating in England and Holland'. Despite attacks on the Society, it continued in favour under Charles II and Philip V, and Feijóo was eventually elected as one of its honorary members. The Count of Peñaflorida, who was later to found the societies of *Amigos del País*, wrote to a

Jesuit friend in Toulouse that 'some years ago there appeared an excellent work, excellent above all for a nation in which the sciences are still in the cradle: I speak of the *Teatro crítico* of Father Feijóo'.[11] Despite this growing attention to his labours, little or nothing was done under Philip V, and in 1742 Feijóo was complaining that 'everyone can hear my voice but nearly everyone seems to turn a deaf ear'.[12]

Fortunately for him the Inquisition also turned a deaf ear. Feijóo, however, was under no illusions about the Holy Office, as we can see by a letter of his to a friend in October 1727:

I speak as a Newtonian . . . However, I am far from beating my head uselessly against a brick wall, such as by buying more books, for I consider that I need the little money that is still left for greater necessities. One must also bear in mind that there reigns today an Inquisitor General who is a devotee of antiquity and who, thunderbolt in hand, threatens any book that says anything of the infinite amount we are ignorant of in Spain. Soon after they put him on his throne I received a letter from a priest in the diocese of Teruel, an Asturian and a friend of mine, who told me that this gentleman was very unsympathetic to me. It is true that I also have news of someone in Madrid who reassured him on this matter, and, as it turned out, in this last edict which condemned and corrected eighty books not an iota of mine was touched. But I always have to fear that the suggestions of the infinite number of ignorant individuals may turn him against my books when one least expects it.[13]

His fears were justified, and subsequently his friend and colleague Padre Sarmineto had to revise and alter Feijóo's work to satisfy the censor.

Official recognition by Ferdinand VI established Feijóo, and turned the tide for the new learning in Spain. By 1730 the first volume of the *Teatro crítico* had been reprinted four times, and fifteen editions of the *Teatro* and the *Cartas eruditas* were issued before 1786. The Benedictine monk became in popularity and in prestige the pioneer of the Spanish Enlightenment. The foreign influences he imbibed were transmitted through him to Spanish readers who could read neither English nor French. One of the first contacts made by a Spanish reader with Jean Jacques Rousseau would have been through the reply published by Feijóo in his *Cartas eruditas* to the 1750 discourse on 'Si le rétablissement des sciences et des arts a contribué a épurer les moeurs', which won Rousseau a prize offered by the Academy of Dijon.[14]

The breakthrough out of the closed society was not easily achieved. All the apparatus of the Inquisition was geared to the defence of the traditional verities, and in this task the tribunal found itself new allies in the eighteenth century. In previous times the Society of Jesus in Spain had distinguished itself by its universal outlook and its liberal ideology. It had never identified itself with the Holy Office, and the only Jesuit to become Inquisitor General (Everard Nithard, under the Queen Regent in 1666) was a German who did so against the wishes of the Society. In the eighteenth century, however, the Jesuits found new enemies and therefore new allies. The struggle in France against Jansenism was now, as we have seen by the instructions to Louville, extended to Spain. But Jansenism, defined as belief in the propositions attributed to the circle round the convent of Port-Royal in France, did not exist in Spain at all.[15] What did exist was widespread opposition to the ultramontane and probabilistic theories of the Jesuits, so that in time the opponents of the Society came to be indiscriminately labelled as 'Jansenists' no matter how orthodox they were. The rise of regalism, conflicting as it did with the rights of the pope in Spain, also aroused the hostility of the Jesuits, so that for the rest of the eighteenth century the political and religious conflicts in Spain were inextricably tangled, with (roughly) the Jesuits on one side and the regalists and 'Jansenists' on the other. In this conflict the Inquisition naturally ranged itself with the Jesuits, who had risen to new and unprecedented importance by their monopoly of the post of royal confessor through the long reign of Philip V.[16]

The alliance between the Jesuits and the Inquisition is of more than purely religious interest, for the tribunal ventured directly into the world of politics when it began to prosecute 'Jansenist' partisans in Spain. One of the first great conflicts was over some of the writings of the Italian Augustinian friar Cardinal Noris, which had been approved by Rome but were in 1747 included in the Index published by the Spanish Inquisition, on the direct instigation of the Jesuits. The controversy over this was not settled until 1758, when the pope eventually succeeded in getting the name of Noris removed from the Index.[17] The Noris affair was typical of the growing split in the Spanish clergy between those who supported the Jesuit position and those who believed in the inherent and independent privileges of the Spanish bishops, men such as Climent, bishop of Barcelona, who was denounced to the Inquisition for praising the 'Jansenists'. It was not until 1761, however, that the other split, between the State and the Inquisition, came out into the open. In that year Charles III, patron of the Enlightenment in Spain, exiled the Inquisitor General Quintano from Madrid for having published in Spain without royal approval the papal bull condemning the *Exposition de la doctrine chrétienne* of the anti-Jesuit French priest Mésenguy. From this time the Inquisition was not allowed to publish any papal decrees without royal permission. Once again it was the Jesuits who had forced the issue by their campaign against Mésenguy. In these circumstances it was not surprising that when the government sought out those responsible for the popular riots in Madrid in 1766 against the widely hated Italian minister Squillace, it was the Jesuits who were chosen as the scapegoat. The extent of their alienation from the great forces in Church and State is shown by the fact that forty-six out of the sixty bishops voted for the decree, issued in 1767, to suppress the Society of Jesus and expel its members from the country. With this measure political 'Jansenism' triumphed in Spain.

But for the Inquisition this was only the beginning of another struggle. In 1768 the Count of Campomanes, who had shared responsibility for the expulsion of the Jesuits, claimed that:

the tribunals of the Inquisition today compose the most fanatical body in the State and the one most attached to the Jesuits; the inquisitors profess exactly the same maxims and doctrines; in fine, it is necessary to carry out a reform of the Inquisition.[18]

Such a reform was never carried out. A few limitations were put on its authority, but no radical steps were taken. To many the furore seemed pointless. With the decline in prosecutions for Judaism, and the apparent loss of its political influence, it seemed as though the Inquisition was moribund, powerless to affect the progress of the Enlightenment in Spain. Let sleeping dogs lie, the reformers decided. Charles III, when asked why he did not abolish the tribunal, is reported to have said, 'The Spaniards want it, and it does not bother me'. This optimistic complacency was shattered soon afterwards by the case of Pablo de Olavide.

The fortunes of Olavide, who will concern us presently, must be set against a background of increasing triumphs for the Enlightenment. In the main, these triumphs were the work of an élite – an élite not of the traditional nobility, but of parvenu servants of the State – drawn from the upper classes, so that the split in the ruling class foreshadowed under Philip V bore fruit at last in the second half of the eighteenth century. While the mass of the nobility continued to be decadent, ignorant and uncultured, unwilling to work or to be of any service to the nation whose natural leaders they were, there remained a cultural and enlightened minority among them, devoted to the Catholic faith and to the Spanish tradition but anxious to learn from other peoples and fired by what Sarrailh describes as an *ivresse de savoir*.[19] The inspiration of this élite came first of all from abroad. The literature of new ideas from across the frontiers began to trickle into Spain, through ports and customs barriers and police controls. Wherever a foreign ship touched Spanish soil, in Vigo or in Seville, a book could get through. Already by the end of the reign of Charles II the works of the philosophers of Europe could be obtained in Spain. When in 1691 the Inquisition of Seville arrested a cleric in minor orders, Juan Cruzado de la Cruz, they found in his possession a vast library of 1,125 books. Among these books were works in French, Italian, English and Dutch. The library included a volume of the works of Francis Bacon; the works of Bartolomé de las Casas; the letters, *Colloquies*, and *Enchiridion* of Erasmus; two works by Descartes; six volumes of Gassendi; Grotius' *Mare liberum*; the letters of Balzac; Hobbes' *Elements of Philosophy* in French; and numerous other volumes showing a distinct interest in the kind of literature prohibited by the Inquisition and available freely only outside Spain.[20] Long before the advent of the Bourbons, then, the outside world had been infiltrating into the country. This development was welcomed by individuals here and there in Spain, but for a long time no official encouragement was forthcoming.

In 1739 we find Feijóo complaining, 'The immense delay in the books from France is causing me much trouble'. He had nothing but contempt for those who spoke 'with affected emphasis of the infected air of the north, which is the usual refrain in such matters; whereas it is admirably suited for en-lightening many good Catholics as well as ignorant Catholics'.[21] It was from the north, from France, that books and men came into Spain; and not only from France. Under Ferdinand VI and his successor the maintenance of cultural and scientific links with England, Sweden and other countries was encouraged and extended. Technical and philosophical literature of every kind was introduced and adopted in Spain. There was an even more startling departure from tradition: Spaniards went abroad. As in contemporary England, the 'grand tour' was now performed by young Spanish noblemen. The Count of Peñaflorida studied in Toulouse and sent his son there after him, and then on to Paris, the Netherlands, Scandinavia, Germany and Italy. The distinguished writer José Cadalso went to England, France and Italy.[22] Perhaps those who did most to undermine the structure of official thought in Spain were the noble ambassadors abroad: the Count of Aranda, friend of Voltaire and envoy to Versailles from 1773 to 1787; the Duke of Alba, friend of Rousseau and likewise envoy to Versailles, from 1746 to 1749; the Duke of Almodóvar, translator of the Abbé Raynal and envoy in turn to Russia, Portugal and England. By their admiration of foreign achievements and the use they made of their official positions to propagate the Enlightenment, these nobles split the defences of the governing class and opened the way to revolutionary innova-tions that toppled the *ancien régime* in Spain.

The great pioneers of the new reform movement in Spain, men who were consciously influenced by foreign culture but who were never divorced from the immediate reality of Spanish problems, were Melchor Jovellanos and the Count of Campo-manes. The reforming party also consisted, however, of men who by their nature and upbringing were alien to the Spanish tradition: of these one was Olavide.

Brought up in Peru, and an emigrant to Europe in 1752, Pablo de Olavide lived in Spain but spent all his most formative years in France, whose thought and culture he adopted to the exclu-sion of all else. Even his reading was virtually only in French, and in 1776 the Inquisition found that his lodgings in Madrid contained only two Spanish books in a collection of about thirty. It was this young man who, in the wake of the reformist victory that followed the Squillace riots, obtained for himself a post in the Madrid administration and was later in 1767 transferred to the exalted position of intendant of Seville and Andalucia. While he was at Seville the government in 1769 accepted a plan for educational reform drawn up by him. This led to the administrative order of 1770 reforming the syllabuses of all the Spanish universities. This important measure was the beginning of a great revolution in Spanish higher education but Olavide was not able to witness it. His already difficult administrative duties in Andalucia had been made worse by the failure of a plan entrusted to him to colonize the Sierra Morena with foreign settlers, and differences with a German Capuchin (an adviser on the German colony) who in 1775 denounced him as 'the most dangerous intellectual in Spain'[23] led eventually to his recall to Madrid and his arrest by the Inquisition in November 1776. The charge was heresy and atheism. A popular song of the time accused him of being everything but a Christian:

> Olavide es luterano,
> es francmasón, ateísta,
> es gentil, es calvinista,
> es judío, es arriano,
> es Maquiavelo, ¿es cristiano?
> Esta cuestión ventilada
> y a un tribunal reservada
> resuelve que aqueste voto
> de todito tiene un poco
> pero de cristiano nada.*[24]

True to inquisitorial practice, Olavide now vanished completely from the face of the earth for two years, and none of his friends knew where he might be or whether he was even alive. It was only on 24 November 1778 that he was brought out to an *auto de fe* held behind locked doors, in the presence of about forty specially invited dignitaries. When during the reading of the sentence Olavide heard himself pronounced a 'formal heretic', he cried out 'No, not that!' and fainted. The sentence passed on him was banishment, and confinement for eight years in a monastery. The ceremony so affected those present that a few

* Olavide is a Lutheran, a freemason, an atheist, a gentile, a Calvinist, a Jew, an Arian, a Machiavel, but is he a Christian? This question was raised and it was resolved by a secret tribunal that he is a bit of everything but not a bit a Christian.

days later one of them, an intimate friend of Olavide, denounced himself for having read Hobbes, Spinoza, Bayle, Voltaire, Diderot, d'Alembert and Rousseau. But the Inquisition refused to absolve him until he had denounced all his accomplices. The final denunciation received by the tribunal therefore contained the names of nearly everyone in the government, including Aranda, Campomanes and Floridablanca.[25] The Holy Office dropped the matter.

Olavide was singled out for prosecution simply to set an example to others, and not because he was the worst offender. It was well known that others, even more highly placed than he, were friendly with the French philosophers and had read their books. Olavide was a warning, and the lesson did not go unheeded. Throughout Spain and abroad in Europe the noise of his condemnation aroused fears that the Inquisition had returned to its old position of power. In Rome the Spanish envoy to the Holy See, Nicolás de Azara, wrote home, 'Is it still possible to witness things such as Olavide has just suffered? I am no friend of his, but humanity makes me weep tears of blood.'[26]

In the literary equipment of Olavide we can study the weapons of the Enlightenment against which the Inquisition was exerting its full powers. His personal library contained an enormous number of French books, many of them on the Index and therefore forbidden in Spain. Among these were all the works of Voltaire; several by Rousseau; Bayle's *Dictionnaire*; the *Encyclopédie*, and so on. The English authors in his collection, all in French translation, were Bacon, Locke, Pope, Defoe (*Crusoe*), Fielding (*Tom Jones* and *Joseph Andrews*), Richardson (*Pamela*), Swift and Smollett.[27] Of these only Fielding, Richardson and Smollett were not on the Index. The necessity of reading such books was accepted without question by the élite in Spain, as the only way to rational knowledge, a way long neglected by the universities. When the plan for syllabus reform initiated by Olavide was presented to Salamanca university in 1770, it refused to co-operate, protesting that all modern philosophers were dangerous, particularly Descartes, 'in whom are found propositions contrary to all natural reason and to Catholic tenets'. 'We have also', the university went on to say, 'heard talk of a Thomas Obbes and of the Englishman John Lochio, but the first is very compendious and the second, besides being very obscure, must be read with extreme care'.[28] Small wonder that José Cadalso poured his heavy irony on the 'most learned University of Salamanca', which taught 'neither mathematics nor physics nor anatomy nor natural history nor international law nor Oriental languages nor other trifles; but produces men who can in an imposing voice construct 77,777 syllogisms on *Baraliptonfrisesomorum* or *Sapesmo*, on the question of the language of the angels in their hosts, or on the constitution of the heavens'.[29] Not all the centres of learning were like this. After 1770 Alcalá and other universities accepted gradual change. By 1784 Valencia university had included Condillac in its course of philosophy. In 1774 the Council of Castile held a competition for a textbook of philosophy, to include the theories of Descartes, Malebranche and Leibnitz: in 1779 approval was given to a text by the Capuchin Villalpando. In 1781 the general of the Spanish Discalced Carmelites urged all teachers under him to read Condillac, Locke, Wolf, Leibnitz, Newton, Descartes and Bacon.

In this successful advance of European and particularly French thought into Spain, a leading role was played, as we have seen, by the élite and the enlightened nobility. The revolution they brought about was not, however, simply one that broke the intellectual stagnation in the peninsula and demolished the spiritual bulwarks of the closed society. The work of Jovellanos and Campomanes was more profound than this. They, like Olavide, planned to adopt the Enlightenment as a tool to further social and economic reform in Spain. To them the urgent economic problems of the country were of far greater significance than the existence of the Inquisition as such. Not that they were indifferent to the tribunal. Jovellanos was certainly aware, in his own words, that 'the Holy Office strikes ceaselessly and does not seem overwhelmed by the growing number of its enemies. It proscribes imperturbably all that is new, all that rises against the past, all that speaks of emancipation and liberty'.[30] But he knew that the reformers still had the mass of unenlightened opinion to contend with and that in the absence of popular approval it would be unwise to come to a confrontation with the Inquisition. Writing to his English correspondent Alexander Jardine, he expressed agreement with the latter's opinions:

You explain yourself perfectly on the subject of the Inquisition. On this point I am in agreement with you and think that there are many, very many, who think the same. But if only this opinion were general! As long as it is not, we cannot attack this abuse directly. We would lose everything. The result would be what has happened before: one would consolidate its foundations still more and render its system more cruel and treacherous.[31]

The Inquisition, it should be remembered, had been far from hostile to the Economic Societies of *Amigos del País* founded by Peñaflorida and devoted to economic reform throughout Spain. But when radical social doctrines accompanied the ideas of the Enlightenment, the Holy Office ceased to be tolerant and turned to the offensive. In 1795 Jovellanos published his famous *Informe de ley agraria (Report on the agrarian law)*. It was denounced to the Inquisition and condemned because it declared immoral the holding of large entailed lands or *mayorazgos*, by Church and nobility. The *Informe*, said the tribunal, should be prohibited as not only 'anti-ecclesiastical but also as destructive of *mayorazgos* and therefore conducive to ideas of equality in the ownership of goods and lands'.[32] In this way the Inquisition ranged itself decisively on the side of property and against any fundamental reform in the intellectual and social structure of the *ancien régime*.

The one powerful weapon remaining to the tribunal in the eighteenth century was that of censorship, but even this did not remain undisturbed in its control. The Inquisition was free to issue condemnatory lists of books, but most actual censorship passed under the control of the Council of Castile. The licensing powers of the Council, first granted in 1544, were reaffirmed in 1705 and 1728, and in 1749 Ferdinand VI made this control of all printing absolute and invariable.[33] Under Charles III a schedule issued on 16 June 1768 affirmed control of censorship and laid down liberal rules by which authors were to be given a hearing, circulation was to be undisturbed until judgment was passed, and all prohibitions were to be approved by the government. Finally in 1773 bishops were deprived of the right to issue an *imprimatur*, which was limited to the government only. The whole apparatus of literary control consequently fell upon the laymen, usually informed intellectuals, who sat on the Council of Castile. This was enlightened despotism at its clearest and purest. One result was the surprising picture of Jovellanos as a

State censor, opposing the publication of Voltaire's *Alcira* in 1784 on the grounds that it was anti-Spanish; and censoring translations from the Latin because they were incorrect.[34]

Ecclesiastical censorship continued to exist side by side with State censorship. This state of affairs was perfectly unexceptionable, and a similar system exists in some countries today. Although the more important censorship may appear to have been that exercised by the State, in fact the inquisitorial Index continued to wield such authority that its dictates could not easily be ignored. Because of this it is essential to study the development of the Index in the eighteenth century.

The first inquisitorial Index of the eighteenth century was issued in 1707. It had been begun by Diego Sarmiento, the Inquisitor General who died in 1699, and was completed by Vidal Marín, bishop of Ceuta and Inquisitor General till his death in 1709. In many ways it is the least interesting of all the Indices. Its date places it between the rigid orthodoxy of the seventeenth century and the infiltration of the Enlightenment in the eighteenth. Consequently most of the books on the 1707 Index are the same as in the previous Index. New arrivals included the *Augustinus* of Cornelius Jansen, bishop of Ypres, and John Milton's *Pro populo Anglicano Defensio* published at London in 1651. Jansenism had begun to trouble the government as early as 1645, when its existence in Flanders provoked Philip IV to issue decrees against it.[35] Under Philip V this and other ideological disputes did not develop appreciably, and although the inquisitors saw fit in 1739 to issue an appendix to the 1707 Index the censors had no serious worries. To 1739 also belongs what seems to have been the only attempt made to censor the *Teatro crítico* of Feijóo. The author gave an explanation of his intention and the matter seems to have been dropped.[36] One of the more notable additions to the Index under Philip V was the *Historia civil de España* of Fray Nicolás de Jesús Belando. The fourth part of this work was banned and ordered to be destroyed because of its open hostility to the Inquisition and Rome in its discussion of the Macanaz affair.

The Index of 1747, a massive work in two weighty volumes, was issued by Inquisitor General Francisco Pérez de Prado y Cuesta. It immediately became notorious because the Jesuits had managed to include in it many of their opponents' works, including that of Cardinal Noris. What particularly aroused hosility was that an appendix to the Index was published under the title of *Catalogue of Jansenist books*. This catalogue was no more than a copy of the *Bibliothèque janséniste*, a list of allegedly Jansenistic works drawn up on his own authority by a Belgian Jesuit in 1722 and condemned subsequently at Rome in 1745. The adoption by the Inquisition of the orthodox side in the Jesuit-Jansenist controversy meant that the Index had now become a tool of faction, and that the era of political conflict had begun.

The new period of censorship differed in other ways also from the earlier period. In the first place, the character of the censors changed. In the sixteenth and seventeenth centuries the most brilliant intellects of Spain had helped to draw up the principles of the Index. Eminent men like Juan de Mariana, Juan de Pineda, and Arias Montano had on occasion helped to prepare Indices. By the eighteenth century ignorant and small-minded clergy had seized control of the apparatus of censorship. Secure in dogmatic and political principles, they condemned to oblivion any work which threatened to illuminate the intellectual darkness in Spain. For this reason more than any other the intelligentsia despised the inquisitorial censorship and belittled its importance until the case of Olavide pulled them up with a shock. In the second place, the nature of censorship changed. Before the eighteenth century, particular care had been taken to expurgate books so that they could be passed for publication, and the greater part of an Index was often taken up with expurgation only. The advent of heretical doctrines with the Enlightenment made it impossible to pick and choose passages in the old way, and books had to be condemned as a whole, so that the balance between condemned and expurgated books was tilted heavily towards the former. The third main change is an obvious one. Most of the old censorship had concerned Protestant and other heresy, and the Index had been weighed down by the names of minor theologians whose errors had incurred censure. The new Indices were less theological and more political. The writers now prohibited had little or nothing to do with heresy. Instead they propagated ideas of freedom, equality and tolerance, political doctrines against which, because of their implications, the Inquisition was determined to set its face.

Provoked by political doctrine, the Holy Office entered the arena of politics.

The first new campaign of the Inquisition in matters of censorship was directed against the 'Jansenists', a term which continued to be used long after it had lost any precise meaning. All the works of the Enlightenment throughout the eighteenth century were now treated as 'Jansenistic'. Since most of the foreign works entering Spain happened to be in French (even English books entered in French translations, since French was the only foreign language at all widely read) the campaign against 'Jansenism' became simply a campaign against subversive French books. When Spaniards read Locke or Pope they read them invariably in a French version, 'English thought through a French pen', as Feijóo put it. Essentially, therefore, we are reduced to studying the fate of French books in Spain.[37]

1747 marked a departure with the condemnation of Pierre Bayle's *Dictionnaire philosophique*. This ban was issued by means of an inquisitorial edict and not through the Index. In subsequent years the growing number of book condemnations were all issued through edicts. Of seventy-four books condemned by edict in 1756 forty-two were in French. From then on the proportion of French books never fell below a third of the total and often exceeded a half. These figures prove the extreme importance of French thought in Spain at the time. From 1747 to 1807 some five hundred titles of books in French were condemned by the Inquisition, the greater proportion of these falling in the period after the French Revolution. Within these years only one more Index appeared, the *Indice último* of Inquisitor Agustín Rubin de Cevallos, bishop of Jaén, which came out in 1790. Between 1747 and 1790 the books condemned by the Inquisition included Montesquieu's *Esprit des lois*, prohibited in 1762; Voltaire's complete works, prohibited in 1762; Rousseau's complete works, prohibited in 1764; Holbach's *Système de la nature*, prohibited in 1779; Pierre l'Etoile's *Journal du règne d'Henri IV*, prohibited in 1750; Algernon Sydney's *Discours sur le gouvernement*, prohibited in 1767; and Vattel's *Droit des gens*, prohibited in 1779. These and many more works, sometimes important, sometimes of little or no significance, helped to open a new world to the reading public of Spain. Despite the efforts of the inquisitors there was no difficulty in obtaining prohibited books. Particularly towards the end of the century, writes the contemporary historian of Charles IV, Muriel, 'it was no longer necessary to go and look for them in the capital or in the main cities, as had been the case till then. The abundance of what was being introduced from France was such that the traffickers themselves went to offer them in thinly populated villages at cut prices'.[38] The zeal of a functionary of the Inquisition in Cadiz, always an open route for illicit goods, resulted in him rounding up no less than 8,000 forbidden books over a period of nine years, of which 2,600 had been collected in 1776 alone. This number he regarded as only a qualified success. In December 1776 he was writing to the *Suprema* that 'they continue to sell prohibited books in the French bookshops in this city, and others can be found in Spanish shops. The town is full of them'.[39]

The same story was true for other seaports in Spain. As a result the censorship exercised by the Inquisition was a signal failure. Part of the blame lay with the tolerant policy of the Council of Castile, which allowed numerous works to circulate in defiance of the Inquisition. Several works of Voltaire were issued in Spain on the understanding that the name of the author should nowhere appear in print, and works by Condillac and the Abbé Raynal were also allowed to circulate. Smuggling continued to be carried on with the full connivance of prominent members of the government. Jovellanos, for example, procured English and French books through his consular friends in Santander and La Coruña. The censorship regulations of June 1768 revealed this official hostility towards the Inquisition. It was also shown explicitly in an edict of 3 May 1768 drawn up by Floridablanca and Campomanes which said that 'the abuse in the prohibition of books by the Holy Office is one of the sources of the ignorance that reigns over a large part of the nation'.[40] With the spread of reforms in university education and the rise of a cultured, largely noble élite devoted to the introduction of reforms based on enlightened principles, less and less attention was paid to the official prohibition issued by the Inquisition. Trials such as that of Olavide could help to alarm people but not to check the infiltration of new ideas into Spain. The collapse of old frontiers witnessed also the rise of timely reforms not only in social and economic life but also in those very provinces in which the Inquisition had left its mark. It was on 12 February 1773 that the Chuetas of Majorca sent a petition for relief to Charles III. In this they were supported by the bishop of Palma and government officials on the island. The result was a series of orders in 1782, 1785 and 1788 prohibiting all discrimination and opening all public offices on the island to them.[41]

At this stage of tension between traditionalism and reform, we should turn aside for a moment to consider the fate of free-masonry in Spain. The exaggerations, myths and legends sur-rounding freemasonry are not our present concern. What is relevant is that for many traditionalists in eighteenth-century Spain freemasonry was the great conspiracy of which Jansenism formed an integral part. Lea gives the date 1726 for the founda-tion of the first masonic lodge in Spain.[42] Whatever the time or place of origin in Spain, there appear to have been many members by the end of the reign of Philip V. In 1738 pope Clement XII issued the first ban on the organization, denounc-ing its secrecy and forbidding Catholics to join it under pain of excommunication. The Spanish government adhered to the terms of the ban by initiating prosecutions of freemasons, who were first condemned by a decree of Philip V in 1740. In 1751 Ferdinand VI repeated the condemnation of freemasonry. Pro-bably the first individual to be tried and punished for this crime was a canon named Roscobel, in 1744. After this several cases came before the courts of the Inquisition, and revealed the existence of an organization whose secrecy might well lead it to become a means of expressing discontent with the regime. By 1760 an independent Grand Lodge was active in Spain, and it was rumoured in subsequent years that men like Aranda, Campomanes, Jovellanos, and the Duke of Alba were free-masons. The political activities of some members came to light in 1796, when a republican conspiracy failed to materialize and all those responsible were arrested. Beyond this there seems to have been no great development until the opening of the peninsular war, when French and English troops on Spanish soil promoted the building up of masonic lodges. Whatever the truth about the extent of freemasonry, it is certain that the Inquisition brought very few individuals to trial for it. Between 1780 and 1815 there were only nineteen prosecutions, followed by 25 in 1815, and then down to fourteen in 1817, nine in 1818 and seven in 1819. These figures suggest that the anonymity of

the masonic organization led to exaggerations about its membership and influence. This is not unlikely, since freemasonry was
looked on with suspicion as something secret, foreign, heretical,
and atheistic. Olavide, in common with other followers of the
Enlightenment, was looked upon as a freemason. Anyone who
supported modern or foreign thought and opposed traditionalism could be labelled a freemason and blamed for any ills
besetting the country. Where a Protestant saw Jesuits under
every bed the inquisitors saw freemasons. The issue is probably
of curiosity value only.

The steady progress of reform, the concurrence of enlightened
ministers, and the obvious impotence of the Inquisition, were
factors enough to give satisfaction to a liberal at the end of the
eighteenth century. All this was stopped in mid-career by the
world-shaking impact of the French Revolution. Very soon
after its outbreak the Inquisition began to discover in Spain
scores of French pamphlets denying the power of kings and proclaiming the doctrine of natural rights. The reaction was swift.
On 13 December 1789 the *Suprema* issued an edict prohibiting all
such papers in Spain. The edict denounced the revolutionaries:

> who, under the specious guise of defenders of liberty, work in
> reality against it by destroying the political and social order and
> consequently the hierarchy of the Christian religion . . . and claim to
> build on the ruins of religion and monarchy this chimerical liberty
> which they erroneously believe to be conceded to all men by nature
> which, they rashly say, has made all individuals equal and in-
> dependent one from another.

This edict was supported by a royal order of 29 December,
signed by Floridablanca, which prohibited all controversial
material from entering the country. The order was repeated in
January 1790. At the same time the ambassador in Paris, the
Count of Fernán Núñez, was told to ask all Spaniards in France
not to send home any news of events in that country. In May
1790 Fernán Núñez wrote anxiously to his government to warn
them of a special depot set up near the frontier by Frenchmen to
send revolutionary pamphlets into Spain. Such precautions
meant that Charles IV, king since 1788, had made an alliance
with the Inquistion to protect the country against the subversive
ideas boiling over north of the frontier. From now on all
revolutionary ideas were to be deemed heretical. A new curtain

of silence was imposed on Spain, but it was never to be as successful as that imposed in the sixteenth century. The presence of a large French colony in the trading centres of Spain, and the volume of commerce with France, meant that information was bound to filter through. To combat this the radical measure was taken of compelling foreigners, particularly Frenchmen, to become domiciled or leave the country. Faced with this choice, thousands left Spain and went home. A further sign of the change from a liberal policy was given with the treatment of Charles III's reformist ministers. Francisco Cabarrús, who had as recently as 1789 been created a Count and was well-known for his liberal theories, suffered denunciation to the Inquisition, was arrested in June 1790, and then confined in a castle at La Coruña in Galicia. His friend Jovellanos, who was at the time in Salamanca, returned home hurriedly in August to intervene on his behalf, but was himself four days later ordered into virtual banishment by being sent on a trifling mission to the province of Asturias. The next year it was the turn of Campomanes, who was deprived of his position as governor of the Council of Castile, although he still retained nominal membership.

The reaction was complete. Fear of the Revolution had driven the conservative circles of the administration into alliance with the Inquisition. On 24 February 1791 Floridablanca, who had now renounced his liberal past to become the leading minister in the government, annihilated the intellectual movement in Spain by a decree which suspended all private periodicals.[43] This decree was accompanied by renewed activity by the Inquisition against the popular press and individual writers. One of these, Mariano Luis de Urquijo, in 1791 dared to publish a translation of Voltaire with the author's name on it. He was immediately summoned before the Inquisition, but before anything could happen there was a change in the government. In February 1792 Floridablanca was replaced by the Count of Aranda, the famous suppressor of the Jesuits, who took Urquijo into his government after the latter had suffered a mild reprimand from the inquisitors.

The change in administration did not improve matters substantially. Restrictions had to be continued because of active republican propaganda emanating from France. In Spain political excitement had been stirred up to a high pitch. One contemporary observed that in Madrid:

> in the inns and over the tables, by the Mariblanca and in the cafeteria, you hear of nothing but battles, revolution, convention, national representation, liberty and equality.[44]

This interest in the issues of the day was fed by French propagandists who magnified the horrors of the Inquisition and represented Spaniards as labouring under clerical tyranny. One typical text was the speech made to the Club des Amis de la Constitution of Bayonne by a young refugee from Spain, the ex-priest José Marchena. It was distributed in Spain under the heading *A la nación española* and called on Spaniards to achieve their liberty by destroying the Inquisition:

> Is it not time for the nation to shake off the intolerable yoke of the oppression of thought? Is it not time for the government to suppress a tribunal of darkness that dishonours even despotism?[45]

In about 1794 another leaflet sent into Catalonia asked the Spaniards:

> Are you fighting for the infernal Inquisition that did not exist in the time of the good *sans-culotte* lord Jesus Christ? . . . the infernal Inquisition that, using the name of a God of peace and goodness, brings desolation to your families and commands thought itself?[46]

These exhortations disturbed nobody, and spoilt their own case by overstating it. The Inquisition under Charles IV had none of the terrible aspects it presented in earlier times, and so hostile a critic as Llorente, contemporary with all these events, described the inquisitors of the reigns of Charles III and Charles IV as 'men of extreme prudence and singular moderation'.[47] If any pro-French sentiment arose, it was soon dispelled by news first of the execution of Louis XVI and then of the commencement of the Jacobin terror. In Spain the rise of the Queen's handsome and brilliant favourite Manuel Godoy led to the dismissal of Aranda in 1794 and the release of Floridablanca from his prison in Pamplona. The pendulum swung back again to the traditionalists. When in 1794 the Inquisition got hold of an inflammatory pamphlet entitled *Exortación al pueblo español para que . . . se anime a cobrar sus derechos,** it tried to set another ex-

* Exhortation to the Spanish people to win their rights.

ample on the lines of the prosecution of Olavide, by victimizing as writer of the tract a professor of jurisprudence at Salamanca, Ramón de Salas, whom it condemned in 1796 to abjure *de levi*, although his authorship was not proven and the tract contained no statement of heresy. The baneful year 1794 was also distinguished by the appointment of the reactionary archbishop of Toledo, Francisco de Lorenzana, as Inquisitor General in place of his liberal predecessor Manuel Abad y la Sierra, who had held the post only sixteen months. This retrogressive step was in keeping with a royal order of 31 July which suppressed the teaching of public and international law in Spain.

The Holy Office was fulfilling its own duties of censorship in perfect tune with the dictates of the *ancien régime*. Condemnations of French books gathered momentum as the pillars of orthodoxy crumbled and the doctrines of the Revolution were sown broadcast on Spanish soil. Attempts to seal off the frontiers failed dismally. As the tribunal of Logroño informed the *Suprema*, 'the multitude of seditious papers coming from France makes it impossible to initiate prosecutions against all the people who introduce, keep, and distribute them, to which is added the lack of theologians conversant with the French language to censor them'.[48] Regardless of its sheer inability to enforce proper censorship, the tribunal continued to issue condemnations as of old. The Index of 1790 contained among its condemnations a French translation of John Cleland's *Fanny Hill*. More elevated foreign books were condemned in the years after this. Among them were the philosophical works of Diderot, prohibited in 1806; a French version of Locke's *Essay Concerning Human Understanding*, prohibited in 1804; Pope's writings in French translation, prohibited in 1804; Adam Smith's *Wealth of Nations* in French, prohibited in 1792; Bourgoing's *Nouveau voyage en Espagne*, prohibited in 1797, and his *Tableau de l'Espagne moderne*, prohibited in 1805; Gibbon's *Decline and Fall of the Roman Empire* in French, prohibited in 1806; Edmund Burke's *Reflections on the French Revolution* in French, prohibited in 1796; Choderlos de Laclos' *Liaisons dangereuses*, prohibited in 1791; the abbé Prévost's *Manon Lescaut*, prohibited in 1797 along with other works, this being a repetition of a ban in 1789; Laurence Sterne's *Works*, and his *Sentimental Journey*, prohibited in French in 1801 and 1804: Restif de la Bretonne's *Les Nuits de Paris*, prohibited in 1806; and a multitude of other works of greater or lesser significance. The lunatic side of censorship showed itself in 1790 with the prohibition of the great Spanish classic *Celestina*, which was forbidden even to those who held licences to read prohibited books. Edicts against these books did nothing to stop their diffusion. A priest in 1778 testified that 'Voltaire, Rousseau and the other leaders of modern impiety have penetrated the furthest corners of Spain', and a preacher in Salamanca denounced 'these books which circulate clandestinely, are sought after at any price, and are read with ardour and delight and devoured even by young girls and boys with the hunger of a disordered appetite excited by novelty and prohibition itself'.[49] Llorente is another witness to the fact that prohibition of books only drew attention to them and increased their circulation. The Inquisition consequently contributed directly by its repressive measures to making the educated public aware of the significance of the literature from France. The truth is that the government had adopted clumsy methods to meet an imaginary threat. Censors might proclaim that foreign literature would increase atheism and induce rebellion in Spain, but the reading public only desired these books in order to satisfy their curiosity and their longing for knowledge. If ardent spirits dreamed of bloody revolution the course of events in France was enough to dampen their ardour. What Spaniards wanted was reform and education, not the overthrow of the monarchy or even of the Inquisition.

The period of reaction in Spain disappeared after July 1795, when the treaty of Basle brought peace after three years of war between republican France and monarchist Spain. Events showed that there was little danger of a republican revolution in Spain, and Godoy became genuinely interested in promoting the Enlightenment now that the threat of subversion and foreign intervention was over. Already in 1794 he had accepted the dedication of a Spanish edition of Adam Smith's works; by 1797 translations of Tom Paine and John Locke were being offered to the public.[50] Then in 1797 the liberals were received back into the government, Cabarrús becoming ambassador to France, and Jovellanos and Urquijo occupying key central posts. Once again it appeared that the 'Jansenist' party had triumphed. But this was shortlived. In March 1798 Godoy withdrew from the government and in August Jovellanos was dismissed. Urquijo remained as chief minister, which gave him the opportunity in 1799 of suggesting to Charles IV that the Inquisition be abolished.[51] But his days too were numbered, and in December 1800 he was dismissed and confined in a prison at Pamplona. The partisan motives behind his dismissal revealed themselves with the publication on 10 December 1800 of the papal bull against the religious Jansenists, *Auctorem fidei*, which had in 1794 been prohibited entry into Spain but was now allowed in by the traditionalists. The defeat of the political 'Jansenists' was crowned by the arrest of Jovellanos in March 1801 and his transportation to Majorca, where he was confined until 1808.

The history of these years shows the Inquisition acting openly as a political institution rather than in its traditional role of a prosecutor of heresy. But whatever the political vicissitudes of the Inquisition, and regardless of its ascendancy in the administration of Charles IV, it completely failed to set the clock back in Spain. The principal reason for this was that it had forfeited the confidence and support of the aristocratic élite in the country, and because the reins of power had passed to a new class composed of the men who promoted the Economic Societies, and the men who sat in the Cortes of Cadiz, which saw in the Inquisition only a barrier to progress in science, industry and agriculture. The bourgeois revolution in Spain demolished the supports on which the tribunal had always rested, and in eliminating its predominance also swept away the barriers confining the closed society.

CHAPTER FIFTEEN

THE ABOLITION OF THE INQUISITION

> Peoples to come, nations who will one day enter the bosom
> of the Church, future generations – will you in time believe
> that there once existed in the Catholic Church a tribunal called
> the Holy Inquisition?
>
> *Ruiz Padrón*, in the Cortes of Cadiz in 1813

By the end of the reign of Philip V the Spanish Inquisition was
well on the way to decline in wealth and numbers. The second
factor probably follows from the first. As the possibilities of income decreased, so the number of laymen who once flocked
around to secure the privileges of services with the Inquisition
decreased. In most tribunals of the peninsula expenses far exceeded the income from all sources. Among the exceptions was
the Inquisition of Seville, which had considerable credit balances
in the 1760s. With income averaging over twenty million *maravedis* and expenditure averaging between fifteen and eighteen
million, the tribunal made a regular profit of between two and
five million.[1] Seville's prosperity was fully consonant with its
position in 1731, when it and Santiago were the only two tribunals to be paying their way with profit, while all the others
(except Valencia, which just made ends meet) were steeped in
debt, leaving an overall annual deficit of well over 55,000 *reales*.[2]
If we go back a little further, however, to the fiscal statements
for 1705, in the slack period before the last great persecution of
conversos, we find that all the tribunals had deficits of considerable proportions.[3] Despite these variations, the final picture in
the eighteenth century is one of growing poverty. In the tribunal of Saragossa, which had been deprived of its seat in the
palatial Aljafería since 1705, the crown had even been subsi-
dizing the inquisitors by a generous grant which continued up

to 1725. This financial decline was accompanied by a great decline in the personnel of the Inquisition. In earlier times it had been usual for the Cortes to complain of the excessive number of familiars in the realm; now it was the turn of the Inquisition to bewail the decrease in membership. By the *Concordia* of Castile, the inquisitors of Toledo stated in 1748, they had a right to 805 familiars but now there were only ninety-nine; in Granada at the same date 554 familiars were allowed by the *Concordia*, but there were only eighty-four; similarly Aragon had a right to 1,215 familiars but there were only thirty-five in the whole province.[4] This contraction in numbers extended to every office of the Inquisition.

In a way the development was a rational one. With the decrease in business and the growth of administrative centralization it became essential to eliminate costs in provincial tribunals, and to concentrate rather on the central apparatus of the *Suprema*. The decline in business can be shown by comparing the first half of the century with the second half. Under Philip V, according to Llorente, there were about 782 *autos de fe* held in all the tribunals and the victims ran into thousands. Under Charles III and Charles IV, on the other hand, only ten people were condemned in *autos* and of these only four were burnt. In the twenty-nine years of their two reigns, only fifty-six people were publicly made to do penance.[5] All other prosecutions and sentences were carried out at private or secret *autos*. Moreover, many of these cases were political prosecutions only, since the Inquisition had now adopted an overwhelmingly political role, so that the number of purely religious cases is even lower than the figures given.

Parallel to this material decay went the decay of inquisitorial influence among the progressive élite in Spain. This new mood, which we have observed to some extent in Jovellanos and others, reflected a fundamental crisis in the *ancien régime*: a crisis which profoundly affected the whole structure of society and in which the Holy Office played only one, though important, part. The development of the crisis can be illustrated by the movement of prices in the eighteenth century. Up to the end of the reign of Philip V the moderate level of prices reflected stable economic conditions in a stable society and this steady development gave birth to no economic or political upheavals. But from this point Spain began to experience a steady inflation which occurred simultaneously throughout western Europe. The first and most important result of this, in a country with a largely agricultural economy, was a revolution in land values, leading to greater stress on agriculture and hence to an interest in land reform. This period saw the rise of Economic Societies, the multiplication of attacks on the feudal privileges of the sheep-owners' Mesta, and a movement against the landed possessions of the Church which received its greatest impetus from the publication in 1765 of Campomanes' treatise *De la Regalía de Amortización*. At the same time the growth of commercial companies under government approval led to a great expansion in trade to the Indies, and to a rise in the import of precious metals from America. On the basis of this expansion a prosperous bourgeois class devoted to trade rose in the great ports, above all in Barcelona. The economic boom, which built up to an inflationary climax at the very end of the century, precipitated new social and political development which revolutionized the attitude of the progressive classes in Spain.

This expansion lay at the root of cultural and social change. The point cannot be stressed firmly enough. When Spanish nobles read foreign books it was not only because they had an interest in foreign culture but because they wished to learn from abroad and to apply foreign methods to Spanish economic problems. Even Olavide, who was so deeply read in French literature, had as the core of his library a selection of works on political economy. Works on agriculture, industry and trade were not only introduced from abroad: they were also drawn up ambitiously and systematically by native Spaniards. This new zeal for productivity looked askance at the deadweight of history represented by the Inquisition under which Spain had laboured so long. Opposition centred in the liberals, who, learning from the Enlightenment and the French Revolution, set about to overthrow the old pillars of the establishment. A perceptive contemporary observed that the bourgeoisie everywhere in Spain were identified with the liberals and that between them the common people and the bulk of the aristocracy composed the traditionalist party.[6] This was the division of parties which had persisted throughout the history of the Inquisition, and which complicates any attempt to identify the revolution as an exclusively popular struggle for liberty.

Events year by year began to prove that the Inquisition was fighting in vain against the tide of change. In 1756 it comdemned and placed on the Index Rousseau's *Origine de l'inégalité*, Voltaire's *Lettres philosophiques*, and the works of Burlamaqui and La Bruyère. Regardless of these edicts the ministers of the crown went ahead with their programme, and in 1758 the feudal privileges of the once powerful Mesta were destroyed when the special tax which had been its financial mainstay was repealed. Every step backwards was followed by two steps forward. In 1766 Rousseau's *Lettres de la Montagne* and Diderot's *Pensées philosophiques* were put on the Index. That same year the Squillace riots destroyed the power of the Jesuits, and on 2 May the government decreed the first of an ambitious series of agricultural reforms in the south of Spain. Only the previous year, in 1765, the Basque society of the *Amigos del País* had come into existence, dedicated to economic reform; and the government had broken the trade monopoly to America exercised by Cadiz, by extending the trade to nine Spanish ports and five American islands. The urge to commercial freedom was part of the demand for political liberty, and the growing pressure for free trade in Spain became based on the principle of man's inalienable liberty. In 1778 the condemnation of Olavide marked a step backwards in history; yet that same year the expansion of Spanish society was signalled by the complete opening of the American trade to all Spanish ports. The Index had obviously become no more than a petty and insignificant brake on processes which had far outpaced any possible restraint that the Inquisition could have exercised. 'The Holy Office', in the words of the contemporary historian Muriel, 'had become no more than a sort of commission for the censorship of books, and even to maintain this position it had to be passive and tolerant'.[7] The clearest indication of this dichotomy between the Inquisition and the society it lived in, occurred in 1797, the very year Condorcet's *Progrès de l'esprit humain* was put on the Index. That same year Godoy passed the first decree of toleration ever known in Spain: his order of 8 September allowed any foreign manufacturer, even if Protestant, to settle in Spain provided he respected the religion of the country. The only shadow from the past was that Jews were expressly forbidden entry by the decree.

The inflationary movement reached its peak in the years 1800-1814. This was the climax to mounting difficulties occasioned by war. From 1793 to 1795 Spanish armies were engaged in struggle against France, and peace was followed only by the outbreak of war with England in 1796. In 1797 the impossibility of maintaining the trans-Atlantic monopoly against British aggression forced Spain to cut the American colonies free and allow them to trade with neutral powers. South America was now for all practical purposes lost to Spain. Military burdens crippled the treasury, and while government credit crumbled the cost of living soared: between 1780 and 1800 a labourer's salary rose by only 12.5 per cent while the price level rose by 50 per cent. In Madrid Charles IV found that the French alliance had in reality become a French occupation. The annexation of Portugal by French troops under Junot in 1807 was followed by the imposition of French garrisons on Spanish cities in 1808, when Murat took over control of Spain. Differences over policy at court led to disagreements between Charles IV and his son Ferdinand, who mounted the throne as Ferdinand VII in March 1808 after Godoy had been displaced and Charles forced to abdicate. The French command, however, refused to recognize the change of monarch, and the royal family was induced to go to Bayonne, just inside the French frontier, to lay any differences before Napoleon. Once at Bayonne, Charles and Ferdinand were in Napoleon's power. The latter persuaded Ferdinand to renounce the crown but immediately had Charles surrender it to France. Napoleon then chose his brother Joseph as the new king of Spain.

The economic distress of these years made popular agitation inevitable. When in addition the people of Madrid found that Murat had seized control from the royal family, they registered their protest on 2 May 1808 by rising against the French army of occupation and so setting ablaze the War of Independence. The bloody suppression in Madrid did not lead everywhere to immediate rebellion. Conservatives in particular had reason to be satisfied by the Constitution of Bayonne, which guaranteed the Catholic religion and had been drawn up in June 1808 by an aristocratic body calling itself a Cortes. The Inquisition saw nothing objectionable in the Constitution and gave its earnest support to the new regime. Already on 6 May it had proved its worth by issuing to all tribunals a circular letter condemning the 2 May uprising as a 'scandalous tumult of the common people', and claiming that 'malevolence or ignorance had misled the unwary and simple into revolutionary disorder, under the colour of patriotism and love of the sovereign'.[8] Praiseworthy as these sentiments might be, they did not impress Joseph, who on his arrival on 4 December issued a decree suppressing the Inquisition and confiscating its property to the crown. The tribunal now ceased to exist in theory, but in practice the French did not go out of their way to interfere with it, and inquisitors continued to operate wherever circumstances allowed. Paradoxically, among the Spaniards who, like the *Suprema*, supported French rule and opposed popular riots against it, were ranged some of the most distinguished liberals of the reign of Charles IV. Among the members of Joseph's government we can find the names of Cabarrús, Urquijo, and Juan Antonio Llorente.[9] These were men of unblemished patriotism and high liberal ideals. Yet they were denounced by their compatriots as traitors to their country, a just description when we realize that they supported a government which was hated by the vast majority of the Spanish people. Why did they take this path? It is clear that their motives were just and justifiable, and in collaboration they sought perhaps the only way to meet the needs of their country.[10] What is important for our purposes is that these men, who can be identified exactly with the reforming ministers of Charles III and Charles IV, formed a moderate party between the two extremes of conservatives and left-wing liberals, who were both anti-French. With the expulsion of Joseph Bonaparte and with him of the *afrancesados*, the two extreme parties stood face to face over a prostrate Spain. And the one great issue standing between them was the Inquisition.

On 24 September 1810 there opened in Cadiz a Cortes representing all the parts of Spain not occupied by French troops. In this historic assembly less than half the number of about a hundred deputies were liberals, according to one historian,[11] but such a division cannot be made both because of the many fluctuating opinions and because of the irregular number of deputies, which rose at times to well over two hundred. The great work of this constituent Cortes was the famous Constitution of 1812, the first break made with tradition by the bourgeoisie of Spain, and the future rallying point of all liberal national aspirations. The main struggle arose, however, over the Inquisition, which was bound to provoke the most irrational arguments on either side. Freedom of debate on the issue was provided by a decree of 18 October 1810 establishing freedom of the press. By this measure the last control exercised by the Inquisition, that of censorship, was taken away absolutely. The tribunal was not yet attacked directly, and it was only in January 1811 that the first clear voices were raised in support of abolishing the Inquisition. A committee was set up to examine the status of the tribunal and in July 1811 it reported in favour of re-establishing the *Suprema*. No action was taken on this, however, and the issue was postponed until the end of 1812. In March 1812 the Constitution was adopted by the Cortes. This decided the form of debate over the Inquisition, and when in December that year two reports were presented to the Cortes, the minority report stated that only the procedure of the Inquisition conflicted with the Constitution, while the majority report claimed that the very existence of the tribunal was incompatible with the Constitution. The majority report based its conclusions on a lengthy historical survey of the Inquisition from its very origins.[12] The discussions that followed, taking up the whole of the month of January 1813, were less historical in content.

The bitter debates carried on in the Cortes over the Inquisition had in fact very little to do with the Inquisition. The melancholy conclusion to be drawn from reading the speeches of the deputies is that very few members present had any knowledge of the part played by the Inquisition in the history of their country. There was a great deal of erudition about the early years of the tribunal, much of it no doubt drawn from Llorente's famous *Memoria Histórica* which had been read before the Royal Academy of History as recently as November 1811. But Llorente's great History had not yet appeared, and for lack of it the disputants battled among generalizations, conjectures, and misconceptions, without beginning to show any understanding of the nature and function of the Inquisition in the seventeenth and eighteenth centuries. What is clear from the debates, however, is that there still remained a firm and inflexible undercurrent of antisemitism among the deputies, whether they were conservatives or liberals. Even more surprising is the fact that not

277

a single voice was raised to attack the primacy and unity of the Catholic faith in Spain. The attack on the Inquisition, in other words, was not based on irreligious motives, but even – as some liberals maintained – on a greater concern for the preservation of Catholicism. If the conservatives strained themselves to defend the tribunal, it was largely because they feared attacks on ecclesiastical jurisdiction and on the Catholic religion. The liberals, on the other hand, appealed to primitive Christianity and reduced their case to three main points:[13] the Inquisition was not essential, since the Church had existed for thirteen centuries without it; bishops were originally the only authorities competent to judge matters of faith and heresy; and the Holy Office was incompatible with the Constitution. Of these points the last was the most cogent. These arguments were fortified from outside the Cortes by intelligent pamphleteers who tried to enlist public support for their cause. Among the conservatives the principal writer was a distinguished Dominican called Francisco Alvarado whose letters on the subject were published under the title of *El filósofo rancio* (*The old philosopher*). On the liberal side the outstanding pen was that of Antonio Puigblanch, whose pamphlets were collected under the title *La Inquisición sin máscara* (*The Inquisition unmasked*), and published in 1811. From an English translation published five years later in London we can extract the following verbatim summary of Puigblanch's argument:[14]

1. The Inquisition being an ecclesiastical tribunal, its rigour is incompatible with the spirit of meekness which ought to distinguish the ministers of the Gospel.

2. The system of rigour adopted by this tribunal is opposed to the doctrine of the Holy Fathers and the discipline of the Church in its most happy times.

3. The Inquisition, far from contributing to the preservation of the true belief, is only suited to encourage hypocrisy and excite the people to rebellion.

4. The form of trial used in this tribunal tramples on all the rights of the citizen.

5. The Inquisition has not only obstructed the progress of science in the countries wherein it has been established, but has also propagated pernicious errors.

6. The tribunal has supported the despotism of kings, and has itself exercised it.

7. As the Inquisition owes its origin to the decline of the discipline and remissness of the clergy, it opposes obstacles to their reform, which is indispensably necessary if the nation is to prosper.

Neither side attempted to debate the history and character of the tribunal rationally: to conservatives it represented all that had been best and holiest in Spain, to liberals it had brought their country into decadence at home and disrepute abroad. In fact, of course, the low standard of the debates was irrelevant. The Inquisition had long been nothing but a pale shadow of its former self, and what the combatants of 1813 were really fighting about was not the past but the future. They were concerned not with the real nature of a moribund institution but with the direction the history of their country might take. In this respect the debates marked the end of one unhappy chapter and the opening of another, perhaps unhappier and even more bloody.

The final victory of the liberals was enshrined in the decree of abolition issued on 22 February 1813, and voted for by ninety votes against sixty.[15] The decree did not actually abolish the Inquisition but only declared that it was 'incompatible with the Constitution'; at the same time all jurisdiction over faith and heresy was given back to the bishops, by reviving the ancient laws of the kingdom. To claim that this measure was a popular one would be far from the truth. The ministers of Charles III had seen that a great deal of support still attached to the Inquisition, as a tribunal necessary to the Catholic faith, and had wisely not attempted to do away with it altogether. The deputies at Cadiz, on the other hand, failed to see that they were by no means representative of the great mass of the people. Already on 25 January, the day before the critical vote in the Cortes restoring jurisdiction over heresy to the bishops, the city of Córdoba had resolved to petition the Cortes to restore the Inquisition.[16] Córdoba was representative of a great tide of opinion, from all parts of Spain, which showed that the liberals in the Cortes had defied a wide body of opposition in order to enforce their own partisan programme: a policy which was to be followed only too often thereafter in Spanish history. The bishops and clergy and through them the mass of the faithful, refused to recognize the dissolution of an institution sanctioned by the pope, who alone could revoke his sanction.

On 5 March the papal nuncio issued a protest along these lines, claiming that the abolition of the Inquisition injured the rights of the Holy See and asking, in a more conciliatory tone, for the abolition to be suspended until the advent of peace and the possible consent of the pope or of the nation as a whole.

By now the indiscretion of the liberals had created a state of virtual civil war in the country. The refusal of Church officials in Cadiz to read the decree of abolition from their pulpits, led to suspicions of an impending *coup d'état* in Cadiz, whereupon the Cortes on 8 March took the emergency step of dismissing the Council of Regency which theoretically ruled Spain in the absence of the king. The regents were replaced by others, and the policy of the government was ordered to be enforced. The papal nuncio, meanwhile, was expelled and retired to Portugal. In this atmosphere of extremes the liberals perhaps lost far more than they gained. When in March 1814 king Ferdinand was restored to his throne in a liberated Spain the moment was ripe for reaction. The king made his triumphal entry into Spain through Catalonia and Valencia, and on 10 May, just before he entered Madrid, the hall of the Cortes was seized and all the prominent liberal deputies were proscribed by royal order. The Cortes was dissolved, the Constitution annulled, and all the work of the liberal revolution undone. On 21 July a royal decree restored the whole machinery of the Inquisition.

However reactionary this measure may have appeared to contemporaries, it in fact did little or nothing to resurrect the Inquisition. The crown still claimed absolute control over censorship, and the damage done since 1808 to the dignity, property and finances of the tribunal was irreparable. Besides, it was impossible to restore to the Inquisition all the confiscations that had been made of its possessions, both private and institutional. Despite royal favour, shown particularly in elevating the Congregation of St Peter Martyr to the status of a knightly order, the tribunal could resume very little of its old authority, and the few cases it dealt with in these years were treated with exemplary patience and moderation. The financial losses suffered were considerable. Papers and books of accounts had been lost or destroyed, so that claims could not be substantiated. Investments such as *juros* had been swallowed up by inflation and by government bankruptcy. Salaries had not been paid for nearly a decade. Between 1808 and 1814 the chief inquisitor of Valladolid had received only one-sixth of the salary due to him, and five years later he and his colleagues complained to the *Suprema* that they were reduced to desperation because their wages were still unpaid.[17] Without money and without authority, the Inquisition realized that it could not hope to re-establish itself. The few prosecutions that occurred from 1814 to 1819 were carried out with what Lea describes as 'a studied courtesy and evident desire to avoid giving offence'.[18] This complete evaporation of its former power was accompanied at the same time by widespread disaffection and resentment against the failures of the Bourbon regime.

The coming of revolution in 1820 brought Spain into line with the whole of discontented bourgeois Europe and proved how fragile was the reaction on which Ferdinand's power rested. As the first signs of rebellion broke out in the provinces the king on 9 March issued a hasty decree abolishing the Inquisition throughout the monarchy. The measure came too late. Already the crowds in Barcelona and Majorca were sacking the palaces of the tribunal. History now began to repeat itself. The Cortes which Ferdinand had summoned on 6 March set about proving that liberals could be as harsh and fanatical as their opponents. In August the Jesuits, who had been allowed back in 1797, were once more suppressed, and succeeding months produced the most extreme collection of anticlerical decrees ever passed in Spain. The country degenerated rapidly into a state of civil war, from which it was not rescued by the intervention in 1823 of French troops who restored Ferdinand to a throne from which he had been deposed only a few months before. Although the king was confirmed in power and denounced all decrees issued since 7 March 1820, absolute control of the country never returned to him. The long list of executions and imprisonments which characterized Ferdinand's resumption of the throne, showed beyond doubt that Spain had split into two bitterly irreconcilable factions which were never again to make common cause.

Despite the revocation of all decrees passed since 7 March 1820, which seemed to imply restoration of the Inquisition, no steps were in fact taken by Ferdinand to bring back the tribunal, perhaps because he considered it to be by now more of a liability than a help. Individual tribunals continued to carry on a shadowlike existence, but any petitions for total restoration, such as that sent by Córdoba in August 1825, which claimed that since the abolition Spain had suffered 'disappearance of Christian morality, which used to be second nature in a Spaniard',[10] were studiously ignored. It was in this last period of the Inquisition that there occurred what was probably the last official execution for heresy to be carried out in Spain. The prosecution was carried out not by the Inquisition but by the episcopal authorities in Valencia. Cayetano Ripoll was a schoolmaster who fought the French during the War of Independence, was taken prisoner to France and there became converted to Deism. On his return to Spain he was denounced for not taking his pupils to mass and for substituting the phrase 'Praise be to God' in place of 'Ave Maria' in prayers at school. He was arrested in 1824, imprisoned and tried, and condemned to hanging and burning after a delay of two years. The burning was only symbolic: a barrel with flames painted on it was placed under the gibbet. The hanging was real, and was carried out on 26 July 1826.

The Inquisition took no part in this and other similar prosecutions. It remained in a state of lifeless suspension until the regency of Queen Christina, who controlled the government after the death of Ferdinand in September 1833, in the interests of her infant daughter Isabella II. Final steps were now taken to bury the Inquisition once and for all. Discussions carried on by the government in July 1834 showed that the tribunal had long been considered suppressed and that to abolish it again would be little more than a formality. Despite this a formal decree was eventually issued on 15 July 1834,[20] by which the Inquisition was definitively suppressed, all its properties and canonries applied to the extinction of the public debt, and just payment of salaries made to all its former officials. From this date the Inquisition ceased to exist in Spain.

The once powerful and dreaded tribunal vanished without a murmur, swallowed up in the ferocious conflicts of the nineteenth century, unaided by the class that had presided over its institution and deserted by the clergy and people for whom its existence had once been synonymous with the existence of Christianity itself. There still remained parties and individuals who regretted its passing, but even for them the Inquisition had long ceased to be a practical consideration and had become merely a symbol of their present political affiliations. After 1834 it only remained to estimate loss and gain, and to count the cost of the Holy Office. This had already been done by the last secretary of the Inquisition, canon Juan Antonio Llorente, who published at Paris in 1817 and 1818 the four volumes of his *Histoire critique de l'Inquisition d'Espagne*.

Of Llorente and his work some mention should be made. Born in 1756, and educated for an ecclesiastical career, by 1789 he had become secretary general of the Inquisition in Logroño. In 1794 he initiated plans to reform the tribunal along more liberal lines, but this was blocked by the fall from power in 1798 of Jovellanos and the other reformers. In 1799 he supported the famous decree of Urquijo by which the Spanish Church was to be driven into virtual schism from Rome; but this support lost him the favour of his superiors and his post in the Inquisition. When the French took control of the peninsula Llorente was one of those who joined the *afrancesados* in support of Joseph Bonaparte. This opened many doors for him, and he was entrusted with the care of the archives of the suppressed Inquisition. It was on the basis of these original papers that in 1811 he read to the Academy of History at Madrid his *Memoria Histórica*. Other work he had in hand was interrupted when the French began to withdraw from Spain, with the result that his history of the Inquisition was not published until 1817, and then in French with a publishing house in Paris, where he had fled with a large number of original documents from the inquisitorial archives. He returned to Spain when the liberals declared an amnesty after the 1820 revolution, and died in Madrid a few days after his arrival, in February 1823.

Llorente's history is interesting not only because it was written before the definitive suppression of the Inquisition, but also because it was the first informed account, drawn from original manuscripts, ever to be given of an institution which had thrived on utter secrecy. Before his time there had existed complete, widespread and wilful ignorance about even the most elementary facts regarding the Inquisition. After his time there was far less excuse for this. With all his faults, and they were many, Llorente attempted to write a factual history of the tribunal. Unfortunately his work was used by partisan minds as so much more grist for the anti-Catholic mill. Propagandists pointed to his credentials as a former secretary of the Inquisition and hailed in his history the triumph of freedom over darkness: his condemnations were repeated and his extenuations ignored; and soon his work became relegated to the lumber room of pseudo-history, as just another vulgar anticlerical production. This was to do Llorente an injustice which has never been adequately righted. In Spain two generations ago the brilliant and vitriolic pen of Menéndez Pelayo found in Llorente the perfect target for his genius, and so thorough was his work of demolition that virtually no writer since then has dared to defend him. Yet there is less solid criticism in Menéndez Pelayo than his partisans will admit. The bias, the errors, the prolix style, these are all rightly castigated. But intemperate abuse and not serious criticism drove Pelayo to claim that Llorente's history 'is so ill written that it cannot even aspire to be called a booklet or a novel', to call it an 'iniquitous work', 'a rambling and disordered relation, obscure and incoherent, full of repetition and confusion, without any art of composition', 'a hateful and repulsive book, ill conceived, ill arranged and badly written, hypocritical and venal, drier than the sands of Libya'.[21] Few modern readers will admit the justice of these epithets, which have become part of the arsenal of conservatives in criticizing unfavourable studies of the Inquisition.

In one matter, however, Llorente justly deserves the censure of historians. In an attempt to reckon up the cost of the Inquisition in human suffering, he tried to deduce the total number of its victims by multiplying available averages, and came up with the incredible figures of 31,912 relaxations in person, 17,659 relaxations in effigy, and 291,450 penitents, a grand total of 341,021 victims.[22] All the historical evidence has shown this greatly exaggerated figure to be without any foundation. Although there is no way of guessing even a probable total figure for the victims, the available records do allow us to discover the actual totals at specific periods.

According to Hernando del Pulgar, the Inquisition in Spain up to about 1490 had burned two thousand people and reconciled fifteen thousand others under the edicts of grace.[23] His contemporary Andrés Bernáldez estimated that in Seville alone the tribunal had burned between 1480 and 1488 over seven hundred people and reconciled more than five thousand without counting all those who were sentenced to 'perpetual' imprisonment.[24] A later historian, the annalist Diego Ortiz de Zúñiga, claimed that in Seville between 1481 and 1524 over twenty thousand heretics had abjured their crimes, and that over one thousand obstinate heretics had been sent to the stake.[25] Another early account shows that in the seven *autos* held in 1485 at Guadalupe, 124 persons were burnt in person and in effigy, and 'innumerable' people were condemned to various penances including imprisonment.[26] All these examples date from the early years of the tribunal and show that great severity was exercised in the prosecution of heretics. For periods after this there is less reliable information and more speculation. We have already studied the toll in some tribunals in the 1720s. It only remains to summarize in table form what other precise figures can be found for local tribunals.

Tribunal	Period	Relaxations		Other Victims
		Person	Effigy	
Ciudad Real[27]	1484–1531	113	129	27
Toledo[28]	1485–1501	250	500	5,400
Toledo[29]	1575–1610	11	15	904
Toledo[29]	1648–1794	8	63	1,094
Badajoz[30]	1493–1599	41		190
Valladolid[31]	1485–1492	50	6	?
Saragossa[32]*	1485–1502	124	32	458
Valencia[31]	1485–1592	643	479	3,104
Barcelona[33]	1488–1498	23	430	420
Majorca[34]	1488–1729	120	496	664
Canaries[35]	1504–1820	11	107	2,145

These figures set in perspective the proportion between executions and punishments, and help us to arrive at some sort of idea of the scale on which the Inquisition operated. But figures do not tell the whole story. The counting of lives is no clue to the impact of the Holy Office. Fewer deaths were caused by the Inquisition than by criminal folly and political repression in other countries of Europe. What is significant is rather the

*Of those burnt in person, 64 suffered in 1486-8, because of the murder of Arbués. From 1503-74 there were 44 relaxations in person.

influence on Spanish history of social and religious interests of which the Holy Office was at once the tool and the champion, at once the instrument and the guardian, bearing in one hand the olive branch of peace and in the other the exterminating sword.

CHAPTER SIXTEEN

A FINAL REASSESSMENT

O duro Oficio, quién te llama Santo?
João Pinto Delgado, AUTOBIOGRAFÍA (1633-4)

'IN the present liberal state of knowledge', wrote Prescott in 1837, at the beginning of a chapter on the Inquisition in his *History of the Reign of Ferdinand and Isabella*, 'we look with disgust on the pretensions of any human being, however exalted, to invade the sacred rights of conscience, inalienably possessed by every man'. A later writer, conversant with an age where liberalism has repeatedly been eclipsed and the human conscience consistently invaded and perverted, would perhaps look on the Inquisition from a rather different point of view. There is little justification for regarding the tribunal purely as an instrument of fanatical intolerance, and the Inquisition must consequently be treated not merely as a chapter in the history of intolerance but as a phase in the social and religious development of Spain. It would be difficult to prove that religious bigotry alone was responsible for the various events we have already outlined in this book. The intolerance of the Spanish Inquisition becomes meaningful only if related to a wide complex of historical factors, and the religious issue was not always the most prominent or relevant of these. The long discarded but still ever-present legend that the Inquisition represented a natural development in Catholicism, need never have arisen had some attention been devoted to the circumstances which brought it into existence in any particular country. The legend originated in the sixteenth century. It was John Foxe the martyrologist who warned his contemporaries that:

this dreadful engine of tyranny may at any time be introduced into a country where the Catholics have the ascendancy; and hence how careful ought we to be, who are not cursed with such an arbitrary court, to prevent its introduction.[1]

For Foxe and others the Inquisition was just another example of the evils of Rome, and in their works the tribunal was presented as the supreme institution of intolerance:

When the inquisitors have taken umbrage against an innocent person, all expedients are used to facilitate condemnation; false oaths and testimonies are employed to find the accused guilty; and all laws and institutions are sacrificed to satiate the most bigoted vengeance.[2]

Protestant pens depicted the struggle of heretics as one for freedom from a tyrannical faith. Wherever Catholicism triumphed, they claimed, not only religious but civil liberty was extinguished. The Reformation, according to this interpretation, brought about the liberation of the human spirit from the fetters of darkness and superstition. Propaganda along these lines proved to be strikingly effective in the context of the political conflicts of the sixteenth century, and there were always refugees from persecution to lend substance to the story. As late as the mid-nineteenth century one of the best examples of such propaganda could be found in John Motley's brilliant history of *The Rise of the Dutch Republic*, first published in London in 1855. Motley adhered close enough to the truth to appear convincing, yet writing half a century after Llorente he could say this of the Spanish Inquisition:[3]

It taught the savages of India and America to shudder at the name of Christianity. The fear of its introduction froze the earlier heretics of Italy, France and Germany into orthodoxy. It was a court owning allegiance to no temporal authority, superior to all other tribunals. It was a bench of monks without appeal, having its familiars in every house, diving into the secrets of every fireside, judging and executing its horrible decrees without responsibility. It condemned not deeds but thoughts. It affected to descend into individual conscience, and to punish the crimes which it pretended to discover. Its process was reduced to a horrible simplicity. It arrested on suspicion, tortured till confession, and then punished by fire. Two witnesses, and those to separate facts, were sufficient to consign the victim to a loathsome dungeon. Here he was sparingly supplied with food, forbidden to speak, or even to sing – to which pastime it could hardly be thought he would feel much inclination –

and then left to himself till famine and misery should break his spirit. When that time was supposed to have arrived, he was examined. Did he confess and forswear his heresy, whether actually innocent or not, he might then assume the sacred shirt, and escape with confiscation of all his property. Did he persist in the avowal of his innocence, two witnesses sent him to the stake, one to the rack. He was informed of the testimony against him, but never confronted with the witness. That accuser might be his son, father, or the wife of his bosom, for all were enjoined, under the death penalty, to inform the inquisitors of every suspicious word which might fall from their nearest relatives. The indictment being thus supported, the prisoner was tried by torture. The rack was the court of justice; the criminal's only advocate was his fortitude – for the nominal counsellor, who was permitted no communication with the prisoner, and was furnished neither with documents nor with power to procure evidence, was a puppet, aggravating the lawlessness of the proceedings by the mockery of legal forms. The torture took place at midnight, in a gloomy dungeon, dimly lighted by torches. The victim – whether man, matron, or tender virgin – was stripped naked and stretched upon the wooden bench. Water, weights, fires, pulleys, screws – all the apparatus by which the sinews could be strained without cracking, the bones bruised without breaking, and the body racked exquisitely without giving up its ghost—was now put into operation. The executioner, enveloped in a black robe from head to foot, with his eyes glaring at his victim through holes cut in the hood which muffled his face, practised successively all the forms of torture which the devilish ingenuity of the monks had invented. The imagination sickens when striving to keep pace with these dreadful realities.

Side by side with this presentation of the Inquisition as a threat to human liberty went a more practical consideration. The tribunal was looked upon as the great instrument of that enemy of the Protestant religion, Spain. Attacks on it, and stories of its horrors, became part of the machine of anti-Spanish propaganda in western Europe, where some Catholic powers no less than Protestant were beginning to dispute Spanish hegemony. In the Netherlands it was bruited about that Spain intended to introduce the Inquisition as a means of subduing the country. In 1566 a pamphlet entitled *Les subtils moyens par le Cardinal Grandvelle avec ces complices Inventez, pour Instituer l'abhominable Inquisition avec la Cruelle observation des Placcartz Contre ceulx de la Religion* called on the Protestant nobility of the Low Countries to defend their liberties against the tyrannies of the Holy Office. In fact, the Netherlands already possessed an Inquisition of its own, which Philip II himself confessed was 'more merciless than the one here',[4] and the rumour was little more than a legend employed to discredit Spain and incite rebellion. William of Orange in his famous *Apologia* of 1581, written in reply to a decree outlawing him, turned the issue into a brilliant exercise in anti-Spanish propaganda. The execution of heretics, he claimed, was a natural occupation for bloodthirsty Spaniards: 'the brightness of the fires wherein they have tormented so many poor Christians, was never delightful or pleasant to mine eyes, as it hath rejoyc'd the sight of the Duke of Alba and the Spaniards'. Then came the unkind cut: 'I will no more wonder at that which all the world believeth: to wit, that the greatest part of the Spaniards, and especially those that count themselves noblemen, are of the blood of the Moors and Jews'.[5] To a racially sensitive *hidalgo*, this was abuse indeed. A legend of Spanish cruelty and barbarism had to be created if Europe were to sympathize with the revolt of the Netherlands, and the Inquisition was the most natural choice of weapon. How effective such propaganda was, is shown by the universal fear in Protestant countries that Spanish or Catholic domination anywhere would result in the introduction of the notorious tribunal. During the religious wars in France the Huguenots feared that Henry II, in concert with Philip II of Spain, planned to establish a native Inquisition. William of Orange and the Count of Egmont were so disturbed about this that they asked Cardinal Granvelle in 1561 to deny the report.[6] Yet apart from his Italian states Philip had little serious intention of exporting the Spanish Inquisition. Even in England, where he exercised some influence as husband of the queen, no steps were ever taken to introduce the tribunal. The truth was that most European countries already had their own machinery for dealing with heretics, and had no need for outside help. Besides this, the Spanish tribunal was not by nature a primarily anti-Protestant body, and would have needed substantial modification if introduced into some European states. Finally, the foreign policy of Philip II was by no means consistently anti-Protestant, so that the picture of Spain as a rabidly Catholic power distorts the reality of sixteenth century international politics.

This then was the context in which the legend arose. The many pamphlets and works written since the sixteenth century on the horrors of the Spanish Inquisition would require considerable space to be studied adequately: the picture they all paint can, however, be easily guessed. Perhaps the most important of all the propagandists was Reinaldo González Montano, a Spanish victim of and then refugee from the Holy Office, who published abroad in Heidelberg in 1567 his *Sanctae Inquisitionis Hispanicae Artes aliquot detectae ac palam traductae.* The vivid style and imagination of its author made this book an immediate international success. It was translated into all the major languages of western Europe, went through several editions in various forms, and served as the basis for further literature on the subject. The year after its appearance it was translated into English by a government official and published with a dedication to the archbishop of Canterbury, Matthew Parker. As history the book is worthless, as an episode in the development of sustained distortion and virulent invective it was important enough to command the admiration of Menéndez Pelayo. Among its other qualities, the book was careful to warn Protestant gentlemen to look to their wives and daughters. The following passage, taken from the contemporary English version, comments on prisoners of the Inquisition who are taken into the torture chambers and are stripped naked, even if they are women.

And here those ranke Rammes declare how they will not lose that devilish pleasure, which they take in that shameful and unseemly sight, though the poore wretches that suffer this, buy it both with payne and shame enough full dearely. The which thing surely is a good occasion, why that after this shameful and impudent dealing of the Fathers of ye faith be once noysed and bruted abroad, they whose wives or doughters either have already or may heareafter fall, or presently are in this ye holy fathers foule handling, suffering this shameful villainly, should be utterly abhorred and shunned of al the people wheresoever they go.[7]

As time went on, the legend grew out of all proportion, thanks to the efforts of zealous Protestants to keep alive the cause for which their martyrs suffered. To a nineteenth-century edition of Foxe's *Book of Martyrs* a certain Reverend Ingram Cobbin, MA, added the following account of the Inquisition, enlivening it with detailed falsehoods with which even Foxe had not sullied his original narrative. During the Napoleonic wars in Spain, the Reverend Cobbin assured his readers, the French liberating troops broke into the secret cells of the tribunal in Madrid:

> Here they found the instruments of torture, of every kind which the ingenuity of men or devils could invent. The first instrument noticed was a machine by which the victim was confined and then, beginning with the fingers, all the joints in the hands, arms and body were broken and drawn one after another, until the sufferer died. The second (was the water torture). The third was an infernal machine, laid horizontally, to which the victim was bound; the machine then being placed between two scores of knives so fixed that by turning the machine with a crank the flesh of the sufferer was all torn from his limbs into small pieces. The fourth surpassed the others in fiendish ingenuity. Its exterior was a large doll, richly dressed and having the appearance of a beautiful woman, with her arms extended ready to embrace her victim. A semicircle was drawn around her, and the person who passed over this fatal mark touched a spring which caused the diabolical engine to open; its arms immediately clasped him, and a thousand knives cut him in as many pieces.[8]

To native Spaniards such grotesque misrepresentation only proved that the outside world was interested, against all the facts, in preserving the Black Legend (*Leyenda Negra*) of an obscurantist, cruel and fanatical Spain. The Inquisition took its place beside all the other historical iniquities attributed to Spaniards, the wars of religion, the destruction of the American Indians, the expulsion of the Jews and Moriscos, and probably outdid them all in the volume of polemical literature through the centuries. No small part in this can be attributed to the Italians who, in their struggle against Spanish imperialism in Italy, gave an impetus to the Black Legend long before the Dutch revolt stirred the conscience of Protestant Europe.[9] It was in the Italian provinces of the Spanish crown that the greatest and most successful revolts against the Inquisition occurred. The risings of 1511 and 1516 in Sicily were caused partly by popular hatred of the tribunal's familiars. Ferdinand the Catholic attempted to introduce the Spanish Inquisition into Naples, which already had its own episcopal Inquisition, but effective protests blocked his bid. The issue did not subside, and both in 1547 and 1564 there were risings in the province because of rumours that the Spanish tribunal was going to be established. Similarly, in 1563 Philip II had to admit defeat when universal opposition greeted his attempt to replace the episcopal Inquisition in Milan by a Spanish one. Italian 'nationalism', and not any particular fear of the Spanish tribunal, was the driving force behind this hostility. The same reason makes it sometimes difficult to accept Italian accounts of the Inquisition at face value, and the very valuable reports of the Venetian ambassadors share this defect, that they invariably depict the tribunal as a despotic body in control of a hypocritical nation. In 1525 ambassador Contarini claimed that everyone trembled before the Holy Office. In 1557 ambassador Badoero spoke of the terror caused by its procedure. In 1563 ambassador Tiepolo said that everyone shuddered at its name, as it had supreme authority over the property, life, honour and even the souls of men. In 1565 ambassador Soranzo reported that its authority transcended that of the king.[10] These accounts were far from being 'unbiased reports', as Lea claims them to be. They were subjective appraisals from which hostile undertones were seldom absent. Francesco Guicciardini, as Florentine ambassador to Ferdinand, was also representative of Italian opinion when he described the Spaniards as 'very religious in externals and outward show, but not so in fact'. [11] Almost the same words were used by the Venetian Tiepolo in 1563. Such hypocrisy in religion, taken hand in hand with the existence of the Inquisition, meant to Italians that the tribunal was created not for religious purity, but simply to rob the Jews. Some conclusion of this sort was certainly held by the prelates of the Holy See whenever they intervened in favour of the conversos. Moreover, the racialism of the Spanish authorities was scorned in Italy, where the Jewish community led a comparatively tranquil existence. As the Spanish ambassador at Rome reported in 1652:

In Spain it is held in great horror to be descended from a heretic or a Jew, but here they laugh at these matters, and at us, because we concern ourselves with them.[12]

This lack of love between two leading Latin countries is of some importance, because it shows that the tide of opinion in Europe was not confined to Protestant countries only, and that contemporary Catholic sentiment could also be added to the general attitude.

But while it is relatively easy to gauge European opinion of Spain and the Inquisition, it is impossible to estimate with any precision what Spaniards themselves thought of the tribunal. This was the difficulty facing Llorente in his *Memoria Histórica*, when he attempted to prove that the tribunal was really hated in Spain. How could it have been hated? Llorente himself admitted that scarcely a single book published in the previous three centuries would be found to be critical of the Inquisition. The cynical observer will comment that the censorship allowed only favourable literature to be published, and that printed opinion in favour of the tribunal was bound to predominate. But this is only part of the story. There is little doubt that in the three or four centuries after the foundation of the Inquisition the Spanish people as a whole, and the Castilians in particular, gave their ready support to its existence. The tribunal was, after all, not a despotic body imposed on them tyrannically, but a logical expression of the social prejudices prevalent in their midst. It was created to deal with a social problem, and as long as the problem was deemed to exist people did not question its necessity. It is worth remembering that virtually no historical evidence exists to show any significant opposition to the existence of the Inquisition, apart from the obvious hostility of the racial category against whom it was directed – the conversos. What opposition there was rested on readily discernible minority motives, such as nationalism in Italy and Aragon; jurisdictional conflicts in the case of secular and episcopal tribunals; and economic interest when lords came to the protection of their tenants. In none of these cases was any plea ever made for the abolition of the Inquisition. Quarrels and discontent did not need to go that far. It is significant, too, that even the most liberal, and at times critical, of Spanish Catholics before the nineteenth century did not omit to give due praise to the Inquisition in their writings. A final indication of the relative popularity of the Inquisition is provided by one negative, but important, piece of evidence. In a period when the popular mind invented refrains of every sort to express disapproval of kings, ministers, prelates and their policies; when the sheer volume of anti-

Jewish verse reflected the depth of antisemitism in society; and when anticlericalism was prevalent in numerous political pasquinades; it is astounding to find no proverbs reflecting any dislike of the Holy Office, apart from the mild and well-known phrase 'Con el Rey y con la Santa Inquisición, chitón!' – 'On the king and on the Holy Inquisition, not a word!'[13]

In this picture of massive support for the Holy Office, the exceptions stand out more sharply and clearly. Yet they are – as far as we know – very few. 'It seems impossible', protested Llorente, 'that as many learned men as Spain has had in three centuries could have been all of the same opinion'.[14] Had there not been any Catholics who considered the existence of the tribunal contrary to the practice of true religion? The fact is that until the eighteenth century the only native opposition seems to have come from Catholic conversos. There were certainly individuals like Juan de Mariana, who expressed his strong disagreement with forced conversions.[15] There was Alonso de Virués, a protagonist of tolerance who also condemned forced conversions and those 'who spare neither prison nor knout nor chains nor the axe; for such is the effect of these horrible means, that the torments they inflict on the body can never change the disposition of the soul'.[16] But effective disillusion only occurred in the eighteenth century. A sign of coming changes was given by a native pharmacist arrested by the Inquisition at Laguna (Tenerife) in 1707. He is reported to have said:

that one could live in France because there there did not exist the poverty and subjection that today exists in Spain and Portugal, since in France they do not try to find out nor do they make a point of knowing who everyone is and what religion he has and professes. And so he who lives properly and is of good character may become what he wishes.[17]

A generation later, in 1741, another native of the Canaries, the Marquis de la Villa de San Andrés, echoed precisely the same sentiments when he praised Paris, where life was free and unrestricted, 'and no one asks where you are going, or questions who you are, nor at Easter does the priest ask if you have been to confession'.[18] This was the spirit that threatened to splinter the defences of the closed society. It was, in one way, an urge to freedom, but in another way it was a demand for justice. The fate of the Jews and Moors continued to be on the conscience of intelligent statesmen. When José Carvajal began to interest himself in the attacks directed by Salucio against the statutes of *limpieza*, his main preoccupation was 'the cruel impiety with which they have treated those who were outside the Catholic religion, barring all human doors of entry against them'.[19] This was in 1751. A similar approach was adopted by Jovellanos in 1798. For him the first blame to be laid against the Inquisition was on account of the conversos:

From this arose the infamy that covered descendants of these conversos, who were reputed infamous by public opinion. The laws upheld this and approved the statutes of *limpieza de sangre*, which kept out so many innocent people not only from posts of honour and trust but also from entering churches, colleges, convents and even unions and trade guilds. From this came the perpetuation of hatred not only against the Inquisition but against religion itself.[20]

Jovellanos argued that the injustices committed against a whole section of society by the Inquisition now needed to be remedied. The tribunal had lost all theoretical justification for its existence, since the modern threat to religion came no longer from Jews and Moriscos and heretics, but from unbelievers. Against these the tribunal would be of little avail, since its ministers were ignorant and incapable. The time had come to get rid of such a superfluous body, to right the injustices of history, and to restore to the bishops their old powers over heresy.

For all this, Jovellanos and his other Catholic colleagues in the government and in the ranks of the nobility were not radical revolutionaries. Their desire for reform, for a change in the nature of society, was limited by the concern for stability. The Catholic liberals who opposed the Inquisition were unwilling to look too far. Jovellanos wrote to his friend Jardine: 'You approve of the spirit of rebellion; I do not. I disapprove of it openly and am far from believing that it carries the seal of merit'.[21] Because of this, the attitude of Catholics as such towards the Inquisition ceased to be of great consequence, and was lost among the waves of turbulence created by those whose hatred of the Holy Office was only part of their distrust and hatred of religion.

But how far had the Inquisition by itself been responsible for the growth of irreligion? A question of this sort can never be adequately answered, and because of this the onus lies on opponents of the tribunal to prove their case. So thorough an historian as Lea gives way to the simplest faults of reasoning in this matter. Beginning with the observations of Italians on the shallowness of religion among Spaniards, Lea goes on to cite other witnesses to irreverent behaviour in Spain and concludes that 'the Inquisition, while enforcing conformity as to dogma and outward observance, failed to inspire genuine respect for religion'.[22] Evidence, reasoning, and conclusions here are all equally absurd. As well might the Inquisition be blamed for any of the other failures of Spaniards and their history. There is some justice in Menéndez Pelayo's satire on those who have blamed the tribunal for all the ills of Spain.

Why was there no industry in Spain? Because of the Inquisition. Why are we Spaniards lazy? Because of the Inquisition. Why are there bull-fights in Spain? Because of the Inquisition. Why do Spaniards take a *siesta*? Because of the Inquisition.[23]

And so on. Besides all this, the tribunal has been discussed in the context of the decline of Spain. In so far as the question of decline is an economic one, the responsibility can only marginally be laid at the door of the Inquisition. The expulsion of the Jews, the prejudice against servile labour, these and other factors were not initiated by the Inquisition alone but by the social temperament in Spain. The guilt to be borne by the Inquisition must be shared with those sections of society that inspired its policies. Antisemitism came first, and then the Holy Office. In a way, the burden of responsibility may be placed on the governing classes of Castile more than on anyone else, since from the time of the Catholic monarchs onwards it was they who guided the destinies of the peninsula, and it was they who imposed the Inquisition on Aragon, Catalonia and Valencia. There is no doubt, of course, that the initial consequences of introducing the Inquisition were seriously felt in the economic circles of the large cities. But even here it is possible to exaggerate. In Barcelona, for instance, the coming of the tribunal caused serious dislocation in the 1480s. We have the names of at least 280 people who fled with their families. Among them were great merchants and leading administrators, including the regent of the Chancellery, Antonio de Bardaxi, who fled to the

Holy See for help. Most of them were able to take their goods with them, thanks to the hostility shown by the Catalan authorities to the Inquisition. But the Inquisition did not by itself cause the decline of Catalonia. That had already begun: the Inquisition merely quickened the pace.[24]

More serious and solid an issue is the question whether the cultural decline of Spain from the mid-seventeenth century to the mid-eighteenth century can be blamed on the tribunal. That there was such a decline is certain. That the Inquisition caused it is less certain. 'It would seem superfluous to insist', argued Lea, 'that a system of severe repression of thought, by all the instrumentalities of Inquisition and State, is an ample explanation of the decadence of Spanish learning and literature'.[25] For Lord Acton the injury inflicted on literature by the Inquisition was 'the most obvious and conspicuous fact of modern history'.[26] It is true that the tribunal in its more conservative years was only too active in moving against certain intellectuals, and here the testimony of Mariana, already quoted, is decisive. There is no doubt that many of Spain's finest theologians, poets and writers had to toe the party line with the greatest possible care, and Saint Teresa (because she was no intellectual) was one of the few who had enough confidence to laugh off this threat to creative liberty. Similarly there can be little doubt that in its role as guardian of the closed society, and by the preservation of orthodoxy through censorship, the Inquisition restricted the development of independent enquiry. But, did it achieve more than this? More than a century after the institution of the tribunal, Spanish language, art and literature dominated Europe and the Europeanized world.[27] In certain sciences among them mathematics, botany, and metallurgy, Spain could compare with any other nation in Europe.[28] If it kept at bay the intellectual achievements of the outside world, it did not therefore cease to project its image on that world. Foreign universities were for the most part closed to Spaniards, but they still came and went as travellers, learned foreign languages and adopted foreign customs.[29] This could hardly be otherwise, since Spanish political interests extended over the whole of the continent up to Muscovy. Within the peninsula no creative literature was forbidden unless it compromised dogmatic essentials as the authorities interpreted them. Yet contradiction and reaction did occur, and intellectual atrophy did set in. By the beginning of the seventeenth century Mariana was explaining that he had translated his history from the Latin because there were now few who understood the language.[30] Classical studies decayed. Had the Inquisition ever been against them? The practice of science died out. But what evidence is there that the tribunal disapproved of science? In the sixteenth century Salamanca led the European world in teaching the system of Copernicus as part of its syllabus and this was laid down in the university's statutes of 1594. Ten years before this, the Spaniard Diego de Zúñiga was expounding and defending the system of Copernicus in a still largely Ptolemaic world. It was to Spain that Galileo thought of retiring in 1612, when persecution haunted him in Italy.[31] Yet two centuries later all this had changed. In 1804 the professor of Astronomy at the same university published a book in which he was careful to explain that Copernicus was not opposed to Holy Scripture.[32] What happened to Copernicus? Where did his name disappear in those two lost centuries? No Index of the Spanish Inquisition ever prohibited a work of Copernicus, and the works of Galileo, Kepler and Tycho Brahe had never been forbidden.

For part of the answer we have to turn to the universities of Spain. Too often in modern history the universities, from the time of the Reformation to more recent memory, have been among the most belated upholders of liberty of thought and freedom from authority. Galileo's enemies were not in Rome but at the University of Pisa. Arias Montano's labours were threatened not by the inquisitors but by members of the academic staff of Salamanca University. El Brocense's career was likewise threatened more directly by his colleagues than by the Holy Office. The academic world came to the parting of the ways under Philip II. A few liberals – Juan de Valdés, Pedro de Lerma, Francisco Enzinas – for intellectual, religious or racial reasons left the country to work abroad. Others remained behind and were slowly silenced or died out. The great universities of Alcalá and Salamanca, open by statute to all Christians of every degree, began in the sixteenth century to lose their democratic character and to become resorts of the aristocracy. The colleges began to be monopolized by young nobles.[33] Under their influence only those courses that satisfied the needs of the aristocracy were developed. By the mid-sixteenth century decadence cast its shadow over the world of learning. The faculties of medicine which had been the glory of Spain, thanks to the great Moorish and Jewish tradition, fell into decline. Part of the reason was certainly the suspicion attached to the culture of the non-Christian races of the peninsula. In addition the spirit of enquiry in medicine carried with it associations of heresy, as in the case of Servet, whose heretical book on the Trinity was published in 1531, twenty-two years before the publication of his findings on the circulation of the blood. On both these counts the Inquisition had a serious responsibility to bear. But it is also significant that the practice of medicine was socially despised as a mercenary career, and in the prevailing scale of values a calling so long associated with Jews was not considered worthy of attention. By the end of the sixteenth century the universities were in reactionary hands. El Brocense had at one time intemperately exclaimed, 'If they prove to me that my faith is founded on St Thomas, I'll excrete on it and find another', but by the seventeenth century St Thomas Aquinas and Aristotle were the unshakeable pillars of philosophy in Spain. The spirit of enquiry and experiment in the sciences was replaced by a conformist obedience to authority: the works of Aristotle and Aquinas were trimmed to fit a syllabus they would have been the first to revolt against. In this way, as Feijóo was later to lament, in Spain the sources of knowledge dried up and science ceased to exist. By the end of the sixteenth century there were no professors of mathematics in Alcalá or Salamanca. It was left to Philip III in 1590 to order a lectureship in mathematics to be reinstituted at Salamanca, because of a lack of experts on artillery! The chairs of physics, natural philosophy, and astronomy at Salamanca were indeed filled from time to time, but by names drawn from utter obscurity. 'They were professors', says la Fuente, 'who held professorships but did no teaching.'[34] What happened to Copernicus was what happened to everyone else, and in this the role of the Inquisition was only a secondary cause. A *trahison des clercs* of enormous dimensions, a complete abdication of responsibility by the academic leaders of the nation, led to the ossification of Spanish thought for well over a century. Added to this, the Inquisition by its willingness to prosecute any divergent ideas in the country helped to repress the development of originality. In the experimental sciences, in physics, biology, medicine, agriculture, mathematics and so on, Spain stopped dead for several generations. Matriculation entries at Salamanca and Alcalá after the mid-seventeenth century reached a record low level and the application sheets for medicine and mathematics contained not a single entry.[35] This decline is all the more remarkable since not a single important scientific book was ever placed on the Index, and the Inquisition only showed itself hostile to scholars who mingled theological speculation with their researches.

The fact is that 'decline' is too complex a concept to be blamed on the Inquisition alone. We have tried to portray the tribunal as an organic function of a corporate whole, inseparable from the social and economic forces which affected the entire body of society. Being a part of the whole, the Inquisition shared in the rise of Spain as it shared in its decline. In this view, the question whether the tribunal was a cause of decline is one that ignores a wide field of related issues. Similarly, the thesis, still fashionable in some quarters, that since the tribunal's greatest period of power coincided with the period of greatest Spanish expansion and achievement, the Inquisition was partly responsible for the glories of the Golden Century, is too obviously wrong to be credible. Both theses err by attempting to identify the Holy Office with either the rise or the fall of Habsburg Spain. In reality, it took part in both without being uniquely responsible for either. In its early years and in the sixteenth century the Inquisition had the support of the greatest statesmen of Spain, and inquisitors such as Ximénez, Manrique, and Quiroga were among the most eminent men of their time. Leaders of society and religion saw in the tribunal the surest defence against decadent ideas prevalent in other countries and the banner of the Holy Office was raised in Mexico, Lima, Goa and Manila. By the seventeenth century, however, the external collapse of Spanish power at the Dunes (1639) and at Rocroi (1643) was accompanied by an internal collapse of confidence. It was an inquisitor who in the reign of Philip IV pressed for the repeal of the statutes of *limpieza*; and under Charles II the election of a Jesuit, for the first and only time, as Inquisitor General led to the political discredit of the *Suprema* and the repeated dismissal of inquisitors under Philip V. Well before the eighteenth century the tribunal had lost all its intellectual eminence, and Jovellanos opposed its continued function of censorship because its 'members were ignorant and incapable of judgment'. This rhythmic identification of the Inquisition with the general movement of Spanish history into and out of the closed society, is as far as the evidence will take us.

All history, Croce maintained, is contemporary history. In a sense quite distinct from the philosophical one, this is true of the events discussed so briefly in these pages. The weight of themes we have been analysing bears down heavily on the modern historian. By far the greater volume of work on the Inquisition now circulating in Spain presents the tribunal as an essential and saving component of the nation's structure, created in a golden age by the legendary Catholic monarchs and for over three centuries thereafter representing all that was sacred in the heritage of a religious people. The ideological presuppositions of this uncritical viewpoint are too obviously a part of contemporary politics to be discussed here. But it is worth citing the explanation for this attitude given by Juan Valera in the nineteenth century. The cause of withdrawal and decadence, he claimed, was 'a fever of pride' that gripped Spain: 'we thought we were the new people of God, and confused religion with patriotic egotism'.[36] In a period of political chaos and uncertainty, conservatives looked back wistfully to the sixteenth century, reading into it a state of political stability, religious unity, and cultural glory within the peninsula, while beyond its frontiers the soldiers, explorers and missionaries of Spain brought the nation to a level of greatness unequalled before or since. It was left to the twentieth century for a regime to adopt the emblem, the yoke and arrows, of the Catholic monarchs, and to sanction attitudes reminiscent of the Golden Century. Since the Inquisition flourished most at precisely this time, since it alone guaranteed unity of religion and purity of faith in a crumbling Christendom, there must have been a necessary dependence of the golden age on the tribunal, or at least no inherent contradiction. Whatever the virtues of this view, and even if one were to grant that a closed society, such as Spain was in the sixteenth century, or as others have been in the twentieth, were best equipped to develop and expand the resources of a country in the most phenomenal way, the question remains whether the ideological pressures imposed on the nation as a whole were such as to benefit the country. The internal peace imposed by the Catholic monarchs, the religious unity enforced by the early Habsburgs, these gave Spain a national identity it had not previously possessed. But the peace and unity of those years created a problem for twentieth-century historians who had to explain to themselves why the whole structure broke down.

For some historians the tranquillity of the sixteenth century was bought at a price. 'We had no religious wars in the sixteenth century', admits Sánchez Albornoz, 'but we have had them in the twentieth.'[37] In other words, the *pax hispanica* of the Habsburgs was a false peace, it was the imposition of order without concern for the maintenance of internal justice. One ideology was proclaimed, and the interests of particular classes and provinces were ignored. If there had been a reconciliation of parties, of conversos and Old Christians, of royalists and *comuneros*, of Castilians and Catalans, it had been only apparent and not real. For Ramón Menéndez Pidal the reconciliation had hardly even been apparent. He believed that a reconciliation had never taken place, and that there had always existed a struggle, often mute, never suppressed, between Two Spains.[38] The interplay between African and European Spain, isolationist and international Spain, liberal and reactionary Spain, caused the tensions that explained the strife in Spanish history. The Two Spains followed 'the fated destiny of the two sons of Oedipus, who would not consent to reign together and mortally wounded each other'. Menéndez Pidal looked forward to an age when reconciliation would eventually occur, and reintegration would lead to unity of purpose in a tolerant society. In their own way, both these explanations are relevant to the impact made by the Inquisition upon Spanish history. The enlightened ministers of the eighteenth century were right to see that the racial doctrines of *limpieza* had created social injustice in the community and had, as an inquisitor had once pointed out, set one half of Spain against the other. The Inquisition and what it represented may have been accepted by the mass of the people in Spain, but there always existed the small minority of those who believed that the propagation of racialism in the seventeenth century, and the defence of absolutism in the eighteenth, were no part of the work of an ecclesiastical tribunal. At a period when the Spanish Church and Holy Office were dedicated to strengthening the barriers between Reconquest Spain and a world in ferment, it was an international order, the Society of Jesus, founded and directed for the first few decades of its existence by Spaniards, that tried to recall the conscience of Spain to values which did not rest on exclusivism. But Spain chose exclusivism, it chose a 'patriotic egotism' which denied existence to dissidents within and denied recognition to dissidents without. It was the fate of the Inquisition not merely to be a tool and executor of this exclusivism, but also to be identified as the author responsible for all the ills that followed from it. In this way it drew upon itself detestation and fear in the sixteenth century and universal obloquy in the nineteenth.

The liberal school in Spanish historiography is large, but so far has not produced many works of revision. It is exceptional to find a general work which presents the Inquisition as a pernicious influence on Spanish religion and society.[39] The principal difficulty in the way of effective revision has been the old approach which presents religious toleration as the centre of the question. With an argument set only in terms of religious toleration, it has been relatively easy to excuse on the grounds that it was an intolerant age and that Protestants executed as many heretics as their opponents did. If figures sufficed, it could probably be shown that single acts of religious fury outside Spain, such as the Massacre of St Bartholomew's in France, or any other religious atrocity in the Netherlands or in Germany, wiped out more people in a single night than were executed in the whole history of the Spanish Inquisition. We have already seen that witchcraft alone claimed more victims in Germany than intolerance did in Spain. The citation of deaths is no argument. For those who have lived under the shadow of Hitler, the whole perspective has changed. A reader of Julio Caro Baroja's essay on the Jews in Spain, or of the seminal works of Antonio Domínguez Ortiz and Albert Sicroff on the cult of *limpieza* in Spanish society, finds himself haunted by the degrading and ever-darkening spectre of racialism. The sufferings of people who in the past and even today in the twentieth century have found themselves excluded from occupation, office and social position because of their racial antecedents, and of those who have been defined out of a society simply because they have been denied assimilation, are considerations which make past history contemporary. The problem of the Inquisition remains no longer exclusively a religious one, but becomes a sociological one, something to be considered as part of a totality and not as an isolated phenomenon.

In these pages we have taken the ruling class of Spain as the demiurge of an ideology which, for good or ill, has dominated Spanish society into modern times. This class content in ideology cannot be too strongly emphasized as the main factor in the creation of the closed society of traditional Spain. Ortega y Gasset in a famous essay in 1922 lamented the decline of Spain as being caused by the failure of the aristocratic class to govern the rural masses.[40] We must stand Ortega on his head to get at the truth. What decline there may have been was caused by the excessive predominance of the noble class. 'The spirit of chivalry and *hidalguismo* penetrated the marrow of Castilian society and weakened its fibre'.[41] Wherever it was established, the Inquisition drew its strength from the common people and from the nobility over them, who together became the steadfast pillars of the traditional order in Spain. This broad mass of support has made it possible for some to denounce attacks on the Inquisition in modern times as attacks on Spain itself, and the number of these denunciations shows clearly that the ideology of the closed society still predominates in certain quarters. One and a half centuries after its abolition the Holy Office still remains a part of contemporary history. The spirit which brought it to birth still roams abroad,[42] and the problem it was created to solve – preservation of the faith – remains more urgent and more intense than it has ever been. There was a time once when the banner of the Inquisition stood in every continent of the world and in every corner of the monarchy on which the sun was reputed never to set. Today, nearly two centuries after the sunset of that empire, there is a need for the ending of myths and the beginning of reconciliation.

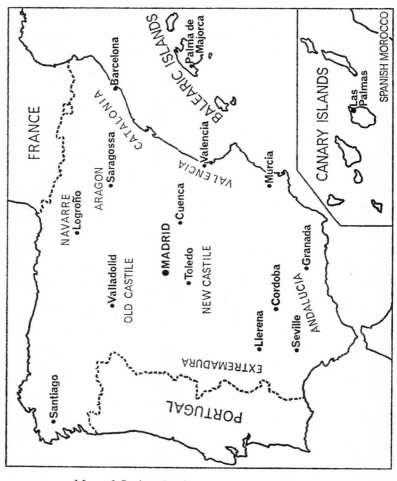

*Map of Spain, showing the permanent tribunals
of the Spanish Inquisition*

NOTES

Chapter One: Introductory

1. Cited in Américo Castro, *The Structure of Spanish History* (Princeton 1954), p. 221.
2. *Ibid.*, p. 225.
3. Jaime Vicens Vives, ed., *Historia social y económica de España y América* (5 vols. Barcelona 1957), II, 417. Cited hereafter as Vicens Vives, ed., *Historia*.
4. E.g. W. H. Prescott, *History of the reign of Ferdinand and Isabella* (London 1841), p. 146 ff.
5. Jaime Vicens Vives, *Historia Económica de España* (Barcelona 1959), p. 269. Cited hereafter as Vicens Vives.
6. Julius Klein, *The Mesta. A study in Spanish economic history 1273-1836* (Cambridge, Mass., 1920), p. 37-8.
7. Vicens Vives, p. 269.
8. See in general *La Reconquista española y la repoblación del país* (Saragossa 1951).
9. Angel del Arco y Molinero, *Glorias de la Nobleza española* (Tarragona 1899).
10. Antonio José Saraiva, *A Inquisição portuguesa* (Lisbon 1956), p. 13: 'O rei abandona o seu papel tradicional de árbitro entre as diversas forças nacionais. O Estado torna-se absorvente, destrói as minorias, sejam elas os lavradores vilãos e livres, os hebreus ou os "mouriscos", impõe uma vigorosa disciplina ideológica, esmagando todas as dissidências e oposições e regressando à ideologia tradicional da grande época do feudalismo.'
11. Vicens Vives, p. 270.
12. *Don Quixote*, book I, chap. 21.
13. *Ibid.*, book I, chap. 28.
14. Guicciardini, *Opere* (Bari 1929-36), vol. IX p. 130, 'Relazione di Spagna'.
15. Ramón Menéndez Pidal, *The Spaniards in their history* (London 1950), p. 131.
16. Américo Castro, 'Algunas observaciones acerca del concepto del honor en los siglos XVI y XVII', *Revista de Filología Española*, III (1916).

17. Antonio José Saraiva, *op. cit.*, p. 10-12.
18. 'La nobleza castellana brilló por su ausencia en la conquista de América', Vicens Vives, ed., *Historia*, III, 422.
19. *Ibid.*, III, 528.
20. For all this see Antonio Domínguez Ortiz, 'Los extranjeros en la vida española durante el siglo XVII', *Estudios de Historia Social de España* (Madrid 1960), IV, ii, p. 293-426. Also André-E. Sayous, 'La Genèse du système capitaliste: la pratique des affaires et leur mentalité dans l'Espagne du XVIe siècle', *Annales d'Histoire Economique et Sociale* (1936), p. 334-54.
21. Domínguez Ortiz, 'Los extranjeros', p. 300.
22. Menéndez Pidal, p. 135.

Chapter Two: The Great Dispersion

1. 'La Biblia de Mose Arragel de Guadalfajara', cited in Américo Castro, *The Structure of Spanish History*, p. 489.
2. Abraham A. Neuman, *The Jews in Spain. Their social, political and cultural life during the Middle Ages* (2 vols. Philadelphia 1944), II, 184.
3. Pero López de Ayala, *Crónica de Enrique III*, cited in Julio Caro Baroja, *Los Judios en la España moderna y contemporanea* (3 vols. Madrid 1962), I, 106 n. 19.
4. See the discussion in Caro Baroja, I, 21-110.
5. Américo Castro, *The Structure*, p. 474-91.
6. Neuman, II, 217; see also Américo Castro, p. 491-6; and Caro Baroja, II, 162-90.
7. Américo Castro, p. 499.
8. Neuman, II, 187.
9. *Ibid.*, II, 221.
10. Fritz Baer, *Die Juden im christlichen Spanien* (2 vols. Berlin 1929), II, 223, 428.
11. Andrés Bernáldez, *Memorias del reinado de los Reyes Católicos* (Biblioteca 'Reyes Católicos', Madrid 1962), chap. CXII, p. 256.
12. Manuel Serrano y Sanz, *Orígenes de la Dominación Española en América* (vol. XXV, Nueva Biblioteca de Autores Españoles, Madrid 1918), p. 46-7.
13. Antonio Domínguez Ortiz, *Los conversos de origen judío después de la expulsión* (Madrid 1957), p. 146.
14. This figure, with no claims to accuracy, is obtained by adding the presumed pre-1492 Jewish population figures to those given in Vicens Vives, ed., *Historia*, II, 417.

15. Bernáldez, chap. XLIII, p. 98.
16. Serrano y Sanz, p. 37-8.
17. 'Copia de los sanvenitos que corresponden a la villa de Aguilar de la Frontera', British Museum (cited hereafter as B.M.) Add. MS. 21447 f. 137-9.
18. A. Rodríguez Moñino, 'Les Judaisants à Badajoz de 1493 à 1599', *Revue des Etudes Juives* (1956), p. 73-86.
19. Quoted in Neuman, II, 264.
20. Henry Charles Lea, *A history of the Inquisition of Spain* (4 vols. New York 1906-8), I, 120. Cited hereafter as Lea.
21. José Amador de los Ríos, *Historia social, política y religiosa de los Judíos en España y Portugal* (3 vols. Madrid 1875-6), III, 242.
22. This was Pedro de Caballería, author of the antisemitic tract *Zelus Christi contra Judaeos, Sarracenos et infideles.*
23. Cecil Roth, *The Spanish Inquisition* (London 1937), p. 30.
24. Luciano Serrano, O.S.B., *Los conversos D. Pablo de Santa Maria y D. Alfonso de Cartagena* (Madrid 1942), p. 23-4.
25. Published by Rodrigo Amador de los Ríos in *Revista de España*, CV-CVI (1885).
26. I have consulted the edition published in Madrid in 1849 by Antonio Luque y Vicens. The *Tizón* is also printed in Caro Baroja, III, 287-99.
27. Caro Baroja, II, 264.
28. Nicolás López Martínez, *Los Judaizantes castellanos y la Inquisición en tiempo de Isabel la Católica* (Burgos 1954), appendix IV, p. 391-404.
29. Fidel Fita, 'Nuevos datos para escribir la historia de los judíos españoles: La Inquisición en Jérez de la Frontera', *Boletín de la Real Academia de la Historia* (cited hereafter as B.A.H.), XV (1889), p. 313-32.
30. Neuman, II, 274.
31. Isidore Loeb, 'Le nombre des Juifs de Castille et d'Espagne', *Revue des Etudes Juives*, XIV (1887). Loeb estimates that 20,000 more died in the process of expulsion, and that 50,000 remained behind in Spain; he thus gives a total of 235,000 as the number of Jews in Spain. For a discussion of other figures on the expulsion, see Caro Baroja, I, 182-9.
32. Quoted in Caro Baroja, II, 15 n. 19.
33. Bernáldez, chap. CX, CXII.
34. Quoted in Lea, I, 143.
35. See Caro Baroja, I, 191-270. Also Cecil Roth, *A history of the Marranos* (Philadelphia 1941).
36. Bernáldez, chap. CXII, p. 262.

Chapter Three: The Coming of the Inquisition

1. Antonio Domínguez Ortiz, *Los conversos*, appendix II, p. 217-19.
2. Cf. Caro Baroja, I, 269-70.
3. For this and the following paragraph I rely on Caro Baroja, II, 162-244.
4. Lea, I, 148-9.
5. *Ibid.*, I, 295.
6. Documentation cited in this paragraph is in Eloy Benito Ruano, *Toledo en el siglo XV* (Madrid 1961), appendices 16, 18, 19, 22, and 44.
7. Luis Delgado Merchán, *Historia documentada de Ciudad Real* (Ciudad Real 1907), appendix 16, p. 419.
8. Caro Baroja, III, 279-81.
9. Lea, I, 134. For the whole case, see Fidel Fita, 'La verdad sobre el martirio del Santo Niño de La Guardia', B.A.H., XI (1887), p. 7-160. Also H. C. Lea, 'El Santo Niño de La Guardia', *Chapters from the Religious History of Spain* (Philadelphia 1890), p. 437-68; and Caro Baroja, I, 165-76.
10. See Cecil Roth, *The ritual murder libel and the Jew* (London 1934).
11. Thus Nicolás López Martínez, *Los Judaizantes castellanos*, p. 193.
12. Hernando del Pulgar, *Crónica de los Reyes Católicos* (vol. V-VI, Colección de Crónicas Españolas, Madrid 1943), V, 337.
13. *Relación Histórica de la Judería de Sevilla* (Seville 1849), p. 24-6.
14. Bernáldez, chap. XLIV, p. 99-100.
15. Bernardino Llorca S.J., *La Inquisición en España* (Barcelona 1936), p. 79.
16. Bernáldez, chap. XLIV, p. 101.
17. Lea, I, 587, appendix X.
18. Lea, I, 233.
19. Lea, I, 590, appendix XI.
20. Quoted in Ferran Soldevila, *Historia de España* (7 vols. Barcelona 1952), II, 432 n. 88, 89.
21. Lea, I, 244-5. Cf. Juan Antonio Llorente, *Memoria Histórica sobre qual ha sido la opinión nacional de España acerca del tribunal de la Inquisición* (Madrid 1812), p. 89, where the date 1485 is given.
22. Quoted in Llorente, *Memoria Histórica*, p. 90-1.
23. Lea, I, 247.
24. Lea, 592-611, appendix XII.

Chapter Four: A Minority Opposition

1. Llorca, *La Inquisición en España*, p. 166.
2. Llorente, *Memoria Histórica*, p. 37.
3. Biblioteca Nacional, Madrid (cited hereafter as B.N.) MS. 1517. For a study of Pulgar's general position see Francisco Cantera, 'Fernando de Pulgar y los conversos', in *Sefarad*, IV (1944).
4. Juan de Mariana, *Historia General de España* (Biblioteca de Autores Españoles, vols. XXX-XXXI, Madrid 1950), XXXI, p. 202.
5. 'Baptizati invite non recipiunt Sacramentum, nec characterem baptismalem, sed remanent infideles occulti': Ludovico a Páramo, *De origine et progressu officii Sanctae Inquisitionis* (Madrid 1598), p. 165.
6. Jose de Sigüenza, *Historia de la Orden de San Jerónimo*, II, 306-7, cited in Caro Baroja, I, 150 n. 61.
7. Bernardino Llorca S. J., *Bulario Pontífico de la Inquisición Española en su período constitucional* (1478-1525) (Miscellanea Historiae Pontificae vol. XV, Rome 1949), p. 113-15.
8. Mariana, *loc. cit.*
9. Bernáldez, chap. XLIV.
10. H. Graetz, 'La police de l'Inquisition d'Espagne à ses débuts', B.A.H., XXIII (1893), p. 383-90.
11. *Colección de documentos inéditos para la Historia de España*, vol. CXII (Madrid 1895), p. 279: Luis Ramírez y las Casas Deza, *Anales de Córdoba*.
12. The issues are lucidly detailed by Lea, I, 190-211.
13. Quoted in Lea, I, 195.
14. Archivo General de Simancas (cited hereafter as A.G.S.), Patronato Real, Inquisición, leg. 28 f. 39.
15. Lea, I, 211-12.
16. A.G.S. Patronato Real, Inquisición, leg. 28 f. 16.
17. Archivo Histórico Nacional, Madrid (cited hereafter as A.H.N.), Inquisición, leg. 4724[2] no. 8.
18. Pascual Gayangos and Vicente de la Fuente, *Cartas del Cardenal Don Fray Francisco Jiménez de Cisneros, dirigidas a Don Diego López de Ayala* (Madrid 1867), p. 261. Cf. Lea, I, 217.
19. Lea, I, 215.
20. Llorente, *Memoria Histórica*, p. 119-31.
21. A.G.S. Patronato Real, Inquisición leg. 28 f. 45.
22. Llorente, *Memoria Histórica*, p. 156.
23. Lea, IV, 250.
24. J. I. Gutiérrez Nieto, 'Los conversos y el movimiento comunero', *Hispania*, 94 (1964), p. 237-61
25. B. M. Egerton MS. 1832 f. 37-40.

Chapter Five: 'Silence has been imposed'

1. Marcel Bataillon, *Erasme et l'Espagne* (Paris 1937), p. 529.
2. Cited in Prescott, *History of the reign of Ferdinand and Isabella*, p. 345.
3. *Ibid.* p. 349. I have rephrased the quotation.
4. *Ibid.* p. 346.
5. Bataillon, p. 302.
6. *Ibid.* p. 298.
7. Lea, III, 415. Also John E. Longhurst, *Luther and the Spanish Inquisition: The Case of Diego de Uceda 1528-1529* (Albuquerque 1953).
8. Manuel Serrano y Sanz, 'Juan de Vergara y la Inquisición de Toledo', *Revista de Archivos, Bibliotecas y Museos* (cited hereafter as R.A.B.M.), V (1901) and VI (1902).
9. Marcelino Menéndez y Pelayo, *Historia de los Heterodoxos Españoles* (8 vols. Buenos Aires 1945. The first edition was in 1881), IV, 129. Cited hereafter as Menéndez Pelayo.
10. John E. Longhurst, *Erasmus and the Spanish Inquisition: The Case of Juan de Valdes* (Albuquerque 1950).
11. Cited Lea, III, 419.
12. Bataillon, p. 529.
13. Ernst Schäfer, *Beiträge zur Geschichte des spanischen Protestantismus und der Inquisition im sechzehnten Jahrhundert* (3 vols. Gütersloh 1902), II.
14. Bataillon, p. 584.
15. For Egidio and other Protestants, see Edward Boehmer, *Bibliotheca Wiffeniana: Spanish Reformers of two centuries, from* 1520 (3 vols. London 1874-1904). For the Seville community, Schäfer, I, 345-67; II, 271-426.
16. Schäfer, I, 233-48; III, 1-813.
17. Menéndez Pelayo, V, 89.
18. A.G.S. Patronato Real, Inquisición leg. 28 f. 37. The last sentence I quote is mistranslated by Lea, III, 435 (basing himself on L. P. Gachard) to read, 'I cannot promise that there will be a king hereafter to do it'. The original reads, 'No me prometo que al adelante sera el Rey ni nadie parte para hazerlo'.
19. Lea, III, 571, appendix VIII.
20. Schäfer, II, 286-8.
21. B.N. MS. 9175 f. 258-60.
22. Schäfer, II, 1-106.
23. López Martínez, *Los Judaizantes castellanos*, p. 375: 'Los focos principales de alumbrados coincidan con antiguos centros de judaizantes. Esta última observación cabe también con respecto a los grupos luteranos'.

24. B.N. MS. 13267 f. 281.

25. Rafael Gibert, 'Las universidades bajo Carlos V', in *Carlos V (1500-1558). Homenaje de la Universidad de Granada* (Granada 1958), p. 475-500.

26. For Luis de León see, *inter alia*, Lea, III, 149-62; Luis Alonso Getino O.P., 'La causa de Fr. Luis de León ante la crítica y los nuevos documentos históricos', R.A.B.M., IX (1903) and XI (1904); *Colección de documentos inéditos*, vols. X-XI (1847).

27. Miguel de la Pinta Llorente, *Proceso criminal contra el hebraista salmantino Martin Martínez de Cantalapiedra* (Madrid 1946), p. 392.

28. *Colección de documentos inéditos*, vol. XLI (1862), p. 316.

29. *Ibid.* p. 387.

30. Antonio Tovar and Miguel de la Pinta Llorente, *Procesos inquisitoriales contra Francisco Sánchez de las Brozas* (Madrid 1941), p. xliv.

31. Américo Castro, 'Erasmo en tiempo de Cervantes', *Revista de Filologia Española*, XVIII (1931), p. 364-5.

32. *Ibid.* p. 366.

33. Bataillon, p. 760. Also Mario Scaduto S.J., 'Lainez e l'Indice del 1559', *Archivum Historicum Societatis Jesu*, XXIV, 47, Jan.–June 1955.

34. Lea, III, 485.

35. *Tres indices expurgatorios de la Inquisición Española en el siglo XVI* (Madrid 1952).

36. I. S. Révah, 'Un index espagnol inconnu', in *Homenaje a Dámaso Alonso* (3 vols. Madrid 1963), III, 131-46. For the indices in general see Heinrich Reusch, *Der Index der verbotenen Bücher* (2 vols. Bonn 1883-5). Also the apologia by Miguel de la Pinta Llorente, 'Aportaciones para la historia externa de los indices expurgatorios españoles', *Hispania*, XII (1952), p. 253-300.

37. Antonio Rumeu de Armas, *Historia de la Censura literaria gubernativa en España* (Madrid 1940), p. 16-20. On the same subject, the apologia by Antonio Sierra Corella, *La censura de libros y papeles en España y los indices y catálogos españoles* (Madrid 1947).

38. 'Dictamen de Jerónimo Zurita acerca de la prohibición de obras literarias por el Santo Oficio', R.A.B.M., VIII (1903), p. 218-21.

39. B.N. MS. 718 f. 30-2.

40. Fray Justo Cuervo, 'Fray Luis de Granada y la Inquisición', in *Homenaje a Menéndez y Pelayo* (2 vols. Madrid 1899), I, 733-43.

41. A list of all the bookshops in Madrid just after 1600 is given in B.N. MS. 718 f. 323, 325.

42. A.H.N. Inquisición leg. 4470^1 no. 3.

43. A.H.N. Inquisición leg. 4517^1 no. 1.

44. A.H.N. Inquisición leg. 4470^1 no. 4; leg. 4517^1 no. 1.

45. A.H.N. Inquisición leg. 4470^1 no. 3.

46. Menéndez Pelayo, V, 482.

47. Juan Antonio Llorente, *Histoire Critique de l'Inquisition d'Espagne* (4 vols. Paris 1817-18), I, 343-5.

48. For all these, see A. Paz y Melia, *Papeles de Inquisición: catálogo y extractos* (2nd edn. Madrid 1947), p. 23, 69, 71.

49. 'Las obras de caridad que se hazen tibia y flojamente no tienen mérito ni valen nada': *Quixote*, II, 36, See A. Castro, 'Cervantes y la Inquisición,' *Modern Philology*, 27 (1929-30), p. 427-33.

50. *The Life of Saint Teresa*, trans. J. M. Cohen (Penguin Books 1957), p. 243.

51. Miguel de la Pinta Llorente, *La Inquisición Española y los problemas de la Cultura y de la Intolerancia* (Madrid 1953), p. 152-3.

52. A. Castro, 'Erasmo en tiempo de Cervantes', p. 365 n. 2.

53. Cf. Pierre Chaunu, 'Inquisition et vie quotidienne dans l'Amérique espagnole au XVIIe siècle', *Annales E.S.C.*, 1956.

54. A.H.N. Inquisición leg. 4480 no. 21. For Las Casas see Lewis Hanke, *The Spanish Struggle for Justice in the Conquest of America* (Philadelphia 1949).

Chapter Six: The End of Morisco Spain

1. Américo Castro, *The Structure of Spanish History*, p. 92.

2. See the documents in H. C. Lea, *The Moriscos of Spain: their conversion and expulsion* (London 1901), p. 409-14.

3. Fernand Braudel, *La Méditerranée et le Monde méditerranéen à l'époque de Philippe II* (Paris 1949), p. 580.

4. Tulio Halperin Donghi, 'Les Morisques du royaume de Valence au XVIe siècle', *Annales E.S.C.*, 1956, p. 165. See also the same author's important article 'Un conflicto nacional en el siglo de oro', *Cuadernos de Historia de España* (Buenos Aires), XXIII-XXIV (1955), and XXV-XXVI (1957).

5. Braudel, p. 579.

6. Lea, *The Moriscos*, p. 95 n. 3; p. 98 n. 1.

7. Lea, III, 375.

8. Pascual Boronat, *Los Moriscos españoles y su expulsión* (2 vols. Valencia 1901), I, 412.

9. B.N. MS. 721 f. 39-46.

10. B.M. Add. MS. 10238 f. 188.

11. Pierre Chaunu, 'Minorités et conjoncture. L'expulsion des Morisques en 1609', *Revue Historique*, 1961, p. 90.

12. Henri Lapeyre, *La Géographie de l'Espagne morisque* (Paris 1959), p. 31-2.

13. Braudel, p. 591.

14. Lapeyre, p. 204-6.
15. Juan Reglá, 'La expulsión de los moriscos y sus consecuencias en la economía valenciana', *Hispania*, 23 (1963).
16. B.M. Egerton MS.1151 f. 323, 336. Cf. Boronat, II, 657-61.
17, A.H.N. Inquisición leg. 4671[1].
18. *Quixote*, book II, chap. 65.
19. John C. Salyer, 'La importancia económica de los Moriscos en España', *Anales de Economía*, IX, 24 (1949), p. 123.
20. Boronat, II, 196-7; F. Janer, *La condición social de los Moriscos de España* (Madrid 1857), p. 114, 116.
21. Reglá, 'La expulsión', p. 213.

Chapter Seven: Race Purity and Racialism

1. Claudio Sánchez Albornoz, *España, un enigma histórico* (2 vols. Buenos Aires 1962), I, 677.
2. Américo Castro, 'Algunas observaciones acerca del concepto del honor', p. 40-1.
3. Marcel Bataillon, 'Honneur et Inquisition', *Bulletin Hispanique*, XXVII (1925), p. 15-17.
4. *Quixote*, book I, chap. 47.
5. Domínguez Ortiz, *Los conversos*, p. 58-9.
6. A.H.N. Inquisición libro 497, f. 22-3.
7. For these three writers, Albert Sicroff, *Les controverses des statuts de 'pureté de sang' en Espagne du XVe au XVIIe siècle* (Paris 1960), p. 36-74.
8. Sicroff, p. 78.
9. For what follows, Sicroff, p. 96 ff.
10. 'Sobre el Estatuto de limpieza de la Sancta Iglessia de Toledo', B.N. MS. 13267 f. 278.
11. 'La contradicion hecha por algunas dignidades y canonigos de la Santa Iglesia de Toledo', B.N. MS. 1703 f. 1-17.
12. Sicroff, p. 138 n. 184.
13. All these cases are documented in Lea, II, 300-6.
14. Caro Baroja, II, 304-5.
15. A.H.N. Inquisición libro 497 f. 50.
16. Narciso Hergueta, 'La Inquisición de Logroño. Nuevos datos históricos', B.A.H., XLV (1904), p. 422-39.
17. Quoted in Eusebio Rey, 'San Ignacio de Loyola y el problema de los "Cristianos nuevos",' *Razón y Fe*, 153 (1956), p. 178-9.
18. Sicroff, p. 272-3.
19. Quoted in Eusebio Rey, *op. cit.*, p. 190. For the hostility of the Spanish clergy and the Inquisition to the Jesuits, see Antonio

Astraín S.J., *Historia de la Compañía de Jesús en la Asistencia de España* (7 vols. Madrid 1902-25), vols. I-III.

20. A.H.N. Inquisición leg. 4994[3].
21. 'Papel que dió el Reyno de Castilla a uno de los Sres Ministros de de la Junta diputada para tratarse sobre el Memo[1] presentado por el Reyno a S.M. con el libro del P[e] Mro. Salucio, en punto a las probanzas de la limpieza y nobleza del refe[o] y demás Reynos', B.N. MS. 13043 f. 116-27.
22. Domínguez Ortiz, *Los conversos*, appendix IV (e), p. 233.
23. B.N. MS. 18718 no. 8.
24. Menéndez Pidal, *The Spaniards in their history*, p. 227.
25. 'Discurso de un Inquisidor hecho en tiempo de Phelipe Quarto, sobre los estatutos de limpieza de sangre de España, y si conviene al servicio de Dios, del Rey y Reyno moderarlos', B.N. MS. 13043 f. 132-71.
26. 'Discurso politico del desempeño del Reyno', printed in Caro Baroja, III, 318-20.
27. 'Que los hijos y descendientes de los nuebamente conbertidos a la fee deben gozar de todas las honras que los Christianos viejos', Bodleian Library, Oxford, MS. Arch. Σ. 130 no. 32.
28. Carvajal to Joseph de Luyando, 28 Sept. 1751, B.N. MS. 13043 f. 130.
29. Domínguez Ortiz, *Los conversos*, p. 129 n. 14.
30. Baruch Braunstein, *The Chuetas of Majorca. Conversos and the Inquisition of Majorca* (Columbia University Oriental Series vol. 28, Pennsylvania 1936), p. 123.
31. Lea, II, 314, citing Tomas Bertrán Soler, *Un milagro y una mentira* (Valencia 1858).
32. Domínguez Ortiz, *Los conversos*, p. 130.
33. *Regla y Establecimientos de la Orden y Cavallería del glorioso Apostol Santiago* (1655), tit. I, cap. 5.

Chapter Eight: The Spanish Inquisition: its Organization

1. Lea, I, 174.
2. This and all previous instructions are contained in A.H.N. Inquisición libro 497.
3. Lea, II, 168-78.
4. Lea, I, 541-55.
5. Salary details based on Lea, II, 194-203.
6. Lea, II, 251.
7. A.H.N. Inquisición leg. 4696[2].
8. Llorca, *Bulario Pontífico*, p. 200-6.

9. All figures from A.H.N. Inquisición leg. 4723³.
10. Lea, II, appendix XVII.
11. A.H.N. Inquisición leg. 5144¹.
12. Hernando del Pulgar, *Los claros varones de España y las treinta y dos cartas* (Madrid 1747), letter 24, p. 252.
13. Diego Ortiz de Zúñiga, *Annales de Sevilla* (Madrid 1677), año 1480, p. 389.
14. Lea, II, 367.
15. Fidel Fita, 'La Inquisición en Guadalupe', B.A.H., XXIII (1893), p. 283-8.
16. A.H.N. Inquisición leg. 4776-4779. Cf. Braunstein, *The Chuetas*, p. 68-9, where a different figure is given.
17. Pedro Sanahuja O.F.M., *Lérida en sus luchas por la fe* (Lerida 1946), p. 162.
18. A.H.N. Inquisición legs. 4535³, 4561³, 4562².
19. A.H.N. Inquisición leg. 5083¹.
20. Lea, II, 8.
21. See Astraín, *Historia de la Compañía de Jesús*, vols. I-III.
22. My account is based on Menéndez Pelayo, V, 9-82; Gregorio Marañón, 'El proceso del Arzobispo Carranza', B.A.H., CXXVII (1950), p. 135-78; and Lea, II, 48-86.
23. Marañón, *op. cit.*, p. 145.

Chapter Nine: The Spanish Inquisition: its Procedure

1. Cf. Caro Baroja, I, plates 82-4.
2. *Records of the Spanish Inquisition, translated from the original manuscripts* (Boston 1828), p. 27.
3. W. de Gray Birch, *Catalogue of a collection of original manuscripts . . . of the Inquisition in the Canary Islands* (2 vols. London 1903), I, 103, 112. Cited hereafter as Birch.
4. Lea, II, 99.
5. *Records of the Spanish Inquisition*, p. 78-113.
6. Lea, II, 572.
7. A.G.S. Patronato Real, Inquisición leg. 28 f. 45. Cf. Lea, I, 585-6.
8. *Discusión del proyecto de decreto sobre el Tribunal de la Inquisición* (Cadiz 1813).
9. *Colección de documentos inéditos*, CXII, 264-5, 270.
10. 'Extracts from a narrative of the Persecution of Hippolyto Joseph da Costa Pereira Furtado de Mendonca, a native of Colonia-do-Sacramento, on the River La Plata', printed in the English version of Philip Limborch's *The History of the Inquisition* (London 1816), p. 521-30. For another description of the Lisbon prisons, see B.N. MS. 718 f. 316.

11. Miguel de la Pinta Llorente, *Las cárceles inquisitoriales españolas* (Madrid 1949), p. 115.
12. Birch, I, 367-8.
13. Pinta Llorente, *Las cárceles*, p. 102.
14. Birch, I, 235.
15. Lea, II, 534.
16. A.H.N. Inquisición libro 497 f. 45-6.
17. Lea, III, 33.
18. Lea, III, 2.
19. Lea, III, 25.
20. Birch, I, 381-2.
21. *Ibid.*, I, 378-9.

Chapter Ten: The Spanish Inquisition: Trial and Condemnation

1. Lea, III, 46.
2. Cited above, chap. 9 note 5.
3. Lea, III, 68.
4. Cited above, chap. 9 note 2.
5. Lea, III, 552-4. What is not clear from Lea's classification of punishments is whether he puts individuals under one category only or under several categories, as he would need to do for a man sentenced to be reconciled with confiscation of goods and the wearing of a *sanbenito*.
6. Lea, III, 156.
7. B.N. MS. 9475.
8. Lea, III, 205.
9. Llorente, *Histoire Critique*, IV, 92.
10. Fidel Fita, 'La Inquisición Toledana. Relación contemporanea de los autos y autillos que celebró desde el año 1485 hasta el de 1501', B.A.H., XI (1887), p. 294-6.
11. Cf. my article 'The Decline of Castile: the last Crisis', *Economic History Review*, 1964.
12. *An authentick Narrative of the original, establishment, and progress of the Inquisition* (London 1748), p. 35-9. The original account is Joseph del Olmo, *Relación Histórica del Auto General de Fe que se celebró en Madrid este año de* 1680 (Madrid 1680).
13. Fidel Fita, 'La Inquisición de Logroño y un judaizante quemado en 1719', B.A.H., XLV (1904), p. 457-9.
14. Jose Simon Díaz, 'La Inquisición de Logroño (1570-1580)', *Berceo*, I, (1946), p. 100-1.
15. A.H.N. Inquisición leg. 4696[2].
16. A.H.N. Inquisición leg. 5047[3].

17. A.H.N. Inquisición leg. 4724[1] no. 1.
18. Braunstein, *The Chuetas*, p. 65.

Chapter Eleven: Special Spheres of Jurisdiction

1. B.N. MS. 9475, MS. 9304.
2. Birch, I, 198.
3. Llorca, *Bulario Pontífico*, p. 215-19.
4. B. M. Egerton MS. 1832 f. 37-8.
5. Lea, IV, 362.
6. Páramo, book III, quaestio 10, p. 838. For a lengthy treatment of this subject, see Lea, IV, 95-137.
7. Lea, IV, 197.
8. B.N. MS. 9475.
9. Lea, IV, 205.
10. *Malleus Maleficarum* (London 1948), an English edition by Father Montague Summers. Summers believes wholly in the book, which constitutes for him 'inexhaustible wells of wisdom'.
11. R. Trevor Davies, *Four Centuries of Witch-Beliefs* (London 1947), p. 153.
12. G. L. Kittredge, *Witcraft in Old and New England* (New York 1956), p. 368.
13. Llorente, *Histoire Critique*, II, 43.
14. Sebastián Cirac Estopañán, *Los procesos de hechicerías en la Inquisición de Castilla la Nueva* (Madrid 1942), p. 196.
15. Llorente, *Histoire Critique*, II, 61-76; Menéndez Pelayo, V, 405-8.
16. B.N. MS. 718 f. 271.
17. B.N. M.S. 20-31 f. 229-32.
18. Lea, IV, 233-4. The italics are my own.
19. B.N. MS. 6751 f. 53-62.
20. Albert Loomie S.J., 'Religion and Elizabethan Commerce with Spain', *Catholic Historical Review*, April 1964, p. 30-1.
21. Consulta of the Consejo de Estado, 31 March 1653, A.G.S. Estado leg. 2528.
22. Lea, III, 447.
23. Lea, III, 462.
24. L. de Alberti and A. B. Wallis Chapman, ed., *English Merchants and the Spanish Inquisition in the Canaries* (Royal Historical Society publications, vol. xxiii) (London 1912), p. 80 n. 1.
25. Birch, I, 221-33.
26. Alberti and Chapman, p. x.
27. A.G.S. Estado leg. 2981.

Chapter Twelve: The last Days of the Conversos

1. Caro Baroja, I, 440.
2. *Ibid.*, I, 449. On the conversos in general, see also I.S. Révah, 'Les Marranes', *Revue des Etudes Juives*, 1959-60, p. 29-77.
3. Lea, III, 239 ff.; A. Herculano, *História da origem e estabelecimento da Inquisição em Portugal* (3 vols. Lisbon 1907), I, 228-86.
4. Lea, III, 259.
5. Lea, III, 265-6.
6. B.N. MS. 721 f. 127-31; Llorente, *Histoire Critique*, II, 400; Lea, III, 267.
7. Bodleian Library, Oxford, Arch. Σ. 130 no. 8; Gaspar Matute y Luquín, *Colección de los Autos generales i particulares de Fe celebrados por el Tribunal de la Inquisición de Córdoba* (Cordoba 1840), p. 65, 127; B.N. MS. 718 f. 375 and MS. 6751 f. 53.
8. Lea, III, 267-70.
9. Elkan Adler, 'Documents sur les Marranes d'Espagne et de Portugal sous Philippe IV', *Revue des Etudes Juives*, XLIX (1904), p. 63-5. See also XLVIII-XLIX (1904); L (1905); and LI (1906).
10. Quoted in Caro Baroja, II, 56-7.
11. For Olivares' philo-judaism, see Domínguez Ortiz, *Los conversos*, p. 110 ff.
12. Caro Baroja, II, 59.
13. For Saravia see A. Domínguez Ortiz, 'El proceso inquisitorial de Juan Núñez Saravia, banquero de Felipe IV', *Hispania*, 61 (1955); also by the same, *Política y Hacienda de Felipe IV* (Madrid 1960), p. 127-37; Caro Baroja, II, 60-7.
14. For this and the cases that follow, see Caro Baroja, II, 68-131.
15. The accounts of the firm are in A.H.N. Inquisición leg. 5096[2].
16. Accounts of the firm of Montesinos are in A.H.N. Inquisición leg. 4971[1].
17. B.N. MS. 718 f. 375.
18. A.H.N. Inquisición leg. 5019[5].
19. A.G.S. Contadurias Generales leg. 190.
20. A.H.N. Inquisición leg. 5047[1].
21. B.N. MS. 9475; José del Olmo, *Relación*; Matute y Luquín, p. 210.
22. *Inquisición de Mallorca. Reconciliados y Relajados 1488-1691* (Barcelona 1946), p. 201-75.
23. *Ibid*, p. 109-99.
24. For what follows, see Braunstein, *The Chuetas*.
25. Caro Baroja, III, 21.
26. Caro Baroja, III, 73-5, 387-91.

27. Lea, III, 553.
28. This table is based on *Spanish Tracts 1683-1725* (B.M. 4625 g. 1);
    Relaciones de Autos de Fe, 1721, 1722, Madrid (B.M. 4071 bb[43]
    1-15); *Autos de Fe* (B.M. 4071 i. 3); and Matute y Luquín.
29. Lea, III, 311.
30. G. Desdevises du Dézert, 'Notes sur l'Inquisition espagnole au
    dix-huitième siècle', *Revue Hispanique,* VI (1899), p. 490.
31. *The Bible in Spain* (London 1930 edn.), p. 155.
32. *A journey through Spain in the years 1786 and 1787* (3 vols. London
    1792), III, 84. Cited in Caro Baroja, III, 26 n. 43.

Chapter Thirteen: Political Conflict

1. Lea, II, 110.
2. B.N. MS. 718 f. 38. See also f. 3-4 and f. 8, for letters in 1518 and
   1519.
3. In B.N. MS. 718 f. 108-110, 'Remisiones de causas hechas por los
   summos Pontifices a la Inquisizion de España', are examples of
   21 appeals thus referred back between 1569 and 1608.
4. Lea, I, 567-9, appendix I.
5. Lea, IV, 249-75.
6. Lea, IV, 252.
7. J. H. Elliott, *The Revolt of the Catalans* (Cambridge 1963), p. 456.
8. B.N. MS. 2569.
9. Quoted thus in Sánchez Albornoz, II, 563. Lea, IV, 250 quotes
   it as four clerics.
10. Gregorio Marañón, *Antonio Pérez. (El hombre, el drama, la época)*
    (2 vols. Madrid 1947). For quotations I use the one-volume
    English edition of 1954.
11. Marañón, p. 11, 13.
12. *Ibid.* p. 53.
13. *Ibid.* p. 276.
14. *Ibid.* p. 52.
15. For this case see Lea, II, 133-57.
16. Menéndez Pelayo, VI, 66.
17. For an estimate of his career see my article 'Melchor de Macanaz
    and the foundations of Bourbon power in Spain', in the *English
    Historical Review,* 1965.
18. *Proposiciones que de orden de S.M. hizo Dn Melchor de Macanaz.* There
    are numerous copies, with varying titles, of this paper, e.g. B.N.
    MS. 10745.
19. Antonio Valladares de Sotomayor, *Semanario Erudito* (Madrid
    1788), VIII, 206-85.

20. B.N. MS. 2768 p. 10.
21. Archives du Ministère des Affaires Etrangères, Paris, Mémoires et Documents (Espagne), 250 f. 177.
22. There is no evidence for the suggestion, reported in Caro Baroja, III, 59-60, that Macanaz favoured conversos, or was one, or wished to abolish the Inquisition.
23. Macanaz to Grimaldo, 14 March 1722, B.N. MS. 767 f. 1.
24. B.N. MS. 10745 f. 37.
25. B.N. MSS. 5958, 10701, 10655.
26. Lea, I, 306.
27. Lea, I, 330-1.
28. Lea, I, 447.
29. Lea, I, 469-70.
30. Menéndez Pelayo, VI, 56.
31. *Consulta que hizo la Junta que mandó formar el Sr Rey Dⁿ Carlos 2° a su Mag^d para reformar abusos de Inquisición*, Real Academia de la Historia, Madrid, Est. 24 gr. 5a B. no. 129 f. 308-352. Other copies in B.N. MSS. 6202 and 5547. Menéndez Pelayo dates this document wrongly to 1693.

Chapter Fourteen: In Defence of the Ancien Régime

1. Marquis de Louville, *Mémoires secrets sur l'établissement de la Maison de Bourbon en Espagne* (Paris 1818), p. 34.
2. Antonio Domínguez Ortiz, *La Sociedad Española en el siglo XVIII* (Madrid 1960), p. 299.
3. Archives du Ministère des Affaires Etrangères, Paris, Correspondance Politique (Espagne), 203 f. 141.
4. Macanaz, *Regalías de los Señores Reyes de Aragón* (Madrid 1879), p. 15.
5. Quoted in Jose Deleito y Piñuela, *La vida religiosa española bajo el cuarto Felipe* (Madrid 1952), p. 330.
6. 'Carta que escribió Don Joseph del Campillo al Señor Don Antonio Gerónimo Mier, Inquisidor de Logroño', *Semanario Erudito*, XXIV, 194-204.
7. Marcelino C. Peñuelas, 'El siglo XVIII y la crisis de la conciencia española', *Cuadernos Americanos* (Mexico) vol. CIX no. 2 (1960), p. 148-79.
8. Quoted in Gregorio Marañón, *Las ideas biológicas del P. Feijóo*, printed as the introduction to *Obras escogidas del P. Fray Benito Jerónimo Feijóo*, vol. II (Biblioteca de Autores Españoles, vol. 141, Madrid 1961), p. xix.
9. *Ibid.* p. xxiii.

10. *Teatro crítico*, VII, xiv, 24; I, vi, 43. Cited Marañón p. lxxv.
11. Marañón, p. cxliii.
12. *Cartas eruditas*, I, xxxv, 8. Cited Marañón p. ciii.
13. Marañón, p. xxiv.
14. See J. R. Spell, 'Rousseau's 1750 *Discours* in Spain', *Hispanic Review*, II, iv (1934), p. 334-44.
15. See Jean Sarrailh, *L'Espagne éclairée de la seconde moitié du 18e siècle* (Paris 1954), p. 702-8. Sarrailh stresses, however, that several Spanish 'Jansenists' could correctly be described as such from a moral viewpoint.
16. Astraín, *La Compañía de Jesús*, VII, 147-68.
17. Lea, IV, 284-91.
18. Quoted in Richard Herr, *The Eighteenth-Century Revolution in Spain* (Princeton 1958), p. 28.
19. Sarrailh, p. 101-41, 147.
20. A.H.N. Inquisición leg. 4695[2].
21. Marañón, p. lxxv, xix.
22. Sarrailh, p. 287-372, 441-470.
23. Marcelin Défourneaux, *Pablo de Olavide ou L'Afrancesado (1725-1803)* (Paris 1959), p. 327.
24. Quoted in Caro Baroja, III, 159.
25. Défourneaux, p. 362-3.
26. Sarrailh, p. 623.
27. Défourneaux, appendix II, p. 476-91.
28. Sarrailh, p. 91.
29. *Ibid.* p. 98-9.
30. G. Desdevises du Dézert, 'Notes sur l'Inquisition espagnole au dix-huitième siècle', *Revue Hispanique*, VI (1899), p. 60.
31. Sarrailh, p. 305.
32. *Ibid.* p. 380.
33. Antonio Rumeu de Armas, *Historia de la Censura*, p. 24-6. See also M. Serrano y Sanz, 'El Consejo de Castilla y la censura de libros en el siglo XVIII', R.A.B.M., XV (1906), and XVI (1907).
34. Serrano y Sanz, R.A.B.M., XV (1906), p. 36; Rumeu de Armas, appendix I, p. 205-11.
35. A.H.N. Inquisición leg. 4477 no. 1.
36. A.H.N. Inquisición leg. 4425 no. 11.
37. For what follows I rely on Marcelin Défourneaux, *L'Inquisition espagnole et les livres français au XVIIIe siècle* (Paris 1963).
38. Andrés Muriel, *Historia de Carlos IV* (2 vols. Madrid 1959, Biblioteca de Autores Españoles vols. 114-15), I, 269-70.
39. Défourneaux, *L'Inquisition*, p. 96.
40. Sarrailh, p. 292.
41. Braunstein, *The Chuetas*, p. 123.

42. Lea, IV, 299.
43. Herr, p. 262.
44. Quoted in Carlos Corona Baratech, *Revolución y reacción en el reinado de Carlos IV* (Madrid 1957), p. 238.
45. Herr, p. 409.
46. Adapted from Herr, p. 290-1.
47. Llorente, *Historie Critique*, IV, 92.
48. Défourneaux, *L'Inquisition*, p. 104.
49. *Ibid.*, citing J. R. Spell, *Rousseau in the Spanish world before 1833* (Texas 1938), p. 91. On the infiltration of ideas see also Défourneaux, 'Les dernières années de l'Inquisition espagnole', *Annales Historiques de la Révolution Française*, 172, April-June 1963, p. 161-84.
50. Herr, p. 358, 361.
51. Llorente, *Histoire Critique*, IV, 108.

Chapter Fifteen: The Abolition of the Inquisition

1. A.H.N. Inquisición leg. 5126⁴.
2. Lea, II, appendix XVII.
3. Figures in A.G.S. Gracia y Justicia leg. 622.
4. A.H.N. Inquisición leg. 5025¹. These figures suggest that the list published by Lea, II, 597, appendix VII, is incomplete.
5. Llorente, *Histoire Critique*, IV, 31-2, 92.
6. Edward Blanquiere, *An historical review of the Spanish Revolution* (London 1822), cited in Caro Baroja, III, 164.
7. *Historia de Carlos IV*, I, 270.
8. Lea, IV, 539, appendix III.
9. Miguel Artola, *Los Afrancesados* (Madrid 1953), p. 109 n. 55.
10. *Ibid.* p. 25-51.
11. Cited in Lea, IV, 403 n. 2.
12. 'Dictamen presentado a las Cortes generales', in *Discusión del proyecto de decreto sobre el Tribunal de la Inquisición*.
13. See Miguel Artola's introduction to *Memorias de tiempos de Fernando VII*, II, xli (Biblioteca de Autores Españoles vol. 98, Madrid 1957).
14. Antonio Puigblanch, *The Inquisition Unmasked* (2 vols. London 1816), I, 10-11.
15. *Discusión del proyecto*, p. 687.
16. *Colección de documentos inéditos*, CXII, p. 260-3.
17. A.H.N. Inquisición leg. 4618².
18. Lea, IV, 432.
19. *Colección de documentos inéditos*, CXII, p. 275.

20. Lea, IV, 545, appendix VIII.
21. Menéndez Pelayo, VII, 21-2.
22. See the discussion in Lea, IV, 518, 524.
23. Pulgar, *Crónica*, chap. 96, p. 336.
24. Bernáldez, chap. 44, p. 101.
25. Zúñiga, *Annales de Sevilla*, año 1524, p. 482.
26. B.A.H., XXIII (1893), p. 283-8.
27. These figures, from Lea, IV, 520, differ considerably from those given in Delgado Merchán, p. 217-25, and in Páramo, p. 170. According to Delgado Merchán, from 1483 to 1485 the tribunal here relaxed 39 in person, 118 in effigy, and penanced 9 others. Fidel Fita, 'La Inquisición de Ciudad Real en 1483-1485', B.A.H., XX (1892), puts the total at about 279 victims, of whom over 160 were burnt in person or in effigy.
28. B.A.H., XI (1887), p. 289-321.
29. Lea, IV, 523.
30. A. Rodríguez Moñino, 'Les Judaisants à Badajoz de 1493 à 1599', *Revue des Etudes Juives*, 1956, p. 73-8. The figure for relaxations includes those in effigy.
31. Lea, IV, 522.
32. Lea, I, 592-611, appendix XII. Cf. José Amador de los Ríos, *Historia . . . de los Judíos*, III, 616-27.
33. Lea, IV, 521-2.
34. Braunstein, *The Chuetas*, appendix III, p. 182-3.
35. Birch, I, xxiv.

Chapter Sixteen: A Final Reassessment

1. *The Book of Martyrs* (1863 edn. London), p. 153.
2. *Ibid.* p. 154.
3. Motley, *op. cit.* (1912 edn. London), p. 165.
4. M. Dierickx S.J., 'La politique religieuse de Philippe II dans les anciens Pays-Bas', *Hispania*, XVI (1956), p. 137.
5. *An Apology or Defence of William the First of Nassau, Prince of Orange etc., in answer to the Proclamation against and Proscription of him by the King of Spain*, a translation in *Phenix*, XIII (1707), p. 497, 530.
6. J. W. Thompson, *The Wars of Religion in France* (New York n.d.), p. 12.
7. Reginaldus Gonsalvius Montanus, *A Discovery and playne Declaration of sundry subtill practises of the Holy Inquisition of Spain* (London 1569), f. 23.
8. *The Book of Martyrs*, p. 1060.
9. For this generally, see Sverker Arnoldsson, *La leyenda negra: Estudios sobre sus orígenes* (Göteborg 1960).

10. Cf. Lea, IV, 514, quoting the *Relazioni Venete*, serie I.
11. 'Relazione di Spagna', *Opere*, IX, 131.
12. Miguel de la Pinta Llorente, *Aspectos históricos del sentimiento religioso en España* (Madrid 1961), p. 37.
13. Cf. Gonzalo Correas, *Vocabulario de refranes y frases proverbiales* (Madrid 1924), p. 124.
14. Llorente, *Memoria Histórica*, p. 38.
15. *Historia General de España*, book 26, chap. 13 (Biblioteca de Autores Españoles vol. 30, p. 256).
16. Cited Llorente, *Histoire Critique*, II, 14-15.
17. Birch, II, 905.
18. Quoted in Vicens Vives ed., *Historia*, IV, 247.
19. Carvajal to Luyando, 28 Sept. 1751, B.N. MS. 13043 f. 130.
20. Jovellanos, 'Representación a Carlos IV sobre lo que era el Tribunal de la Inquisición', in *Obras*, vol. 5 (Biblioteca de Autores Españoles vol. 87, Madrid 1956), p. 333-4.
21. Sarrailh, p. 317.
22. Lea, IV, 504.
23. Menéndez Pelayo, *La Ciencia Española* (Madrid, 1953 edn.), p. 102-3.
24. Pierre Vilar, *La Catalogne dans l'Espagne moderne* (3 vols. Paris 1962), I, 507.
25. Lea, IV, 528.
26. Lord Acton, *Essays on Church and State* (London 1952), p. 393.
27. Julián Juderías, *La Leyenda Negra* (13th edn., Madrid 1954), p. 99 ff. One wonders why a work so full of xenophobia and rabid nationalism called for thirteen editions.
28. See Felipe Picatoste y Rodríguez, *Apuntes para una Biblioteca Científica Española del siglo XVI* (Madrid 1891).
29. Menéndez Pidal, *The Spaniards in their history*, p. 223-4.
30. *Historia General de España*, prologue (Biblioteca de Autores Españoles vol. 30, p. li).
31. Picatoste, p. 339-44. The reference to Galileo is on p. 341 n. 2.
32. Corona Baratech, *Revolución y Reacción*, p. 122-3.
33. Vicente de la Fuente, *Historia de las Universidades, colegios y demás establecimientos de enseñanza en España* (3 vols. Madrid 1884-5), II, 428.
34. *Ibid.* II, 487.
35. Alberto Jiménez, *Ocaso y Restauración. Ensayo sobre la Universidad Española Moderna* (Mexico 1948), p. 49.
36. 'Del Influjo de la Inquisición y del fanatismo religioso en la decadencia de la literatura española', in *Disertaciones y Juicios literarios* (Madrid and Paris 1878), p. 107.
37. *España, un enigma histórico*, II, 563.

38. *The Spaniards in their history*, p. 204-45.
39. One example is José Deleito's work, cited chap. XIV note 5.
40. *Invertebrate Spain* (London 1937).
41. Sánchez Albornoz, II, 348.
42. Cf. the opinion of Caro Baroja, III, 258: 'La Inquisición ha desaparecido, pero no el espíritu inquisitorial'.

GLOSSARY OF SPANISH TERMS

Alguacil. Officer of the peace. In the Inquisition, usually the prison officer.

Aljama. A word of Arabic origin, signifying the ghetto in which Moors or Jews lived apart from their Christian neighbours.

Almorávide Moors. The intolerant Muslim invaders of the eleventh century.

Auto de fe. Literally 'act of faith', the ceremony at which penitent heretics were 'reconciled' to the Church. *Autos* were held either in public (*auto pública*) or in private (*auto particular*). It should be remembered that the execution of heretics did not officially form part of the proceedings at an *auto*.

Censo. An annuity consisting either of ground-rent or of interest on loans to municipalities.

Comunidades. The rebel governments set up in Castilian cities by the *Comuneros* in 1520-1.

Converso. Literally 'convert', applied generally to Christianized Moors and Jews.

Cortes, or parliament. In Castile, it consisted at first of representatives of the three estates (nobility, clergy and towns), but was later restricted to representatives of specified cities. Aragon, Valencia and Catalonia continued to have Cortes in which all the estates were represented.

Ducado, or ducat. Castilian unit of account. See *Vellón*.

Familiar. Lay associate of the Holy Office.

Fueros. The constitutional liberties enjoyed by certain towns and provinces in Spain.

Hermandad. A peace-keeping brotherhood, organized as a police force by towns in the fifteenth century.

Hidalguía, 'nobility', the status of an *hidalgo* or noble.

Juez de bienes. In the Inquisition, the official in charge of confiscations.

Juro. An annuity consisting usually of interest on loans to the government, drawn directly from taxes assigned for the purpose.

Libro verde. Literally 'green book', a term applied particularly to genealogical accounts current after the sixteenth century, tracing the Jewish ancestry of the nobility.

Limpieza, 'purity'. In this book the term refers to *limpieza de sangre*, the doctrine of 'purity of blood'.

329

Maravedi. See *Vellón.*

Marranos. Derogatory term to describe Christianized Jews. There are various explanations of the origin of the word.

Mayorazgos. Entailed estates held by the Spanish nobility.

Moriscos. General term applied to Christianized Moors.

Mozárabes. The Christian minority living in lands under Moorish rule.

Mudéjares. The Muslim minority living in lands under Christian rule.

Real. See *Vellon.*

Sanbenito. A corruption of *saco bendito,* the penitential garment prescribed by the Inquisition.

Vellón. 'Vellon was originally a mixture of silver and copper used for fractional coins. Through debasement the silver content was reduced and finally eliminated. The maravedi, originally a large Moorish coin, was the smallest unit of account in the monetary system. A real, for example, contained 34 maravedis and a ducat 375 maravedis': Earl J. Hamilton, *War and Prices in Spain 1651-1800* (Cambridge, Mass., 1947), p. 38 n. 7.

INDEX